Neo-Confucianism in History

Harvard East Asian Monographs 307

Publication of this book was partially underwritten by the Mr. and Mrs. Stephen C. M. King Publishing and Communications Fund, established by Stephen C. M. King to further the cause of international understanding and cooperation, especially between China and the United States, by enhancing cross-cultural education and the exchange of ideas across national boundaries through publications of the Harvard University Asia Center.

Neo-Confucianism in History

Peter K. Bol

Published by the Harvard University Asia Center
Distributed by Harvard University Press
Cambridge (Massachusetts) and London 2008

© 2008 by the President and Fellows of Harvard College

Printed in the United States of America

The Harvard University Asia Center publishes a monograph series and, in coordination with the Fairbank Center for Chinese Studies, the Korea Institute, the Reischauer Institute of Japanese Studies, and other faculties and institutes, administers research projects designed to further scholarly understanding of China, Japan, Vietnam, Korea, and other Asian countries. The Center also sponsors projects addressing multidisciplinary and regional issues in Asia.

Library of Congress Cataloging-in-Publication Data

Bol, Peter Kees.

Neo-Confucianism in history / Peter K. Bol.

p. cm. -- (Harvard East Asian monographs ; 307)

Includes bibliographical references and index.

ISBN 978-0-674-03106-7 (cl : alk. paper)   ISBN 978-0-674-05324-3 (pbk : alk. paper)

1. Neo-Confucianism. I. Title.

B5233.N45B66 2008

181'.112--dc22

2008027466

Index by the author

❀ Printed on acid-free paper

Last figure below indicates year of this printing

18 17 16 15 14 13 12 11 10

Frontispiece: Xu Qian (1270–1337), known as Master Baiyun, established the Bahua Academy in the mountains of Dongyang County (Zhejiang) to teach Zhu Xi's learning. Today the academy is a religious site and Xu is worshipped as a god who will "respond to any supplication." Above the altar hang two late Ming plaques, reading "Leading Progenitor of the Learning of the Way" and "His Honor Xu Baiyun." Photograph by the author, April 2000.

for

Kees and Margaret Bol

and

Satomi Matsumura and Christopher Bol

Acknowledgments

Ideas for this book were developed first as part of a paper for the 1997 ACLS Conference on the Song-Yuan-Ming Transition, published as "Neo-Confucianism and Local Society, Twelfth to Sixteenth Century," in *The Song-Yuan-Ming Transition in Chinese History*, edited by Paul Jakov Smith and Richard von Glahn (Cambridge: Harvard University Asia Center, 2003), 241–83. Early versions of some of the argument appeared in "Neo-Confucianism and Chinese History," *Chinese History/ Chūgoku shigaku* 6 (1997): 1–22; and in "Shier zhi shiliu shiji de wenhua, shehui ji lixue" 十二至十六世紀的文化, 社會及理學, *Zhongguo wen-zhe yanjiu tongxun* 中國文哲研究通訊 9 (1999): 89–103.

I am grateful to the participants in the several colloquia at which parts of this book were presented: as a Specially Invited Visiting Scholar of the Institute of Chinese Literature and Philosophy at Academia Sinica in spring 1999, the Tompkins Lectures of Department of East Asian Languages and Cultures of the University of California at Berkeley in spring 2000, the *New History* Lectures at the Institute of History and Philology at Academia Sinica in spring 2000, the Department of History at the Chinese University of Hong Kong in spring 2000, the Historians at Harvard faculty seminar in the Department of History at Harvard in spring 2000, the Tang Junyi Lecture at the University of Michigan in spring 2005, the Harvard China Humanities

Seminar in fall 2006, and at various meetings of the Columbia Seminar in Neo-Confucian Studies. I thank the Chiang Ching-kuo Foundation for a Senior Scholar's Grant during the spring of 2000.

My particular thanks to Chu Ping-tzu, Kim Youngmin, and Ong Chang Woei for reading and commenting on the manuscript. Their dissertations, and those of Chen Wenyi, Hilde De Weerdt, Peter Ditmanson, Robert Foster, Anne Gerritsen, Min Byounghee, Douglas Skonicki, Song Jaeyoon, and Curie Virag have contributed to my thinking about Neo-Confucianism. Detailed reports from Robert Hymes and an anonymous reader were invaluable in revising the manuscript.

I have been fortunate to be in a department of exceptional colleagues and students, who over the years have broadened my view of China and its history. But I have also benefited from having more wonderful teachers than anyone has a right to expect. I thank Virginia P. Zimmerman for getting me to think about the world beyond the United States, Henry N. Drewry for showing me how interesting the study of history could be, Aisin Gioro Yü-yün for demonstrating his way of taking the Four Books and Five Classics seriously, and Willard J. Peterson for guiding me in studying China's intellectual traditions as part of its history.

P.K.B.

Contents

Neo-Confucianism in History

INTRODUCTION

Neo-Confucianism in History

Where does Neo-Confucianism—as a school of thought built on the teachings of eleventh-century moral philosophers and as an elite social movement that took shape in the twelfth century—fit into our story of China's history? In the study of China's intellectual traditions, there has always been a special place for the thinkers and texts of early China, the age when people began to argue over the ideas that should guide rulers and individuals. The religious movements that took mature form during the medieval era, especially Buddhism, continue to garner attention for the new ways of thinking they introduced and the new kinds of communities they created. Modern Chinese thought deals with the pressing question of what values should guide China in a global context. Neo-Confucianism is caught in the middle. It is a kind of Confucianism, but one that claims to be rediscovering what Confucius and Mencius really meant and that often speaks through its interpretations of the ancient texts. Zhu Xi, its Confucius, wrote too much rather than too little, and he assumed readers already well schooled in Confucius and the Classics. Some modern scholars hold that it gave traditional ethics a new philosophical foundation by co-opting basic concepts from Buddhism and Daoism, although the first Neo-Confucians thought they were making Buddhism and Daoism unnecessary. It was the orthodoxy of the late imperial system and for that reason was condemned by those seeking to create a modern nation-state. And the modern philosophers who have become the primary interpreters of Neo-Confucian doctrine are caught up with questions of finding an intellectual and moral basis for a China in a global context. Neo-Confucianism is, moreover, not easy to teach, or so my colleagues tell me; it is too abstruse, too esoteric. It is as difficult to grasp as medieval Christianity would be in a Chinese college classroom.

Neo-Confucians were not greatly interested in history or literature, except to the extent they could put them in service of their own program of moral cultivation, and few historians or literary scholars have wanted to spend much time on Neo-Confucianism. Some would say there is good reason for this, that Neo-Confucianism was little more than the ideological justification for the order of things during the last thousand years of imperial China's history: a society stagnating under the exploitation of an ever more autocratic state and a ruling class that had turned in on itself, ignoring everything that was happening in society and the world around them. I disagree with every single phrase in the preceding sentence, but it is still, I fear, a way of summing up the final millennium of "premodern" or "traditional" China. And it is not entirely without a basis in historical fact, its defenders will remind you, pointing to the pervasiveness of the Chinese civil service examination system. The examination system extended to every county school from the eleventh century on, and in every one of those schools students practiced writing essays based on the Neo-Confucian Four Books. Although, of course, they did not do so until two hundred years after Neo-Confucian philosophy first appeared, and only then, in 1315, at the order of the ruling Mongols, who were not Chinese but had incorporated all of China into their empire forty years before.

All this has made it difficult, or perhaps simply less pressing, to think about Neo-Confucianism in history. This lack of attention is all the more ironic given how much Neo-Confucians wrote—many important philosophical writings have been translated into English—and how much we can know about the times and places in which they lived. Neo-Confucianism was spreading at precisely the moment when commercial printing was becoming common, and many counties had a printer or two, thus ensuring that more texts were put into circulation and more survived; communities were investing in local schools and academies, providing intellectuals with careers and students with places to gather; local historical records were being compiled, giving local people a way to record their accomplishments and providing us with details unavailable for earlier periods; and private wealth was increasing, making it possible for Neo-Confucians to raise the money necessary to print their books, build their shrines and academies, organize charitable activities, and gain fame locally when they could not nationally. In other words, we can know more about the Neo-Confucians themselves and the world in which they lived than we can about intellectuals of any earlier period.

But how did Neo-Confucians fit into the world in which they lived and what difference did they make? These are not questions that either the philosophically or the historically minded have asked in much depth, although for different reasons: the philosophically minded rightly deny that social interests explain philosophical ideas, and the historically minded rightly doubt that ideology determines the course of history. I find myself caught in the middle, between those who think that we are all Neo-Confucian by our very nature as human beings and those who think Neo-Confucian philosophy is solipsistic drivel. I see Neo-Confucianism as a movement that from the twelfth century into the seventeenth profoundly influenced the way people understood the world around them and made choices about how to respond to that world, and thus I see it as of the greatest historical consequence. In looking at Neo-Confucians in their times we must be historical, and in understanding their ideas we need to be philosophical. I hope that doing so will speak to the study of both philosophy and history in China's past.

This is a good moment to be considering the connections between Neo-Confucianism and history, because so much has been done to revise our understanding of the history of China's middle period and of the south, where Neo-Confucianism first became established among the social and political elite. A more interesting story has been emerging, making it far easier to see how Neo-Confucians were speaking to their times. During the past two decades, there has also been an explosion of interest in Neo-Confucianism in China, something that may be more than a passing academic interest. For Neo-Confucianism began, in the late eleventh century, as one of several attempts to find an alternative to the orthodoxy of that day, which held that the human condition could be improved only if the state worked to transform social, economic, and cultural life.

This is an interpretive, at times polemical, inquiry into the Neo-Confucian engagement with the literati as the social and political elite, with local society, and with the imperial state during the Song, Yuan, and Ming dynasties, from the eleventh century into the seventeenth. It is also a reflection on what makes this period different from preceding periods and the kinds of questions that we might ask in thinking about it. I have tried to offer an inquiry into Neo-Confucians' engagement with the world, rather than the kind of history of Neo-Confucian philosophy that has already been written in many languages. In writing, I have tried to remember that we still need books for those who do not already have the kind of knowledge of Chinese history and thought that the Neo-Confucians assumed, although at times this tends to lengthen my explanations. I hope that those who study Chinese thought will find the historical context worth re-examining, and that those who study China's history will find Neo-Confucians and their ideas worth thinking about.

I begin with an account of the many differences between the world of the great Tang empire at the height of its power in the mid-eighth century and the smaller, but no less ambitious state of Song in the eleventh. The differences—all that was lost and all that was new—set the stage for a re-examination of the ideological grounds of the imperial state and the role of literati in it. This re-examination, the subject of Chapter 2, resulted in what we know as the "New Policies," the concerted effort to create government institutions that would transform society by increasing wealth and spreading education on one hand and strengthen the state on the other. The Neo-Confucians, whose history is surveyed in Chapter 3, began on the margins, as moral thinkers who opposed the New Policies. In the late twelfth and thirteenth centuries, despite the court's attempt to suppress them, they succeeded in persuading large numbers of literati to share their vision. What that vision entailed is the subject of the final four chapters. Chapter 4 argues that the Neo-Confucians' view of politics shifted moral authority away from the political system and toward the individual, with a new conception of the self as grounds for morality in society and politics. The basis for this shift was a theory of learning, set out in Chapter 5, which explains how, through the practice of Neo-Confucian teachings and the study of Neo-Confucian texts, one can realize one's innate potential to be a moral actor in society, a potential that every human being possesses equally as one of the living things in the larger organism of the natural world. Much of Neo-Confucian writing was devoted to theories of learning, and the practice of teaching and lecturing, sometimes to audiences numbering in the tens of thousands, was known as "discoursing on learning." Learning was meant, ultimately, to enable the individual consistently and spontaneously to do the morally correct thing whatever the circumstances. But, as Chapter 6 argues, the idea that a choice could be called morally right rested on a belief essential to the Neo-Confucian idea of morality: a belief in unity and coherence as the fundamental nature of all things in the universe. In effect, the idealized unity of empire was internalized and made the foundation for individual morality and social action. The final chapter argues that, as Neo-Confucians put their learning into practice in local society, they created a new social ideal, in which society at the local level would be led, with the backing of the state, by the voluntary efforts of literati. The spread of this ethic in the south during the thirteenth and fourteenth centuries culminated, during the early Ming dynasty, in the state's promotion of Neo-Confucian learning and mandating the creation of self-supervising local communities throughout the country. When these legislated institutions began to fail, Neo-Confucian learning regained its social mission, and with that came a second era of local activism and literati voluntarism. Even after Neo-Confucianism lost its hold on the center of intellectual culture in the seventeenth century, it continued as the foundation of local education and the late imperial order continued to accept local elite leadership as necessary to the state's own existence. It is the contention of this book that Neo-Confucianism made that order possible.

1

The New World of the Eleventh Century: 750 and 1050 Compared

The first Neo-Confucians appeared in the latter half of the eleventh century during a period of intense ideological debate, when many claimed that they had found the one way of learning, the way of learning that all could share and that could guide all their choices. The Neo-Confucians differed in the particulars—they were more concerned than most with personal ethics—but they shared their contemporaries' general belief that there ought to be a real basis for knowledge, meaning, and action. The search for certainty in the eleventh century was both a product of the belief that now, at last, it had become possible to create a new order of things, a society better than those of the early imperial dynasties of Han and Tang, and a reaction to the political elites' doubt and uncertainty about what they should do. Whether they were hopeful or fearful, eleventh-century writers assumed that something had changed, that the present was different from the past. And since it was, then the constitutional ideas of the Han (202 B.C.–A.D. 220) and Tang (618–907) empires—their ways of tying together politics, culture, wealth, and status—could not guide modern times. If the two greatest empires did not provide answers, then there was not only reason for uncertainty but also a need to find new guides. We begin thus with an exploration of the ways things had changed by the eleventh century.[1]

———

To see how different the world had become, let us speculate about how in the mid-eleventh century a literatus, a *shi*, an educated man who saw himself as a participant in public life, could have plotted the differences between his times and Tang at its height.

To begin with, he had reason to think that the founding of the "Great State of Song" was a success. It had been proclaimed in 960 at Kaifeng in the north China plain by a general, Zhao Kuangyin (Taizu, r. 960–76), who had usurped the throne from the infant ruler of the preceding Zhou. At first, Song was merely the sixth in a string of short-lived states that held the northern plain after the collapse of Tang in 907. But Song was the first of the six to subdue the independent states in the south that had been established after the Tang and to protect it-self from internal usurpation. Once domestic challenges to a unified empire had been suppressed, the first emperor, known as Emperor Tai-zu, and his brother and successor, Emperor Taizong (r. 976–97), turned their attention to state building: defining the border, controlling inde-pendent military governors, recruiting civil administrators, regularizing tax collection and military provisioning, and re-establishing a national legal system.

By 1050 the institutional success of Song was clear. Literati of this generation no longer compared themselves to what they now called the "Five Dynasties." Instead they looked to the two great empires of the past, Tang and Han, the only two times in history that a centralized bu-reaucratic state had governed so much territory in both north and south for such an extended period. Han was distant, Tang was not. A literatus could read Tang's legal codes and study the works of its great classicists, literary intellectuals, historians, and learned clerics. He could also read its history from a Song perspective, for in 1057 Ouyang Xiu and Song Qi (998–1061) finished rewriting the official history of the Tang dynasty in the more accessible literary style of the day and in a manner that re-flected their own ideas. This 225-chapter work, now known as the *New Tang History,* gave a chronology of political events and contained trea-tises on all the major areas of state activity: court rituals, the tax system, the military, the calendar, the examination and recruitment system, the catalog of the imperial library, and so on. Charts listed the chief councilors at court and the governors of the provinces over the course of the dynasty. And it had over 150 chapters of biographies for those who had achieved fame in Tang: as members of the imperial clan; as the military and civil officials who had shared in power; as men noted for their political integrity, their loyalty, their personal morality, their administrative expertise, their mendacity and cruelty; as Confucian scholars—men who had prepared the official commentaries on the Classics, compiled great collections of documents, edited histories, or defined rituals and ceremonies—and as literary men; as exemplary women; of eunuchs; and finally, as the leaders of the many foreign states with which Tang had relations, peaceful and hostile.

But when our literatus looked at the Tang past more closely, it was less grand than its three-hundred-year existence suggested. Working back from its final collapse, he would have learned of the devastating rebellions of the 870s and 880s that had sacked the capital and pillaged whole regions. Before that, military governors had been steadily eviscerating the Tang court's control over the provinces by withholding taxes from the center and appointing their own successors. Most important, he would have known of the An Lushan rebellion of 755, at the very height of Tang power, when General An (ca. 703–55) swept down from his garrison on the northeastern border and took the capital of Chang'an in the northwest, putting the emperor to flight. Our literatus might have concluded that from the mid-750s the Tang was in decline, or he might have emphasized the Tang court's subsequent moments of success in restoring central authority. We, with hindsight, see the rebellion as marking the moment when the unified hierarchy of power, wealth, culture, and status that Tang had tried to maintain began to give way, allowing a series of fundamental changes in the order of things to unfold. A literatus with intellectual ambitions would have known that some of the great Tang poets and essayists, Du Fu (712–70) and Han Yu (764–824) for example, whose works were very much part of his own intellectual universe, had lived through the rebellion or were born soon after it; these were men who had begun to ask not how to restore the pre-rebellion past but what the world ought to become. The An Lushan rebellion marked the advent of a series of institutional and socioeconomic changes to which the Song was heir, but it was also an intellectual divide between the glories of empire and the search for something else.

Let us suppose that our literatus had compared his times, the 1050s, against the Tang at the height of its power in about 750, on the eve of the great rebellion. What were the most obvious changes?

Foreign Relations

He would have known that that Song no longer was sending great armies west to maintain a dominant presence along the Silk Road as Tang had once done, and that it had only limited ability to incorporate the many tribes, confederations, and states to the north, south, and west into its empire. The current situation was almost a case of "China among equals."* This was not because Song was weak but because the tribal peoples had learned how to become strong. Song had large armed forces (although it was weak in cavalry), it had superior technology (including bombs and rockets using gunpowder), and it could afford to keep strings of forts provisioned. But in the north the Khitans had learned from Tang how to fashion a state, something that to Song looked like a traditional empire with an emperor and to Inner Asian peoples looked like a traditional khanate. Their Great State of Liao, proclaimed in 907, had occupied the northeastern region between the Song frontier and the state of Koryŏ (918–1392) on the Korean peninsula. The Liao had also defeated the Song armies that had tried to take from it sixteen former Tang prefectures around modern Beijing. A treaty in 1004 had ended hostilities after the Liao armies had advanced to the Song capital, but at an initial cost to Song of an annual compensation to Liao of 200,000 bolts of silk and 100,000 ounces of silver.

In the northwest, along the upper loop of the Yellow River and continuing westward, the Tanguts had been learning as well. Once a tribal people who accepted both Song and Liao hegemony, their king and

---

*Morris Rossabi (*China Among Equals*) demonstrates that Song foreign relations did not realize in practice the rhetoric of one ruler to whom all under heaven paid tribute. But as David Wright (*From War to Diplomatic Parity*, 2; see also 8–38) notes in his review of Song-Liao relations: "The concept of an entire international community of equally sovereign and independent states did not exist in East Asia in Sung times. Northern Sung China did not see itself as one state among many equals but as a state with only one equal: Liao" (see also Tao, *Two Sons of Heaven*).

khan had established a dynastic state with the name Great Xia (known usually as Xi Xia, "Western Xia") in 1038, a year after the Tanguts had promulgated their own unique writing system. Xia expanded further northwest along the Silk Road and successfully defended itself against Song attacks; in 1044 Song agreed on an annual payment of about half of what it was giving Liao. In the far south, there had also been a major change; the area of northern Vietnam had become independent in 939 and was now known as Dai Viet. The southwest (modern Yunnan) remained an independent kingdom, although what had been the country of Nanzhao in Tang times was now Dali.

What did our literatus think about all this? He might have agreed with those statesmen who pointed out that older ideas about barbarian peoples coming to pay tribute to the civilized empire did not describe the reality of the present, in which both the Song and Liao recognized the right of their respective emperors to claim the title of "son of heaven."[2] He might have sided with those who saw the treaties and indemnities as national humiliations and called for a more aggressive foreign policy, or with those who believed that long-term peace was possible, or with those who argued for constant vigilance against foreign incursions but opposed Song aggression abroad. How onerous the subsidies to foreign states really were depends on the frame of reference. Computed as a direct outlay from the central government's discretionary funds, they were significant, but as a percentage of central revenues they could not have been more than 3–4 percent. Moreover, some proportion of the subsidies flowed back into the Song economy through trade at the border markets and related taxes.[3] A more serious issue was the proportion of the budget devoted to defense: over 80 percent of cash revenues in 1065.[4]

The cycle of state building among the northern peoples would continue for centuries to come. Song was richer than any previous dynastic state, but its neighbors to the north were better organized than ever before—so well organized, in fact, that tribes further out began to learn from them. In 1115 the Jurchen tribes, hitherto subordinate to Liao, proclaimed their own state of Jin (1115–1234) and attacked the Liao. Song, seeing an opportunity to capture the sixteen prefectures around Beijing, turned on Liao in its moment of crisis. But in the end, Jin, victorious but not content with the destruction of Liao, turned on Song.[5] Both the reigning emperor and his retired father were captured and taken north. The Song court was reconstituted in the south at Hangzhou and the dynastic line re-established, but the northern plain had been lost to Jin. Jin held it until it fell to the Mongols in 1234, a fate that would befall Song in the 1270s. After defeating Song, the Mongols, using the dynastic name Yuan for that portion of their territory that included their Jin, Xia, and Song conquests, possessed an empire that extended to eastern Europe. Yuan lasted for nearly a century, and the Mongols remained a threatening presence on the northern border after being driven out by the newly founded Ming (1368–1644).

In the early seventeenth century, the Jurchens re-emerged, renamed themselves Manchus, adopted the dynastic name of Qing, and took the Ming capital of Beijing in 1644. In the 1680s, they gained direct control over all Ming territory. Although this was the richest prize, the Manchus continued to expand for another century, doubling their territorial holdings. Much of their empire is claimed by the Peoples' Republic of China today. In sum, for roughly half of the last millennium peoples from outside the Great Wall have governed all or part of what was called the "central country," the place we call "China."* Even if this might have been unimaginable to an eleventh-century literatus, he would have known that Song's international relations in the 1050s were substantially different from those of Tang in the 750s.[6]

The ideological question was how to make sense out of this international reality of multiple states without a single, even nominal, ruler over all. Emperors more than others experienced it as an affront to their dignity, for imperial rhetoric treated the ruler as the universal monarch—and emperors were, in the eyes of some contemporaries, the driving

---

*I translate *zhong guo* as "central country" rather than as China, because for Song, Jin, Yuan, and Ming literati it was the claim to centrality that mattered. *Zhong guo* was both a territorial term, commonly signifying the area of the northern central plain in which the "central states" of the Eastern Zhou feudal lords were located, and a cultural term, for those areas loyal to the culture of Zhou. I use "country" for *guo*, otherwise translated as "state," because in middle-period usage the term refers to a culturally coherent spatio-temporal entity in which dynastic states have come and gone. "Middle Kingdom" is a popular rendering of *zhong guo*, but unfortunately reduces this entity to a political construct. As the Mongols showed, it was possible to hold the northern plain without being loyal to what literati saw as its cultural tradition.

force behind the resumption of an aggressive border policy in the 1070s, whose disastrous consequence was the loss of the north in 1126.

One possibility was to move toward a notion of ethnicity, in which each state was legitimate because it governed a distinctive and separate people. Song could thus have relations with Liao, Jin, and Yuan as the state for the "Chinese" in contrast to the states for other peoples. Paintings suggest that the Song could imagine its neighbors in what we would call ethnic terms, as people who were different because of the way they looked, spoke, and lived.[7] Such a solution would have been quite different from that of the Tang, when the operative distinction had been between those who participated in the empire and those who remained outside it. Those who came from afar—from Japan for instance—could serve in high positions in the Tang system even if they were seen as "belonging" to states and tribes that offered tribute to the Tang court but were not governed by it.[8] This was less viable in Song, although it did happen. In practice, however, all states included ethnically diverse populations, and to take territory across a frontier meant, in effect, to incorporate the people living there. This was particularly true for the northern peoples, who once they held Song territory became the conquering minority. At the political level, treating the state as the national community of an ethnic group was not plausible. Liao and Jin documents refer to "people of Song" (Song *ren*), and mentions in Song documents of the people of Liao and Jin indicate that state affiliation trumped ethnicity. The point at which a distinction needed to be made was when large numbers of different cultural groups lived under a single political authority. Thus a few Song documents distinguish between peoples who lived intermingled along the frontiers by referring to the people similar to themselves as "Han people" (Han *ren*) and the tribal peoples as *fan* (border). In Liao, Jin, and Yuan sources, there are frequent references to culture groups within their population; a Jin edict, for example, ordered: "When officials draft announcements, the Jurchen, Khitan, and Han people are each to use their own writing systems."[9] This fits the Liao, Jin, and Yuan governing practice of using different institutions and special quotas for the various culture groups in their states; the group in charge saw itself as a minority and needed to maintain cultural distinctiveness if it was to continue to make a special claim on power and wealth. But even apparently ethnic terms such as

Han, Khitan, and Jurchen turn out to have been unstable: the Mongols sometimes lumped all three together as the "Han people" of the north, and when they conquered the Southern Song (1126–1279), they labeled its population "people of the south" (*nan ren*).

In 1368 the Ming founder attempted to have it both ways in announcing his reign to his population and to foreign states. After Song, he explained, heaven's mandate to rule had gone to men from the desert (i.e., the Mongols) who "entered the central country and became rulers of all under heaven," but now "I am the ruler of the central country."[10] He was, he acknowledged, from the southeast, rather than the "central plain" (*zhong yuan*) or "central land" (*zhong tu*), but now he had conquered the north, driven out the "nomads" (*hu ren*) who had befouled the "florescent civilization" (*hua xia*) with the "rank odor of sheep and goats." In this implicit distinction between the political order and civilization, political legitimacy stems from the possession of the territorial center, but the justification for driving others from this pivotal area was loyalty to its historical civilization.[11]

In the post-Tang world, political universalism—the rhetoric of a greater empire—was problematic. Although the Mongols claimed it, the Great State of Ming, asserted at best to be the holder of the central country in a larger world of many countries. The other extreme, the sort of ethnic particularism associated with much modern nationalism, was not a possibility, especially for the tens of thousands of literati who lived in Liao, Jin, and Yuan.

But in the eleventh century, universalism was not dead. Instead, two other kinds of universalism were conceived (and to some extent resurrected) during the eleventh century. One was cultural: civilization was something all could learn and all could share; it did not depend on one's birth. This, as we shall see, was an argument for recognizing that men from families with no history of government service could become literati through learning. The same logic could be applied to Jurchens as well. This would become the mainstream position among Han literati under the Jin dynasty and, to some extent, among Jurchens at the Jin court.[12] The other was the product of Neo-Confucian moral philosophy: all beings are endowed with the same moral nature, a position that also appeared in Jin.[13] Neo-Confucians had originally called for the recovery of the north after the Jin conquest, but ultimately they chose another course. Although the Neo-Confucians defined particular texts (such as the Four Books) and particular ideas (such as the doctrine that all humans are endowed with the same innate moral nature), and although they were loyal to the states they served, they proclaimed that morality could be shared by all and that Jurchens and Mongols should at least honor the tradition of learning that taught men how to cultivate their moral natures. In the end, then, the Tang-Song transition brought not the end of universalism but a transformation of it.

North and South

When literati turned their attention to the south, they could see another kind of difference, not in control over territory but in the population of the territory. The most important demographic change in history to this point was the rise of the south. In 752, slightly under half of all registered households (4.07 million) lived in the south and in the Sichuan basin, with the remainder (4.86 million) dwelling in the broad north China plain extending from the Huai River in the south to the northern and western mountains and in the river valleys to the west and northeast of the bend of the Yellow River. By 1085, registered households in the north had increased by 16 percent, to 5.66 million, but the registered population of the south and Sichuan had more than *doubled*, to 10.94 million registered households. To cut this somewhat differently: in 742 the middle Yangzi, lower Yangzi, and southeast coast physiographic macroregions held 27 percent of the registered households but in mid-eleventh century they had 50 percent. The registered population by the end of Northern Song was almost 21 million households, 110 million individuals.[14]

The idea of a "south" and of a north-south divide already had a long history, one of particular importance in the late sixth century when Sui (581–618) conquered the last southern dynasty and reunified north and south, linking its capital at Chang'an to the south by constructing the Grand Canal. However, the "south" in 1050 was no longer a single area centered on the lower Yangzi River, as it had been during the period of "northern" and "southern" dynasties prior to Sui and Tang. Now the south had clearly become multiple regions. Between the Tang and Song periods, there were five successive dynasties in the north, and independent kingdoms in the south that effectively divided the region into five simultaneously viable polities. In other words, the "south" had grown from one area in the southeast to five self-sustaining regions, approximately equivalent to modern Zhejiang and southern Jiangsu, Fujian, and Guangdong, along the coast, and Jiangxi and Hunan inland. This institutional, economic, and demographic articulation of the south as a *multicentered* terrain contrasted fundamentally with the north, where, outside the northwestern river valleys, most of the population lived on a single continuous plain. In Song, three of these southern regions were particularly important, Zhejiang–southern Jiangsu, Jiangxi, and Fujian. After the Southern Song, the Guangdong region gained in significance; in the seventeenth century, the middle Yangzi became a new center of growth. The geography of the river and mountain systems of the south versus the broad plain of the north ensured that the south would continue to have multiple centers as its population grew, and even today the language map of China reflects this diversity.

It is hard to separate cause from consequence in accounting for this shift. The south always had the potential for higher agricultural productivity and, given the river systems, lower transportation costs; so the question is why it happened so late in history. One part of the answer is that warfare and instability in the north after 755 prompted southward migration, although the south itself was not free of destructive rebellions and the breakdown of local government. Another reason is that it became the focus of government attention and investment—first from the Tang court, which increasingly relied on it for revenue after 755, and then from the local kingdoms in the tenth century. Finally, the south had not been made to conform to the pre-rebellion Tang tax system, which was, for the non-elite population, extremely egalitarian. In principle the Tang government distributed to each household, based on the number of productive members, a set amount of land in return for a set amount of grain, cloth, and labor. At the end of a farmer's productive life, the land could be redistributed. In a sense tax was the rent farmers paid for the land they were lent by the state (or by the official families or monasteries that had been given that land). This land redistribution system evidently worked in the northern plains, but there is no visible evidence that it was applied in the south.[15] In the hilly and wet south, a combination of swidden farming and rice agriculture precluded a land redistribution system, but this also meant that investments could be made in paddy fields and in terracing with a reasonable expectation that the fields would be kept in the family. The Twice a Year Tax (*liang shui fa*) reform of 780, a measure meant to secure revenue for the court, recognized the reality of private ownership: it taxed the household's property rather than the individual. The state had in effect surrendered control over land tenure to the private market and allowed households to amass landholdings without state interference.

Between the eighth and eleventh century, the necessary critical mass of factors was reached, and the south began to grow. By one estimate, 95 percent of land was in private hands by the eleventh century, despite occasional attempts to return to a state redistribution system. Three-fourths of the households in the north held title to their own land; in the south, farmers were more likely to be tenants. The steady advance of rice agriculture in the south, bringing with it the terracing of fields, the draining of wetlands, and the building of irrigation systems, enabled the south to support a growing population and ship a far greater amount of grain to the north. In 748, the high point in Tang, the south annually shipped 2.5 million *shi* (1 *shi* = 60 kg) of tax rice north along the Grand Canal. In 1007, and for the rest of the eleventh century, annual shipments reached 6.2 million *shi*. At the same time, Champa rice, a new early-ripening strain from southeast Asia, was introduced with state support; time to harvest was reduced from 150 to 120 days and, by the twelfth–thirteenth centuries, to 60 days. This allowed farmers to plant another crop. By the mid-eleventh century, according to one estimate, 80–90 percent of fields in the south were growing Champa rice, yet the government did not accept it for tax payments. Higher-quality tax rice was thus a relatively small proportion of southern production.[16]

All this meant a greater share of wealth in the south and, consequently, an increasing proportion of affluent families there. Already by the 1050s southerners accounted for the majority of literary men; within a century southerners would tower over intellectual culture, as they would continue to do for centuries to come. By the 1070s officials from the south had come to dominate policy-making offices.[17] Literati knew this, but in the latter half of the eleventh century they were divided over the solution. Some called on the court to institute regional quotas for the civil service examinations but some defended a system that would favor talent above regional representation. Tension between northern and southern officials (and among southern officials from different regions) would become one basis for the formation of factions. By maintaining two capitals, one at Nanjing and the other at Beijing, the Ming dynasty recognized the differences between north and south, as well as the priorities of national defense and economic growth.[18]

North and south had different regional priorities. For the north, defense of the frontier was the main concern. The northern border was a military zone, a drain on the manpower and economic surplus of the northern plain and the northwest. However, for southerners that border was far away. Their most important foreign border was the coast, and their great coastal cities made money from trading networks that extended overseas, a fact that helps explain the extraordinary development of Fujian.[19] The south had exploitable internal frontiers as well, as villagers extended settlements up through river valleys. For the south, in other words, economic development was more important than the defense of the northern frontier. From this perspective, it is not surprising that a southern chief councilor (Wang Anshi, 1021–86) adopted policies that promoted economic development, whereas his foremost opponent, a northern chief councilor (Sima Guang, 1019–86), gave priority to social stability and insisted that economic growth was a function of the size of the population.[20] The southern conviction that infrastructural investment and marketing networks led to greater wealth for both population and government drew support from improvements in agricultural technology, grain stock, and boatbuilding, and greater investment in roads and water conservancy.[21] During Tang, water conservancy projects had been evenly split between north and south; during the Northern Song, 75 percent of all projects were in the south, and the total number of projects doubled; during the Southern Song, this figure doubled once again.[22] The draining and poldering of marshlands created new lands for agriculture in the southeast: 3.5 million *mou* (1 *mou* = 1/6 acre) in the area around Lake Tai in southern Jiangsu alone.[23] These developments help explain why, according to one rough estimate, agricultural productivity doubled between Tang and Song.[24]

The difference between north and south in the cost of transportation was also significant. The Tang court maintained ties to its empire by a network of roads radiating out from Chang'an, the capital in the northwest, and the Grand Canal, which linked it to the southeast. The all-important provisioning of the borders was necessarily by road. But in the mountainous south, where land transport would have been even more expensive, the river systems provided an alternative. Of course, the north did have rivers and canals and the south did have roads, but what mattered were the proportions—downstream transportation by water cost about *one-fifth* of land transport.[25] If we think of river systems as economic networks in which larger downstream settlements served as markets for smaller upstream settlements, we can see that prices would be lower in the south and profits greater. There were also major improvements in the water transport system during this period. In 1000 boats averaged 18 tons in size and could make three trips along the Grand Canal per year; by 1050, thanks to improvements in locks, water management, and boatbuilding, boats averaged 25 tons and made four–five trips a year.[26]

The south carried less of the burden of national defense, it produced more, its transportation costs were lower, and it made more money through commerce; all of which meant the south was richer. In the north the government had to be concerned with control over the land in order to secure provisions and labor for the military, whereas in the south it could see facilitating commerce as a means of increasing the general well-being and gaining revenue. One might say that the north tended toward a tributary mode of production, in which the production and circulation of goods were guided by state requisition, whereas the south tended toward a petty-capitalist mode of production, and legions of small traders kept the economy thriving.[27]

Although the area around the capital at Kaifeng was still the most active economic region in 1050, the lower Yangzi River drainage basin was already becoming the economic heartland. Its cities were growing, better water conservancy techniques allowed settlement of the wet low-lands, and tax quotas were relatively lower. The south received a further boost seventy years later when the north China plain was held in succession by Jurchens, local warlords, and Mongols, and the Song capital was moved south to Hangzhou. The loss of the northern plain also greatly reduced the defense budget by reducing transport costs to the frontier.[28] The north suffered greatly from the successive conquests of the north China plain, and its suffering was compounded when a shift in the course of the Yellow River in 1194 destroyed a large part of its water transportation system.[29] When Ming registered the population in

1391, it had fallen by over 30 percent from 1100, with great losses in the north, northwest, and Sichuan.

The rise of the south also had consequences that presented ideological challenges. Two of these, which are related to changes in the economy and society, are discussed below. Here I note a third: the relationship between the size of the administrative apparatus and the population. Adjusting for changes in territory, there was little overall change in the total number of counties and prefectures between 750 and 1050, yet Song taxed and governed about twice the population. This point has been used to support the thesis that the administrative apparatus failed to grow in step with the population, resulting in an overall decline in governance.[30] This was in part ameliorated by a shift in the spatial distribution of administrative units, as Map 1 illustrates. Still, given that there was a doubling of population without a doubling of the administrative apparatus, the point remains valid.

In practical terms this meant that the government was not prepared to maintain the degree of control over local society that it had in 750, when it still had an elaborate land redistribution system that in theory guaranteed land to all farmers. How, then, was the government to realize its responsibility for the general welfare? The conservative position was to call for an end to social change and the stabilization of the social order (which presumably would have stopped growth), combined with effective but limited government. Activists wanted more. Some literati called for a return to land redistribution, in the interest of creating a society where all had a place, each had enough, and harmony reigned. Others called for expanding the government to boost its institutional ability to intervene in society and guide economic expansion. This was the more popular position from the mid-eleventh century until the Jin conquest in 1126, especially under Wang Anshi and the succeeding New Policies regimes. An idealistic literatus around 1050 would have thought, at least at first, that the New Policies activism was true to the founding faith of the Song: the power of civil institutions to bring order to the world.

After the loss of the north to the Jin, two other positions appeared in the most developed parts of the south, both of which called for a diminished role for government. Those who put their faith in the private market and commerce called on government to reduce its share of the national wealth, maintain the money supply, and facilitate economic

Map 1   County seats in the southeast, 750 and 1050. The increase in county seats in the southeast, marked by red circles, took place in the areas of the greatest population growth. This was balanced by a sharp decrease in the number of seats in the far south, largely a result of the Song abolition of Tang and Southern Han administrative outposts in this region.

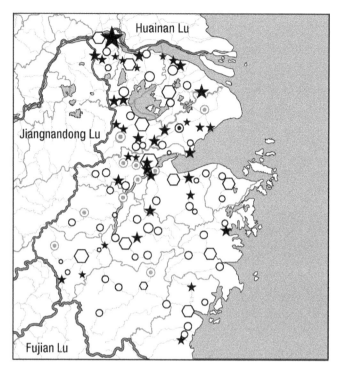

county seat quota		market town quota		prefectural seat quota	
○	1-249	★	1-249	○	4000-7999
○	250-499	★	250-499	○	8000-15999
○	500-999	★	500-999	⬡	16000-31999
○	1000-1999	★	1000-1999	⬡	32000-63999
○	2000-3999	★	2000-3999	⬡	64000-127999
○	4000-7999	★	4000-7999	◉	prefectural seat w/o quota
○	8000-15999	★	8000-15999	◉	county seat w/o quota
		★	16000-31999		

Map 2   Commercial tax quotas in the Liangzhe circuit for 1077 as measured in strings of cash (*guan*). Black symbols are used for market towns, yellow for county seats, and red for prefectural seats. Symbols of the same size represent equal amounts. Not only are there towns with tax quotas greater than those of their county seats and county seats with quotas greater than those of their prefectural seats, there are administrative centers with no quotas as all, indicating an absence of significant commercial activity. The area covered is the Liangzhe circuit (modern Zhejiang, southern Jiangsu, and eastern Anhui provinces). SOURCE: Xu Song, *Song huiyao jigao*, for tax data; China Historical GIS for the administrative hierarchy of 1077.

growth led by the private sector. Those who put their faith in the moral leadership of local literati communities asked what could be done outside the bureaucratic apparatus to promote the common good. From the start the Neo-Confucians rejected the expansion of government activity and centralization called for by the New Policies. Instead, they spoke of local control, moral leadership, voluntary institutions that would organize local literati elites, such as private academies (*shuyuan*), and establishments that could provide a means of doing good for the community, such as charitable granaries. Neo-Confucianism was more successful in gaining followers in the south than in the north, even after north and south were reunified in the late thirteenth century.[31]

Commerce and Urbanization

In 750, urban and commercial centers were simultaneously administrative centers, and the government supervised and limited commercial activity. By 1050, urbanization and commercialization were developing independently of the state administrative system. The difference between the Tang capital of Chang'an and the Song capital of Kaifeng illustrates this. Chang'an was a great square imperial city, built to an architectural plan, strategically located within the mountain passes in the Wei River valley on the corridor that connected Central Asia to the northern plain. Its defense depended on garrisons of conscripts, and its provisioning on the importation of tax goods from outside. Chang'an was *the* city in Tang, and the court was the epitome of its civilization. It had the best of everything. Exotic domestic products were delivered from the prefectures, and merchant and tribute missions brought luxuries overland from Central Asia and by sea from Southeast and South Asia to be sold in its two great market districts. The fashionable wards of Chang'an were home to the mansions and gardens of high official families, although many preferred the more pleasant environs of the secondary capital at Luoyang to the east. These elite families stored their wealth more in land and in bolts of silk than in money or silver. The government granted them estates in return for service, something that was possible because the state in 750 still had a high degree of control over land and labor. But Chang'an has also been described as the arch-example of a "closed" city, in contrast to the new style of "open" city, such as Kaifeng. Our literatus would have had some sense of the difference, for a map of Chang'an produced around 1080 showed a plan of wide avenues dividing walled and gated wards with commerce strictly limited to the two market wards in the east and west.[32]

In contrast, the Song capital of Kaifeng, located near the junction of the Yellow River and a canal from the south, was just as much a commercial city as an administrative one. At first the court considered returning to the Tang model, but in the end it allowed commerce along the streets and, except for critical government sites, left urban development in private hands (although Song built a massive square wall around the city to make it look properly imperial). By 1050, the government was taxing commerce rather than trying to control it. Certainly Kaifeng was the largest and richest city in its day, with an urban and suburban population of about a million, but it was neither the only major city nor the only cultured city. Yangzhou, Suzhou, and Hangzhou, all in the south, attracted merchants and officials as well, and they were much less likely to adhere to the square grid plan of the northern past.[33] In Tang a city or town of importance was simultaneously a prefectural or county administrative seat, but by 1050 there is clear evidence that market towns that were not administrative seats were becoming economically important in both north and south, and new commercial networks connected villages to market towns, thence to small cities and on to larger cities. In 1084, Song officially recognized 1,837 market towns. From the Song on, the economic hierarchy of cities and towns continued to develop, and the administrative system tried to adjust to it.[34]

The transition to the more open, commercial Song city had its roots, first, in the breakdown of government authority after 755 and, second, in the growth of commerce. In the 780s, the government introduced a commercial tax. In Song this was a 2 percent *ad valorem* transit tax and 3 percent *ad valorem* sales tax. But in creating a new revenue source, the government was in effect surrendering control over commerce in favor of taxing it, just as it had given up control over landownership in favor of taxing it. Similarly, the introduction of sales monopolies for salt, liquor, iron, and eventually tea, also instituted in the late eighth century to garner revenue from areas the court did not fully control, was also an impetus to private trade. By Song times the relative proportions of

Table 1.1
Sources of Revenue in 1077

Source	Value (in strings of cash)		Percentage
Land tax	Collected in:		
	rice	12,521,000	
	cash	5,586,000	
	silver	60,000	
	textiles	1,629,000	
	fodder	3,530,000	
	other	64,000	
SUBTOTAL		23,390,000	36.2%
Monopolies	From:		
	salt	12,030,000	
	wine	7,865,000	
	tea	2,029,000	
SUBTOTAL		21,924,000	34.0
Commercial taxes		8,680,000	13.5
Privatized revenue sources (such as wineshops and ferries)		6,027,000	9.3
Customs		540,000	0.8
Mines (mainly copper)		3,973,000	6.2
GRAND TOTAL		64,534,000	99.8%

SOURCE: Liu Guanglin, "Wrestling for Power," based on Bao Weimin, *Songdai difang cai-zheng shi*, 318.

these types of revenue show that for the first time the commercial economy had become the foundation of government revenue. Table 1.1 shows the sources of revenue in 1077.[35]

By the 1050s, the state had learned that it could effectively tax the market, but it had also learned that it had to support the market by maintaining the money supply. The difference from Tang is evident: the highest annual mint in the 740s was 327,000 "strings" of bronze cash (one string was nominally 1,000 cash), but output soon declined to a third of that, with deflation as the result.[36] In 1050 the annual mint was about 1.5 million strings of cash. By the 1080s the annual mint was about 4.5 million strings.[37] (Some scholars bring into the calculation silver as a means of storing wealth and think that the equivalent of about 360,000 strings was entering the economy annually in about 750 and over 9 million strings by 1080.) In terms of value, these figures are equivalent to 4.6 million bushels of rice in 750 and 21.6 million in 1080.[38] In the eleventh century, convertible bills of exchange began to be widely used in private commerce and already in the 1020s the government was circulating paper currency in one area. Yet despite the growth in mintage, some areas suffered debilitating cash famines. A century later, in the 1160s, the government began to issue well-backed paper money with great success. In the long term, silver would become more important than paper as a means of storing value, but in Song bronze coins and paper overshadowed silver.[39] The Song economy had reached a degree of monetarization unprecedented to this point in China's history.

We will probably never know total aggregate government revenues, but in 1050 (a period of inflated prices) the central government recorded total *cash* receipts of about 40 million strings from commercial tax stations (of which there were over 2,000) and monopoly sales of salt, liquor, and a few other commodities.[40] How extensive was the commercial network? A list of commercial tax quotas from 1077 shows that 127 out of the 284 prefectural capitals had annual quotas of over 10,000 strings. The quotas provide a kind of ranking of urban commercial centers and show that a multilevel network was emerging, as we see in Table 1.2.[41] What this table does not show, however, is that 33 county seats and market towns had quotas in excess of their prefectural seats, and 22 county seats and market towns had quotas of more than 10,000 strings, an indication that economic networks and the administrative system were becoming distinct (see Map 2).[42]

It is much more difficult to say how many people actually lived in cities in 1050 since the records we have do not discriminate between urban and rural population (although the Song tax system treated rural and urban households differently and Song was the first dynasty to register and tax urban dwellers). Fairly reliable figures for registered population in the Southern Song show that some prefectures must have had fairly large urban centers. The capital, Hangzhou, was not even the

Table 1.2
Commercial Tax Quotas for Prefectural Seats in 1077
(in thousands of strings of cash)

	Annual quota (000s)			
Location	400	50–100	30–49	10–29
Number south of the Huai River		5	8	40
Number in Sichuan and north of the Huai River		2	12	59
TOTAL	1*	7	20	99

*Kaifeng

largest city in the south, although its population grew from about 100,000 to 190,000 households between roughly 1170 and 1270, or from 500,000 individuals to about 1 million (based on a calculation of five persons per household). Even so, cities such as Wuchang (called Ezhou in Song) in Hubei and Chengdu in Sichuan each had 100,000 households, Nanjing had 170,000, and Quanzhou, the Fujianese port, had 50,000. Prefectural totals give some sense of the kind of growth that was possible: for example, Suzhou had a population of almost 80,000 households in 740; it was smaller than that at the beginning of the eleventh century, but it had reached 200,000 households by 1080, 330,000 by 1275, and 475,000 by 1369.[43]

Two final notes conclude this survey of the economy. First, marked differences appeared in foreign trade and its relationship to the money economy. Tang armies kept the routes to Central Asia open into the mid-eighth century; in Song this trade soon came to be controlled by the state of Xia, with which Song traded tea for horses.[44] The importance of tea in domestic and international trade is suggested by the spread of tea planting from 52 counties in 742 to 80 at the Song founding to 277 by the end of Northern Song.[45] The Central Asian trade would later grow even further under the protection of the Mongols.

Overseas trade increased dramatically between 750 and 1050. The invention of the mariner's compass in the eleventh century freed ships from the need to rely on coastal landmarks. Its economic effects during this period are probably impossible to measure, but the eleventh century saw a stream of official trading missions as well as private trade. Wrecks of Song ships carrying tens of thousands of pieces of pottery, metal tools, and other goods have been found in Southeast Asia. Ships from over 40 states and principalities arrived in Canton alone.[46] Quanzhou in Fujian became the great entrepôt for trade with Southeast Asia. Some have argued that the need for revenue eventually destroyed this trade, but others contend that commercially friendly administrative institutions significantly reduced transaction costs and created an incentive structure conducive to maritime trade.[47] The size of the coastal trade can be estimated from Southern Song sources, which record 19,287 registered vessels in nine Zhejiang coastal counties alone. Given crew sizes, there could have been as many as 700,000 people in the shipping business.[48]

The second concluding point bears on the extent of the commercial revolution and the growth of the money economy from Tang to Song. Did this revolution create a national market for non-luxury goods, or were regions still largely separate economies? Was the growth of the economy driven by the market, or was what we are seeing in Northern Song in particular the result of fiscal policies aimed at maintaining the economic power of the state and enticing merchants to deliver provisions to the northern frontier garrisons? Did the private market begin to drive the economy only in the sixteenth century? It seems to me that the preponderance of evidence supports the conclusion that the economy was rapidly commercializing, the importance of merchants was being recognized, long-distance trade was growing, cash cropping was increasing, and the government was willing to invest in infrastructural improvement and enlarge the money supply in a manner that increased both its revenue and private wealth.[49] One problem is that much of the evidence stems from government documents relating to its fiscal policies during a period when it was simultaneously encouraging economic growth and increasing its revenues. Nevertheless, one recent study has made a persuasive case that the economy and per capita wealth reached a peak in Northern Song that would not be equaled for centuries to come. Although a lack of realistic data on registered households in the sixteenth century makes it difficult to estimate per capita wealth, the evidence at hand suggests that the late Ming economy, long seen as the great commercial revolution in China's history, did not attain Song levels.[50] Expansion in the south increased agricultural output, but it was the availability of cheaper transport there, profits from maritime trade, the greater distance from the troubled northern border, and limits on the collection of commercial taxes that ensured that this increased output resulted in greater per capita wealth.

In 750, the ideal order was one in which the political hierarchy also controlled the distribution of wealth. This was no longer true in 1050. What ideological problems did this pose? The fundamental question was how the state should relate to private wealth. Wang Anshi's New Policies regime aimed to increase the state's role in the economy at the expense of landlords, who controlled rural credit, and great merchants, who controlled the distribution of goods. But this was not an attempt to restore the Tang model of 750: the New Policies encouraged economic growth, fostered long-distance trade, and increased the availability of money and credit. Others urged the government to reduce its revenues on the grounds that the economy was a zero-sum sector: the more the government took, the less there was for private use. Still others called for less interference in trade and credit, in effect allowing the market to take care of the economy. Some early Neo-Confucians proposed a more radical policy: end the private land market, distribute the estates of landlords in equal portions to farmers, and restore an egalitarian rural society based on the idealized "well-field system" of antiquity. Ultimately the question for Neo-Confucians and others was not whether they should accept the reality of economic inequality (in Southern Song times they generally did), but what morality would mean in a world in which economic power operated independently of political power. Southern Song and later Neo-Confucians defended the independence of private wealth, but they also insisted that morality could not be equated either with profit or with political power. At the same time, they found numerous ways in which private wealth could be used to support their own agenda: for example, supporting publications, building shrines and academies, endowing charitable granaries, or investing in lineage building. One consequence of this was that the Neo-Confucian movement did not have to depend on state support to survive, although its adherents certainly wanted the court to recognize the authority of Neo-Confucian learning.

Social Change

Much of what we know about society in the past comes from elite writings and government documents, and in what follows I focus on changes in the elite. The Tang-Song transition did affect the general populace as well, however. In general, it is thought that the transition resulted in greater legal protection for the entire population (agricultural laborers now had legal standing in court) and greater reliance on written contracts in economic transactions. In short, personal bonds were giving way to a new recognition of the majority of people as legally responsible social actors.[51] We should add two caveats. First, there was regional variation, with commoners in the most developed areas having greater rights. Second, the legal system favored landlords over tenants: crimes by tenants against landlords were punished more severely than crimes by landlords against tenants.[52]

Who were the elite? In their terms, they were the *shi*. The use of the term *shi* to refer to an upper stratum of society that played a leading role in political and cultural life was already 1,500 years old in 1050. But what it meant to be a *shi* had changed over time. In the mid-eleventh century, to be a *shi* in political terms meant to serve in government—to be a *shidafu*; in cultural terms, it meant having the education befitting someone serving in civil government (thus the translation of *shi* as "literatus"); and in social terms, it meant coming from a family in which previous generations had been educated and served the government.[53] In 1050, our literatus would have acquired the kind of education tested by the civil service examinations, even if he did not need to take them; once he became eligible for appointment to office, he could expect to begin his service with a staff position in a county or prefecture. If he then secured the sponsorship of higher officials or had successfully held low-ranking posts for a number of years, he could be promoted into the senior administrative ranks. Men with relatives in higher government office could enter the bureaucracy through the "protection privilege," which allowed a high-ranking bureaucrat to secure official rank for a number of his kin. Those without relatives in high offices, those trying to break into officialdom, and those who wanted to be on a more prestigious career track had to participate in the increasingly competitive civil service examinations.

In 1050, the consequences of the course on which Song was embarked were beginning to become clear. The government had been encouraging literati to take the examinations, and literati had been calling on the government to establish schools in the counties and prefectures to better prepare them for the examinations. The numbers of examination candidates were beginning to increase dramatically, but the opportunities for government service were not growing. Some thought it was time to cut back on the use of the protection privilege and make more places for examination degree holders; others argued that access to the examinations should be narrowed rather than broadened; and still others believed that if the government tried to accomplish more, it would necessarily create more positions to fill. What was clear, however, was that the examination system was creating an ever-growing number of men with political aspirations and ever-fewer prospects of government employment. As we shall see later, the existence in local society of large numbers of men who considered themselves to be literati by virtue of their education was both a challenge to the authority of the government and an opportunity for those who sought an audience for their doctrines.

Some Song literati were well aware that what it had meant to be a *shi* in Tang was very different. At its upper reaches, the Tang government was dominated by an oligarchy of great *shi* clans, the *shi-zu*, something close to a state-sponsored aristocracy. These were families who had served at court for centuries and had intermarried with other families of equal stature. And they could be certain of their stature because until 755 the court maintained a national list that ranked the clans and had an office that checked the genealogies of applicants to office. The great clans of Tang had once been the great lords of the countryside as well, but they had traded their local power for court ranks and emoluments. The best families expected their sons to spend their career at court, leaving provincial service to officials of less illustrious pedigree. In Tang the protection privilege and promotion from the ranks of senior clerical personnel supplied most of the needed officials.

How we understand the transformation of the *shi* elite from Tang to Song bears on how we conceive of the audience for new ideological programs.[54] There are, I think, three views. The earliest, and once the most influential, holds that the great clan aristocracy that had dominated the government disappeared when Tang fell. It was succeeded by a new "ruling class" drawn from among the landholding commoners, who were brought into government through a competitive examination system. These new men proceeded to perpetuate themselves as a scholar-official elite, known as the *shidafu*. However, the *shidafu* lacked the aristocratic pedigrees that in Tang had made high officials the emperor's social equals, and as a result Song officials found themselves subordinate to and dependent on the ruler, the only remaining aristocrat. Moreover, the examination system, now capped by a palace examination overseen by the emperor himself, meant that officials owed their position to the ruler directly. The *shidafu*, as dependents of the emperor, supported his centralization of bureaucratic power. But when those policies proved detrimental to their own economic interests as landlords, they were torn between their institutional loyalty to the state and their economic loyalty to their families. Ultimately, they tended to follow their economic interests; they became corrupt and self-interested. Thus China was left with an autocratic ruler and a self-interested elite, and its progress toward modernity was thwarted. In this view, Neo-Confucianism offered no alternative and made no difference.[55]

This account, in which the "feudal" aristocracy of Tang gave way to the "modern" bureaucracy of Song, was soon challenged by Marxist historians. They tended to the view that state control over land and labor in Tang in effect bound farmers to the land, to be disposed of as the state saw fit, and officials controlled that population on behalf of the state, which they constituted. When the Tang system broke down, it became possible to acquire large estates without holding office, with the result that the landlords became a feudal ruling class.[56] It was in the interest of those who controlled the means of production (the landlords) to increase the central authority of the state because they needed it to defend their interests against their tenants, and they needed an ideology that justified this arrangement. Some have argued that Neo-Confucianism supplied that ideology.[57]

More recently, a third view of the social transformation has emerged, one that I think better fits how Song literati thought about culture, family, and political service and the realities of their lives.[58] In 750 it could still be assumed that one's moral quality and cultural refinement was largely determined by one's ancestry. *Shi* clans were not just court officials; they were the "best" people from whom officials could be chosen (in fact Tang also employed men from non-*shi* backgrounds as officials). Pedigree mattered, and so the court ranked the great clans and checked the genealogical claims of office seekers. Given what they represented, the presence of great clans in government helped legitimate a dynasty, but what made a clan great was the line of ancestors with high government office extending into the distant past.

We cannot, in other words, separate the Tang great clans as social elite—which they were—from their focus on holding official rank, for ideally the hierarchy of political power and the hierarchy of social status were the same. But to do this, Tang had to make it institutionally possible for members of great clans as the social elite to maintain the office and rank befitting a political elite. Tang accomplished this with a system that allowed large numbers of people to have some kind of official status. If officials could not secure positions in the regular bureaucracy for their sons and grandsons, then they could place them in various "guards," register them as "students," or find them places on the professional staff of a government office (in Tang, but not in Song, senior clerkships were still a major route into higher office). Men in such status groups were "officials outside the stream" for regular promotion (*liu wai guan*), but they could qualify for promotion into the Nine Ranks at the apex of the bureaucratic system and thus become "officials within the stream [for regular promotion]" (*liu nei guan*). In the 730s, there were about 18,000 regular officials (the Nine Ranks), but beyond this there were about 140,000 men in these other official categories "outside the stream." In addition, there were 300,000 minor office functionaries who lacked such status. In 749 the government listed 398 clans, each of which had several branches.[59] Of the 140,000 men of status, some 60,000 were listed as students, yet the Tang examination system aimed to garner only twenty or thirty talented (usually aristocratic) men a year for those court offices that required knowledge of the Classics or literary talent. Passing the examination merely made one eligible to be considered for an appointment; it did not guarantee one. After 755 the examination supplied a maximum of some 15 percent of civil officials.

The genius of the Tang system was that it sharply limited the number of men who could become officials (an intake of about 600 a year was enough to staff the Nine Ranks) while absorbing a very large number of their relatives into honorable official status groups. This allowed the great clans to shift the focus from power in the localities to life as part of the government system. But making the clans dependent on the government was a tragedy for the great clans in the end, for when Tang lost control over the provinces to military men and when rebels sacked its cities, it lost its ability to provide clansmen with stations and incomes, and out in the provinces pedigree mattered ever less. Great clan status mattered as long as someone was there to reward those who maintained it; once the dynasty fell, the great clans faded away.

What had changed by 1050? At this point there were 12,700 men holding civil (rather than military) rank. (We do not know how many actual posts there were in the civil administration, but we do know that some posts, tax station managers for instance, were regarded as beneath civil officials and held by officials with military rank.) About half of the 12,700 would have entered the ranks by passing the regular civil service examination, as many as 30 percent might have gained rank (but not necessarily an official post) by passing special "facilitated" examinations for those who had repeatedly failed the regular exams, and an uncertain number (perhaps over 30 percent) could have held rank by virtue of a father's or grandfather's office. In other words, by 1050 the examinations had become the primary means of entering the bureaucracy and the only means of rising to high office.

This led to a debate over what made a *shi* a *shi*. Some argued that the examinations were meant to choose officials from among the *shi*, and that the *shi* were in fact those cultured families with traditions of government service; in other words they saw the *shi* as a hereditary group. This was not a claim to great clan ancestry in most cases, but a sense that the state ought to be managed by men from families with the right values, the right education, and traditions of service. Families whose fortunes came from commerce or who had no traditions of service did not belong. But others argued that since the examinations tested education and talent, anyone who had the education of a *shi* ought to be regarded as a *shi*. In other words, education made a person a *shi* and fit for government service. This was particularly important in the south, where families had little history of officeholding.

This debate had not yet been resolved by 1050. Some contended that to be a *shi* meant to belong to that group of families who had made government service their occupation. The great northern conservative Sima Guang, whose family had served the dynasty since its founding, even proposed that admission to the examinations be limited to those who had secured the greatest number of recommendations from officials at court![60] Predictably, incumbent officials developed a variety of special examinations to lower competition for their sons at the entry level.[61] Such developments pointed toward the creation of a new state aristocracy. Why, then, did this *not* happen?

It did not happen because in practice a consensus formed around an alternative model: those who governed should be the most talented men, talent could be cultivated through schooling, and competitive examinations should be used to select the best. This made it increasingly difficult for families to count on rank and office for their descendants. Moreover, by 1050 both the entry-level prefectural examinations and the capital examinations were blind, making it difficult for examiners to be sure they were passing people of a preferred background. (In Tang the examinations were not blind, and candidates typically circulated their writings to the examiners prior to the exam. Under these circumstances the examination offered a chance to compare the examiners' favorites.) Opportunities to prepare for the exams were increasing as well, as prefectures and counties built schools to prepare local students for the examinations, but even before that the number of candidates had been steadily increasing. In addition, the old Tang system of supporting many official status groups outside the Nine Ranks of regular officials had disappeared. Being a clerk, for example, no longer made one eligible for promotion into the Nine Ranks, and although occasionally the court proposed employing surplus literati as clerks, very few accepted that being a clerk was an honorable alternative for a *shi*.[62] Being a student brought no special status unless one held a place at the National University at the capital, and by 1050 this was no longer restricted to the sons of officials. In short, the government no longer could provide all *shi* family members honorable official careers. Furthermore, when it later extended relief from the labor service obligation to households of students who had passed the entry-level examination, it encouraged yet more families to prepare their sons for the examinations.[63]

Literati families were thus confronted with a problem. If they could not expect the government to favor them by excluding others or provide honorable careers for their sons, then how were they to help their descendants keep their status as *shi*? "What do families wish for their descendants?" asked the great twelfth-century writer and poet Lu You; "That their food and clothing will be sufficient and marriages will be made at the right age; that they will be *shi* and not slide off into being artisans and merchants, nor descend to being clerks, nor depart to become Daoist and Buddhist clergy."[64] How could an elite family maintain its status as *shi* if every generation did not serve in government? At least by the middle of the twelfth century a solution to this problem had taken shape in the south.

The solution, which involved both new social practices and a reconceptualization of what it meant to be a *shi*, entailed the formation of local communities of literati families. During the early Tang, the great clans had transformed themselves from local magnates who held rank in government into a bureaucratic aristocracy; ultimately in Song the *shi* transformed themselves from literati who served in government into local literati elites, families whose males were educated for the examinations they rarely passed and who aspired to government offices they rarely obtained but played important roles in local society. This happened through social movements in two directions.

The first direction was the rise of well-to-do local families to *shi* status, made possible by shifting the requirements for being a *shi* away from officeholding and toward the acquisition of the kind of education the examinations tested. As the late Song statecraft writer Ye Shi observed: "All the common people can become *shi*, but not all do; nor do all *shi* become officials."[65] The number of county and prefectural local schools increased, and in the twelfth century the government began to grant certain tax breaks to the families of those who registered at such schools. Families that had long been rich and powerful in their hometowns began to invest in education; they began to convert to being *shi*. It was to their advantage to do so. This can be illustrated with a story about the Guo family of Dongyang county in Zhejiang, as told by a family friend in the mid-twelfth century. Grandfather Guo amassed a great fortune, thousands worked his lands, and the Guos were known throughout the region as a powerful family. But to be powerful, rich, and smart did not protect the family from the jealousy of its neighbors, and when the Guos transgressed the law, even the *shi* families extorted everything they could from them. The examination system mattered, the writer explained, for two reasons. From the perspective of locally powerful families, it was a means to join the *shi* and better defend their interests, and from the perspective of the public good, it led powerful families to accept constraints on their behavior in order to gain the acceptance of the local *shi*. The Guos eventually figured this out. The son saw to the education of the grandsons, and one of them in turn associated himself with the leading *shi* of the day.[66] From other sources, we know that this family went on to become the most important sponsors of private academies in Dongyang county.[67]

The second direction of change was the greater efforts of official families to solidify their position in local society. Families who in the eleventh century had been successful in placing sons in office began to turn their attention to maintaining their social position without the guarantee of making government service the family occupation. They did this by shoring up their position in their home locale by building marriage alliances with other leading local families and playing a greater role in the social and cultural life of their native region, rather than seeking marriage ties with officials from elsewhere in order to create bureaucratic alliances. An example will illustrate this family strategy. Hu Ze (963–1069) was the first in Yongkang county (near Dongyang) to pass the examinations and rise to high office at the capital. When he retired, he did not return to Yongkang but moved his household to Hangzhou, the administrative center of Zhejiang, where it was easy to stay in touch with other high officials and make connections for his sons. Other Hus stayed in Yongkang. But in the twelfth century, when some Yongkang Hus were successful in the examinations, they stayed in Yongkang and tried to maintain solidarity among their local kin. Their descendants have remained a force in local society into the present.[68] In the eleventh century in places such as Yongkang, an official who wanted to marry his children to families of the same status could look abroad instead of marrying locally. By the twelfth century, the number of official and literati families in Yongkang had increased, and it was much easier to find marriage partners of equal status.[69] Not everywhere in the south was like Yongkang. In Jiangxi, where there were many well-established official families in the eleventh century, a demonstrable shift took place from the Northern to Southern Song period away from seeking external marriage partners to marrying locally.[70]

In some instances establishing a local base was not so easy. The northern official families who were able to escape to the south after the fall of the Northern Song in 1126 needed to find a place to settle, and they needed to intermarry with powerful families like the Guos, families who themselves aspired to *shi* status and benefited from the social status of such a marriage. Lü Zuqian (1137–81), a scholar and official who helped spread Neo-Confucianism, was descended from one of the most illustrious bureaucratic families of Northern Song. After the Jurchens took Kaifeng, his branch of this family moved south to Jinhua (next to Yongkang), where the local government lent them a house. Lü Zuqian's father married him to the daughter of one of his bureaucratic colleagues, but Lü Zuqian (who passed the examinations and held office for a time) married his daughter to the son of one of the wealthiest local families, which in the previous generation had established itself as *shi*.[71] However, the Lüs did not establish a strong economic base of their own, and they did not become one of the great local families.

I am not sure that a literatus in 1050 could have foreseen these developments, although the course had already been set. Some twelfth-century observers were aware that in the past illustrious pedigrees and high-status marriages had mattered more.[72] But in 1050 it was clear that the number of *shi* was increasing, that southern families were more competitive than ever, and that the most important factors behind these trends were increases in wealth and the spread of education. By the start of the twelfth century, the government was investing in schools and supporting their students. Some have argued that in Song the term *shi* really applied only to those serving or eligible to serve as officials, and that their numbers were sharply restricted by the fact that only the *jinshi* degree counted (in contrast to the many different kinds of degrees in Ming and Qing)—in this view the great expansion of the *shi* had to wait until after 1447, the year the Ming government removed the quota on the number of students who might be granted the special rights of local degree candidates.[73] I am more persuaded by those who think this expansion happened by the end of Northern Song, when there were as many as 167,662 registered students in state schools supported by rents from over 1.5 million acres of land with annual expenses amounting to almost 3 million strings of cash.[74]

The growth of local literati communities in the south continued through the Mongol invasion. The role of schools in this is evident: in Fujian, Zhejiang, Jiangxi, and Hunan, between 80 and 100 percent of counties had schools (in the north incomplete sources show between 10 and 25 percent had schools), and there is mention of another 350 private schools, most of which appeared after 1126.[75] In Southern Song the numbers of triennial prefectural examination candidates are quite amazing: up to 20,000 in Fuzhou in Fujian, over 10,000 in Jianning in Fujian, over 10,000 in Jizhou in Jiangxi, 7,000 in Yanzhou in Zhejiang, and 7,000 and 8,000 in other prefectures in Zhejiang.[76] With numbers like these, one can understand why it is possible that by 1250 there were as many as 400,000 candidates taking part in the examinations. By this point all agreed that such men could be called *shi*. The chance that any one of them would gain office was minuscule, but as families compiled genealogies and strengthened kinship connections, it became ever more likely that an examination candidate would be kin to someone who had passed the examinations and gained office.[77]

The transformation of the *shi* from official families to the community of the educated depended on the spread of education. Printing played an important role. By 1050 our literatus would also have read some of his books in printed form, either at a library in a government school or at home after purchasing them at a commercial book store, whereas his counterpart in 750 could have read only handwritten copies. This, too, was a long-term trend. In the north the National University had completed the printing of a set of the Confucian classics in 130 fascicles between 932 and 953; in the south local government offices and, increasingly, commercial firms were printing books. By the end of the eleventh century, one could buy various editions of the Classics and commentaries, printings of Buddhist and Daoist texts, historical and political writings, philosophical tracts, literary anthologies, and the collected writings of individuals. Although movable type was invented in around 1050 and occasionally used, most printing was done with woodblocks: a whole page was written out and pasted face down on a plank, the spaces around the characters cut away, the block inked and a page struck off. The great advantage of this system was that once the blocks were cut, copies could be printed on demand. Some people sent their manuscripts to well-known printers in the cities, but often teams of journeymen traveled to the family, school, temple, or government office that offered work for them. The result was that many places were producing printed books—above all, books for the examination market and religious texts—and often competing with one another to issue new works, even pirating other printers' editions.[78]

The result was a far more literate and well-published society than in Tang. We know the names of about 2,200 writers of poetry in Tang, but over 9,000 for Song; some prose writings from about 10,000 Song figures are still extant, but only a quarter as many from Tang. These differences may reflect the greater chance of survival for Song works, but they also fit the larger trend.[79] The literate national elite was not only larger but also better informed. County and prefectural schools gave students access to local officials, with their connections to the political center. There were also other means of staying informed. By the late eleventh century, a system had been established for distributing the official court gazette to the prefectures, and local governments were required to inform the public of new rules and procedures through public placards. There were also privately published papers aimed at informing literati who lacked official connections.[80] Despite official prohibitions, the printing industry saw to it that government documents relating to current events were published, thus enabling local literati communities to stay informed of current events.[81] The volume of private and public publishing continued to expand. For Wuzhou in Zhejiang (which included the counties of Jinhua, Dongyang, and Yongkang cited in examples above), there are references to books by about 150 Song period authors for this prefecture alone, compared to less than ten for all periods prior to the Song.[82]

In 1050 a literatus could know that some things set him apart from the *shi* of 750. He no longer claimed descent from a family with a pedigree stretching back through the centuries, but he knew that the civil administration was now almost exclusively in the hands of people who identified themselves as *shi*. He was ever more likely to view learning as that which defined him as a *shi* and thus as the best route into government service, but he also saw that the competition was increasing. He knew that he lived in a wealthier and more commercial world. He knew that international relations, regional development, and education were central concerns of government. And, as we shall see in the next chapter, there were a fair number of literati who had been writing about how and what he should think about all these matters and how government ought to respond to the problems of the day. Some literati were aware that current policy was creating far more aspirants to office than the bureaucracy could absorb and called for cutting back the number of officials who did not have active appointments, but others appealed to the growing pool of talent with plans to increase the size of government and to use its powers to create a better society. This was the position taken by Wang Anshi and his successors, whose New Policies would double the number of officials within a generation.

In 1050 I think the expectation was still that literati could and should make government their occupation. Since few writers at the time were seriously considering what the alternatives might be, the solutions appeared to be either to reduce literati numbers or increase the size of government. But by the end of the twelfth century, in the south it was clear that neither option had been realized: opportunities for education continued to increase and literati numbers continued to grow, yet the bureaucracy was trimmed to the size it had been around 1050, and those with office had developed new means to advantage their own descendants.[83] The new social order in the south kept the literati in place, but the sense that to be a *shi* was to serve as an official was much weaker. Continued literati growth supported ever larger numbers of scholars: well-to-do families wanted private teachers, academies needed famous names to draw students, publishers wanted authors, and so on. Now, however, literati were increasingly engaged with their locality. In 1050 the south had known only three generations of Song rule, by 1200 there had been eight generations. One consequence of this was that the numbers of local families with histories of education and officeholding increased, and as they increased, there was ever less reason for the rare literatus who gained office to move away from home.

This had two consequences, which the Neo-Confucians would address more successfully than most others. First, as the numbers of families who saw themselves as being the equals of the local officials increased in a locality, they constrained the scope of action of local government.[84] Second, those local literati families began to see themselves as a community capable of acting in concert, and even, some Neo-Confucians thought, of transforming society from the bottom up.

2

Searching for a New Foundation in the Eleventh Century

Let us return to our literatus as a young man in the 1050s. Let us suppose he had concluded that the Tang order could not be revived. Let us also suppose that he was ambitious, both for himself and for his country, that he hoped not only to pass the examinations and hold office but also to define a common purpose for contemporary society. When he looked around for answers, he would have found disagreement among the literati over what the goals for the times should be and how they could be attained. This chapter traces the unfolding of these debates and locates the first Neo-Confucians within them by discussing three successive developments that shaped ideological arguments in the eleventh century.

The first trend was the politicization of learning. As the importance of examinations for literati political careers increased, so did calls for reforming the examinations. From the start, changing what the examinations tested was seen as a way of changing what literati learned and how they thought about politics, culture, and morality. These controversies were an outgrowth of an emerging national debate over what the Song should try to achieve, but they were also a cause of that debate, because careers depended on examination success.

The second development was the undermining of the ideological foundation of empire. Layer by layer, mid-eleventh century intellectuals were taking apart ideas about history and the cosmos that in Tang times had justified empire. Although this deconstruction of the early imperial model did not produce a new consensus, in retrospect we can see that shared convictions about how the individual was connected to history and cosmos were taking shape. Neo-Confucians contributed to these new convictions, to be sure, but they were not their sole authors.

The third element was the imposition of an ideological program on government. For most of the last fifty years of the Northern Song period, one group of literati—those associated with Wang Anshi's New Policies, not the Neo-Confucians—held power at court and put their answer to the question of what the Song should accomplish into effect. The new social and economic policies aimed to transform society, and a nationwide school system and a new curriculum aimed to transform how literati learned, but they also split the literati into ideological factions. Neo-Confucianism was one of the alternatives to the New Policies program. Its eventual success represented a rejection of the New Policies path and had profound consequences for the rest of Chinese history.

Literati Opinion and the Civil Service Examinations

In 1050 the court was led by men who were merely trying to cope: to maintain dynastic continuity with an emperor who lacked an heir, to balance the budget in the face of rising deficits, and to maintain defenses against the Khitans to the northeast and the Tanguts to the northwest. But literati knew that some of the most famous writers of the day had once proclaimed more ambitious goals. From the 1020s into the 1040s, they had accused the court of losing control over circumstances and had called on the emperor to take charge or, at the very least, to bring to court those who wanted to accomplish something. Their rhetorical strategy had been to measure their own times against antiquity, not the great Tang empire, and to condemn the reigning approach to government as a misplaced Daoistic ideal, inappropriate to a great state, of not interfering in society and letting the people take care of themselves. Fan Zhongyan (989–1052), the leader of this group, had argued that this was not the time for a quietist vision of rulership: in antiquity the kings "personally oversaw transforming society through their instruction, thus making the populace pursue the good."[1] One of Fan's propagandists, the gifted writer and scholar Ouyang Xiu (1005–72), set up the problem in 1042 in his "Essay on Fundamentals." His "antiquity" featured a militarily powerful and economically rich country, which distributed a fair share of land to all and saw to everyone's education and moral instruction, and in which social harmony reigned. No dynasty during the early imperial period had attained this ideal, and Song had not yet either. But more important, the reason to look to antiquity was to understand the principles through which the ancients had accomplished this: "There is a necessary order of things in affairs of the world, and there is a necessary sequence for putting them in order. The documents of [the ancient sage-kings] Yao and Shun are too summary. Yet in later ages good governance of the world has always taken its models from the Three Dynasties, because by inferring from the order of things one can know the necessary sequence [of action]."[2] Hu Yuan (993–1059), whose style of teaching Fan had held up as a model for the world, called on his students to be sages, but his sage aimed at more than detached omniscience: "A sage will penetrate all things and illuminate all events. A sage will make himself available to society. It is appropriate for him to complete his worldly enterprise by giving assistance to the emperor, bringing welfare to the people, and facilitating the myriad things."[3]

Fan, Ouyang, and Hu had called for a government with a vision of what the proper order of things should be and willing to work to realize it. To accomplish that, they wanted men like themselves to have power. They succeeded, but only briefly. The emperor summoned Fan and his allies to court in 1043–44 when foreign threats loomed and critics needed to be accommodated. Among the several measures Fan instituted was a change in the civil service examinations meant to favor literati with big ideas, men like himself and his supporters. The reforms were soon rescinded, but out of power Fan's group, with growing persuasiveness, called on younger literati to adopt a politically engaged approach to learning and writing.

Unless he had a close relative in high office, a literatus who aspired to serve in 1050 had to prepare for the examinations. At the prefectural level and at the capital, the examinations were now blind tests—before being sent to the examiners to grade, examination papers were copied by clerks and names replaced by code numbers; what the candidate said mattered more than who he knew. The examinations offered a choice between two tracks, both inherited from Tang. One track tested the memorization of texts, usually one or more Classics and their commentaries or alternatively ritual codes, the legal code, or the first histories; the other tested the ability to compose poetry and prose.

THE CLASSICS IN THE EXAMINATIONS

In 1049, 550 degrees were awarded in the various fields of the memorization track, making it the most popular choice.[4] Our literatus would have thought of "the Classics" as the five major Classics in the first instance, although he could have spoken of the "Six Classics" by including the lost *Music* classic or the "Nine Classics" by including additional texts.

Today we see the texts of the Classics as being of various dates, some antedating Confucius and others being compiled centuries later in the Han dynasty. Despite scholarly doubts, the official view in the eleventh century was that the texts of the Classics were works of the times and persons they claimed to represent—in some cases the sage-kings and the beginning of government and civilization in the third millennium B.C.—and had been edited by Confucius in the sixth century B.C.

The *Documents* was seen as a compilation of texts from the eras of the sage-kings. The *Odes* was a collection of ancient hymns, songs, and poems, which were read as celebrating events of state or expressing the feelings of society about the quality of governance. The *Book of Change* had 64 hexagrams (the set of possible permutations of six full or broken lines) and commentaries attributed to the sages. It was regarded as a guide to understanding the outcomes of human events because the process of divination and the structure of the text itself embodied the fundamental patterns of natural process. The *Rites* usually referred to the *Book of Rites*, a collection of essays on ritual, broadly conceived, as concept and practice. To act according to the rites was supposed to bring about social harmony. The phrase "ritual and music" stood for governing through noncoercive means rather than laws and punishments. There were two other ritual classics: the *Rites of Zhou*, seen as a detailed account of the Zhou dynasty's structure and government around 1000

B.C., and the *Ceremonial*, which spelled out a series of rituals for the political elite. The *Spring and Autumn Annals* was a chronology from 722 to 484 B.C. edited so as to reveal Confucius' judgments of political events during an age of decline. Students were expected to read it together with the historical narratives in the *Zuo Transmission of the Spring and Autumn Annals*, although it could also be read with the *Gongyang* or *Guliang Transmission*s, which sought to uncover Confucius' judgment of political behavior by interpreting the wording in the *Annals*.

Han dynasty scholars, with patronage from the court, had established these texts as "the Classics." They had made two claims for them. First, the Classics revealed how the sage-kings had created civilization, governed the empire, and created an ideal integrated social order. Second, the way the sage-kings had done this was applicable to later periods as well, an idea we see the young Ouyang Xiu adopting at the start of his "Essay on Fundamentals." These claims could be contested, and were, but they depended on how one interpreted the Classics. Han dynasty scholars developed the art of writing extensive commentaries on the Classics to make arguments about what the standards for political and personal life should be, and the writing of commentaries had continued even after the Han empire fell apart into separate kingdoms in A.D. 221.

When Tang created a new unified empire almost 400 years later, the court commissioned a grand synthesis of past interpretations. The work that resulted, *The Correct Meanings of the Five Classics* (*Wu jing zheng yi*), adopted one commentary as the standard interpretation for each classic and supplemented it with a subcommentary that sought to rhyme the many interpretations that had appeared during the centuries past.

But what could justify making officials out of literati who simply had memorized the Classics and knew the commentaries? As the record of the creation of empire in antiquity, the Classics were the foundation on which history ought to unfold, the basis for a unified empire, and the necessary education for all those who participated in governing that empire. The Tang court asserted:

Now the Classics are the subtle pointers of the most intelligent of men and the affairs that were possible for the sages; with them one can make heaven-and-earth constant, regulate *yin* and *yang*, rectify social norms, and promote morality.

On the outside they show how to benefit everything in the world, yet on the inside they contain behaviors for being good as a person. Those who learn them will grow; those who do not learn them will fall. When in the great enterprise of governing the ruler honors [these texts], he completes his imperial virtue; when a common fellow can recite them, he wins the respect of nobles. What king has not proceeded along this Way of ours to establish his influence, spread his title, glorify his transforming power, and change social customs? Thus it is said, "When one is compliant and sincere, it is thanks to the teaching of the *Songs*; when he sees the larger picture and can think ahead, it is thanks to the teaching of the *Documents*; when he is accommodating and harmonious, it is thanks to the teaching of the *Music*; when he is reverent and respectful, it is thanks to the teaching of the *Rites*; and when he writes judgments and finds analogies between cases, it is thanks to the teaching of the *Spring and Autumn Annals*."[5]

Yet despite such grand claims, by 1050 a memorization degree had come to be regarded as a bit second-rate, something that required more effort than intelligence to pass. With such a degree, one was unlikely to reach a prestigious office at the capital.

The problem was twofold. First, since the late Tang scholars had been writing their personal interpretations of the various classics, starting with the *Spring and Autumn Annals*, and they departed from the orthodox Tang commentaries in order to show what the Classics meant for their own times. To really understand the sage-kings of antiquity and Confucius, Ouyang Xiu and others thought, literati had to read the original texts of the Classics, divorced from the commentaries of the past. What were the values that had guided the sage-kings, they asked. What kind of society had they created? What had to change before the present could match it? Since there were many views but no new consensus, the memorization tests had little choice but to ignore these developments. Second, as the new spate of commentaries made clear, literati wanted to interpret the texts in ways meaningful to themselves. But the highly objective memorization examinations tested mastery of texts, not of meaning and relevance. Ouyang and others tried to save the situation by creating a third examination track in 1057, one that combined a test of knowledge of the texts of the Classics with interpretive essays on the "greater significance" (*da yi*) of various passages.[6] This had less appeal than they had hoped, and in 1073 the memorization fields were abolished altogether.

EXAMINATION LEARNING AS *WEN-XUE*

In 1050 our literatus had a second choice, he could compete in the "literatus presented [to the court]" or *jinshi*, examination. This required some rote knowledge: a candidate was tested on his memorization of the *Analects* of Confucius and asked ten factual questions about the *Spring and Autumn Annals* or the *Book of Rites*. But the heart of the *jinshi* examination was a literary test. First, he had to compose a poem and a rhapsody on set themes according to strict rules of Tang prosody, followed by a prose essay on a set theme and three or five "treatises" in response to questions on current issues of government policy or scholarship.[7] The "creative" composition requirement made the *jinshi* unique, although our literatus was probably more concerned with recognizing the themes set for the compositions and avoiding mistakes in poetic composition, for too many mistakes resulted in instant failure.[8]

What logic justified using literary composition to decide who would serve in government? In Tang the examinations recruited a small number of officials for certain kinds of offices—a literary test was a way of recruiting men who were not only well read but also skilled in literary composition; in 1050 the exams had become the pre-eminent means of recruitment, for without high-ranking relatives there was no other way of becoming a civil official. This was not an accident. By the end of the tenth century, the Song court had come to believe men devoted to a certain kind of learning should govern.

In Tang, and still in 1050, the examinations, both the memorization and the literary composition tests, tested what was acquired through "learning" (*xue*). As it was understood at the time, this meant that the examinations tested *wen*. When the Song founders expanded the examinations to recruit literati (rather than military men, for example), they were "using *wen* to broadly draw in the literati."[9] For better or worse, they were closing the road to office to those who were "simple and without *wen*."[10] In these contexts, *wen* meant the writings from the past thought to provide models for the present (thus memorization of the Classics) and the ability to write in a good style (thus literary composition). A person who "had *wen*" was someone who knew how to write well, and this in turn required being well read in the textual tradition: the Classics, the histories, philosophical writings, and the works of past writers in literary genres. But, of course, in a society in which writing well was defined as being able to write in sophisticated styles of poetry and prose, being well read did not mean one was able to write well. Literati who passed a memorization examination had read well, albeit narrowly, but were presumed to be lacking in literary skill, the highest individual form of *wen*.

This would have made sense to our literatus. He could see examination learning as one aspect of what it meant to be a good literatus as defined by Confucius. He was expected to maintain the highest standards of "ethical conduct" (*de-xing*), that is, he should practice filial piety (by showing respect to his parents and mourning the deaths of his relatives according to his degree of kinship to them) and generally conduct all his relations with others according to well-defined ethical standards. He was expected to be well educated, which meant that he was successful at *wen-xue* (learning that was concerned with the acquisition of *wen*). And he was expected—contingent on passing the examinations in this case—to participate in the "work of governance" (*zheng-shi*).* Together these three represented areas of personal, social, and political achievement. They were also distinctive perspectives: a person who believed ethical conduct mattered most could object to a good writer who behaved immorally, the politically minded to a person who let a concern with integrity get in the way of political effectiveness, and literary men to a successful politician's lack of intellectual cultivation.

Early in the Song period there had been a general consensus that *wen*, and men with literary ability in particular, were crucial to the success of the dynasty. "*Wen* is of pre-eminent value for the age," one literatus wrote, for "even though past and present differ in form, and north and south vary in tone, its essentials are simply to broadcast the kingly beneficence and transmit the feelings of those below and, without departing from the Way of the sages, to accomplish the common goals."[11] And another: "Man's possession of *wen* is the great way of governing; he who has apprehended this Way can control the process of transfor-

---

*These are three of the four categories (*si ke*)—the fourth being speech—to which ten of Confucius' foremost disciples (the *shi zhe*) were assigned in *Analects* 11.3. These categories were frequently used in Tang and Song to define areas of elite endeavor and ways of gaining good reputations. As such, these were also values, the relative weight of which literati debated.

mation through instruction."[12] To govern through *wen* was to govern in a *civil* fashion, relying on proper forms, communication, and education rather than the coercion and violence that had marked the previous century. Officials who could write well—officials who had acquired *wen* through learning—were men who could be trusted to realize the idea of a civil order in practice.

We need to pay attention to this concept of *wen* for two reasons. First, we tend to assume that intellectual history is defined by the history of philosophy and not by concepts that seem to be more literary than philosophical. Second (as we shall see in the next section), some intellectuals were beginning to question whether it was adequate. In early Song the term *wen* stood for the overarching value the dynasty claimed for itself. There was a precedent for this: *wen* had been used in the Han dynasty to characterize the guiding value of the ancient Zhou dynasty, in contrast to the values of the preceding Xia and the Shang dynasties.[13] Over time the term had accumulated several levels of meaning. It was the manifest aspect of cosmic process (astronomy, *tian-wen*, being the study of the *wen* of heaven), the forms of human society (the *wen* of humanity), the cumulative textual tradition that stemmed from antiquity and the Classics, the complex of political and social values and normative cultural forms associated with the sage-kings (*wen-jiao*, the teaching of *wen*), and eventually individual literary accomplishment. A person with *wen*-learning was one who had mastered the textual tradition and the skills of writing; he could compose *wen* in the present that was "cultured," in that it drew on the texts and styles and models of the past. Thus in preparing for the *jinshi* examination, our literatus was learning to "do *wen*" (*wei wen*) and produce literary works, *wen-zhang*, which, if successful, might enter the corpus of *wen* as the larger textual tradition that included the Classics, histories, and philosophical and literary writings. All this was implied when literati used the phrase term *si-wen* (This Culture of Ours), which Confucius had used to define his connection both to the founder of the Zhou dynasty and to heaven itself.[14] When literati used the term *wen* to denote the "civil" versus the military, we should understand "civil" in a normative sense: the style of government that drew on ancient sociopolitical models and the textual tradition, operated through writing, and valued literary ability. The connection between civil government and literary/textual learning was evident to the emperor when he commanded in 963 that henceforth the personal staff of the military governors "should have *wen-xue*."[15] As the rhapsody theme for the examination of 1000 expressed it, Song was "perusing the *wen* of man to transform all under heaven."[16] The dynasty's success in creating a unified empire was, one scholar asserted, the "clear result of valuing *wen* and honoring learning."[17]

In pursuing his education, our literatus thus had every reason to agree with his predecessors that "the task of Confucians (*Ru*) is *wen*."[18] By attaching rewards to *wen-xue*, either the passive knowledge of textual traditions or the ability to compose *wen-zhang*, the examinations reinforced this orientation. In the examinations, the dynastic interests of the imperial family and the corporate interests of the literati met on the grounds of literary idealism. The examinations did not create this culture, which had emerged from the aristocratic court circles of medieval China; nor were they an insurmountable obstacle to those who sought to change it from within.

THE ANCIENT STYLE (*GU-WEN*) IN WRITING
AND THE ATTACK ON EXAMINATION LEARNING

The problem for our literatus in 1050 was that the conception of learning as the mastery of *wen* was under attack from within, from men like Fan Zhongyan, Ouyang Xiu, and Hu Yuan. They did not equate skill in composing poetry in the Tang court style with a commitment to or understanding of the ideals implied by *wen*. An ability to compose well-written literary works—the edicts and memorials and the patents of appointment with which the bureaucracy formally conducted its business, and the odes and songs of celebration, letters of friendship and remonstrance, biographies and inscriptions with which bureaucrats conducted their lives—did matter. To be skilled in literary composition was to possess the very qualities of style and culture—of *wen*—that made it possible to serve as a civil official and manage an empire with civil (*wen*) rather than military means. But, beyond the establishment of a civil order, it did not answer the question of what the larger purpose of the dynasty should be.

In 1050 our literatus would have known that examination learning had come under sharp attack from those who believed that the examination system was not testing the right *wen*. Instead Fan Zhongyan, Ouyang Xiu, and many others promoted what they called "the *wen* of antiquity" (*gu-wen*). As Ouyang had written in "Essay on Fundamentals," this "antiquity" (*gu*) was to be thought of as a period in time—the Three Dynasties of Xia, Shang, and Zhou—and as an ideal world, one in which government made everything work so that all needs were met and all people lived in harmony and prosperity. The *wen* of antiquity meant both the texts—the Classics—that gave access to that ideal world and the *style* of those ancient texts, for the way in which they were written was presumed to manifest the values according to which the ancients acted. The logic of this proposition was straightforward: to the discerning eye, the way a person wrote inevitably revealed the values that guided him; thus one could infer the qualities of the person and how he would act from the style of his writing. So studying the "ancient *wen*"—in functional terms we might say to study the "ideal culture"—was really about learning the *values* of the sages and making them one's own.

The idea that the values of sages could be appropriated through learning had been articulated by the founder of the Ancient Style (*gu-wen*), the great post-rebellion Tang literary intellectual Han Yu, who had argued that learning the *wen* of antiquity and writing in the style of the ancients required comprehending the "Way of the Sages" (*shengren zhi dao*). For Han Yu and his Song followers, learning the Way of the Sages was a process of literary transformation. By studying the texts of antiquity in a synthetic manner—by drawing on many texts to grasp the integrated system of the ideal world and the values that guided it—the student would gradually transform the way he wrote. His writing would become "ancient," idealistic. The resulting change in literary style would mean that he no longer would write in the highly ornate and embellished parallel style of the medieval aristocratic court; rather, he would break with conventions and make the way he wrote fit the ideas he was trying to express. One consequence of this, the emergence of a distinction between "prose" and "poetry," was already apparent by 1050. It is not clear that Han Yu saw a sharp distinction between the two: in his day all genres of cultivated writing, all *wen*, had their appropriate models. But the ancient style was not about genre and prosody; its form and subject matter could be unconventional and unpredictable, and it was concerned more with articulating the writer's ideas about how things should be than with elaborating on received models. This better fit nonpoetic styles of writing, and *gu-wen* thus came to mean "ancient-style prose."

Han Yu's ideas about how every literatus could create his own works in his own style yet share the vision of an ideal antiquity and the understanding of later history that he set out in his famous ideological essay, "Finding the Source of the Way" ("Yuan dao"), gave eleventh-century ancient-style writers an intellectual agenda. Writing in the Ancient Style meant learning for oneself rather than slavishly following the socially acceptable style of the day tested in the literary examination. And learning the Way of the sages of antiquity meant recognizing, as Han Yu said, that the integrated social order of antiquity had been cut off with the Zhou, the last of the Three Dynasties. The great empires of Han and Tang had not recovered it, despite their claims to having done so. Song had to look to antiquity, not to imperial history, for only by breaking with that history could it match the achievements of antiquity.

Our literatus could not have escaped knowing about this view, which is not to say he would have agreed with it. The Ancient Style writers had their opponents, who warned that calls for the transformation of society were based on idealistic literary speculations and were more likely to destroy the dynasty than to improve society. He would have known, for example, that when Fan Zhongyan and his allies were given a brief chance to set policy at court in 1044, during a national crisis brought on by war with the Tanguts' new state of Xia, they had tried to change the way officials were chosen. They had wanted to reduce the number of literati who entered office through family privilege, thus forcing more people to go through the examination system; to require that candidates supply written affidavits attesting to their "ethical conduct"; to change the order of the examination so that the two prose parts would go first, a rearrangement that would ensure that passing would be determined by writings on statecraft and scholarship rather than poetic skill; and to greatly increase the number of local schools.

The Fan group was a faction, but rather than avoiding the label, it embraced it. In theory factions were not acceptable, since they implied that some officials were working together to further their own private interests rather than the dynastic interest. Ouyang Xiu's 1044 essay "On a Party of Friends" argued boldly that the only real political division was between those morally superior men who joined together to pursue their ideals, whom it was the emperor's duty to support, and the self-seeking, narrow-minded careerists who opposed them. A "party of friends," Ouyang wrote, were united by their values: they shared the same Way, and they were of the same mind.[19] This was a dangerous argument, as Su Shi (1037–1101), one of Ouyang's most loyal admirers, later pointed out: if you thought you were right and that everyone you disagreed with was merely self-interested, then if the emperor did not side with your party, you would, as a man of principle, have to resign from office. Since that would leave the government entirely in the hands of those you said would destroy the state, you ultimately were responsible for its destruction. Better to be more accommodative, to make sure that those who did not share your vision received the rank and emoluments they wanted so that they would leave you alone to decide on policy.[20]

Ouyang's thesis had merit in one sense: his was the foremost political faction that based itself on ideology, and it promoted a reform agenda. Perhaps in 1050 our literatus thought he could avoid the choice—Fan and Ouyang were out of power—and at least in the capital many of the most promising young men, who had a better chance in the examinations because their high-ranking relatives had secured them places in the National University, avoided the Ancient Style. But in 1057 Ouyang Xiu was appointed director of the examinations. Not only did he ask questions that favored literati who sought the way of the sages in the Classics with their own minds, he also changed the grading standards to reward those who wrote in the Ancient Style. Some of the most sophisticated literati of the day failed and rioted outside Ouyang's house, but several men who would become the leading intellectuals of their generation passed.

The spread of the Ancient Style made learning an ideological enterprise. It encouraged its proponents to write about the great issues of the day, irrespective of their rank, and to aspire to gain control of government so that they could put their vision into effect. And it pushed those who disagreed with them to argue for their own alternatives. Paradoxically, by defining learning as a way of apprehending and embodying the ideals of the antiquity, it made *wen* less central, for ultimately it gave ideas priority over culture.

The idea that learning gave literati the authority to challenge those in power at court put an end to government by consensus. Looking back a generation later, Su Che (1039–81), one of the brilliant Ancient Style writers who passed the examination in 1057, addressed the conservative view of the senior statesman Zhang Fangping (1007–91), who believed that there ought to be a single hierarchy of intellectual authority, with the court at the top. Zhang saw in recent history the seeds of dynastic decline, not because the number of foreign states the Song had to deal with had multiplied or because their demands had grown, but because what Zhang called "private opinion" (by which he meant self-serving rather than impartial and fair views) had increased. In the past, he held, the court's pronouncements had been accepted as final, but during the 1040s and 1050s this had changed, and the court had lost much of its leverage. Indeed it had changed, Su Che agreed, but in the old days powerful ministers could do as they pleased, and those below them could do nothing about it. Su Che did not believe the court had an institutional *right* to control opinion, although he agreed that it had an institutional *role* to lead. In fact, he argued, the weightiness of the court's view had to do not with whether the less powerful had views of their own—and thus the suppression of dissent was not the solution to political disagreements—but with the quality of the people in power and the policies they set. "If we really could have the right people in power, men who did not serve special interests but took the actions that were right and necessary, then those below would have nothing to complain about and the court would be in control." But then Su moved toward a different and less imperial point of view. Could, he asked rhetorically, the court prevent people in lower positions from having views of their own and being critical? Since the answer was clearly no, Su concluded, the court should instead worry lest the "feelings of those below not pass through to those above." And when those feelings and criticisms are right, he continued, they should be followed. For the court to accept correction from literati opinion did not make the court less important.[21]

Taking Apart the Tang Model of Antiquity

During the second half of the eleventh century, literati opinion divided into camps, each with its own ideas, creating one of the great eras of debate in China's history, not unlike the "hundred schools" of thought in the Warring States period. Yet the differences are instructive. Eleventh-century writers looked back to a history that included the Warring States thinkers, the Han commentators on the Classics, the many schools of Buddhism that had taken shape after Han, Daoism, and the numerous works of history, philosophy, classical exegesis, and literature that had accumulated over time. They could not think they were finding ideas for the first time. Moreover, their diversity worried them. For many of them, the profusion of schools of thought in the Warring States period and the later spread of Buddhism and Daoism were signs that humankind had lost its one common way. In turning back to the origins of civilization, they were searching for the key to the unity that they believed had existed under the sage-kings in antiquity.

Let us suppose our literatus passed the examinations and was pursuing both an official career and a reputation for learning. What was the map of the intellectual terrain? If he believed culture—that is, the cultural forms that mediated between oneself and the world—mattered most, he could turn to Ouyang Xiu from Jiangxi in the south and his successor as the arbiter of cultural standards, Su Shi from Sichuan in the west. Su, together with brother, Su Che, gathered a circle of like-minded literati (and some Buddhist monks) who continued to believe in the importance of *wen*. If he believed that serving the common interest required harnessing the powers of government to transform society, he could turn to Wang Anshi (1021–86) from Jiangxi, who had gained an increasing following through his Ancient Style essays on the political ideals of the Classics. Wang would gain power at court at the end of the 1060s and launch the New Policies, the most radical program of state activism in many centuries. But our literatus might have shared the doubts of the historian Sima Guang (1019–86) from Shaanxi in the northwest, who argued that reform of the bureaucratic system, not the transformation of society, was the key to stability. When Sima became the chief councilor in 1086, he tried to abolish all the New Policies. Finally, if he thought that how people behaved as individuals—whether they were ethical in their personal conduct or not—was the foundation upon which society and government rested, he might have sought out Zhang Zai (1020–77) from the northwest. Zhang and his kinsmen Cheng Hao (1032–85) and Cheng Yi (1033–1107) from Luoyang in the north anchored the idea of morality in theories of the natural world. All these figures gained national fame and large followings in their own lifetimes, and all of them left records that spoke to a wide range of issues.

All claimed to have understood truths about how literati should learn and how government should work that had been lost for the previous millennium, that is, throughout imperial history. And most of them claimed that the truths they had grasped were exactly those that the sages had practiced, rediscovered by turning back to antiquity and the origins of civilization to find guides for the present. Yet the notion that this made Song thinkers fundamentally different from earlier times was problematic, for the Tang court had also claimed that its empire was true to the origins of civilization in antiquity. The difference between Tang and Song lay in how they understood antiquity and their connection to it. All the various intellectual streams of the eleventh century alike were involved in dismantling the Tang claim to antiquity. From the perspective of the Song thinkers, they were right to think that they represented a new beginning in history. But what was the Tang model of antiquity, and what came out of the undoing of it?

THE TANG MODEL: HEAVEN-AND-EARTH, ANTIQUITY, AND EMPIRE

We can analyze the Tang model of antiquity as a set of cumulative, interrelated layers. As depicted in Table 2.1, its ultimate foundation lay in heaven-and-earth and humanity's existence as one of the myriad things of creation. This was followed by the appearance of the Former Kings (the sage-kings) who were the first to organize humanity and whose institutions for ordering the world established civilization. This accomplishment was represented in the texts that became the Classics, which Confucius edited in order to show society the right way, an effort that unfortunately did not forestall the "decline" (*shuai*) of civilization. The

Table 2.1
Modeling Antiquity

Post-Antiquity

Han and Tang	The two great unified empires; they "restored antiquity"; that is, they re-established the empire and restored continuity with antiquity, thus reversing the decline.
Qin	The empire that purposefully broke with the institutional legacy of antiquity.

Antiquity

The decline of the Three Dynasties, the decline of the Zhou	The decline of the system created by the Former Kings, which made possible the appearance of institutions and practices that were discontinuous with antiquity.
Confucius (Kongzi)	The person who put in order the Classics so as to clarify the model of the Former Kings of antiquity for the future at a point when the decline had become apparent. He was seen as the First Teacher, and eventually as a sage himself.
The Classics (*jing*)	The texts that represented the works and world of the Former Kings and their ministers; later edited by Confucius and extensively commented on beginning in the Han dynasty.
Civilization (*ren wen*)	The writing, rites, implements, calendars, institutions, etc., created by the Former Kings to enable a harmonious human community. Although transformed, diversified, and elaborated, these have continued into the present.
Former Kings, sage-kings (*xian wang, sheng wang*)	The Former Kings brought humanity out of the realm of nature by creating civilization. They looked to the manifest patterns of the natural realm and translated them into the constant guides for the organization of society (e.g., creating a calendar, establishing hierarchies, organizing space). Although there would be no true sage-kings after the early Zhou dynasty, the unified state and integrated social order they created were in resonant accord with the organic system of nature itself.
Heaven-and-earth and the myriad things (*tian di wan wu*)	The realm of nature, the organic system that produces and sustains all life. Humankind began in the realm of nature, where it competed with the birds and beasts for survival.

decline culminated in the Qin dynasty, which disavowed any ties to the ancients, but those ties were restored, first by the unified empire of Han and then, after another period of decline, by Tang.

Tang court scholars used this model to accomplish two things. First, it justified the reimposition, after the failed Sui unification, of a centralized unified empire. In their view, Tang was a restoration of an ancient order that was in fundamental agreement with the workings of the universe (for the Former Kings had modeled civilization on the patterns of heaven-and-earth). Second, it explained that, to succeed, the new empire needed to restore formal continuity with the civilization created by the Former Kings, a system that could be known from the Classics, which Confucius had edited to preserve the model of the ancient system as it was being lost. In the Tang view, antiquity was the starting point of a continuously and cumulatively (but not progressively) evolving totalistic political, social, economic, cultural, and moral order. At times the connection to antiquity faltered and empire failed, and at times the threads were rewoven and empire was restored; Han had restored antiquity after Qin, and Tang could restore it once again. When empire succeeded, it brought about the proper functioning of both the activities of humans and the workings of the cosmos, so that there was no gap between the politically constructed realm of human activity and the self-constructing realm of nature. Continuities with the past were not achieved by blind imitation, yet they were expressed by creating continuities between ancient and modern cultural forms.

The early Tang treated this understanding of antiquity as the constitutional grounds for empire. This was evident in the rhetoric and ritual of the founding; in the history of court-sponsored scholarship, which dominated intellectual and literary culture into the mid-eighth century; in Empress Wu's adoption of the dynastic name of Zhou (even as she patronized Buddhist texts and models of rulership); and, on the eve of the An Lushan rebellion of 755, in the institution of the new ritual program of the Tianbao reign period and the composition of the *Six Canons* (*Liu dian*), which represented the Tang imperial system according to the Zhou model.[22]

CHALLENGING THE TANG MODEL

The attack on this model began soon after the rebellion of 755. Han Yu, for example, denied that Tang had ever established real continuity with antiquity. There had been a rupture (*jue*) in the transmission of the sages' way after Confucius and Mencius, Han argued, and no dynasty had yet succeeded in returning to the origins of civilization. Han's position did not gain general currency in post-rebellion Tang, but by 1050 it had become the credo of many literati. During the lifetime of our literatus, he would have witnessed the intellectual world reconsidering every layer in the Tang model of antiquity—the processes of heaven-and-earth, the sages, the system of civilization, the texts of the Classics, the position of Confucius, and the status of the earlier empires—and challenge the supposedly seamless connections between them. Let us consider this layer by layer.

Confucius.   Confucius still remained the editor of the Classics, but more attention began to be paid to the content of what Confucius was trying to communicate. For Wang Anshi, for example, Confucius was the one who had understood that the cumulative achievement of antiquity was based on constant principles of social organization. He was not simply reaffirming the validity of the Yao and Shun as models; Confucius was, Wang wrote (echoing Mencius) "wiser than Yao and Shun."[23] For others such as Cheng Yi, Confucius as interpreter of the system of civilization was less important than Confucius as the teacher of the *Analects* who, as Cheng saw it, was trying to teach students how they could become sages themselves.[24] For the moral philosophers Zhou Dunyi and Zhang Zai, Confucius was not simply one who transmitted the achievements of the past; he was a philosopher who used the *Book of Change* and other texts to show how human morality was grounded in the organic processes of heaven-and-earth.

The Classics.   The Classics were reinterpreted and problematized. The differences between early Tang exegetical strategies and those of the Song are often described as a shift from a philological (*xungu*) approach to a moralistic (*yili*) one. This is too simple a dichotomy. A more useful distinction is between the goals of interpretation. In early Tang, the aim was to synthesize the history of classical exegesis so as to arrive at a definitive understanding of what the words of the Classics said, on the assumption that what the Classics said was both descriptive and normative. In the eleventh century, the goal became to grasp the conceptions that the sages had in mind, for these conceptions had made possible the sociopolitical achievements the Classics described. The challenge for Tang was to sort out a body of contradictory exegetical texts; for Song to develop strategies that could reveal the hitherto unapparent significance of the Classics themselves. This happened first with studies of the *Spring and Autumn Annals* in the eighth century, was revived in the early eleventh century by Sun Fu's (992–1057) *Exposing the Subtleties of the Spring and Autumn Annals' Respect for the King (Chunqiu zun wang fa wei)*, and soon spread to the other Classics. This undermined the authority of the exegetical tradition of Han through Tang even as it liberated the new generation to read the Classics for themselves with the aim of developing their own insights.[25]

There were various ways of historicizing the Classics. For Wang Anshi, the Classics were an after-the-fact compilation from which the logic of the system of antiquity could be known. For Su Xun (1009–66), father of Su Shi and Su Che, they were byproducts of mutually reinforcing strategies that the ancients had developed to get people to accept the imposition of government.[26] Some raised questions about the accuracy of the received editions and even their authenticity, a tendency that has been labeled "doubting the Classics." Ouyang Xiu's works on the *Songs* and *Change* are examples. In the *Original Meaning of the Odes (Shi ben yi)*, he argued that the modern *Odes* resulted from four historical stages or layers (composition, collection, editing, and exegesis). Hence, the meaning of *Odes* had to be understood in terms of this historical process, rather than derived from any supposed systematic arrangement of the texts.[27] Ouyang's attack on the received text of the *Book of Change* was part of his program to deny a connection between heaven-and-earth and the society the sages created.[28] Su Xun took this a step further: the *Change* was merely a strategy aimed at mystification, a means of getting the populace to think that the order being imposed on them was not a political construction but somehow a natural one.[29] Once one raised enough questions about the Classics, it was possible to conclude, as Ouyang eventually did, that because the Classics mediated the present's understanding, it was not possible to be sure of anything about antiquity.[30]

Civilization.   The civilization created in antiquity was also re-examined. A fundamental issue, already articulated in the eighth century, was whether civilization began as a ritual order intended to socialize people who would otherwise be guided by selfish desires, or whether it began as a socioeconomic order that, because it enabled people to satisfy their material needs, made it possible for them to live in mutually supportive communities. The first view, common in early Tang, continued to be promoted, for example by Cai Xiang (1012–76)[31] and, most famously, Zhang Zai. Among those who wrote at length for the materialist view, the strongest statement came from Li Gou (1009–59), whose seven essays on "ritual" (*li*) expanded and transformed the concept.[32] Li Gou recognized that behind this was a fundamental moral question: a material view implied that civilization was based on an appeal to interests, to profit and advantage (*li*). Li was untroubled by this prospect, but others were convinced that civilization had to be grounded in "righteousness" or "morality" (*yi*). But what this meant in practice remained in dispute. Was it defined by external cultural forms? Was it connected to something real in human experience? Was it grounded in the biological makeup of the human being? One could, of course, have it both ways, either by denying that the ancient order necessitated any real distinction, as Ouyang Xiu did in introducing the "Treatise of Rites and Music" in the *New Tang History*,[33] or by pointing out that both were necessary (even if the material aspect had priority), as Zhang Fangping and also Ouyang did.[34]

Texts mediated debates over the origins of civilizations, but texts were not the only legacy of antiquity. The Song period witnessed a new interest in ancient objects, particularly bronzes. Yet despite the immediacy and authenticity of the real thing, their meaning was a matter of interpretation, as was the depiction of ritual objects and the re-creation of ancient rituals.[35]

The Former Kings. The Former Kings were also scrutinized. Were the Former Kings to be taken as examples for rulers who had the responsibility to govern society, or were they models for thinking and acting at the individual level that all could share? Did they merely observe and act, or did they think and reflect? Was it the fact of their being sages that mattered—and if so, what did this mean—or did they owe their accomplishments to their political position? Those who took the problem of being a sage seriously included all the natural and moral philosophers—Zhou Dunyi, Zhang Zai, Shao Yong, and the Cheng brothers—although they reached different conclusions. But it also includes figures we might not expect, such as the Su brothers, for whom the Way of the sages represented a way of thinking that required individual realization.[36] Wang Anshi was also concerned with explaining how the sages had been so effective.[37] But in contrast to these figures, for whom the sage represented the realization of universals, some, such as Sima Guang, saw them as historical political figures, as "former kings" rather than sages.

Heaven-and-earth. Finally, new theories of heaven-and-earth and the myriad things were advanced. Shao Yong developed a cosmology that explained both the generation of natural phenomena and the cycles of human history. Notably, Shao's "numerical" system dispensed with the five phases of change, the main tradition of cosmology, in favor of a quadripartite system based on *yin* and *yang*. Zhang Zai developed a theory of the processes of heaven-and-earth based on *qi* (energy-matter or material force), which he held both explained the nature of life process and asserted the reality of the phenomenal world—against the Buddhist view of the phenomenal as illusory. Cheng Yi reworked the concept of *li*, transforming it into the principle that gave all things their coherence of organization, process, and function. Others set out their understandings of heaven-and-earth as well: Sima Guang in his *Hidden Vacuity* (*Qian xu*), Su Shi in his *Commentary on the* Change (*Yi zhuan*), and the many others in their commentaries on the *Change*. Although Wang Anshi did not propose a new way of understanding the cosmos, by the end of his career he also argued that there were principles that were "so-of-themselves" (*ziran zhi li*), that is, were part of the natural order of things and the foundation for the system of civilization.[38]

It is just as important to see what those who wrote about heaven-and-earth were not talking about: although they occasionally used "cosmic resonance theory," the theory of cosmic process that had dominated the early empire, in criticizing court policy, they largely ignored it.[39] The theory had supposed that all things and processes belonged to specific categories as a result of the qualities of the energy-matter (*qi*) that constituted them and that things of the same category "resonated" with one another (for example, strings tuned to the same note on different instruments all resonate when one is plucked). Cosmic resonance theory held further that the categories into which all things and activities fell were valid for both the natural and the human order. It was this last proposition that had great political significance: since the natural order was of itself constant, predictable, and harmonious, any aberration must be the result of human actions. And since the emperor was the central figure in the human order and had the power to orchestrate his own and others' actions, it followed that when those in government went against the proper order of things, heaven-and-earth responded with unusual events (which could be taken as portents of even greater harm to come) or even with full-fledged natural calamities, such as floods and earthquakes. It was incumbent on the emperor to adhere to the rules of the natural order (which the organization of antiquity was assumed to reflect) and to ensure that all society conformed.*

SOME SIGNS OF COMMON GROUND

In short, it could have been evident to our literatus that he lived in a world that was making impossible a return to the imperial order of Tang times and that the leading intellectuals of his day were undermining the model of antiquity that had justified the Tang imperial order. Eleventh-century intellectual culture as a whole agreed that antiquity had meaning for the present but not on what that meaning was. Every

---

*The idea that the phenomenal world was constituted by *qi* remained part of later thinking about natural process and, of course, continued to be a core concept in Chinese medical theory. For Neo-Confucians as well, *qi* was understood to be resonant, which explained why external phenomena could stimulate feelings in a person spontaneously and why sincere devotion in performing a sacrifice to ancestors would cause their dispersed *qi* to gain a certain spectral presence.

part of the Tang model—heaven-and-earth, the sages, civilization, the Classics, and Confucius—was being re-examined. All these matters were imbued with political significance, as increasingly politicized thinkers and increasingly ideological politicians came to define the factions of late eleventh-century political and intellectual life.

And yet with hindsight we can see that there were certain fundamental commonalities in the ways Song literati problematized the Tang model, not in their understanding of the layers themselves, but in how they understood the ways in which the layers were connected.

The Tang model held that the multiple layers of antiquity were linked together by imaging, replicating, and elaborating on natural patterns, received models, and texts, from the sages who translated the patterns in heaven-and-earth into the patterns of civilization, to Confucius as the transmitter of ancient texts, to the long-lived empires of Han and Tang. That is why in early Tang understanding the "meaning" of the Classics depending on knowing what the words of the Classics referred to. Eleventh-century thinkers saw this as a misapprehension of how those linkages were created. As they saw it, the vital—and hitherto unexplored—connection between the layers of antiquity was the mediating role of cognition, of the "mind," *xin*, which was capable of grasping the patterns, principles, commonalities, and systems that underlay what was manifest in heaven-and-earth, in the deeds of the Former Kings, and in the words of the texts. As Wang Anshi wrote, the sages comprehended the Way with their minds and thus everything they did over many generations formed a perfectly coherent whole. Later generations failed because they imitated the forms of the past instead of comprehending the Way with their minds, which would have enabled them to change institutions to meet the needs of the times. It was Confucius who figured this out, and he compiled the Classics in such a way that what was truly fundamental could be inferred.[40] What the sages were grasping with their minds were the necessary principles that organized things into systems. This was the basis for Wang's claim that in antiquity writing had been developed in such a manner that the internal structure of each written character embodied a "principle of what is so by itself" (*ziran zhi li*) and thus defined the proper function of its referent. Despite changes in orthography over time, Wang held, these principles could be identified through a comparative analysis of the structural elements of contemporary written characters.[41] Thus, meaning lay in the system of relationships between things, as revealed by the words themselves and the structure of the text, rather than in definitions of the meanings of the words.

Did the sages understand this themselves? Wang's *Meanings of the Rites of Zhou* (*Zhou li yi*; later known as *Zhou guan xinyi*) suggests that he was content to demonstrate that the way things were organized in antiquity, according to the Classics as filtered through the mind of Confucius, was in accord with necessary principles, but that it was up to people in the present to figure out and articulate those principles, to make what had been implicit explicit.[42] In 1058, well before writing this commentary, he had spelled out his basic stance:

The two emperors [Yao and Shun] and the three kings [Yu, Tang, and Wen] were removed from each other by over a thousand years. Order and chaos following one upon the other, and periods of splendor and decline were fully present. The changes they encountered and the situations they faced differed, and the measures they adopted varied as well. But their conceptions (*yi* 意) in governing society and state were always the same in [what they treated as] root and branch and [in what they did] first and last. I therefore say: we simply ought to imitate their conceptions. If we imitate their conceptions, then whatever changes and reforms we make will not shock people and cause complaint, yet they will surely be in agreement with the policies of the Former Kings.[43]

Zeng Gong (1019–83), Wang's cousin, also located the link between heaven-and-earth, the sage-kings, and civilization in the mind and asserted that the sages had cultivated their minds so that they could gain knowledge of the principles of heaven-and-earth and apply them to ordering the world. The task of "learning" in the present was the same, he concluded: to understand the principles of the world and apply them.[44]

Wang's leading opponent, Sima Guang, had always opposed trying to change society radically on the basis of an interpretation of antiquity and rarely had taken recourse to antiquity as a justification for policy, yet he also supposed that cultivating the mind, maintaining it in a state of equilibrium, and keeping it free of distractions were the keys to being *gong*—making impartial judgments that were in the common interest. For Sima, the solution was to keep external things from unbalancing the equilibrium necessary for the mind to arrive at a balanced judgment.[45]

Su Shi detailed his understanding of connections between heaven-and-earth, the sages, civilization, and the Classics in his commentaries on the *Change* and the *Documents*. For Su, the process of learning and acting by a true sage replicated heaven-and-earth's process of creation. Both had an inexhaustible source within, but they maintained constancy by changing with the times, creating new things as they responded to events. The sages created things that others could imitate and be guided by—people could live according to the hexagrams or the institutions of the sage-kings—but the real teaching of Confucius and the Classics was to train men how to transcend the specific creations of the sages and become creators of things themselves. The sages succeeded in creating civilization by being undogmatic creative thinkers, not by being imitators, and this was the lesson earlier Ru had missed.[46]

The moral philosophers, the founders of Neo-Confucianism, gave even greater weight to the sages' minds: it was the mind that grasped heaven-and-earth's principles and guided the construction of civilization. For Zhang Zai the learning of the sages involved cleaning up one's *qi* so that one could become aware of the heavenly nature and thus be in tune with the process of creation. Although Zhang had a theory of the natural world based on a conception of *qi*, he was content with identifying its basic coherence; his real interest was in the sages as a model for the cultivation of the mind. A pure mind was in a state of disinterestedness and thus could sense what was in accord with the principles of integrated and harmonious life process. This was its moral knowledge (*de-xing zhi zhi*), something qualitatively different from cumulative factual knowledge.[47] Zhang's sage had a mind that had expanded its awareness to the point that it could sense the creative process operating in human life. The sages were mirrors at the center of all activity, reflecting accurately the unfolding of the many strands of the life process. Free of bias, they took in everything and saw the incipient springs of developments; hence, when they were stimulated by events, they responded spontaneously yet appropriately. Thus, through their engagement with the world, they continued the process of creation without interfering in it. Because they could see patterns of development and change, they could guide the populace, as, for example, when they identified the seasons and the agricultural cycle, regulated human affairs with ritual, and stimulated the minds of others by their personal example.[48]

Cheng Yi presented a more complicated picture. The way of heaven-and-earth was simply another name for *li*—the necessary principles of a thing's coherent operation. All things, being products of heaven-and-earth, embody *li*, and all things are inherently coherent. And *tian li* ("heavenly *li*"), the very coherence of the universe as a whole and all things within it, is equally endowed in all human beings as their nature (*xing*) and can provide an innate moral sensibility. The mind mediates a person's perception of the *li* in things and of one's own *xing*. The sages, being born with minds of the purest *qi*, fully and completely perceived the *li* of things and were in accord with *tian li* when they responded to events. Thus, they created civilization incrementally in response to the human condition of the moment. Civilization was not in any sense an artificial construct, since, thanks to the sages, it was in full accord with *li*. What makes this complicated is that Cheng does not, I think, suppose that the sages knew what they were doing. They were responding spontaneously. In other words, they did not themselves conceptualize the mental process through which they operated. Cheng granted that they appeared to be operating at the level of form and appearance, but he denied that this was what was actually taking place. This lack of understanding of the actual process involved explained why non-sages in antiquity had no choice but to imitate the sages and maintain the forms of the institutions and rituals they created. As a result, when rulers appeared who were not sages and when the quality of *qi* declined, humanity was lost. Confucius understood the mental workings of the sages and was able to explain how the process actually worked. That is, Confucius was able to set out the program of learning that enabled people to become sages once again, and his teachings provide the clues to the theoretical foundation for learning as a process of mental cultivation.[49]

LEARNING AND THE SELF RECONCEIVED

What might our literatus have deduced from all this? He could conclude that returning to the origins of civilization in antiquity went beyond studying the institutions and texts of the ancients and imitating them in policy and in writing. Rather, it meant realizing in oneself the process by which the sages were able to create things of enduring value. They used their minds to see something that was not of itself apparent:

the principles, intentions, and conceptions that gave things their coherence. It was this that freed the sages from blind imitation and allowed them to accommodate change. This had implications for policy-making: literati could deal with the changes that had taken place since the Tang if they could figure out how to integrate them into a new system. And it had implications for learning: to learn meant to use the mind to see for oneself. The point of learning was not so much to assist the ruler in carrying out "transformation through instruction" (*jiaohua*) or even to communicate the feelings of those below, but to be able to tell the ruler what he should do.

This new view of learning fits well with Fan Zhongyan's reform proposal of 1044 to recruit literati who would take initiative and with Ouyang Xiu's revision of the examination standards in 1057 to favor proponents of the Ancient Style. In a long memorial to the emperor in 1058, Wang Anshi made the transformation of the nation dependent on a school system that produced literati capable of formulating policy. Su Shi saw literature and art as paradigms for a process of cultivation that combined learning from past models with understanding fundamental commonalities to produce new things of enduring value. The moral philosophers treated learning as the essence of moral self-cultivation and the foundation for a good society.

A literatus may not have recognized it in 1050, but his conception of his own self was also changing in a way that fit this new view of learning. An early Tang literatus would have supposed that for better or worse every person had his own personal character, and social harmony depended on training oneself to conform to correct models. Or, if he adopted a Buddhist perspective, he might have thought that his personal character was the product of his desires and cravings, which could be overcome only by realizing that in fact that was nothing real and permanent there, that the real "Buddha nature" was simply emptiness. This could support a similar conclusion: that the alternative for those who could not detach themselves from their cravings was to conform to proper social forms. The Song literatus, however, was beginning to think that there was something important and enduring in the self that he should apprehend. Increasingly, eleventh-century literati were asking what all humans possessed innately. Moral philosophers such as Cheng Yi argued that every person, by virtue of his or her biological existence as one of the myriad things, was equally endowed with a nature (*xing*). For Cheng, this was nothing other than the *li* of heaven-and-earth, and it was capable of providing moral guidance to those who developed the mind's awareness of it.[50] Those who rejected the idea that human nature contained moral guides, such as Ouyang Xiu, and argued that something all possessed equally was not adequate as a guide to human action, still believed that humans were innately capable of understanding things and could cultivate this ability.[51] Su Shi's position was more nuanced: there certainly was a *xing* there, but our knowledge of it was mediated by what arose from it, and it could not be known absolutely or defined. Just as cooked meat cannot be equated with the fire that cooked it nor the son with the man who fathered him, so the *xing* could not be defined by what arose from it. Yet Su had no doubt that there was a "master within," and that the individual should rely on it, and that it was the ultimate source of his creativity.[52] Wang Anshi did not argue that knowledge of human nature should guide the formulation of policy, but he supposed that there was something there that was common to all humans and that successful policy would necessarily be in harmony with it.

The counterpart to the idea that the individual possessed something substantial that enabled him to understand things in a new way was the positive re-evaluation of the emotions (*qing*) as something that enabled human interaction with the world. For some, it was important to distinguish the emotions from selfish desire (*yu*), which led one to attempt to subordinate the interests of the other to one's own.[53] Figures who claimed to be uninterested in cosmology and the natural processes of heaven-and-earth and who rejected the idea of defining human nature in moral terms still sought to show that emotion, and sometimes desire as well, were biological givens that could play a positive role in the organization of social life. They were not obstacles to social harmony that had to be regulated, controlled, or suppressed. There was a fundamental commonality between proponents of a normative human nature and those who conceived of humans as motivated by desire and emotion; both believed they were taking into account something that was real about human beings, something that could not be willed away. What had lost ground by the end of the eleventh century was the old atomistic view of the human condition: namely, each person had a particular character, whose varying moral quality was manifested in its responses to things that impinged on the self. And as this view was abandoned, so were the conclusions that had once been drawn from it: that social harmony required that humans conform to proper forms and that morally superior individuals could be produced through good breeding and good bloodlines.[54]

The belief that learning meant cultivating the grounds of independent judgment in oneself created greater intellectual uncertainty among literati. This may explain their increasing tendency to align themselves with men who they believed had the answers. Nevertheless, literati were becoming used to the idea that the state of the world depended on how they themselves thought and acted, that it was not a matter that could be left to the government alone.

The New Policies: Legislating a System

In the eleventh century, these trends—the idea of recruiting literati devoted to Ancient Style ideals through examinations, the rejection of the early imperial claim to antiquity, the view of learning as thinking systematically about ordering the world—culminated not in the triumph of Neo-Confucianism but in the New Policies program of Wang Anshi and his successors. For most of the years between 1069 and 1124, the court was led by men loyal to Wang's vision, and three successive emperors were steadfast in their support. (The empress dowagers were not, however, and during the regencies of 1085–93 and 1100 they reinstated opponents of the New Policies, who were purged once the emperor began to rule in his own right.)

At first there was widespread support for Wang's initiatives. A young and ambitious emperor had just taken the throne, and following decades of cautious and conservative policy, many saw Wang as someone committed to ancient ideals who would lead the state in transforming society. We can imagine that our literatus would have been one of them, but perhaps he was one of those who soon grew dismayed by the way Wang was going about it. If he did, he still had to choose between the opposition factions of Sima Guang, Su Shi, and Cheng Yi.[55] Literati opinion shifted firmly against Wang's legacy after the loss of the north to the Jurchens in 1126, and as a result we know much more about Wang's opponents than about his advocates.

Wang Anshi had a vision. He was convinced that there was a system—an arrangement of the different parts so that all contributed to create a self-sustaining whole—necessary for the mobilization of society. A decade before he gained power, he had given an extended example of his approach in his famous long memorial. He had proposed a system of governance in which local schools would draw in all the local literati, provide them with material support, educate them through a wide range of texts and thinking about what could be done to improve local society, select the best of them for further education, and finally appoint them to office, where they could develop new initiatives for local society.[56] The necessity of a systematic organization of society in which all the parts were interdependent and mutually supporting was proved by the experience of antiquity, Wang argued, which, thanks to Confucius, could be rediscovered through the study of the surviving Classics and contemporary realities. The Classics agreed with the necessary and universal order of things.

For long the world has not seen the complete Classics. If one were to read only the Classics, it would not be enough to know the [system of the] Classics. I thus read everything . . . and I inquire of everyone, down to the farmer and the craftswoman. Only then am I able to know the general structure and purpose of the Classics and be free of doubt. The later ages in which we learn are different from the time of the Former Kings [of antiquity]. We must do this if we are fully to know the sages.[57]

The fact that the world had changed, that the present was different from antiquity, did not mean that the principles for knitting everything together into an integrated, self-sustaining system had changed. The key was to figure out the principles (*li*) of things, their coherent system of organization. "Every one of the myriad things has a perfect principle," he wrote, and "the way to attain a refined grasp of its pattern lies simply in grasping unity."[58] As his cousin and confidant explained: in the ideal world of antiquity, "morality was the same for all, and customs were uniform"; those who "spoke about principles (*li*)" always reached the same conclusions, "because when the principle fits the thing, then there can be no alternative." This is why the Classics are coherent, like "the theorizing of a single person," and the intellectual diversity of later periods resulted from "not fitting principles," from having values that "did not fit the conceptions of the sages."[59] Although the Classics did not contain everything that existed in the present, what they revealed agreed with the necessary order of things. Building on them, one could take other phenomena into account. The New Policies attempted to establish a coherent system in practice, based on ideas about how different kinds of activities ought to be linked together and on the investigation of local needs and opportunities.

Wang's policies were a programmatic response to the larger social, economic, and cultural changes between 750 and 1050:[60]

1. In response to the privatization of landholding, the state began to implement a cadastral survey to register all land and reassess the land tax. A program of spring loans was instituted to ensure the availability of credit to farmers, thus making them less dependent on wealthy landlords. Local government rented out state lands.

2. In response to the growth of commerce and the monetarization of the economy, the money supply was steadily increased with paper notes and higher denomination coins, facilitating trade; state trading offices engaged in wholesale trade in urban areas, ensuring a steadier supply and greater price stability. Certain tax liabilities, which had hitherto been met through payment in kind or the provision of labor, were converted to cash taxes, allowing government to hire workers rather than rely on corvée labor.

3. In response to the rural instability that accompanied a private land market and the spread of commerce, a mutual responsibility system that incorporated all rural households was instituted. Males were to be given military training, with the goal of having farmers serve as soldiers and play a role in local security. The system was also to be used for the collection of taxes. In addition, the tradition of requiring the wealthiest households to supply local government with clerks and tax managers was abandoned, and in its stead larger number of households were ordered to pay a cash tax that would be used to hire the necessary personnel.

4. In response to the foreign states on the borders, an expansionist policy was adopted on the northern, western, and southern borders, the aim being to bring border communities whenever possible into the Song order.

5. In response to the demand for local education and examination access, the government invested in prefectural and county schools; created a graded school system linking the county and prefectural schools

to the National University with the aim of shifting from an examination system to a school graduation system; gave tax breaks to students (and their households) according to the grade they had passed; reformed the examination system to test a candidate's ability to interpret the Classics rather than demonstrate skill in poetry; and promulgated a national curriculum with new official commentaries on the Classics.

The New Policies approach made the government the leading player in society and economy and the engine of change. There were voluminous sets of new rules for the various parts of the plan, but the institutions were constantly changing as the "bureaucratic entrepreneurs" who managed them took advantage of new opportunities to extend the scope of their activities and enlarge their revenue streams.[61]

From the start, Wang wanted to bring the literati into the system— popular opposition to changes would, he assured the emperor, dissipate as people discovered that the system served their inherent interests— but the literati who would manage the government had to be taught to think systematically if they were to integrate new developments and ensure continued growth. Education was essential to "making morality the same for all and unifying customs" (*tong daode yi fengsu*) in a world filled with disagreement and individual views.[62]

Once in power, the New Policies regime turned quickly to creating a new education system. It abolished the memorization examinations and dropped the poetic sections of the *jinshi* examination in favor of interpretive essays on the meaning of the Classics. It wrote new commentaries on certain of the Classics to show literati how to learn from antiquity. Although critics regularly accused Wang of wanting to make everyone the same as himself, Wang denied that he was calling for imitation and warned students that the ideal order of antiquity had begun to decline when men started imitating appearances and forgot that the sages acted creatively on the basis of their own understanding; students should grasp the conceptions of the ancients for themselves.[63]

Wang retired permanently from office in 1076, but he remained the foremost theoretician of this grand attempt to transform society. In his own estimation, he was the successor to Confucius. In introducing his *Explanations of Characters* (*Zi shuo*), the dictionary he wrote for use in government schools to explain the principles inherent in written words, he adopted Confucius' claim that he, as the one who was continuing the civilization of the Zhou, had Heaven's protection.* "Heaven, not being about to allow 'This Culture of Ours' to perish," Wang wrote of himself, "has used me to illuminate its beginning. Therefore, teaching and learning must start from this [book]. Those who are able to understand it will have gotten nine-tenths of the ideas of morality."[64] In the eyes of supporters such as Shen Liao (1032–85), Wang had, with his "New Learning," coherently integrated the essentials of human nature and the foundations of ethics while maintaining creative insight, the intent of literary writing, and the proper form of Classical scholarship.[65] In 1104, Wang was included in the Confucian temple and thus officially recognized as one of history's true worthies and an authoritative interpreter of Confucius and the sages.

Not all literati were persuaded. A literatus who had taken office in the 1050s may have seen that the New Policies effort to improve the material well-being of the population, to spread education, to make people responsible for one another, to enlarge the market economy, and generally to transform the world into a smoothly functioning system did not always work as intended and that in some fragile local economies the sweeping changes being mandated were counterproductive.

There were other things that might have disquieted our literatus. The court under the New Policies forced leading critics from office and eventually took to blacklisting and exiling them. It ordered the destruction of the printing blocks of writings of Su Shi and his circle, proscribed the teachings of the Cheng brothers, and posthumously attacked Sima Guang. The New Policies explicitly targeted the powerful local families who increased their wealth at the expense of others. Literati families who traditionally had seen to their own education now were required to send their sons to government schools if they wanted to take the examinations. The court set itself up as the great patron of literature and the arts—the last of the New Policies emperors (Huizong, r. 1100–1125) was himself a great exponent of the sophisticated new court painting style—but it did so in opposition to those like Su Shi

---

*The *Analects* of Confucius 9.5: When under siege in Kuang, the Master said, "With King Wen dead, is Culture (*wen*) not here with me? Had Heaven intended that This Culture of Ours (*si-wen*) should perish, those who died later would not have been able to participate in This Culture of Ours. Heaven is not yet about to let This Culture of Ours perish, so what can the men of Kuang do to me?"

who believed that literature and art ought to reflect the insights and cultivation of the author. It sought to improve trade and commerce, but by having government offices take over the wholesale trade of the great private merchant houses. It offered farmers loans at the expense of the wealthy families who had hitherto been the source of all rural credit. It encouraged new knowledge and technology, but it repeatedly crushed dissent. The emperors played a role in this as well, and in return for their support, they demanded initiatives that would serve their own self-aggrandizing imperial aspirations. The aggressive foreign policy ultimately ended in unforeseen disaster: after the Jurchens' Jin dynasty overthrew the Liao empire in coordination with Song armies, the Jin marched across the North China plain and took the Song capital, carrying off the last two emperors in 1126.

For those who did not accept that the New Policies had established a new order and made further debate unnecessary, the challenge was to show that they had an alternative. This brings us to the Neo-Confucians. Toward the end of his life, Cheng Yi, the man whose teaching would become the foundation for the Neo-Confucian movement, assessed himself in direct challenge to Wang Anshi's claim to have been the first since Confucius and Mencius to revive "This Culture of Ours": "The learning of the sages had not been transmitted for a long time," Cheng wrote. "I, born so many generations later, aspired to illuminate This Way of Ours and revive This Culture of Ours after it had been cut off."[66] The questions of how it came about that Cheng's claims were accepted, how they came to be understood, and what consequences followed from their spread are taken up in the following chapters.

3

The Neo-Confucians

Neo-Confucians and Confucians

As used in this book "Neo-Confucian" refers to people who identified themselves as participants in the intellectual streams that emerged from the philosophical teachings of the eleventh-century brothers Cheng Yi and Cheng Hao; to the doctrines on human morality, human nature, and the cosmos developed from that foundation; and to the social activities that linked adherents of these views together and allowed them to put their ideas into practice. "Neo-Confucianism" is a modern, foreign term. The common Chinese names for this movement are quite different—in the order of their appearance: *Dao xue* (the learning of the Way), *Li xue* (learning of the principles that give all things their coherence), *Xin xue* (the learning of the mind), *Xing li xue* (the learning of nature and principle/coherence), and sometimes merely *Sheng xue* (the learning of the sages). *Li xue* has become the standard term in Chinese today. Each of these names emphasizes one aspect of the philosophical discussions at the expense of the other. "Neo-Confucian" has the virtue of allowing us to refer to all of them without committing ourselves to any one. The English term also recognizes that its proponents thought of themselves as *Ru*, a term commonly translated as "Confucians," and as possessing the true understanding of the teachings of Confucius, while allowing us to view them as "new" and different in important ways. As an intellectual persuasion and as a social movement, Neo-Confucianism was a cumulative tradition, one that became central to literati life in the twelfth century and remained central for many centuries thereafter. But cumulative traditions can include diverse, even contradictory, views and practices.[1]

One characteristic of early Neo-Confucianism, before it came to be widely accepted among the literati, was the assertion that its proponents were different from those in the imperial past who had been thought of as Ru. In 1068, Cheng Yi questioned the value of the "later Ru," those who came after Confucius and his first great interpreter, Mencius:

All later Ru have been concerned with literary composition and mastering Classical studies. Literary composition is nothing more than making words pretty and showy and ideas novel and unique in order to please the ears and eyes of others. Classical studies is nothing more than explicating glosses and differing from previous Ru in order to establish your own unique interpretation. Can such kinds of learning actually arrive at the Way?[2]

In Cheng's view, what ought to distinguish Ru from other intellectuals was the search for "the Way," by which we may understand something like "the values all should share." He excluded those seen in the past as Ru, the Classicists of Han and the literary men of Tang, on the grounds that they were not seeking to know the Way itself. Rather, they were concerned with the vehicles through which knowledge of the Way could be made accessible—the Classics as the source of knowledge and writing as the means of communicating knowledge. Applying this view to his own times, he dismissed literary men and scholars of the Classics: "Those who learn today have divided into three. Those of literary ability are called literati of culture, and those who discuss the Classics are mired in being teachers. Only knowing the Way is Ru learning."[3] By the end of his life, Cheng Yi was convinced that he and his brother had found the true method of learning. And once Neo-Confucianism captured the center of the intellectual landscape, it was easier to grant that "Confucianism" was what he said it was.

But from a historian's perspective, saying who was a Ru and who was not does not require our adopting a particular definition of Ru doctrine. Rather, we would say that being a Ru is merely a matter of doing what the self-proclaimed Ru of that era were doing: Confucianism is what Confucians do. Because Cheng Yi approached the question from a philosophical perspective, certain that he understood what it means to know the Way, he could conclude that Confucius and Mencius were the last true Confucians before the eleventh century, and that the Classicists and literary men were either failed Confucians or not Confucians at all.

The Neo-Confucians wanted ideological consistency and coherence, and they fit Confucius and Mencius to what they believed to be true. The fact that their reading of the *Analects* of Confucius differed in important ways from earlier interpretations, for example, does not mean they were wrong, but it does show that they had departed from the received tradition.[4] The conclusion I reach from the contradiction between historical and philosophical approaches to Confucianism is that it is not possible retrospectively to define the essence of Confucianism as a doctrine or a practice through all of history. Others have resolved this by writing a history of Confucianism as an unfolding tradition constituted by all the major Ru through history.[5] What we can say is that, beginning with the Cheng brothers, the Neo-Confucians associated being a Ru with a commitment to ideology, and that they juxtaposed this with what they saw as the false ways of being a Ru prevalent in their age: Classical studies and literary composition.

But I think we can see the Neo-Confucians as participants in a broadly construed "Confucian tradition" without having to accept their claim to define its true essence. Instead of defining Confucianism in doctrinal terms, I propose a general distinction between those throughout history who have shared certain assumptions, questions, and concerns and those who did not.[6] People who called themselves Confucians were likely to see these as core issues, as did the eleventh-century thinkers discussed in the previous chapter. Buddhist and Daoist religious specialists were less likely to do so, or had at their disposal ways of thinking that did not require them to, although one can find religious figures who shared some of them, and there may even have been some who shared all of them. I think on reflection many readers will find that they are concerned about such matters as well, and that what might be called a "Confucian orientation" is largely a this-worldly and pragmatic perspective found in many cultures.

The first of these was the assumption that in some form or other there would be relations of power: there would be government, there would be war; some would be rulers, others would assist them, and still others would be ruled. One did not have to think that government was the ultimate expression of human community or that the ruler should be obeyed under any circumstances, only that government and rulers were unavoidable. Not all assume this to be so; even in ancient times, some asserted that the Former Kings' instituting of government had ended the golden age, not begun it. But those who assumed that relations of power were inevitably part of life could then ask how to improve government and how one should relate to it. To act as if power did not exist or were irrelevant to one's own effort to be a moral person was, from this perspective, to act irresponsibly.

The second assumption was that kinship and family mattered. It was possible to deny this; after all, some argued, the world would be a better place if one did not distinguish kin from non-kin but instead treated all equally (if one respects one's own father, why not extend that respect equally to all fathers?). But for those who believed that the family was here to stay, the questions became how relations within the family should be conducted, how far they should be extended, how families should relate to one another, and how to balance the interests of the family and of the community and state. Everyone was necessarily born of someone— the question was what to do with that fact.

Third was the assumption that the division of labor was inevitable. In antiquity—and in later times in some religious communities—some were drawn to the idea of creating a self-sufficient community of pure people whose survival did not depend on others. Those who assumed that ultimately no one could be truly self-sufficient saw that the differentiation of productive work meant that some worked with their hands and some with their minds, some would be workers and some would be managers, some would be rich and others poor. The question was what to do about the pursuit of wealth. Should it be limited? Should it be controlled by the state? Should wealth remain with families? With individuals? Was there a moral way of acquiring wealth and disposing of it?

A fourth assumption was that the historical accumulation of cultural forms—the media by which people shared meanings with one another— could not be ignored. This applied most obviously to the language with which people spoke and wrote, but it also pertained to forms of behavior such as ritual. Words in speech and writing had agreed-upon meanings, and language could be used to convey what one had seen and heard or what was on one's mind. Examples of speech and action, of writing and government, existed from the past. They could be consulted or ignored for better or for worse, but their existence could not be denied. Again, this did not prompt universal agreement. Some granted only limited reliability and adequacy to language; some believed that the past had no authority as a guide to the present. But accepting what might be called the burden of culture led to questions about the relationship between texts and the phenomena to which they referred, the rules for interpreting language, and the ability of authors to fix their intended meanings.

Fifth was the assumption that some of the things that impinged on human life operated independently of human intention. The most important of these was heaven-and-earth (what we would call "nature"), although some also included the ghosts-and-spirits. Government, family, economy, and culture all unfolded within the larger context of the natural world. How were they related to it? What implications did that have for society? Similarly, death was a fact of life, but what was the relation of the living to the dead and what did that imply for the living?

Most Song, Yuan, and Ming literati, Confucians, and Neo-Confucians shared these assumptions and the concerns with government, family, economy, culture, and nature that followed from them. They were heirs to traditions of writing about these concerns. The Neo-Confucians stood out among Confucians in their time not only in the way they answered the questions these concerns raised but also in their desire to form a "school" of their own, with master teachers and student disciples.[7] Cheng Yi eventually began to call the kind of learning he believed he and his brother had rediscovered the "Learning of the Way" (*Dao xue*), the kind of learning that would result in insight into the true Way. The name was not essential; as later Neo-Confucians pointed out, since this was what it truly meant to learn, it could simply be called "learning," free of any qualification. I think Cheng was pointing out that other ways of learning did not lead to the Way. In particular, he wanted to make sure that literati would immediately sense that *Dao xue* stood in contrast to a term more common at the time: *wen xue*, which linked learning with *wen* and implied that enterprise of learning amounted to mastering texts and composing literary works.

From Cheng Yi on, some literati did use the term *Dao xue* to refer to the approach to understanding morality and values that distinguished Neo-Confucians from others who called themselves Ru. Historians gave the emergence of Neo-Confucianism formal recognition when they compiled the official history of the Song dynasty in the fourteenth century. Traditionally the official histories had had sections for biographies for Ru and for literary figures; now they added a new section, "Dao xue," for the Cheng school as it had been defined in the twelfth century by Zhu Xi and his successors, and they placed it before the section on Ru. They recognized that, first, Neo-Confucianism differed from traditional Confucianism and, second, that there were people who could be called Confucians but did not accept Neo-Confucian claims. The challenge for us is to combine an internal view—to recognize that how Neo-Confucians thought of themselves was important to how they acted—with an external view that acknowledges both that they made claims that not all of their contemporaries accepted and that they had concerns that others shared.

An External Reading of the Internal History

In contrast to prior common Confucian intellectual practice, the Neo-Confucians wrote and rewrote their own history. Only the first part of the story was fairly constant—the part that told of their rediscovery of the Way in the latter half of the eleventh century—but over time the rewriting of the history of Neo-Confucianism also became a way of justifying particular doctrinal positions within the Neo-Confucian camp.[8] It seems to me that this interest in having a "genealogy of the Way" was in tension with the claim (to be explored in a later chapter) that that the truth of Neo-Confucian ideas was evident from a correct understanding of reality. Internal histories were in effect a way of identifying who had authority and where it came from; they invited the student to trust the teachings of someone else, so that his task was to understand and enact what others meant rather than thinking he had to figure it out for himself. This, of course, helped ensure that Neo-Confucianism would be a cumulative tradition.*

We can see this happening right from the start, with the announcement Cheng Yi posted at the grave of his brother, Cheng Hao. The brothers were from an eminent northern family—their ancestors had held positions at court from the beginning of the Song dynasty—that apparently could have placed them in office through the protection privilege, but they choose to compete in the examinations. Cheng Hao passed Ouyang Xiu's famous Ancient Style examination of 1057 and entered the bureaucracy. He initially supported Wang Anshi, who sent him out to investigate local conditions and propose remedies. But the reforms Cheng Hao proposed for education, the military, the tax system, and local society were not what Wang wanted; when Cheng Hao turned against the New Policies, he was demoted and soon released from service. His bureaucratic career never got back on track, but he and Cheng Yi gained fame as teachers. Cheng Yi wrote:

When the Duke of Zhou [the regent of the third king and savior of the ancient Zhou dynasty] died, the Way of the Sages was no longer practiced. When Mencius died, the Learning of the Sages was no longer transmitted. Once they stopped practicing the Way, that was the end of good government for a hundred generations. Once they stopped transmitting the Learning, that was the end of true Confucians (Ru) for a thousand years. Even though good government did not exist, literati could still understand the Way of it by studying about it indirectly through others, and they could transmit that to later times.†
But once there were no more true Confucians, everyone was lost; they did not know where to turn. They let their desires go wild; "Heavenly Principle" [the moral guide that all humans innately possess] was extinguished. My brother was born 1,400 years after [Mencius]. He apprehended the Learning that had not been transmitted in the surviving Classics; he was determined to use This Way of Ours to enlighten This People of Ours.[9]

---

*Neo-Confucian internal histories are, as Thomas Wilson shows, a way of establishing a genealogy of doctrinal transmission and authority. There was a Buddhist precedent for this, for example, in the lists of Chan patriarchs. There was also a Confucian model—the Tang and Song Ancient Style writers, who would sometimes list the successive sages whose Way and *wen* they sought to emulate.
†*Mengzi* 4B22: "I have not had the good fortune to have been a disciple of Confucius. I have learned it indirectly from him through others" (*Mencius*, 132).

This is the basic genealogical claim: Cheng Hao was the only true Confucian in fourteen centuries because he understood the Learning of the Sages, which made him the second starting point in history and his surviving brother his successor.

To support this claim—which might have seemed far-fetched at the time, given that Ancient Style writers since Han Yu had been claiming to have grasped the Way of Sages that had not been transmitted after Mencius—Cheng made a crucial distinction between correct governance and correct learning. Those who wrote about the Way of the Sages were talking about government, and they were more or less on target, but they had not understood that the "Learning of the Sages" was something different.

Cheng Yi's Learning of the Sages is not the old idea of education as the counterpart of governance; that is, it is not *jiao hua*, teaching people how to behave through instruction from the political center communicated to them by officials and the court's writers. It can be accomplished by scholars outside the bureaucracy, and it can be effective even if these scholars do not control the government. I think Cheng also meant to suggest that moral learning requires direct, personal contact with a "true Confucian" teacher, in contrast to knowledge of good government, which can be obtained at second hand. This makes his brother all the more extraordinary, because he found it on his own, 1,400 years after it had been lost.

Cheng Yi, in his grave biography of Cheng Hao, explained how his brother found it.

My late brother engaged in learning from his fifteenth or sixteenth year. Once he heard Zhou Dunyi from Ru'nan discuss the Way, he stopped bothering with examination studies and turned all his attention to seeking the Way. He did not yet know its essentials; he drifted through the various schools of thought and was involved with Daoists and Buddhists for nearly a decade before he turned back to seek it in the Six Classics and found it.

In other words, he had seen what examination learning had to offer, he was conversant with many doctrines, and he had explored Buddhism and Daoism, but he found none of these adequate.

He had insight into natural things and human norms.

That is, he took into account both natural processes and social life.

He knew that fully realizing the nature to arrive at the decree [i.e., developing one's innate potential] was based on filial piety and respect for elders and that fathoming the spiritual and understanding transformation [i.e., true insight into the mysteries of change] came from comprehending ritual and music.

That is, Cheng Hao understood that the most abstract and apparently transcendent matters were integrally connected to ethical and cultural practices. In other words, higher truths could not be detached from the mundane.

He identified the things in Buddhism and Daoism that seemed to be correct but were false; he freed us from the delusions that had blinded us for so many generations. Since Qin and Han no one had yet reached This Principle/ Coherence (*li*)[10] of Ours. He said that the Learning of the Sages was not transmitted after Mencius died and he took reviving This Culture of Ours as his personal responsibility.[11]

Thus, he could explain why religious doctrines were wrong, although they seemed right, and he freed people from false belief. Being the first one since antiquity to grasp the truth, he made it his mission to spread the truth and thus, like Confucius, to revive the culture of the ancient sages.*

Neo-Confucianism became a cumulative intellectual tradition starting with the Cheng brothers, especially Cheng Yi, who outlived his brother by twenty years. Their disciples had recorded their discussions of learning, and these "records of speech" became the key source for Neo-Confucian theory. However, the codification of their teachings was largely the work of Zhu Xi (1130–1200), to whom we shall turn shortly. Zhu Xi also produced the first history of Neo-Confucianism, the *Records of the Origin of the School of the Two Chengs*.[12] Zhu Xi's account identified five figures in the first generation. But he gave the role of "founder" not to Cheng Hao but to Zhou Dunyi (1017–73), with whom the Cheng brothers studied in 1046 when they were still in their early teens. The historical claim Zhu made, that Zhou gave the Chengs the crucial cosmological concept of the unity of coherence (*li*) with his idea of the "supreme ultimate" (*taiji*) is unlikely, and Zhu's understanding of what Zhou meant by the "supreme ultimate" was seen by some as a willful misreading, but his

---

*In making this claim Cheng is also contradicting Wang Anshi's claim to be the first to revive This Culture of Ours.

sense that Neo-Confucianism required an assumption of unity is, I think, quite right.[13] Zhu also included Shao Yong (1011–77), who had more frequent contact with the mature Chengs in Luoyang, but Shao represents a path the Chengs did not follow: the definition of a systematic structure of relationships, modeled on a numerical system, both among the things and processes of the natural world and in the historical development of human society.[14] Finally he included Zhang Zai, also from a northwestern bureaucratic family, who worked out a coherent understanding of the cosmic process in terms of the circulation of *qi*, the matter and energy that makes up all things. Zhang was an older kinsmen of the Chengs who had his own following and influenced the brothers. He died well before them, however, and some of his disciples moved to Luoyang and joined the Chengs.[15]

These "Five Masters of the Northern Song" shared the Ancient Style writers' concern with thinking about the larger order of things but did not see *wen* as integral to understanding true values, opposed the New Policies, and were from the north. What set apart them from other eleventh-century intellectuals was their interest in showing that the process of heaven-and-earth, the process that gave rise to all life, was the real foundation for morality and thus for politics. Whether humans saw it or understood it, there was something real on which human judgment could be based, something that was true irrespective of how literati interpreted antiquity or what the court ordered the schools to teach or what people thought it ought to be, and this real foundation could be personally known with absolute certainty by engaging in learning in the proper fashion.

The disciples who gathered around Cheng Yi in Luoyang following his brother's death came mainly from the north, but of the famous disciples—Xie Liangzuo (1050–1103), Lü Dalin (1046–92), You Zuo (1053–1123), Yin Tun (1071–1142), and Yang Shi (1053–1135)—it was Yang who, after the loss of the north to the Jurchens, actively promoted the Cheng Learning as the only true alternative to the New Learning of Wang Anshi. Yang was from Fujian, and it was Fujian that, thanks to Yang and above all to Zhu Xi, became the new center of Neo-Confucianism.[16]

Cheng Yi did not authorize a "successor," in the Chan Buddhist model of a patriarch choosing his successor, and in the decades after his death his leading followers went in different directions.[17] Some even took up with Buddhist masters, such as Dahui Zonggao (1089–1163), who addressed his message to literati.[18] After the loss of the north in 1126, the Neo-Confucians' place in political culture rose and fell. An initial attempt to assert themselves at court as an alternative to New Policies ideology during the first years of the dynastic restoration was undone by their opposition to accepting peace with the Jurchens at the expense of fighting to recover the north, and "Cheng Learning" was banned until 1155.

The Cheng Learning stood for something different from the political program of Wang Anshi and the cultural program of Su Shi, both of whom still commanded attention in the south.[19] It spread at first as a way of thinking that gave primacy to personal morality, as an ideology opposed to the New Policies, which could be blamed for the loss of the north, and as a principled rejection of a peace treaty that recognized the Jin dynasty's possession of the north. Thus, it could speak for those opposed to the powerholders at court. Although there was a common commitment to the Cheng's teachings, different figures promoted their own understanding. There was Hu Anguo (1074–1128) from Fujian, for example, who had devoted many years to applying Cheng Yi's philosophy to the interpretation of the *Spring and Autumn Annals*, which had been excluded from examination education under the New Policies. His son, Hu Hong (1105–55), lived in Hunan for twenty years and became an influential teacher and thinker in his own right. Zhang Shi (1133–1180), who had settled in Hunan, was the son of a famous military leader from Sichuan opposed to making peace with the Jurchens. He was influenced by Hu Hong and saw himself as representing the true line of the Chengs. Lü Zuqian, a descendant of the most illustrious of northern bureaucratic families, whose father had found refuge in Wuzhou in Zhejiang, tried to combine Neo-Confucian teachings with literary and historical scholarship.

The most important of those inspired by the Chengs' teaching was Zhu Xi, also from Fujian. Zhu was a systematic thinker who worked through all the major concepts associated with the Chengs; a master teacher whose devoted students numbered in the hundreds; a great intellectual entrepreneur who wrote, compiled, and published a body of historical, philosophical, and literary works that gave Neo-Confucianism a firm textual foundation; and a social organizer who persuaded literati families to work together to support Neo-Confucian education, rituals, and social programs in their own locales. Zhu had a remarkable ability to persuade others to accept his leadership and to lend their support to his causes, while being quick to point out their errors. Zhu trimmed and reworked the several possibilities that had emerged from the Cheng brothers so as to create a single coherent program; it is almost right to say that, after Zhu Xi, Neo-Confucianism becomes "Zhu Xi-ism."[20]

The exception to this was Lu Jiuyuan (1139–94) from Jiangxi. Lu criticized Zhu for overtheorizing sagehood and undermining practice by diverting attention to textual studies. In retrospect, Lu became the spokesman for those who believed that it ought to be possible to realize one's innate moral capability through an act of will. Lu had a message, and he had followers; he was a moving public lecturer and corresponded with many, but he did not try to make arguments and establish theories by writing commentaries or producing systematic treatises.[21] Lu acknowledged that the Chengs had had insight into the Way and a degree of practice that surpassed the Confucians of Han and Tang, that they differed from the Ancient Style intellectuals of their own day, and that true learning had not been transmitted after Mencius. In my view, his teachings were tenable only in the context of the Chengs' philosophical assumptions, but Lu himself was not willing to credit them with the rediscovery of the Way, thus implying that he himself was the first since Mencius to get it right. Lu was certain that one could feel that he was in a state of coherence with the world, something that could not be achieved by cumulative and careful learning. He was, as Zhu Xi understood, a serious competitor, and his message continued to have a following. Lu represented one possibility within the context of Neo-Confucian doctrine, and for some Zhu and Lu came to represent a polarity that constituted the Neo-Confucian whole. This was not the common view, but Wu Cheng (1249–1333), one of the most influential southern Neo-Confucians during the Yuan dynasty, held that Lu and Zhu represented two sides of Neo-Confucianism (which he, Wu Cheng, could combine), and there were similar attempts to rhyme Lu and Zhu during the fifteenth century. It seems to me that such efforts signaled a desire to maintain the Neo-Confucian view of learning as a single all-encompassing doctrine.[22]

The Neo-Confucians sought the support of the larger literati public, that is, both officials and the multitude of examination candidates, but they also pressed the court and emperor to recognize that their understanding of the Learning of the Sages was correct. This endeavor did not meet with success during Zhu Xi's lifetime, although several attempts were made. To the contrary, during the late twelfth century, criticism of the Neo-Confucians increased: they formed a clique and thought they were superior to everyone else, they used jargon that excluded others, they ignored the value of literary and bureaucratic accomplishment, and they were too quick to condemn those they opposed. In 1198, the court, which had long ago given up any aspiration to transform society, included Zhu and his followers in a ban that labeled ideological opponents of the regime as promoters of "False Learning," a pointed rejection of their claim to possess the Learning of the Way. Zhu died while the ban was in effect.[23] But during the following decades, Neo-Confucian learning continued to spread among the literati, and whether those in power liked it or not, both examination candidates and the examiners were adopting its language and concerns.[24] The court retreated, and in 1227 an imperial announcement proclaimed that Zhu's most important commentaries illuminated the Way of Confucius and Mencius. In 1241, the court went even further and placed Zhu and the Northern Song masters in the Confucian temple at the capital, and thus also in the Confucian temples in every prefecture and county. Those honored in the Confucian temple, literally the Temple of Culture (Wen miao), were officially recognized as the authoritative Ru of their age, and from the emperor down to county magistrates, the government made offerings to their spirits. In the process the court removed Wang Anshi from the temple and adopted the Neo-Confucians' own version of history: the Way that had been lost after Mencius had been recovered by Zhou Dunyi, the Chengs, and Zhang Zai and was transmitted in the south by Zhu Xi.[25] When the Yuan dynasty restored the examination system in 1315, it required knowledge of Zhu Xi's commentaries.

NEO-CONFUCIANISM IN SOUTH AND NORTH IN YUAN

The examinations were reopened in 1315, with the first section of the four-part test requiring essays based on Zhu Xi's commentaries on the Four Books. Neo-Confucianism would remain part of the examination system almost continuously until 1905. Neo-Confucians had long had an uneasy relationship with the examination system, although few were reluctant to participate in it, because they saw a written test as an unreliable indicator of moral cultivation. But some Neo-Confucians saw 1315 as a triumph: they had succeeded in getting the Yuan dynasty to recognize the correctness of their position, just as they had succeeded in doing in Song when the court placed Zhu Xi and the Northern Song masters in the Confucian temple in 1241. Now, Cheng Duanli (1271–1345) from Zhejiang asserted, true learning and examination learning had been formally united.

Since Xu Heng aided the age with the learning of Master Zhu . . . all the scholars under heaven have known they should honor the Classics upon which Master Zhu commented in order to find their way back to Confucius and Mencius. Xu's merit is great. Our examination system also follows Master Zhu's "Private Proposal [on the Examination System]." The Classics section takes the interpretations of Cheng and Zhu as principal but uses the old commentaries and subcommentaries at the same time, and the essays on the meaning of the Classics do not have to conform to a set form of composition. The essays [these students] write on the Classics are able to compare the Cheng-Zhu interpretation with the old commentaries and subcommentaries item by item and define the failings and achievements of the Han scholars' exegeses. We have completely washed away faults of the late Song, their meaningless emptiness, literary excess, and despoiling of the Classics. We have united Classical studies, the Learning of Principle (*Li xue*), and examination training, thus making it easier for literati devoted to the Way. How could the examinations of Han, Tang, or Song compare![26]

Cheng's celebration of the Yuan examination system was excessively optimistic,* but his comments do make the point that this was now a system that obtained for both the north (represented by Xu Heng) and the south (Zhu Xi).

---

*The Yuan examination system was neither generous in granting degrees nor consistently maintained. In practice personal connections, teaching positions in the school system, and clerical positions in local government were more important ways of entering office for literati. The Yuan imposed a quota and had different examination requirements for Mongols, Central Asians, Hanren (northern Chinese, Jurchens, and Khitans), and Southerners. No group was awarded more degrees than the total given to the Mongols.

For Cheng it was the southerner Zhu Xi who defined Neo-Confucianism, and despite the presence of Xu Heng in the north, from the Southern Song on most influential Neo-Confucian thinkers were from the south, a few from the northwest, and almost none from the vast central plain of the north. The spread of Neo-Confucianism in the south during the Southern Song period was centered on the prosperous regions of Fujian, Zhejiang, and Jiangxi, home to most of Zhu Xi's 500-odd disciples;[27] there were some leading figures in Sichuan as well.[28] Although the Northern Song masters had been northerners—the Cheng brothers' base was in the old capital of Luoyang—and most of the followers of the Chengs were from the north, the New Policies proscription of the Cheng Learning, followed by the Jin conquest, had largely erased Neo-Confucianism from the north.

But this turns out not to be an adequate explanation for the discrepancy. Although during most of the Jin dynasty Neo-Confucianism was absent from the north, other Northern Song intellectual traditions thrived in Jin. The intellectual culture of Han literati under the Jin was oriented toward the literary examinations and admired figures such as Su Shi, rather than the teachings of the Cheng brothers. After the 1160s, the Jin recruited a large number of literati into government through a generous examination system; once in office these officials and the Jurchen court were interested in finding common ground and defending the civil order against the ever-present threat of Jurchen militarism. Cultural continuity with the Northern Song was also evidence of the legitimacy of the Jin. Moreover, the north went into economic decline after 1126, a decline that only worsened when the Yellow River changed course in 1194 and floods devastated part of the central plain. The Mongol invasions in 1209 and the 1230s further ravaged the north. The survival of literati depended to a far greater extent on the goodwill of political authority.[29]

In the south, proponents of Neo-Confucianism had at first hoped to gain court support for their learning as an alternative to New Policies learning, but they had aligned themselves with those who opposed making peace with Jin (which meant accepting the loss of the north) and fell out of favor once the court decided to make peace. Later chapters will explain what happened in greater detail. In essence, Neo-

Confucianism in the south spread among literati in local society and came to depend on private patronage from local literati and the occasional support of local officials. The growing number of private academies, funded with public and private support, anchored local literati communities and provided an audience for Neo-Confucian teachings. The general prosperity of the south below the Yangzi made it possible for many families with wealth to support their sons' studies, whether or not they had a history of officeholding. Moreover, Zhu Xi's Neo-Confucianism gave particular attention to the ways in which local literati could become actively involved in public life in their home locales.

When the Mongols established a dynastic state in the eastern part of their empire, taking the name Yuan, in 1271, they also granted privileges to literati and their families. This prepared them to accommodate the much larger numbers of literati in the south, which they did by funding great numbers of schools and giving literati office as teachers, well before re-establishing the examination system until 1315.[30] With the unification of north and south in the 1270s, after 150 years of separation, northern literati and the Yuan court discovered that Neo-Confucianism had become a central feature of the intellectual landscape of the south. Although the teachings of the Chengs and to some extent of Zhu Xi were known by the late Jin, knowledge of their importance in the south drew increased attention to them in the north after unification.[31]

The difference between north and south was, I think, a difference in literati orientations. Southern Neo-Confucians had learned that they could rely on local resources, whereas northern Neo-Confucians looked to the state. Xu Heng (1209–81) from Henan, whom Khubilai Khan placed in charge of education at the capital, was the most famous advocate of recognizing Cheng-Zhu Neo-Confucianism in the north. Xu was particularly drawn to the idea that if rulers did not take responsibility for morality, then their officials could. Moreover, Xu believed, Neo-Confucianism could be used to transform the foreign rulers as well as to guide officials.[32] It seems to me that Xu, brought up under Jurchen and Mongol overlords and living at the capital, thought in terms of order imposed from above and that he saw in Neo-Confucianism a justification for the greater centralization of bureaucratic authority in a regime given to ad hoc procedures and personal favoritism.

From Southern Song on, southern literati had two options: they could develop contacts and gain fame through their involvement in local traditions, or they could pursue a state-oriented career. But for northern literati, there was only one possibility: absent local traditions, there was only the state.[33] Thus, for example, the Neo-Confucian teacher Xu Qian (1270–1337), from Wuzhou in Zhejiang, made his career at home, although a number of his students went on to serve, whereas Wu Cheng from Jiangxi sought connections to leading officials and national fame. Wu appears to have been concerned more with resolving differences among the literati and unifying the Zhu Xi and Lu Jiuyuan camps of Neo-Confucian doctrine than with making the state successful.[34] Although it is commonly said that the barbarian Mongols did not respect the Chinese literati and that Chinese literati had no chance to serve in government, literati in the south did participate in the Yuan order, even if their opportunities for policy-making positions in government were far more limited than in Song. And just as some Southern Song officials and their families had been loyal to Song and sacrificed themselves when the dynasty fell, the fact that the rulers were Mongols and their most trusted lieutenants were Central Asians did not stop literati from remaining loyal to the Yuan when it came to an end. Ethnic difference seems rarely to have trumped either a desire for official rank or a sense of moral duty.[35]

Southerners provided the great majority of Neo-Confucian thinkers during the Ming dynasty as well, now with the addition of Guangdong literati. Southerners led the two great upsurges of Neo-Confucian activism—the Wang Yangming school of the early sixteenth century and the Donglin Academy of the early seventeenth—whose greatest followings were among southern literati. The Yuan created a unified empire and the Ming continued it, and thanks to the examination system, Neo-Confucian texts and doctrines reached a national audience. Yet southerners and their concerns dominated the Neo-Confucian movement. My answer to the question of why that was so, which will be documented in later chapters, is that Neo-Confucianism better fit the local orientation of southern literati and did not easily lend itself to cooptation by the state.

NEO-CONFUCIANISM AND THE
IMPERIAL STATE DURING THE MING

Including Neo-Confucian doctrine in the state examination system made Zhu Xi's commentaries on the Four Books a necessary part of education.* Although little suggests that the Yuan court was seriously interested in ideology in general or in establishing a national intellectual orthodoxy, the founder of the Ming dynasty was. This has led some modern observers to conclude that with the Ming dynasty Neo-Confucianism became a state-sponsored orthodoxy and the ideological foundation of imperial autocracy. I will take up this question in greater detail in the next chapter. Here I want to trace the tensions between the court, which at times sought ideological control, and Neo-Confucians, who saw themselves as the proper source of ideology.

The Ming began as a southern dynasty, with its capital at Nanjing on the Yangzi River; Beijing became the primary capital only in 1421. Zhu Yuanzhang, the founder, who reigned from 1368 into 1398, became increasingly suspicious of his own bureaucracy and initiated bloody purges in which as many as 45,000 officials, their kin, and their associates were executed. In 1370 he opened and then closed the examinations and then in 1384 reinstated them permanently, but he also demanded that students study his own pronouncements. He restructured the government so that he would have direct authority over the civil administration, censorate, and military. Some have read the writings of his literati advisors as justifying his autocratic centralization of authority and feeding his conviction that the emperor should be teacher to the populace.[36] Zhu's attitude toward literati elites varied; at times he was determined to destroy the power of literati elites in the southeast, a center of Neo-Confucianism and home to these same advisors, and at other times he was anxious for their support. For their part, elite families' responses to Zhu's policies ranged from resistance to support.[37]

The Ming founder did find some common ground with this group of southeasterners, men who were well acquainted with Neo-Confucian

---

*The examinations tested skill in literary composition in the third section; however, this section carried far less weight.

ideas, in the formation of early Ming social policy. In a way that resonated with the Neo-Confucian movement in Southern Song and Yuan
and was quite unlike the Tang and Song foundings, Ming social policy institutionalized the authority of the local community. From this perspective, which will be elaborated on in the final chapter, the Ming founding
can be seen as building on the local orientation of the Neo-Confucian
movement in the south, although the emperor did not grant that anyone
had greater authority over social morality than himself.[38] By the end of
his reign, Zhu's early advisors had died, retired, or been executed. Yet the
leading intellectual figure in his successor's short reign was Fang Xiaoru
(1357–1402) from Ningbo, a protégé of Zhu's early advisor Song Lian
(1301–81) from Wuzhou (Jinhua) in Zhejiang. Fang became the spokesman for the Neo-Confucians after the purges; he shared the local orientation of southern literati and envisioned a less legalistic and less draco-
nian social order in which community interests were tied to local literati
leadership.[39] Zhu Yuanzhang's reign had the title "Overflowing Martial-
ity" (Hongwu); his grandson and successor (reigned 1399–1402) took the
reign title "Establishing the Civil" (Jianwen).

The imperial actions that most look like an effort to make Neo-
Confucianism a state-sponsored orthodoxy date from the third emperor's reign. The Yongle emperor, a son of the founder who had been
given command of the area of the former Yuan capital (modern Beijing), led his army south and usurped the throne in 1402. He executed
those leading officials who refused to support the coup, including Fang
Xiaoru and hundreds of his kin. His usurpation, which made him a
regicide in effect, also made it imperative that he soothe the bureaucracy. He did this in various ways. He backed off from the founder's
style of constant interference in the processes of government and controlling the bureaucracy through terror and instead turned his attention
to foreign policy, sending military expeditions to the frontiers and great
fleets to South and Southeast Asia and as far west as Africa. He offered
some recompense for the execution of the southerners connected to
the previous reign by holding an examination in which all but 39 of the
472 who passed were southerners. Finally he funded large scholarly
projects that employed a multitude of literati. Among these projects
were the creation in 1415 of three official compendia of Neo-Confucian
thought: the *Great Compendium of [Neo-Confucian Explanations of] Nature*

and Principle, Great Compendium of [Neo-Confucian Commentaries on] the Four Books, and *Great Compendium of [Neo-Confucian Commentaries on] the Five Classics.*[40]

The bureaucracy's acceptance of the usurpation, the patronage of Neo-Confucian learning, the emperor's own public avowal of his devotion to Neo-Confucian learning, the continued requirement of Zhu Xi's commentaries in the examination system, and the patronage of Neo-Confucian texts all suggest that this was the moment when Neo-Confucian teachings were subsumed into a state orthodoxy that narrowed and closed literati minds.[41] Neo-Confucian thinkers who spoke for subordinating Neo-Confucian learning to imperial interests are hard to identify; those who gained fame were men who distanced themselves from the court.[42] Yet among them there appears to be a distinction between a northern and southern orientation. Xue Xuan (1389–1464) from Shanxi, for example, identified with Xu Heng, whom he saw as the true successor to Zhu Xi, and spoke for a state-oriented Neo-Confucianism.[43] From a late Ming perspective, however, the seminal Neo-Confucian thinker of the era was Wu Yubi (1391–1469) from Jiangxi. Wu's influence carried over into the next generation with his students Hu Juren (1434–84) from Jiangxi and Chen Xianzhang (1428–1500) from Guangdong, who turned away from examination studies and bureaucratic careers to devote themselves to learning and teaching. Wu, as we shall see later, had no interest in state orthodoxy and pointedly rejected the idea that rulers such as Yongle had moral authority.

There was considerable discontent in political and intellectual circles by the end of the fifteenth century.[44] The emperor had been captured by Mongols while on an expedition beyond the Great Wall in 1449, a sign of incompetent leadership and a humiliation to boot. At court there were rancorous factional disputes, eunuchs who dominated the throne, and the harsh punishment, even execution, of overzealous protesters. Among scholars there were challenges to the intellectualism of Zhu Xi, although that was not new, but there were also beginning to be philosophical arguments against such basic Neo-Confucian assumptions as the equality of human moral potential.[45] At the same time, the economy in the south was beginning to recover, after having declined sharply during the latter half of the fourteenth century.[46] Economic recovery meant that more families could prepare more sons for the examinations, and more students meant a resurgence in private academies, an increased demand for teachers, and a greater demand for books. In many locales the reblossoming of local intellectual life brought with it a resurgence of community building among local literati, and in some places a renewed interest in Neo-Confucian activism. More students increased literati frustration, for it meant that even more of them would not pass the examinations. Like their Song and Yuan predecessors, they were interested in finding something they could do on their own that would have some public value.[47]

The person who caught the tide of the swelling interest in Neo-Confucian morality and became its great spokesman, and the most influential thinker since Zhu Xi, was Wang Yangming (1472–1529) from Zhejiang. "Our time seems to understand the way of sages well enough," wrote Wang, "and yet when I look around I see no sages."[48] Wang's message to literati and non-literati alike was that it was time to work at being sages once again. His criticism of Zhu Xi and the contemporary practice of Zhu's teachings was that they had substituted learning about morality through texts for acting morally in person. Wang's persuasiveness was heightened, I think, by the fact that he proved himself to be morally courageous in politics, an able civil administrator in government, and a victorious military commander against a rebellion by an imperial prince. Before his death, he was already the most famous Neo-Confucian of his generation, eclipsing educators such as Zhang Mou (1437–1522) from Zhejiang and Zhan Ruoshui (1466–1560) from Guangdong. As Wang and others saw, his belief in the direct intuition of one's moral faculty put him on the same side of the fence as Lu Jiuyuan in Southern Song, whom Zhu Xi had sharply criticized for relying too much on intuition. Wang at one point tried to persuade people that his message was not at odds with Zhu's—he argued that toward the end of his life Zhu had in fact reached the same conclusions as Wang—but the differences were too apparent. However, some of Wang's most important ideas could be understood in contradictory fashion, as Wang himself recognized, and his students went off in different directions. One branch resulted in the radical subjectivism of what came to be called the "Taizhou school," which began with Wang Gen (1483–1541), a somewhat poorly educated merchant who with great earnestness decided to be a sage and then accepted Wang as his teacher, and reached its denouement with the iconoclasm and relativism of Li Zhi (1527–1602).

We should not let the fact that Li Zhi eventually denied the possibility of a shareable ethic, which suggests that he fell outside the Neo-Confucian framework, blind us to the revival of Neo-Confucian activism and commitment during the sixteenth century, which was led by proponents of both Zhu Xi and Wang Yangming, or to the hostility toward that activism from those in power at court. We can find both a generation later when in the 1620s Gu Xiancheng (1555–1612) and Gao Panlong (1562–1626) created the Donglin Academy in Wuxi, Jiangsu, as the center for a national literati intellectual society. They were supportive of Zhu Xi's ideas about learning, hostile to the subjectivism of the Taizhou school, critical of the court, and committed to transforming politics and society. The court proscribed the academy and blacklisted its members in 1626.[49]

Two conclusions can be drawn from this survey of Ming developments. First, the revival of Neo-Confucian engagement occurred largely outside the court and examination system; it was not a product of official patronage but a reaction against the status quo. Second, the differences between Wang Yangming's and Zhu Xi's teachings made it clear that that there were now in fact two kinds of Neo-Confucianism. Some associated Zhu Xi-ism with the status quo and established authority, against which activist scholars who wanted to make their mark on the world could agitate. The divisions between the court and the literati, particularly in the southeast, were evident in the court's brief attempt in the 1570s to close the academies, on the grounds that they were fomenting local opinion against court policy, and its resistance to the activists' calls to place Wang Yangming in the Confucian temple (which did not happen until 1584).[50]

The Ming fell to the Manchus' Qing dynasty in 1644. As the Kangxi emperor (r. 1661–1722) consolidated his power, he presented himself as the great patron of Zhu Xi's brand of Neo-Confucianism, a ruler who would not allow the excesses of the late Ming iconoclasm, relativism, and self-indulgence. From the perspective of intellectual history, this is the end of the story, for by the end of Kangxi's reign it was apparent that the leaders of intellectual culture had broken with Neo-Confucianism and settled on a new way of learning; Neo-Confucianism had become one part of a landscape whose contours its proponents had lost the ability to define. But from a social-historical perspective, Zhu Xi's Neo-Confucianism lived on in examination education and thus it remained a core element of literati society.

NEO-CONFUCIANISM AS PHILOSOPHY, NEO-CONFUCIANISM AS CULTURE

The internal history of Neo-Confucianism was a narrative of loss and recovery. For Zhu Xi, the Way had been lost after Mencius, but Zhou Dunyi and the Cheng brothers had recovered it in the eleventh century. From Wang Yangming's perspective, there had been a second loss and recovery: personal moral engagement had been lost due to Zhu Xi's focus on intellectual learning, but Wang Yangming had recovered it. Not only was this narrative the internal history of one school of thought, but it also was a new periodization of China's history. The traditional view of history had conceived of human time in terms of the cycle of the rise and decline of empires: an empire was created when all under heaven were united under one ruler, and then the empire would fall apart. In this older view, the material, cultural, and moral well-being of society was contingent on the state of empire, and the ideal state of the world was one of political unity.[51] But for the Neo-Confucians (and Ancient Style writers before them), there had been a rupture in time between antiquity and the early imperial period.

The Neo-Confucian periodization was *not* based on dynasties and empires. Instead it divided historical time into three periods. First came antiquity, the first sage-kings and the three successive dynastic empires founded by later sage-kings, when the Way was put into practice in government and correct learning was propagated.[*] Second was the period when the Way was neither practiced in government nor understood by scholars. In other words, the Way had been lost during precisely the period of the great centralized bureaucratic empires of Han

---

*Each of the ancient dynasties had also eventually declined, but sage-kings had appeared who restored the proper order of government and learning. Traditionally Han and Tang had been seen as restorations of the ancient model, but in the Neo-Confucian view Han and Tang had established empires without recovering the learning of the sages that was the only basis for moral government.

and Tang, which many would see as the practical standard for measuring the success of a dynasty. Third was the new age, when the Way, although not yet practiced in government, was once again understood by scholars. In this new age, some individuals had realized that humanity was responsible for its own destiny and understood how to realize in human society the harmonious coherence of that which was inherent in the working of the natural realm of "heaven-and-earth and the myriad things." This third age, which began not with the founding of the Song dynasty in 960 but in the 1060s–1070s with scholars who lacked political power, was fundamentally different from the imperial history of the second age. It represented a second break in time, the point at which moral men began to take responsibility for society, whether or not the government cooperated.[52]

The difference with the early and medieval Christian progressive sense of time is instructive. In Christian historiography, the pagan era of Greek and Roman antiquity was the first period, the advent of Christianity marked the second period, and it represented a rupture with antiquity. The third era, in which the faithful would be saved, was yet to come; the task in the second era was to prepare people for that future time. This vision of time as progressive stages, with salvation promised for the future, reappeared in Marxism in the nineteenth century.[53] But for Neo-Confucians, antiquity was an ideal period, the second stage was one of decline, and there was no promise of salvation in the future. There was no promise that the third era, the present, would turn out well; its fate was in the hands of the literati.

Neo-Confucianism's internal history implied that the Song period, simply by virtue of the emergence of Neo-Confucianism, was a new beginning in China's history. In the words of a seventeenth-century observer: the Song period was the "antiquity that came after antiquity" (*sandai hou zhi sandai*). And as Yan Fu (1853–1921), the nineteenth-century translator of European social thought, put it: "The way China has become today, for better or for worse, is eighty to ninety percent attributable to the Song period."[54]

Neo-Confucians buttressed their claim to having a true understanding of antiquity, and thus deserving of a special place in later history, in both cultural and philosophical terms. On one hand, they provided an interpretation of the origins of civilization in antiquity and its texts.

Although they had competitors in the eleventh century, and although in later periods there were always some who doubted their claims, their view of antiquity was widely shared until the seventeenth century. On the other hand, they provided a kind of unified field theory that explained the connections between human society, psychological experience, and heaven-and-earth. To assert, as they did, that the coherence of heaven-and-earth inhered in human beings and all things that came into being through the processes of creation—a philosophical concept that will be taken up in later chapters—was a universal claim about the constitution of reality. It did not depend on any text to be true. The fact that for 1,400 years humanity had not known that this was so did not make it any less true. Zhu Xi recognized that the ancients had never spelled things out as he did—he explained this by saying that essential truths were expressed in a manner that made sense to the age[55]—but Neo-Confucian philosophy could "account for" what the ancients had accomplished and why their way worked. In short, the Neo-Confucians were making a cultural claim—they had grasped what was historically fundamental to "our" antiquity and "our" civilization—as well as a philosophical claim—that this civilization had been successful because it was in accord with the fundamental principles of life itself. In their terms, they had understood how to unify "heaven and man"; that is, they had found the link between natural processes and human sociopolitical endeavors. This was not unlike the Han and Tang view that the ancients had relied on the patterns of heaven-and-earth to create a civilization that came to have a historical existence, except that for the Neo-Confucians this depended on individual learning rather than the state system.

These two claims—to be simultaneously recovering the truth about "our" particular historical and cultural origins and discovering the truth about the natural processes that sustain the universe—do not necessarily entail one another. If the philosophy was right, then in theory it was not necessary to resurrect writings and models from a time that the Neo-Confucians agreed was quite different from the present. If human society could be made to operate according to the right principles, principles that transcended history, culture could change; there was no need for loyalty to an ancient past—a position some Neo-Confucians took. However, if antiquity represented the only possible model of a benevolent and harmonious society, then the challenge was to replicate that model to the greatest degree possible—as some Neo-Confucians indeed thought—in which case there was no real need for the philosophy. In general the Neo-Confucians tried to have it both ways and to present themselves as both a philosophy and a culture. Doing so allowed them to position themselves in intellectual terms in opposition to the Buddhists, and to a lesser extent the Daoists, on one hand, and the traditions of literati culture on the other. (How they accomplished this in social terms is discussed in the final chapter.)

A standard account of the history of Neo-Confucianism as philosophy goes something like this: in the medieval period, Buddhism and Daoism gained strength and Confucianism declined. In the Song period, Confucians responded to the (primarily) Buddhist challenge and revived Confucianism by giving traditional Confucian ethics a better foundation by borrowing philosophical concepts such as *li*, principle or coherence, from Buddhism and *qi*, energy-matter or material force, from Daoism. The origins of this view seem to lie in the critique of Qing scholars, who sought to supplant the intellectual authority of Neo-Confucians by arguing that Song and Ming Neo-Confucians did not have a correct understanding of the Classics and antiquity because they had been influenced by Buddhism and Daoism. Modern historians who accept this view have accounted for it in various ways, for example, by positing that Neo-Confucianism was an outgrowth of an eleventh-century desire to combine the "Three Teachings" of Confucianism, Buddhism, and Daoism[56] and by pointing to parallels between contemporary developments in Buddhism and Confucianism.[57] Certainly there were literati who aimed to synthesize the Three Teachings, just as there were Buddhist monks who asked how they could bring together Buddhism and the literary Ancient Style that was spreading among the literati.[58] I doubt we can account for the rise of Neo-Confucianism simply in terms of philosophy. Much recent scholarship has shown that the most useful contexts for explaining the rise of Neo-Confucianism are debates among literati, the centrality of literary production and textual studies in literati intellectual life, and the search for an alternative to Wang Anshi's New Policies.[59] For present purposes, the more important point is that the rhetorical stance Neo-Confucianism adopted, coming from the Tang Ancient Style writer Han Yu, held that Buddhism and Daoism had spread because the political elite after Mencius did not understand the true meaning of antiquity and the Way of the Sages. If they had, there might not have been a disjunction between morality and politics and the ideal order of antiquity might not have ceased. Han Yu was making a polemical claim—in order for his view of the Confucian way to be correct, Han Confucians and Tang Confucians prior to him could not have been true Confucians—clearly his (and the Neo-Confucian) goal was to assert a fundamental difference between the Confucian way and Buddhism and Daoism.

In fact, it was Wang Anshi and his New Policies successors and Su Shi and his circle who were open to Buddhist and Daoist philosophical ideas, rather than seeing themselves as leading the fight against them.[60] This does not preclude the Neo-Confucian borrowing of Buddhist ideas—students of Neo-Confucian philosophy sometimes studied Buddhist ideas and practices,[61] and there were a plentitude of occasions for exchanges between literati and monks.[62] The rhetoric of literati who wrote on behalf of Buddhist institutions did change from Tang to Song somewhat in favor of the literati, but it is clear that Buddhism was widespread and deeply embedded in literati society.[63] By and large, those Neo-Confucians who found compatibilities between their own and Buddhist ways of thinking were those who found a shared interest with Chan masters in the practice of introspection, perhaps the most anti-theoretical of Buddhist traditions.[64]

Neo-Confucianism's philosophical borrowings from Buddhism were more accidental than purposeful. Ideas about all things sharing the same principle and, above all, the importance given to the "mind" in moral cultivation were in origin Buddhist but by Song times had become current in literati society. But let us grant that Buddhist philosophizing was a longer and deeper tradition than the Neo-Confucian and that Buddhism made claims about the nature of reality and how the individual was connected to it and, on that basis, about the proper organization of social and political life. This is where the two-sided Neo-Confucian claim to know *both* the particular origins of "our" culture and the nature of reality became salient. It worked against Buddhism and Daoism, since neither could claim, at least in a way that withstood serious scrutiny, to have an integrated understanding of and a true commitment to antiquity and the Classics as the origins of a common culture. There was a boundary between the Neo-Confucians and Buddhists; it could be crossed, but to do so threatened the idea of one's duty to a particular cultural tradition.

On the other hand, the Neo-Confucians also saw other modes of literati learning as rivals. Literati generally shared an interest in the cultural traditions that stemmed from antiquity, and during the eleventh century other thinkers had set out their visions of how learning could unify morality and politics. Against them—Zhu Xi took particular aim at Wang Anshi and Su Shi—Neo-Confucians could not deploy the charge of cultural disloyalty. Instead, they accused them of philosophical incoherence.

The cultural and philosophical two-sidedness of Neo-Confucianism probably served its followers well. Those who were uninterested in philosophical universals could devote themselves to the Neo-Confucian cultural program, beginning with the interpretation of antiquity and the Classics, and still claim to be serious about morality. Those interested in the philosophy and the internal basis for morality could still claim to be loyal to "our" culture. But the larger challenge for the Neo-Confucians was to show that their philosophy did in fact fit with the culture in a way meaningful to their primary audience, the literati. They did this, beginning in the twelfth century for the most part, by reworking existing materials to bring them into line with their philosophical ideas and by adding new elements. The result was not the total eradication of previous traditions but a new layer on top of the cultural production and rhetoric of the early imperial period, something that was both an alternative cultural system and a filter for sorting out what did not conform. From the Neo-Confucian perspective, this was the platform that would give humanity a second chance to get it right.

To see how well the Neo-Confucians succeeded, we may consider the materials they produced for literati to read in the four traditional categories of writing: Classics, Histories, Philosophies, and Literary Collections.

Until the twelfth century, the Confucian Classics meant the five major classics, but by the fourteenth century the Five Classics had lost much of their importance to the Four Books. In the process, the focus of Classical learning shifted from the sage as a ruler in antiquity to the sage as a scholar who cultivated himself. The *Analects*—the original collection of conversations and pronouncements of Confucius and his followers—had long been required in the examinations. The *Mencius*—a far longer work in which Mencius defended his version of the Confucian approach to statecraft and individual moral cultivation—had been popular with Wang Anshi but not with Sima Guang, who thought its teachings threatened a hierarchical political system. The *Doctrine of the Mean*—a chapter in the *Book of Rites* presented as the teachings of Confucius, which linked together the individual, the cosmos, self-cultivation, spirituality, and social responsibility—was being read by many during the eleventh century. Only the *Great Learning*—another chapter from the *Book of Rites*, which connected social and political order to individual self-cultivation through apprehending the coherence of things and affairs—gained both an importance and a reading it had never had before. Zhu Xi, who spent many years working on clearly argued commentaries, made the Four Books a primary vehicle of Neo-Confucian ideas.[65] This encouraged others to write their own commentaries, and when the examinations were reinstituted in 1315, they were already being widely taught. The examination system ensured that the Four Books with Zhu Xi's commentaries would be read by all literati until the early twentieth century, but even today the Four Books are read and taught, and commentaries continue to be written.[66] The Five Classics did not disappear—they now came with Neo-Confucian commentaries—but until the mid-eighteenth century students had to master only one of the five for the examinations. This set the stage for the compilation of the great compendia of Neo-Confucian commentaries on the Four Books and Five Classics and teachings on human nature and coherence in 1415.

Zhu Xi's school also rewrote history. The *Digest of the Comprehensive Mirror for Aid in Government* reworked Sima Guang's *Comprehensive Mirror for Aid in Government*, a chronology of 1,400 years of Chinese political history, to apply Neo-Confucian judgments of right and wrong to historical events. Zhen Dexiu (1178–1235) set out to show rulers that Neo-Confucian cultivation applied to their position as well. His *Extended Meaning of the Great Learning* argued that to rule well meant to cultivate oneself properly but ignored what we might call the practical issues of politics and government. In the fifteenth century, Qiu Jun produced the *Supplement to the Extended Meaning of the Great Learning*; although devoted to statecraft, for the most part it remained within the Neo-Confucian framework.[67] Northern and Southern Song history also received its due with Zhu Xi's *Records of the Words and Deeds of Leading Officials* and a later continuation. These and similar works also provided a biographical history of the Neo-Confucian movement and a Neo-Confucian view of modern political and scholarly figures. In the Yuan and Ming, local compilations appeared as well. Neo-Confucians often played roles in the compilation of local histories, a vehicle for their views on local society and local worthies.[68] The greatest, and still very influential, collections of Neo-Confucian intellectual biography are the *Records of Ming Confucian Scholars* by Huang Zongxi (1610–95) and the more broadly inclusive *Records of Song and Yuan Scholarship*, begun by Huang and completed by Quan Zuwang (1705–55).

The Neo-Confucians also asserted their pre-eminence as the premier "school of philosophy" with a series of works. In *Reflections on Things at Hand*, Zhu Xi and Lü Zuqian compiled passages primarily from the Cheng brothers to explain how to think about the cosmos, learning, social relations, political service, and other topics. Later Wang Yangming's followers would provide their alternative, *Instructions for Practical Living*, drawn from Wang's teachings and writings.[69] There were glossaries for key philosophical terms: Cheng Duanmeng's (1143–91) brief *Glosses of Terms for Nature and Principle*, which explained 30 terms, and Chen Chun's (1159–1223) much longer *Meanings of Terms*.[70] There were even collections of charts explaining how key concepts were connected, for example, Li Yuangang's *Diagrams of the Sage Enterprise* from 1172 and Wang Bo's (1197–1274) extensive *Diagrams for Investigating the Subtle*.[71]

Finally, the Neo-Confucians made their claim to literature as well. Zhu Xi offered a new view of the nature of aesthetic experience, one that subordinated it to moral meaning.[72] His *Collected Commentaries on the Elegies of Chu* gave his interpretation of the foundational text of belletristic literature. Lü Zuqian's *Key to the Ancient Style* analyzed Ancient Style prose. Zhen Dexiu produced *The Correct Tradition of Literature*, an anthology of belles lettres according to Neo-Confucian principles. And, adopting Zhou Dunyi's claim that "Literature is a vehicle for the Way," the Neo-Confucians advanced a simple standard for "good" literature that was intended not only to rule out what they saw as the superficial and frivolous but also to deny the independence of literature from moral philosophy.

The occasional state patronage of Neo-Confucians and the role of Neo-Confucian texts in the examination system did not mean that

Neo-Confucianism so dominated the mental landscapes of the Song, Yuan, Ming, or Qing literati that different intellectual positions were impossible. Neo-Confucians were never really free of the need to compete with others. Other areas of literati activity, such as literature and art or historical and statecraft scholarship, did not automatically reflect Neo-Confucian ideas. And just as Neo-Confucians could not ignore the competition, their competitors could not easily ignore them, as we can see from studies of connections between Neo-Confucianism and other areas of literati thought and practice and religious movements.[73]

Approaches and Questions

Neo-Confucianism was one aspect of the great transformation from early to later imperial China. Its claim on our attention stems from its centuries-long influence over how literati understood the methods and goals of learning. It was also, in a way that earlier Confucianisms had not been, a cumulative and self-referential tradition whose advocates sought to maintain ideological continuity. But in considering the history of Song, Yuan, and Ming China, it is useful to distinguish Neo-Confucianism as a position, an identity, and a social movement.

Neo-Confucianism was a rhetorical *position* that literati could learn from teachers or from texts. The Neo-Confucian position involved philosophical ideas that explained certain things (e.g., why people could learn to behave morally and how morality should be understood), that had a certain history (e.g., they had been lost after Mencius and rediscovered in the Song), and that had certain implications for literati action (e.g., what responsibility did one have to the ruler). By the middle of the thirteenth century, the literati were generally conversant with the Neo-Confucian position. Many accepted that, in discussing morality, it was the position they were expected to take, or even that it was correct, without, however, concluding that therefore they should devote their lives to being Neo-Confucian or that personal morality should be the first among their concerns. Song Lian from Wuzhou in Zhejiang, one of the great literary intellectuals of the fourteenth century, held that his world was heir to a diverse intellectual traditions, including those of Wang Anshi and Su Shi of the Northern Song, Southern Song statecraft thinkers such as Ye Shi and Chen Liang, and intuitionist moral thinkers such as Lu Jiuyuan. Song Lian, and others like him, still thought that Neo-Confucianism had something essential that no other Song intellectual tradition offered, but he did not grant that it was the only thing he wanted to know about.[74] Eventually everyone preparing for the civil service examinations would have to learn the Neo-Confucian position well enough to write essays on passages from the Four Books, but this did not mean that this was all that person knew or that he was living his life accordingly. Examinations grade what one writes, not what one believes or how one behaves.

Neo-Confucianism could also be an *identity*. At some times in some places, some literati took the Neo-Confucian position as an "identity" for themselves. By this, I mean that they tried to play the role of men who were living according to the Neo-Confucian position as they understood it. Neo-Confucianism had its own history; they could learn about it and decide to participate in it. If they gained a following of their own, they might come to be regarded as authoritative transmitters. I shall call Neo-Confucians only those literati who made a public point of taking the Neo-Confucian position as the basis for their identity. To see the difference between those literati who recognized the existence of the Neo-Confucian position and those who strove to make it their identity, consider the following passage in which a Yuan dynasty literatus explains how he first heard of the Neo-Confucian position and then decided to take it as the guide for all his activities, both moral thought and literary composition. The passage is from his introduction to his own literary collection.

When I was an ignorant teenager, when I still had not chosen to believe in any "former sayings and past deeds," I heard others reciting the words of Master Zhu Xi. I felt as if they were coming right out of my own mouth. When I heard them speaking of his Way, I felt as if it was they expressing what I was thinking about. Since I liked his teachings so much, I put all my effort into them. I took him as the authority not only for moral principles but also for literary composition. Once I became thoroughly versed in his teachings, I lost any awareness of the difference between us. I did not know I was studying the ancients but felt that the ancients were just like me. A man laughed at me: "Taking the writers Han Yu and Liu Zongyuan as the authorities for literary composition and the Song philosophers Zhu Xi and Cheng Yi as the authorities for moral principle is one thing everyone agrees on. Isn't the way you learn mistaken?"[75]

Other literati compartmentalized: they agreed that the Neo-Confucian position was appropriate to the discussion of moral principles, but they believed it should be limited to that one clearly defined piece of literati life. But this author understood that the Cheng and Zhu teachings were supposed to inform all areas of life and so he applied them to his writing as well, even though his peers believed that the appropriate models in that department were the Tang "Ancient Style" writers Han Yu and Liu Zongyuan.[76] For most literati, a Neo-Confucian identity was not an all-or-nothing proposition. An individual could compartmentalize in practice, as the passage above recognizes; in conducting family rituals, for example, he might follow Zhu Xi but then decide that his daughter ought to remarry after her husband's death or might agree to a parent's request for a Buddhist funeral. Moreover, Neo-Confucianism did not have a complete program for all aspects of literati life, and thus there was much that depended on the individual and the social interpretation of what was right.

Third, Neo-Confucianism could be a *social movement*. Some literati who made the Neo-Confucian position the basis for their identity persuaded other literati to join them in group activities, in influencing local government, in creating local institutions, and so on. There are numerous examples, particularly from the south during the Southern Song, Yuan, and Ming periods, of local literati who were concerned not only with transforming themselves but also with improving their locales by creating community institutions—that is, institutions that were not dictated or directed by local government and were not limited to a single family or kin group. Here, too, there was variation: literati families might join together in establishing a Neo-Confucian academy but not cooperate in releasing their surplus grain to the market during a famine.

This three-part distinction of "position," "identity," and "movement" reminds us that the ability to use the vocabulary of Neo-Confucianism did not necessarily mean living one's life according to it, and that those who decided to try to live their lives that way did not necessarily collaborate with others to create community institutions.

But what was the Neo-Confucian "position" that literati learned, and sometimes followed in part or in whole? As we have seen, Neo-Confucianism had an internal history as a cumulative intellectual tradition, which was continually being defined against other traditions, particularly Buddhism and Daoism, but other literati modes of thought and practice as well. It had its founding figures, authoritative texts, a conceptual vocabulary, and ritual practices. Participants argued over the interpretation of earlier figures and texts, over what and who should be included in Neo-Confucianism, and who in the present was authoritative. Some of them asserted that they had the one correct understanding, but the claims to know the one way were plural. One reason literati became famous Neo-Confucians and entered the history of Neo-Confucianism was that they persuaded others to pay attention to their views. Studies of major thinkers have traced this process and have shown that sometimes the path to articulating one's own position involved arguing against the ideas of one's erstwhile allies.[77]

And yet over the centuries, I think, there are recurring themes in Neo-Confucianism as a position, an identity, and a movement that can contribute to the way we think about later imperial history. These themes bear on politics, philosophy, belief, and community. Neo-Confucians were also historical actors with political and social purposes. Above all, they were literati and they spoke to literati concerns. In subsequent chapters, rather than investigate the substance of the Neo-Confucians' political proposals, I ask how they saw their relationship to political power and the state system. Philosophical thought was central to Neo-Confucianism, and I take their philosophy seriously, yet in assessing Neo-Confucianism in history, I am not tracing the history of Neo-Confucian philosophy over six centuries, which others have done with care. I am more interested in the fact that Neo-Confucians were so engaged in philosophical discourse—in contrast to many other participants in intellectual culture—and in the beliefs that were fundamental to their philosophical claims. Similarly, I am interested less in the content of the Neo-Confucian curriculum and community activities than in the fact that Neo-Confucians established academies and other community institutions.

In the end an author decides what questions to ask, and readers judge their usefulness. My goal in the following chapters is to identify what might be called recurring dispositions, even as Neo-Confucians reinterpreted and transformed their history and themselves. I ask how Neo-Confucians understood their relationship to the imperial state and politics, their conception of learning as self-justification and practice, the beliefs that were necessary for their learning to be effective, and their work among the literati and in local society.

Appendix

The literature on Neo-Confucianism is extensive, and surveys of it take up whole books.[78] Scholarship in recent times has explored Neo-Confucianism in terms of its philosophy (what ideas did Neo-Confucians have, where did they come from, how did they fit together), its internal history (how did it evolve over time and how did Neo-Confucians construct their own tradition), and its context (how did Neo-Confucianism fit the sociopolitical order of the later imperial state). These are not mutually exclusive, but they are not the same. A philosophical approach is found in studies primarily concerned with clarifying ideas and explaining concepts as a means of understanding Neo-Confucianism. There are those that lump various thinkers from different periods together in order to define fundamental commonalties, such as a grand attempt to create a synthetic picture of a timeless "Confucianism."[79] Generally, however, writers of philosophical studies are splitters, who see differences between thinkers and divergences over basic concepts.[80]

Largely overlapping with the philosophical studies are works that take the internal history of Neo-Confucianism as their organizing principle and describe the ideas or philosophies of leading Neo-Confucians.[81] Many internal histories focus on subdivisions within Neo-Confucianism. The most important of these is that between an intellectual "Cheng-Zhu" line and an intuitionist "Lu-Wang" line, a division that is sometimes labeled as "Song" versus "Ming" Neo-Confucianism or the "Learning of Principle" versus the "Learning of the Mind," although the historical validity of a separation into rival schools prior to the appearance of Wang Yangming has been challenged.[82] Traditionally the internal history has been taken at face value, as a true record of the past, but in fact Neo-Confucians themselves constructed, and contested, versions of their own internal history. Rewriting and revising the internal history of Neo-Confucianism were means by which later figures placed themselves in a particular line of intellectual authority or made a historical case for the validity of a point of view.[83]

A third approach aims to explain why Neo-Confucianism emerged and why it changed the way it did. This is, in most instances, understood to be a historical problem. Such explanations often assume that any mode of thought that receives official patronage must be serving the interests of the state or a ruling class. The difficulties with such explanations have long been obvious.[84] Nevertheless, they are still prevalent in the Peoples' Republic of China, even if the official Marxist-Leninist historical explanation does not persuade many who write about Neo-Confucianism. The difficulties of challenging an orthodox line may unfortunately have kept scholars from proposing a view of history that can better account for Neo-Confucianism.

An example of an orthodox Marxist-Leninist explanation of the appearance of Neo-Confucianism, from 1983, argues that Neo-Confucianism should be understood in the following way. (1) The Song dynasty marked the transition from the early to the later feudal stage of history and saw a strengthening of feudal autocracy and the further centralization of power. The contradiction between the peasant class and landlord class sharpened, and peasants revolted. Thus the landlord class needed to strengthen both its political and its intellectual control. (2) On the intellectual front, Confucian idealism had already become the guiding thought of the landlord class. However, to withstand criticism from materialism, it needed to draw on Buddhism and Daoism to strengthen its philosophical system. At the same time, Buddhism and Daoism had begun to play a role in teaching social morality in order to secure their own position in the polity. The result of this was a long-standing intermingling of Buddhism, Daoism, and Confucianism, which was especially strong in Song. (3) Moreover, since the Tang moral order had been based on a clan system that had collapsed, Song depended on feudal autocracy to maintain order. (4) There were advances in the natural sciences and technology (e.g., gunpowder, the mariner's compass, and movable type). This explains why (a) Cheng-Zhu learning mixed Confucian ethics and politics with Buddhist and Daoist philosophical principles to create an ethical philosophical system yet (b) even as it blended social ethics with the Buddhist denial of desire, it rejected Buddhism as heterodox. This corresponds to asceticism and the attack on heresy of the feudal medieval period in Europe except that it is not based on belief in God. The correct assessment of Neo-Confucianism is that: (1) it was the last and highest form of pure idealism; (2) it was the culminating ideology for a feudal society; (3) it was the new Confucianism of the later feudal period; and (4) it was the bureaucratic philosophy that supported feudal autocracy. The final judgment is that Neo-Confucian thought was wrong and its social effect negative, but Neo-Confucianism did contribute to the development of epistemology.[85]

The common alternative to the Marxist explanation goes something like this. After the collapse of the Han empire, China was in disarray, and no government was able to re-establish an orderly society. Buddhism spread in China during this period, because it offered an alternative means to salvation that did not depend on the restoration of empire. As a result, Confucianism became moribund, a doctrine lacking social relevance. Faced with the Buddhist challenge, Confucianism looked for a way to recover. It recovered by learning from Buddhism how to create a philosophical foundation for traditional Confucian ethics. Confucianism was thus revived and became a pillar of the late imperial order. Variations on this, for example, see the rise of Chan Buddhism with its focus on individual enlightenment as leading to a Confucian revival that resulted in Neo-Confucianism.[86]

My own view, which will be elaborated gradually, is that Neo-Confucianism was initially successful because it offered education, connections, self-justifications, opportunities for local leadership, and ways of acting morally to the literati as local elites with great ambitions but poor prospects.

4

Politics

This and the following chapters refer to the series of connections in the opening section of the *Great Learning*, translated here according to Zhu Xi's understanding. It begins by explaining that the greater learning is a process with two aspects, the first focused on the self and the second on others, and an ultimate goal.

The way of greater learning lies in keeping one's inborn luminous virtue unobscured, in renewing the people, and in coming to rest in perfect goodness.

It then turns to the cognitive process enabled by having a clear goal.

Knowing where to come to rest, one becomes steadfast; being steadfast, one may find peace of mind; peace of mind may lead to serenity; this serenity makes reflection possible; only with reflection is one able to reach the resting place.

However, moral cognition is more than having a clear sense of the goal. It requires knowing the inherent order and coherence of things and making that the basis for action.

Things have their roots and branches; affairs have a beginning and an end. One comes near the Way in knowing what to put first and what to put last.

The process of greater learning requires knowing what to put first and what to put last based on an understanding of the relationships of dependency (roots and branches) and sequence (beginnings and ends) in things and affairs. Getting this right makes possible the connections between cognition, the transformation of the self, and social and political action.

Those of antiquity who wished that all men in the world keep their inborn luminous virtue unobscured put governing their countries well first; wishing to govern their countries well, they first established harmony in their families; wishing to establish harmony in their families, they first cultivated themselves; wishing to cultivate themselves, they first set their minds in the right; wishing to set their minds in the right, they first made their thoughts true; wishing to make their thoughts true, they first extended their knowledge to the utmost; the extension of knowledge lies in fully apprehending the principle in [or: the coherence of] things.

By beginning with the fundamental work of apprehending the coherence of things, it becomes possible to advance step by step to a world at peace.

Only after the coherence of things is fully apprehended does knowledge become complete; knowledge being complete, thoughts may become true; thoughts being true, the mind may become set in the right; the mind being so set, the person may become cultivated; the person being cultivated, harmony may be established in the family; family harmony established, the country may become well-governed; the country being well-governed, the world may become tranquil.

The conclusion is that self-cultivation is fundamental for all people.

From the Son of Heaven on down to the commoners, all without exception should regard self-cultivation as the root. It is impossible that the root be unhealthy and the branches healthy. Never should the important be treated as trivial; never should the trivial be treated as important.[1]

The *Great Learning* is useful to discussions of the Neo-Confucian view of politics and the question of whether Neo-Confucianism contributed to a transformation of the imperial system, because it treats successful government as dependent on a process of personal and social transformation that should be adopted by all people. In short, it places government in a larger, nonpolitical context. As both Zhu Xi and Wang Yangming read it, the *Great Learning* holds true for all people, and thus also for ruler and officials.

Arguing that Neo-Confucianism made a difference involves intro-ducing a traditional view of politics, the structure of the imperial system, and the challenges to it already under way in Northern Song. I begin with two current scholarly debates. The first deals with whether the Neo-Confucians were really committed to politics. It has been argued that the Neo-Confucian concern with moral philosophy and personal cultivation led to a turn inward, away from political solutions to the problems of the day.[2] This echoes the twelfth- and thirteenth-century critics who accused Neo-Confucians of devaluing government service.[3] Against this it has been argued that Zhu Xi, like the eleventh-century reformers, was trying to gain the ruler's support for his agenda—but that the politicians who dominated the court thwarted him (and the sympathetic emperor).[4] I think it is clear that Neo-Confucians wanted to have an impact on government policy and the conduct of officials and the ruler, and they wanted the court to recognize the correctness of their views formally, but, as this chapter suggests and the final chapter on Neo-Confucians in society demonstrates, I do not see them as pro-ponents of the kind of governmental activism that Wang Anshi repre-sented. The second debate deals with whether Neo-Confucianism in ef-fect served as a pillar of autocracy. It has been said, for example, that Neo-Confucians held that the "subordination of the subjects to the ruler must be absolute and unqualified. This was the major reason why Zhu Zi [i.e., Zhu Xi] was elevated as a Sage and Neo-Confucianism promoted as official orthodoxy by all later emperors, from the Yuan through the Ming and Qing dynasties." And further that "the new Con-fucianism was more totalitarian in intent than the old had been, and it gave the monarch authority to police all private as well as public morals and customs, to extirpate heresy, etc."[5] It is with this view that I begin.

The Question of Autocracy

One of the more common narratives of China's history holds that gov-ernance became more autocratic as a result of the Tang-Song transition, with "autocracy" often understood as the emperor's unrestrained exer-cise of power over the government and populace. This can be seen as ideologically sanctioned, as the quotes above would have it, or as an un-intended consequence of the weakening of alternative centers of au-thority that had the constitutional ability to block the imperial will.

Those who see this as an unintended consequence argue that the disappearance of the medieval great-clan aristocracy during the Tang-Song transition left the imperial family the only aristocratic clan. Song literati, chosen for office through competitive examinations, lacked the hereditary social prestige necessary to challenge the emperor. The conclusion this implies is that all the positive, progressive developments toward modernity in the Tang-Song transition were thwarted and China stagnated for the next millennium.[6] In this view, the power of the emperor is taken to define the political system generally.

Those who begin from the assumption that the emperor had absolute power over the political process have asked whether Neo-Confucians created a "constitutional" challenge to imperial autocracy. They have reached quite similar conclusions: although in theory Neo-Confucians had the potential to create an alternative center of authority, they did not.[7] Neo-Confucians "never questioned the notion that the center was where all values should be deposited."[8] Zhu Xi's philosophy provided a justification for seeking external authority in the ruler.[9] For Neo-Confucians "the responsibility for transforming the world falls entirely on the ruler and those who assist him," and when the ruler misappropriated their ideas for his own purposes, they lacked the institutional basis to resist effectively.[10] There have been doubters, but they have not yet won the day.[11]

It seems to me that we need to distinguish between autocracy as the emperor's having unrestricted power over the officials that staffed the government and autocracy as the government's having unrestricted power over the general population. But we should be cautious about assuming that, during the later imperial period, government, in which the emperor was no doubt central, determined the course of history. The long-term trends in later imperial history—the privatization of land, the commercialization of the economy, and the spread of education, new literary forms, and Neo-Confucian philosophy—were not the result of state policy. We might better see the imperial state as reacting to such developments in an effort to maintain a centralized political system and itself. Moreover, any discussion of the political history of the later imperial period needs to take into account the hundreds of thousands of literati in local society, men who had the same education as those who had been selected for office, the very people whom the Neo-Confucians came to see as the largest audience for their teachings.

This chapter argues that in fact Neo-Confucians offered a new approach to the relationship between ruler and officials, one quite different from the early imperial model and one that encouraged local literati to see themselves as part of politics and public life. This was a change in the rhetoric of empire, and it was a change in political practice. I would suggest that Neo-Confucianism contributed to a transformation of the political system comparable to that in Europe between the sixteenth and early eighteenth centuries. That is, the early imperial vision of a powerful ruler who commanded the populace and kept nature on course, a ruler who mediated between heaven and man and was the center around which all revolved, whose rituals had the power to move heaven and humanity, lost credibility. Instead, the ruler became a more human figure, who was expected to cultivate himself through learning in the style of the literati and whose ability to maintain the support of the populace depended on his success in managing the government so that it served the common good.[12]

The Rhetoric of Empire

The early imperial model of empire was established when the state of Qin created a unified empire in 221 B.C. It centralized power with the aim of ensuring that authority went from the emperor at the top down to the populace below through a hierarchical bureaucratic organization that exercised control from the capital at the center out to the provinces through a field administration of prefectures and counties. This differed from the feudal system of the Zhou dynasty, in which the Zhou king enfeoffed his kin and allies as lords with hereditary rights over their own domains, and those lords mustered their resources in their own and Zhou's defense. However much Confucian scholars of Han and Tang disparaged the short-lived Qin and its reliance on laws and punishments to enforce its policies, in practice they combined the Qin governmental system with the rhetoric of the Classics in service of the idea that there should be one king holding sway over "all under heaven."

There were differences between the early imperial model and the ancient model found in the Classics, and Song writers and philosophers exploited them. The idea that the right to rule belonged to a dynastic house was true for the Three Dynasties of antiquity, but the Classics traced the origins of universal kingship to the sage-kings Yao and Shun, who chose their successors based solely on their worthiness. From an idealistic perspective, rule by hereditary right was second best, and some in Song urged the emperor not to model himself on Han and Tang rulers, despite their success in creating long-lived empires, but on Yao and Shun. The idea that the prefecture-county system was the only viable form of governance was challenged as well, and some Neo-Confucians called for a return to a decentralized form of governance modeled on the feudal system and greater local leadership.[13] Finally, the equation of the *tianxia*, "all under heaven," with the "empire" and the idea of rulership as universal kingship had lost viability because Song accepted that it existed in a world of multiple dynastic states, which exchanged ambassadors and signed peace treaties. An examination question from the early thirteenth century—when Song had lost the historical political center in the north, was at war with the Jin, and beginning to learn of the expanding Mongol empire—recognized the diversity of the world and proposed an alternative to unity through empire: "The sage sees all under heaven as one family and sees the central country (*zhong guo*) as one person."[14]

Rather than thinking of Song, and particularly Southern Song, as an "empire," I think it is more useful to recognize that in its own nomenclature it was the "Great State of Song" (Da Song guo). Our use of the term "Song dynasty" conflates five things that we sometimes need to distinguish: the state apparatus, the ruling house, the place, the population, and the period. The state apparatus had about 20,000–40,000 officials. The Zhao family supplied rulers, who lived in palaces and were surrounded by an "inner court" of personal servitors, whereas the state apparatus was managed by the "outer court" of ranking civil and military officials. The place at its greatest extent, in about 1100, was composed of about 1,200 counties, overseen by about 300 prefectures and 26 circuits, with a population of over 100 million. The Song central government sent regular civil officials no further than the county level, where there were usually only three centrally appointed administrators. To manage its local tax, justice, and security systems, the county had to recruit a clerical staff of local residents. The period when the Zhao house supplied the emperor extended from 960 to 1279, although Song lost the north China plain to the Jurchens' Jin dynasty in 1126 and much of Sichuan to the Mongols in 1235.

These distinctions remind us that "loyalty" to the dynasty involved choosing priorities and thus debate. Was maximizing territory more important than the population's welfare or dynastic survival? Neo-Confucians began by calling for recovering the lost territory in the north but eventually turned against war in favor of domestic interests. Was maintaining the authority of the emperor and the dynastic house more important than the health of the state apparatus? Neo-Confucians joined in deposing Emperor Guangzong in 1194. Did increasing government revenues outweigh the social importance of protecting private wealth? Neo-Confucians sided with those who defended private wealth from the state's fiscal demands. Moreover, there were inherent differences in institutional interests: between the ruler who sought to stay in charge of the government and the court officials who managed it; between the central government, which required goods and labor to fund armies, infrastructural projects, and support the court and the bureaucrats, and the local governments, which had to collect taxes and maintain order; and between local government and the local population, who had to provide for themselves and meet the demands of local officials. When these interests conflicted, Neo-Confucians had to chose sides. In general they chose for the interests of the local population against the demands of local government, defended the flexibility of local officials against central policy, and sided with the civil bureaucracy against the inner court.

But we should not think in terms of the state apparatus alone. Although in the south there were still "powerful families" capable of acting illegally, it seems to me a more important phenomenon was the spread of the lineage, first among literati families in Song and Yuan and then among the populace in general in Ming, which gave those families that maintained kinship solidarity greater importance over the long term. Buddhist monasteries and a smaller number of Daoist temples continued to hold far more land and buildings than the local government and provided nongovernmental public space, education, and community. And Southern Song saw the formation of local literati communities, a subject addressed in the final chapter.

EARLY IMPERIAL MODELS FOR
RULERS AND MINISTERS

The "mandate of heaven" (*tian ming*), the famous Zhou claim that heaven gave it the mandate to rule and heaven would take it away if the king did not rule well, provided the rulers of the early empires with a rhetorical justification for their possession of the throne. But the Tang court understood this in two ways. One stressed the need to accord with heaven, taken to mean the integrated processes of the natural world, or heaven-and-earth, which sustained human life.

When Kings acted, they necessarily took the standard from the path (*dao*) of heaven-and-earth so that not a single thing failed to fulfill its nature. When they moved, they necessarily accorded with *yin* and *yang* so that not a single thing was harmed. Therefore, being able to hold together the cosmos and respond intuitively, their dynastic line was never exhausted and their fame never diminished. This was possible only because [their] path attained the ultimate of the mysterious and subtle.[15]

If properly managed, the human realm would be perfectly coterminous with nature, and all creation would spontaneously function in a harmonious manner. In effect, this made the ruler, the *huang di* (the term usually translated as "emperor" but more literally the "august thearch"), the master of the universe, answerable only to the cosmic order.

The other way the court understood the mandate of heaven focused on the ruler's relationship to the populace. From the emperor's point of view, he was supreme, as Taizong, the greatest of Tang emperors, explained in his *Model for Emperorship*:

The populace is the beginning of the state; the state is the basis for the ruler. The proper form for the ruler of men is to be as lofty and unmoving as a high peak, to be as bright and all-illuminating as the sun and moon. He is the one all the populace look up to, the one to whom all the world returns. He extends the scope of his concerns to include all; he makes his heart balanced and correct so that he can make [impartial] judgments. Without awesomeness and virtue, he cannot make those who are far-off attend; without kindness and firmness, he cannot cherish the populace. He soothes his kin with humaneness; he treats his ministers with ritual.[16]

In the Tang case, the emperor claimed the right to legislate the lives of all.

The *Tang Code* assumes a world in which the hierarchy of rank, privilege, and duty has been legislated for all, from the nobles and officials down to the common people, so that even the amount of land farmers were to be given and their obligations to the state were specified.[17]

We can see how these ideas enhanced the grandeur of the ruler, but how could officials challenge a ruler with such a self-image? Beginning in the Han, they appealed to the same theory of heaven-and-earth that was used to show that the dynasty had received heaven's mandate. This theory, known as "cosmic resonance," held that the empire not only was based on the model of nature but also resonated with it: if the empire ran correctly, the natural world would as well. When it was misgoverned, however, heaven-and-earth would be thrown out of kilter, natural disasters would strike, and eventually, if society was not put back on track, chaos ensued. The ruler, as the principal human agent, was responsible; thus any irregularity in nature—a flood, an earthquake—was a portent of even greater trouble to come. This naturalistic explanation of "heaven's mandate" also allowed for positive portents (a radiance in the sky, double heads of grain) as signs of heaven's pleasure. Typically a dynasty collected such positive portents when it was founded or when a new emperor came to the throne, a tradition that continued in Song. Officials became adept at using natural disasters to justify demands that the ruler change those in power at court and their policies, and this happened in Song as well. Cosmic resonance theory thus justified emperorship and empire even as it provided grounds for challenging those in power.*

---

*To elaborate: all things are made of *qi*, a term that can be translated as "energy-matter" or "material force," which can be rarified or solid, stable or fluid. One can understand changes in the seasons, for example, as changes in the state of *qi*. Things changed because their *qi* was changing, and their *qi* was changing because *qi* was in fact polarized into two kinds, *yang qi* and *yin qi*, which were constantly rising and falling. Thus, for example, *yang* (hot, male, dry, bright) *qi* peaked in summer, and *yin qi* (cold, female, wet, dark) peaked in winter. Yet another system for understanding change, known as the "Five Phases" was tied into *yin-yang*, with *yin* and *yang* being the motor, so to speak, that drove the five phases of a cycle. Cosmic resonance theory held *qi* stimulated a response in *qi* of the same sort. Thus, for example, the lodestone picks up metal, bodily processes slow at night, plucking a string on a lute will cause the same string on other lutes to reverberate. When human society goes out of kilter, it disturbs the otherwise harmonious pattern of *qi* flow. When this happens, it causes irregularities in nature's workings. The ruler and his court were responsible for orchestrating and managing the collective

The Classics and the histories were two other sources that both justified empire and provided grounds for challenging those in power. The Classics provided models for maintaining cosmic harmony and civilized life. In the words of the Tang court scholars:

Now the Classics are the subtle pointers of the most spiritual of men and the affairs that were possible for the sages; with them one can make heaven-and-earth constant, regulate *yin* and *yang*, rectify social norms, and promote morality. On the outside they show how to benefit everything in the world, yet on the inside they contain behaviors for being good as a person. Those who learn them will grow; those who do not learn them will fall. When in the great enterprise of governing the ruler honors [these texts], he completes his imperial virtue; when a common fellow can recite them, he wins the respect of nobles. What King has not proceeded along this Way of Ours to establish his influence, spread his title, glorify his transforming power, and change social customs?[18]

This imperial vision existed in a world of texts, but precisely because it had a textual existence, it could be reproduced, interpreted, and promoted through writing, and it could be acted out through the rituals of state and elite life. Those who had an active command of the Classical tradition were positioned both to speak for the imperial system and to challenge it by pointing out the ways in which modern political and social practice failed to live up to the ancient models.[19]

The writing of history could serve the interests of both rulers and ministers. Beginning in the Han dynasty, history served both as a repository of past experience and as a record of the actions of the current ruler and government. Parts of the first great history, Sima Qian's *Records of the Historian*, read as a critique of the current emperor; the second history, Ban Gu's (32–92) *History of Han*, justifies the restoration of the Han dynasty after Wang Mang's (45 B.C.–A.D. 23) usurpation. Tang developed an elaborate system at court for creating a historical record of the dynasty, which became the model for Song and later periods.[20] Song historians, such as Sima Guang in his *Comprehensive Mirror for Aid in Government*, created a new form of interpretive history, one that combined chronological narrative with a clear articulation of the principles history taught, which in Sima's view determined the fate of every dynastic state.

———

qi of society. Some argued, in fact, that if the ruler cultivated his *qi* correctly, by conducting the rituals appropriate to the season, for example, then he would harmonize the *qi* of both his subjects and the natural world.

During the early imperial period, the prevailing assumption was that the court ought to determine the course of history and society's values, and thus the only secular way to be socially responsible was to have a position within the state system. Those who disagreed with the court could remonstrate. But if their protests and proposals were ignored, they had to leave the court for local service or "withdraw" from politics as they waited for a political change. Their goal was to be brought back, to be employed in the only enterprise that mattered.

Song literati knew monastic institutions were an alternative. They had wealth, they often had high political connections and influence at court, and they played vital economic and cultural roles in local society. In the eleventh century, those who called for an activist state that would serve the general good could cite popular support for Buddhism as evidence that government had failed to fulfill its ancient obligations to society. But generally the decision to enter the religious life meant standing apart from bureaucratic participation in the political system, and for Confucian thinkers that was not an acceptable alternative.

To argue that Neo-Confucians contributed to a substantial change in politics in theory and practice requires showing that they articulated a different justification for political power and authority and that this offered literati a different way of relating to the state.

QUESTIONING IMPERIAL AUTHORITY
IN NORTHERN SONG

By fits and starts, Song intellectuals undermined the glorification of the emperor as the master of the universe and the pivot of human society. In small and large ways, the claims of imperial power were being diminished. No longer did emperors prepare grand tombs for themselves—Song tombs were smaller affairs, built quickly and only after the emperor's death.[21] No longer were imperial edicts received at the local level with the extraordinary pomp and ceremony that the Japanese monk Ennin described on his visit to Tang.[22] Song treaties with Liao recognized Liao rulers as equally "sons of heaven," hardly support for the view that there could only be one true empire and one true king.[23] Some officials, reformers and conservatives alike, denied that "heaven's mandate" was real, recognizing instead that dynasties were founded through power struggles. Natural irregularities were being understood in terms of *qi*, not as heaven's warning to the ruler,[24] and some who defended treating natural disasters as portents did so on the grounds of political utility: they made the ruler reflect on his governance.[25] Eleventh-century political leaders, and again this is true of both reformers and conservatives, agreed that the ruler had the right to choose his chief councilors while insisting that policy-making was the task of the ministers, not the ruler. The degree to which imperial authority was being questioned is apparent in the rivalry between Wang Anshi and Sima Guang, the two leading political figures of the time. In describing an ideal system in the 1050s, Wang Anshi ignored the role of emperor, even though his proposals were addressed to him, and in the 1080s, when the New Policies regime restructured the government, it had all arms report to the State Council rather than the emperor.[26] Against this, Sima positioned himself as the great defender of imperial authority, constantly warning the emperor that he was in danger of losing control,[27] but even Sima was unwilling to serve an emperor who would not listen to him.

All this suggests that during Northern Song autocratic rulership was decreasing. A more nuanced view links autocracy to particular emperors rather than to the system itself, particularly to the two founding emperors, who believed that dynastic stability required a greater centralization of authority.[28] Others argue that the emperor had become a central part of the administrative system, not something apart from it.[29] I am persuaded by those who argue that the true characteristic of the Song political system was not autocracy but "scholar-official (*shidafu*) government," made possible by the existence of the examination system as a means of validating political authority.[30] Over the long run, the emperor shifted from being a figure with administrative power to one with symbolic power, tightly constrained by the system he was part of, even if he did not always act according to the ideals his ministers urged upon him; the emperor was not the top of a pyramid but the keystone in an arch, whose successful functioning depended on his staying in his place.[31] Actions that seem to be an assertion of imperial supremacy can also be interpreted as a recognition of local interests, rather than as evidence of autocracy.[32]

The paradox, particularly evident in the case of officials calling for reform—and thus for a change in power at court—was that they had to urge the ruler to reassert his authority over his ministers at the same time they were insisting he listen only to them.[33] Still, most Northern Song political leaders continued to assume that only government could transform society. Given this, it was still possible for emperors to envision their role in early imperial terms. The last New Policies emperor, Huizong, is a particularly clear example of this. In 1103, having just exiled the leading opponents of the New Polices, he put himself forward as a sage-king in a palace examination question.

In the past when the sages managed the empire, they assigned duties in it according to the Way, they established it with policies, and they protected it with the right men. Therefore when they promulgated the five norms for social relations, they worked, and when they perfected the nine offices, they functioned; when they employed the many craftsmen, they accepted regulation, and when they succored the surrounding foreign peoples, they submitted. This is what we aspire to, but we do not yet understand the method to be employed to do this.

We are ever mindful of the complete virtue and great eminence of the preceding emperors, whose works have extended benefit to us today. We shall restore them; we would never let them be lost. To promote harmony in the [imperial] clan, they gave [imperial kin] rank and salary and graded them by kinship. To form the literati with the Classics, they instituted great numbers of Confucian teachers and promoted teaching through the school system. They equalized market prices and balanced distribution, and thus perfected policies for managing wealth. They made clear the rewards for military achievement and recovered border territory, and thus proclaimed barbarian-controlling majesty. They glorified the good and faulted the bad to make clear the principles between ruler and minister, father and son, and older and younger brothers. . . .

Yet why is it that morality is still difficult to make clear and social customs are not unified?[34]

Huizong, perhaps at the urging of councilors who wished to use him to silence the continuing opposition, not only came to see himself as a ruler in the early imperial style but also used lavish patronage of Daoism to claim divine status for himself. He celebrated auspicious portents (but punished those who claimed that natural disasters were a response to bad policy) and sought new ways to glorify himself.[35] In 1124, in the final examination question of his reign, he claimed control over nature itself.

In the past, the sages used the Way to control *qi*, *qi* to control change, and change to control phenomena; they orchestrated heaven and earth and *yin* and *yang* and completed the myriad things. They accorded with their rise and fall, odd and even, and many and few; with the schedule of filling and emptying, the record of being left and right, the ranking of being superior and inferior; and thus the way of creating institutions based on imitating [heaven-and-earth] was clear. Later ages were too biased, shallow, and narrow-minded to see this. We follow Heaven's example and find a model in high antiquity and think about how to bring about perfect harmony and agreement and benefit the common people.[36]

Yet in retrospect Huizong's use of early imperial rhetoric was an aberration. Emperor Gaozong, who oversaw the restoration of dynasty after the loss of the North China plain to the Jurchens in 1126, rejected Huizong's view of emperorship in his first palace examination question, refused to accept auspicious portents, and announced that the court would not favor any single school of thought.[37] The emperor did not want to be ignored, but what was the alternative to Huizong's posturing? And if the New Policies were unacceptable, what was the proper relationship between government and society?

Neo-Confucianism and Politics

Beginning with Han Yu, Ancient Style writers asserted that the Way of the Sages had been lost after Mencius and that they were recovering it by making the Way of the Sages and the *wen* of the Sages their own.[38] Cheng Yi redefined the problem. What had been lost after Mencius, Cheng argued, was not the Way of the Sages, which was their way of governance and could be known from the texts, but the Learning (*xue*) of the Sages, without which a moral order in the world was impossible.[39] Thus even if government was correctly structured, the world would not return to morality unless true learning was practiced. Moreover, as Cheng saw in the case of the New Policies, it was possible for learning to be correctly understood and practiced by some even when government had gone awry. The opposition Cheng created between governance and learning differed also from the common distinction between governance and "instruction" or, more fully, "transformation through instruction" (*jiaohua*).[40] Learning was something people did to themselves, whereas instruction was something government did to the populace. For Cheng and later Neo-Confucians, "learning" was the process through which individuals came to know what was moral. "Transformation through instruction" had Classical sanction, Zhu Xi recognized, but it was better to speak of "renewing the people," which meant helping each person to reactivate the moral nature he possessed.[41] This implied, as Neo-Confucians would later point out, that the unity of politics and morality would require recognizing, first, that they could be distinguished and, second, that authority over politics belonged to those who learned correctly, for they were the ones with moral knowledge. Cheng Yi held that he and Cheng Hao had accomplished exactly that. For Neo-Confucians, the idea that they had recovered correct learning on their own, independently of the state of politics, and that it had survived and spread despite the court's repeated attempts to suppress it, was clear evidence that the kind of learning essential to morality could not be equated with the political system.[42]

CHALLENGING THE IMPERIAL
CLAIM TO MORAL AUTHORITY

A century later Zhu Xi embedded in his interpretation of the Four Books the claim that the Neo-Confucians alone had recovered the Learning of the Sages. But whereas Cheng Yi had allowed that it was still possible for government to be more or less true to the ancient model even when correct learning was not in effect, in a widely read debate Zhu Xi went beyond Cheng to challenge the moral standing of all early imperial rulers. Their achievements in governance that seemed to be unquestionably good, such as the establishment of great unified empires in Han and Tang, did not make them good or what they accomplished good. There was, Zhu contended, a real difference between the sage-kings of antiquity, who embodied correct learning and ruled accordingly, and the early imperial emperors, who governed but did not know how to learn. The sage-kings were truly "Kings," but the emperors of later times were merely "hegemons," men who ruled through power and were motivated by self-interest.[43]

The implication of this view was that no imperial dynasty could claim "heaven's mandate" or assert, by virtue of its power, that it had the right to instruct people in morality. The Neo-Confucian standard for assessing rulers was whether their actions were guided by the moral conscience (*tian li*, "heavenly principle" or "universal coherence"). They concluded that not a single emperor had met this standard.[44] Nor could they have. Only a person born a sage could be guided innately by the moral conscience. For everyone else, this could be achieved only through learning, and the way of learning had been lost for 1,400 years. In antiquity there had been sage-kings, but in imperial times rulers had merely been hegemons, men who held onto power through the use of force. It followed that, merely because they held political power, the emperor and court were not the final arbiters of how people should act and think.

It was not simply that dynastic claims to "heaven's mandate" were false, but that heaven's mandate had in fact shifted away from rulers to those who practiced true learning, as Hu Anguo argued in his commentary on the *Spring and Autumn Annals*. Hu was one of the most important collectors and defenders of Cheng Yi's teachings in the early Southern Song,[45] and he set out to apply Cheng Yi's ideas to the *Annals*, the one Classic excluded from the New Policies curriculum. When the Yuan government officially adopted the Neo-Confucian curriculum in the examination system in 1313, it included Hu's commentary, which remained the official interpretation until 1793.[46] Why was this Classic so important? Because, Hu explained, it showed that Confucius had claimed authority over politics; he had in effect appropriated the right of the ruler as "son of heaven" to pass judgment over right and wrong, and he created a book that enabled students in the present to do so as well. Hu's preface states (italics added):

In antiquity each of the many states had historiographers to record events of the day. The *Spring and Autumn Annals* was the chronicle of Lu, but Confucius revised it so that it became the essential text outside the historical record that *transmits the method of the mind*. Mencius understood the point of it when he said that *Confucius was doing the business of the son of heaven*.[47] The way of Zhou had declined until it had almost disappeared, and the ruler's authority had come undone. Regicides and patricides went on without stop. Human desire ran rampant, and the moral conscience was being extinguished; *Confucius was where the moral conscience (tian li) was located*. If he had not taken it as his personal responsibility, who could have? The five canons were being disregarded; it was up to him to set them in order. The five rites were not being correctly used; it was up to him to put them into a system. The five robes of rank were not being worn by the right people; it was up to him to assign them. The five punishments were not being correctly employed; it was up to him to impose them. That is why he said: "With King Wen dead, is Culture not here with me? Had Heaven intended that This Culture of Ours should perish, those who died later would not have been able to participate in This Culture of Ours. Heaven is not yet about to let This Culture of Ours perish, so what can the men of Kuang do to me?"[48] The sage thought that Heaven had made the survival of This Culture of Ours dependent on him, not on others. Therefore he said, "If I wish to convey [my way], abstract language is not as cogent and exact as showing it in actual affairs."[49] Abstract language can transmit only the principles, but in deeds one sees their practice. Thus he used the Lu chronicle as a vehicle for the model for a true king and to bring order to chaos. . . . This was an accomplishment as great as [the sage-king Yu's] draining of the floods . . . .

The most important thing is that all these were the business of the son of heaven. . . . Those who fault Confucius say that he was so distressed that he *took over the ruler's authority for 242 years without having the rightful position to do so*, in order to make rebellious ministers and murderous sons restrain their desires from running wild. . . .

We are far from the sage. It is not easy to espy the working of the sage through a transmitted Classic. But there is something in the human mind that is the same for all through all time. *If I can apprehend that which is the same, then it will be as if I am in the presence of the sage, and the standards of judgment of the Spring and Autumn Annals will be present in me.*

Recent times have exalted the new theories of Mr. Wang [Anshi] and treated them as state orthodoxy. Only the *Annals* was not used in selecting literati. . . . Those who decided policy lacked the means to weigh alternatives, and no one knew where to turn. By the day, human desires increased, and the moral conscience (*tian li*) decreased; as a result the rebellious chaos [of invasion] went unchecked.[50]

In Hu's reading, Confucius had the right to take on the authority of a king, because he, not the Zhou king, had become the locus of moral guidance. In this he took issue with the official Tang commentators who had tried to avoid the conclusion that Confucius was claiming authority over the ruler and insisted instead that Confucius was simply applying the precedents of the Zhou kings to his own time.[51] (In the late ninth century, after a revival of interest in the *Annals* as a key text of the sage, when the Tang court was beset by threats from all sides, it got around the problem by raising Confucius' posthumous title from "first teacher" to "king.")

Given that all the sages before Confucius had held political authority, the implication of the *Annals* as Hu read it was that when Confucius, a sage but not the son of heaven, took to himself the prerogatives of the ruler, the locus of legitimate authority shifted from rulers to a man of

learning. When we put this together with the idea that one could become a sage through learning, that sagehood was not reserved for some
fortunate few born as sages, we see the Neo-Confucians' boldness.
Learning to be a sage was, Cheng Yi explained in his earliest extant
writing, what Confucius taught his students.[52] So if what made a sage a
sage was not political authority but his access to moral conscience, and
if it was possible to learn to be a sage, and if there had been no rulers
since antiquity who were sages, then it followed that the only truly
moral source of authority in the world lay with those who understood
the Learning of the Way.

Although Zhu Xi had less to say about the *Annals* than any other
Classic, he accepted Hu's commentary and recognized that the key to
Hu's reading was the view that Confucius was taking over the ruler's
role.[53] Zhu Xi himself argued that there was a separate line of authority
over the Way outside rulership; he and his successors called this the
"Succession of the Way" (*dao tong*). It had been initiated by Confucius
and recovered by Zhou Dunyi and the Chengs, who had "repossessed"
the sage's way of learning that had been cut off since Mencius. Zhu Xi
wrote this into his preface to the *Doctrine of the Mean*.[54] The *dao tong* thus
came to stand alongside the older political term for a "correct succession" (*zheng tong*) of dynasties that were "legitimate" successors to the
sage-kings of antiquity as possessors of heaven's mandate.

The bifurcation of the political and the moral served a dual purpose.
On one hand, it allowed Neo-Confucians to recognize that the political
continued to exist and had a history worth arguing over even if it no
longer should be seen as possessing moral authority. On the other hand,
it allowed them to claim that moral authority transcended the political.
Thus, for example, we find the historian Li Xinchuan (1166–1243) asserting in 1239—in his *Record of the Way and the Mandate*, a text written to justify placing the Neo-Confucian masters in the Confucian Temple—that
"the security of all under heaven and the survival of the state are tied to
the flourishing of the Learning of the Way."[55] In the Yuan dynasty, the
historian Yang Weizhen (1296–1370) asserted that political legitimacy
(*zheng tong*) followed moral authority (*dao tong*). For Yang, this meant that
the Yuan government had an obligation to compile a dynastic history for
the Song dynasty but not for the Jin and Liao dynasties. (Yang lost the
debate, and official histories of the Jin and Liao were compiled.)[56]

The claim that Neo-Confucian learning was the only true foundation for a moral politics could be nothing more than the kind of self-serving argument that those who were out of power might make to persuade an emperor he should bring Neo-Confucian officials to court. Hu Anguo's commentary on the *Spring and Autumn Annals* is typically read as arguing that the emperor needed, on one hand, to centralize authority in his own hands and, on the other hand, to appoint the kind of people who would mobilize the state to take back the north from Jin. Hu submitted his work in 1137, but the following year the emperor entrusted policy to a chief councilor who spoke for those who sought to make peace with Jin.[57] Given that, through much of the twelfth century, Neo-Confucians were among those calling for recovering the North, this seems plausible, but it does not negate the point of Hu's preface. Given such views, what was the Neo-Confucian model for the ruler to be?

THE NEO-CONFUCIAN RULER

Zhu Xi's memorials to the emperor, written over a thirty-year period, set out a new model for rulership. Many are devoted to what Zhu referred to as "learning for emperors and kings" (*di wang zhi xue*),[58] a subject on which moral thinkers had begun to write in the late eleventh century.[59] Some, reading statements such as this:

All affairs in the world have their basis in one man, and the person of that one man has its master in one mind. Thus once the mind of the ruler of men is correct, then all affairs in the world will be correct; but once the mind of the ruler is deviant, then all affairs in the world will be deviant.[60]

see Zhu as elevating the ruler to the position of being the ultimate foundation of world affairs and thus justifying obedience to his authority.[61] We might read this instead as a morally neutral statement—in a hierarchical world the ruler is the single most important force for good or evil—that leads to a moral conclusion: if the ruler has such responsibility, then he must correct his mind. What it cannot mean is that the ruler has moral authority simply by virtue of his political position. In Zhu's view, a ruler with a correct mind would be guided by moral principles, would not make dogmatic decisions from self-interest, and would not suppress public opinion.[62] The ruler needed to be corrected and guided, and, here Zhu agreed with Mencius, evil rulers could be overthrown. As noted above, Zhu and other Neo-Confucians joined the effort to force Emperor Guangzong off the throne in 1194 for his failure to honor his father, the retired emperor Xiaozong (r. 1162–89). Zhu objected to those who exalted emperors, arguing that in antiquity rulers and ministers were close to equals.[63]

There are two great themes in Zhu's writings to and about the ruler. The first is that the ruler is a human being like every other human, with the same moral and intellectual potential and the same susceptibility to corruption. Like all humans he possesses "*tian li*, the original state of the mind," which can guide him to fairness and correctness, but as a person made of *qi*, he is susceptible to desires, which lead him to self-ishness and bias.[64] To develop his potential to see clearly and impar-tially and arrive at judgments in the common interest, he must "learn," and the point of learning is to transform his "mind." The idea that a program of mental transformation through learning was the key to good rulership is, I believe, quite new. Even the ancient sages, men who were born as sages, Zhu told the emperor, still engaged in learning. He quoted to him four lines from *Book of Documents*, said to be the sage-emperor Shun's instruction to his successor, Yu, lines that Zhu held were the fundamental precept of the Learning of the Sages:

> The human mind [*ren xin*, the mind's awareness of
>   *qi* stimulation] is precarious.
> The moral mind [*dao xin*, the mind's awareness of
>   *tian li*] is subtle.
> Maintain attention; maintain coherence.
> Hold fast to the mean.[65]

No matter how smart the ruler may be or how lofty his conduct, with-out learning he will not be able to see what is good or discern how things should be. How should the ruler learn? Zhu insisted that he study the *Great Learning*, which the Cheng brothers, "who recovered the learning of Confucius and Mencius that had not been transmitted," said was the first priority for all who would learn because it showed how learning was connected to social and political life. The ancient sage's dictum "Maintain attention" was the same as "fully apprehending the coherence of things to extend knowledge" in the *Great Learning*, and "Maintain coherence" was the same as "setting the mind in the right and making the thoughts true."[66] *Li*, principles or coherence, have no form, Zhu Xi pointed out the next year; thus fully apprehending *li* required learning to infer them from things. If the emperor invited "true Ru" to discourse on learning with him, he could learn how to learn, and he could apply this method to the Classics and histories.[67] Go back and read my memorial from 1162, he told the emperor in 1180, to see how to set your mind in the right. You cannot correct your mind on your own; you need worthy men to help.[68] Learning involves constant work, and when the ruler stays hidden away in the palace, "whether your mind is biased or set in the right is rather hard to tell."[69] In sum, the ruler should devote himself to learning exactly as the literati did, for if he did not, he could not function. Zhu also argued for his position that learning for the ruler was exactly the same learning as was necessary for everyone else in a formal lecture on the *Great Learning* he gave to the emperor at the "Classics Mat," an institution the Neo-Confucians valued as a means of speaking directly to the emperor about how their teachings applied to his concerns.[70]

Zhu's second theme was that the ruler was *part of* the administrative system, in which counties were coordinated by prefectures, prefectures by circuit commissioners, commissioners by ministers of departments, and ministers by the chief councilors, who obtained the ruler's approval before orders were issued. Without devoting himself to learning, the ruler could not fulfill his duty to keep the structure of government in order, for he needed learning if he was to see the overall situation, select the right men for high office, and judge their sense of policy priorities.[71]

Zhu Xi held that what he was trying to accomplish with the ruler—to persuade him to learn to be a sage and thus possibly to become a sage-king—was true to the Classics and antiquity, but its foundation went beyond the Classics or antiquity: "You should know that what your minister has said is not a theory your minister has made up but the theory of the former sages and worthies of antiquity, and it is not a theory the sages and worthies made up but the inherent principles of heavenly norms and earthly standards . . . which even the sages could not contravene."[72] Moreover, this theory of learning had to be understood through its modern articulation by the Cheng brothers.

For Zhu the principles of this way of learning were true to antiquity, but the present was not beholden to the cultural and institutional forms in which the principles were embedded or from which they were inferred. The crucial difference is that the ancients relied on instructing and transforming others, whereas in modern times literati had to transform themselves. For example, in his introduction to the *Book of Odes*, the ancient classic of poetry, Zhu noted that the sage-kings originally used many of the poems to transform people. When their rule had ended and the world entered decline, Confucius edited them as a vehicle for instructing students. The direct, unmediated transformative power of the odes, when odes had their effect simply by being recited, was lost, and instead they became the subject of a scholarly discourse. But in writing his own commentary Zhu not only added another layer in which he acted as the interpreter of the first interpreter, Confucius, he also added a layer of pedagogy in which he spelled out a method of reading the odes for oneself. The ancient kings used poems to directly transform people, but rather than proposing that modern kings try to do the same, Zhu provided each individual a method to transform himself by learning the ancient texts.[73]

In a similar fashion, Zhu Xi presented the *Great Learning* in terms of both an ancient idea and a modern one. The sage rulers and teachers of antiquity had been select men, who had realized their innate potential; they had instructed a populace that had exactly the same nature as they but were not yet enlightened to it, so that "their natures would be restored." But although people are the same in past and present, that world is gone. Now, after the Chengs have recovered the learning of the sages, literati can turn to the text to discover how the sages taught and the point of their teaching, but rather than simply receiving instruction they must do it for themselves.[74] Cheng Yi had repeatedly made a similar distinction between learning in antiquity and modern learning: in antiquity people were largely transformed by the environment created for them: the decorations they saw, the music they heard, and the ceremonies they performed. But none of these were available to modern students: "Those who learn today only have moral principles with which to cultivate their minds."[75]

Zhu Xi repositioned the ruler by demanding that he adopt what the Neo-Confucians understood to be universal standards for learning based on what is common to all people. Precisely because the ruler is at the apex of government, he should serve as a model for the learning that all men can share. This fixes the ruler in position and opens him to criticism when he strays from those standards. Zhu went to some lengths to argue that past scholars had misunderstood the ancient idea of the ruler as "august pivot" (*huang ji*) of the world, a figure who kept his centrality by shifting his position as circumstances changed. No, said Zhu, what this really meant was "the ruler serves as the standard" against which others could measure themselves.[76] In short, Zhu offered the ruler grounds for claiming moral authority in addition to his political role, by providing the world with a model of learning for oneself.

Zhu recognized, of course, that the rulers he was addressing were not sage-kings and that the Song was not antiquity. Ancient rulers were at once political and moral authorities who could instruct others, and the most outstanding sage rulers among them were people who had gained power through their worth rather than by hereditary right. Moreover, he acknowledged in his memorials that the ruler had inclinations toward literary learning, that he saw value in utilitarian statecraft, and that he was also interested in Buddhism and Daoism as the source of transcendent principles. It is fair to say that in his lifetime emperors were willing to listen to Neo-Confucians, among others, but they did not accept the role the Neo-Confucians aimed to cast them in.

After Zhu's death, the best-known vehicle for this view of rulership was Zhen Dexiu's *Extended Meaning of the Great Learning*. This text, Zhen announced, was to be studied by ruler and minister alike, so that the ruler would have the means to "purify the source [in himself] whence governance comes, and the minister would have the means to fulfill his duty to correct the ruler."[77] Zhen followed Zhu Xi's interpretation of the *Great Learning*, but limited his extension to what he called the basis: the various steps leading from "fathoming the principles of things" to "cultivating the person," and except for "establishing harmony in the family," skipped the sections on "governing the country" and "making tranquil all under heaven." Nevertheless he made an extraordinary functional claim: "I hazard to say that this one book, the *Great Learning*, is the full legal code (*lü ling ge li*) for him who is ruler to all under heaven. What is based on it will always be in good order; what transgresses it will always fall into chaos."[78] Zhu had used the *Great Learning* to explain how the emperor and the literati should cultivate themselves; Zhen made the book itself the point of reference, a code for imperial conduct. Emperors may not have lived by anyone's code in practice, but the question is what they said they subscribed to, for that provided a framework for legitimate criticism from the ministers who sought to set them right. Zhen presented his work to Emperor Lizong (r. 1225–64), the same emperor who in 1241 agreed that the Cheng brothers and Zhu Xi should be enshrined in the Confucian temple as authoritative interpreters of the way of the sages.

The *Extended Meaning of the Great Learning* continued to be an important text after Song, especially once Neo-Confucian ideas became an essential part of the examination system in 1315, and rulers found it politic to pay respect to the Neo-Confucian view of rulership. The *Extended Meaning* was translated into Mongolian at least twice for the edification of the Yuan emperors, who proceeded to write encomiums attesting to the importance they attached to it.[79] We shall deal with the Ming dynasty case shortly.

The Neo-Confucian Mission and the Literati

As we shall see in greater detail in the final chapter, during the Southern Song, Yuan, and Ming periods Neo-Confucians also found ways in which literati without office could work to transform society in their own locales. Here I want to address the narrower question of how Neo-Confucianism in Southern Song redefined participation in political life for officials and for local literati.

A FACTION AND A FELLOWSHIP

Ideally officials put the interests of the dynastic state before their own and loyally served the ruler; they did not form factions. In fact, power at court was held by coalitions of powerful officials, who might be dislodged due to a crisis, growing discontent among the bureaucrats, or the emperor's distrust. During the Northern Song period, the nature of factions changed, and the behavior of officials out of office changed as well. Factions became increasingly ideological, and, as Ancient Style writers like Ouyang Xiu demonstrated, those who wanted to gain power at court or who had been driven from it could spend their time promoting their views through their writings. The response of those in power became increasingly harsh and ideological as well: twice during the New Policies period, the government published lists blacklisting its critics as a "faction" and even made it illegal to circulate their writings and teachings.

Neo-Confucians in Southern Song formed an ideological faction that sought to gain the emperor's ear and overthrow their rivals at court. But they were not only a political faction within the bureaucracy. They were, as Hoyt Tillman has put it, a "fellowship" of officials and literati devoted to the Learning of the Way. We do not find this sort of fellowship, in which teacher-student relationships were formed around the teaching of philosophical ideas, during the Northern Song, except for those who gathered around Zhang Zai and the Cheng brothers.

Central to the formation of this fellowship was the Neo-Confucian claim to moral authority. During his own lifetime, Zhu Xi and others had already shown that one could build a national reputation without high office, and Zhu had shown that it was possible to spend one's time in retirement creating a fellowship of like-minded men. Zhu held official rank from the time he passed the examinations in 1148 until his death in 1200, but he spent only a few years in actual offices and served less than 40 days at court. His influence came from his work as the preeminent Neo-Confucian organizer of his times. He was constantly writing letters, publishing books, lecturing to literati and officials, and building networks and alliances that crossed the boundaries of region and social status. His justification was simply that responsibility for the Way lay with scholars.[80] The authority of Neo-Confucian teachers as participants in the succession of the Way depended on recognition by their students and friends, not the court—although, of course, they also wanted the court to agree and honor them accordingly. When Cheng Yi and his students had given his brother Cheng Hao the posthumous name of Mingdao (Illuminating the Way)—as the students of Zhang Zai had earlier done for him—they were claiming for themselves the right to grant an honor that hitherto had been the prerogative of the court, an honor reserved for officials of exceptional merit. Neo-Confucians continued to give themselves posthumous names, they compiled their own histories, both of their own lineage and of the country, they built their own schools, and they established shrines to worship their founders and later masters.

Such behavior did not go unnoticed, or uncriticized. When high officials at court began to attack the Neo-Confucians in the 1180s, they accused them of being something more than a faction: they were proponents of "false learning," who recognized one another through the use of a particular jargon and rituals; they formed a religious sect like Buddhists, Daoists, and Manicheans.[81] The proscription, which named leading statecraft thinkers as well as Neo-Confucians, lasted from 1198 to 1202. It seems to have only had a momentary effect on the spread of Neo-Confucianism, and those who were attacked are better remembered than those who attacked them.[82]

In Southern Song, the proliferation of private academies, rare in Northern Song, provided ready audiences for Neo-Confucian teachers. Some, such as Zhu Xi's ally Lü Zuqian, sought to institutionalize the cohesion among their students with rules and compacts.[83] The attractiveness of this course became apparent in the thirteenth century, both before and after Song fell to the Mongols, when mainly in the south various Neo-Confucian figures, some of whom had no official rank at all, established themselves as teachers and claimants to the "succession of the Way."[84] This phenomenon, in which people with political interests and a national perspective found space to take on cultural, social, and economic projects outside government, seems to me to be far more characteristic of Chinese history after Song than before it.

LEARNING AS POLITICS

Zhu Xi and other Neo-Confucian officials spoke and wrote about political events. Even if they did not limit themselves to doing so in memorials to the throne, at least they were officials. The majority of their literati students were not, and some officials were disturbed that they encouraged men without any official status not only to talk about politics but also to engage in activities that could be seen as prerogatives of the government. Zhu Xi had used the *Great Learning* to instruct the emperor on his duties, and he applied it again to rebut this challenge.

Governing the country and bringing tranquility to all under heaven, and making their thoughts true, setting the mind in the right, cultivating oneself, and establishing harmony in the family are a single coherence (*li*). What is called fully apprehending the coherence of things and extending knowledge also means nothing but this. This is the fundamental purport of the *Great Learning*.

Now if one regards governing the country and bringing tranquility to all under heaven as the task of ruler and ministers and thinks that these are not a scholar's task, does this not make the way of inner and outer separate and divergent, exactly opposite the fundamental purport of the Classic? [Kings] Yu and Chi and [Confucius' student] Yan Hui shared the same Way. How could it be necessary that one be in an official position in order to govern (*weizheng*)? I have never heard such a disturbing and heinous idea. What this piece [the *Great Learning*] discusses starts from the individual and extends to all under heaven.[85]

Wei Liaoweng (1178–1237), the leading Neo-Confucian teacher in Sichuan, made a more pragmatic argument to the same end: it would be fine if the ruler could unify all under heaven, he wrote, but if he could not, then we should take the power to do so ourselves, just as Confucius did with the *Spring and Autumn Annals*.[86]

Here we see the counterpart to the Neo-Confucian insistence that rulers had no natural authority. Rulers had to cultivate their potential to learn to be worthy of an office they had inherited. But literati, and all people, had the same potential to learn, and the process of learning was the same for all. This further empowered officials, who could in any case claim a political voice by virtue of their offices; more important, it empowered literati as men who learned but held no office. Zhu Xi was not simply defending the right to speak openly about affairs. The abundance of state schools and private academies and the circulation of books with sensitive political content, despite court prohibitions, made this a given.[87] He was insisting that literati had the right to *wei zheng*, a term that included both making policy and putting it into practice. He could argue for this because the Neo-Confucians had a vision of the social order in which local literati could act.

A VISION OF THE SOCIAL ORDER

The near-constant problems of national defense in Southern Song drew the court's attention away from activist policies aimed at improving conditions in local society. But the kinds of local sociopolitical roles that Neo-Confucians took on—their involvement in education, in relief, in community building, in tax fairness—was more than a matter of public-minded men filling the space from which government had withdrawn. From the start, Neo-Confucians had rejected the New Policies

approach to government and had denied that the centralized bureaucratic system that had emerged after antiquity was itself capable of
bringing about a harmonious and productive society; local leadership by
virtuous men of learning was better for all. Although they differed
among themselves, in general they supported (as did a number of
prominent statecraft thinkers) decentralizing the administrative structure and reducing central government revenue and expenditure, while
allowing local officials greater flexibility and calling on local literati to
assume new roles. Here I sketch aspects of their social vision, reserving
a detailed account for the final chapter.

During Northern Song, the idea of resurrecting a pre-imperial feudal
system in which responsibility for territory would devolve upon a modern equivalent of the feudal lords of antiquity and in which land would
be distributed through a system in which communities of households
held equal shares (the "well-field" system) was decidedly marginal.[88]
Proponents such as Zhang Zai believed that the new local lords would
be men of learning with a moral commitment to the well-being of the
people, whose local roots would incline them to do all they could for
the local population.

Prior to his death, Zhang Zai had been preparing to put together a
parcel of land where he could institute the well-field system. Zhang
recognized the practical difficulties involved in doing this in a society in
which land was privately held and could be bought and sold. But the
appeal of an egalitarian society led by an elite of men engaged in learning to be sages was great.[89] When Zhang took a cosmic view, government was at best simply a vehicle for helping those in need. His influential "Western Inscription" gave a vision of government and society as
a family:

Heaven is my father and earth is my mother, and even such a small creature as
I finds an intimate place in their midst.

Therefore that which fills the universe I regard as my body and that which
directs the universe I consider my nature.

All people are my brothers and sisters, and all things are my companions.

The great ruler is the eldest son of my parents, and the great ministers are
his stewards. Respect the aged—this is the way to treat them as elders should
be treated. Show deep love toward the orphaned and weak—this is the way to
treat them as the young should be treated. The sage identifies his character
with that of heaven-and-earth, and the worthy is the most outstanding man.

Even those who are tired, infirm, crippled, or sick; those who have no brothers and children, wives or husbands, are all my brothers who are in distress and have no one to turn to. . . .

In life I follow and serve [heaven-and-earth]. In death I will be at peace.[90]

Others echoed Zhang; Hu Anguo's son Hu Hong was a particularly strong advocate of feudalism and land distribution. It would end poverty, everyone would have a home and community, people would stop suing one another over land rights, and the schools would not be overwhelmed by literati aspiring to office.[91]

Zhu Xi disagreed, not with the fairness of such a system but with its practicality, given the realities of private landownership and the difficulty of finding the right people to manage such a feudal system.[92] Zhu's alternative was not so much a solution as an attempt at amelioration. He also thought that the Song system was too centralized and that, as a result of the New Policies, too much power and flexibility had been taken away from local government.[93] He called for giving local government more authority to act flexibly so that it could work with the kind of strong literati community Zhu himself encouraged. He thought more needed to be done to ensure the fair apportionment of taxes. He supported an intrusive state in one important respect: he argued that it might be possible to limit the size of private landholdings according to family size, and thus to contain what he and many others saw as the great disparities between rich and poor.[94] In general, Zhu argued for a smaller government that would reduce its demands on the population, and a government that was moral and transparent, from the emperor on down, and dealt in a fair and predictable manner in its transactions with private interests.[95] This vision of a more egalitarian society, with strong local communities and literati leadership, would remain part of the Neo-Confucian vision.

The Neo-Confucian institutional agenda envisioned voluntary community institutions but was not, as far as I can see, an agenda for innovative government programs to improve the material and moral well-being of local society on the order of the New Policies. When a mid-fourteenth-century writer introduces a book on institutional history with the words "since the rise of learning of the human nature and coherence, scholars have seen the affairs of government and the Learning of the Way as two separate paths," his goal may have been to heal the apparent divorce between Neo-Confucianism and working through government institutions, but it recognizes the actual situation.[96] One might reach the same conclusion from Qiu Jun's (1420–95) *Supplement to the Extended Meaning of the Great Learning*, in that he thought it necessary to argue that the practical affairs of government were still important and not incompatible with the focus on self-cultivation at the heart of Zhen Dexiu's *Extended Meaning of the Great Learning*.[97]

The Neo-Confucians had their greatest success in encouraging the formation of local literati communities and voluntary leadership at the local level in the south. This was realistic because of the burgeoning numbers of local men who identified themselves as literati. Their numbers probably did not diminish during Yuan, for although there were fewer opportunities for an official career, the number of schools did not diminish. The Neo-Confucian sense of local community contrasts with the view of those who saw local society as composed of self-interested taxpayers, who were to be encouraged to take care of their family affairs and discouraged from becoming too involved with their neighbors.[98] Neo-Confucians encouraged the spread of private academies (*shuyuan*) and practically all of them spent time teaching. They published texts to provide their own curriculum. They helped organize local relief. They encouraged the formation of lineage organizations. Their focus was in the first instance not on preparing literati for office or in aligning themselves with local officials but in creating lateral relationships among the literati, and the most successful of them drew in literati from beyond their own localities. In many places in Southern Song and in the south during Yuan, they became a force in local society that could not be suborned by powerful families and the local government staff.[99]

The Later Imperial State and Neo-Confucianism: The Significance of the Early Ming

More than anything else, imperial support for Neo-Confucianism in the early Ming has given rise to the idea that Neo-Confucianism became the ideological justification for the imperial state. Zhu Yuanzhang, the Ming founder also known as Emperor Taizu or the Hongwu (reign period) emperor, rose from being an illiterate orphan to become the most successful of all rebel commanders. In 1368 he proclaimed the Ming dynasty and made Nanjing his capital. Taizu centralized power over the bureaucracy in his own hands and used terror to cow officialdom—in two terrible purges of military and civil officials whom he suspected, perhaps rightly, of plotting against him; over 40,000 officials and their associates were executed.[100] Yet this same ruler saw himself as being totally devoted to the well-being of the population. Zhu Yuanzhang is the best example before Mao Zedong of a ruler who terrorized the bureaucracy while exhorting the people to behave as he wished.[101] In 1398 he was succeeded by his grandson, whose court included well-known Neo-Confucians. However, in 1402 his uncle in Beijing, Zhu Di, Emperor Chengzu or the Yongle (Everlasting Joy) emperor (r. 1402–24), revolted and usurped the throne. Yet more than any emperor heretofore, Yongle identified himself with Neo-Confucianism.

Those who see the early Ming as the beginning of the co-optation of Neo-Confucianism have made several arguments. One looks at the Confucian advisors the future founder brought together in the 1350s, who were in sympathy with the Neo-Confucian positions, and reads them as arguing that only a strong central authority could set the world aright after years of chaos. The next generation of Confucian scholars realized just how mistaken their predecessors had been, but rather than blaming them, they blamed the emperor. They tried to correct the error in the next reign, only to have it stamped out by the usurper, Chengzu.[102] A second argument is that the early Ming emperors were pretending to a Confucian ideal of rulership and that the political elite, eager to keep its position, chose to act as if the actual ruler were in fact an ideal ruler.[103] Finally, it has been proposed that Neo-Confucianism provided the cultural language that allowed Ming rulers to claim to be sage-kings and to have reunited sage learning and sage politics. As a result, Neo-Confucianism was transformed into imperial ideology and could be used to induce public support for the Ming and succeeding Qing regime.[104]

I would rather turn this around and ask what influence the Neo-Confucian position had on early Ming views of rulership and the local community. In choosing models of governance, Taizu at times rejected the authority of the imperial past and gave preference to antiquity. He spoke repeatedly of correcting the structure of governmental organization. And he sought to find the right people to staff it by going outside examinations (perhaps sharing Neo-Confucian doubts about the reliability of examinations). He emphasized the importance of schools and the role of Confucians as teachers to both the populace and the ruler. He called for and rewarded remonstrance. He spoke of the fundamental importance to the affairs of state of the ruler's "setting his mind in the right" and praised the program of the ruler's self-cultivation set out by Zhen Dexiu's *Extended Meaning of the Great Learning*. He quite rightly saw himself—in contrast to his Yuan predecessors—as an example of a hardworking official who performed the duties of his role. He saw that punishments alone could not transform society and spoke of the dangers of flattery from below and arbitrariness from above.[105]

His reign also legislated the formation of local community institutions and empowered local leaders.[106] The village tithing (*li jia*) and tax captaincy system used local leaders from leading lineages rather than a clerical bureaucracy to organize and supervise tax collection and delivery. The village elder system appointed local men to adjudicate lower-level disputes and gave them the right to bypass local officials and deal directly with authorities in the capital. Schools and community rites were established at the village level to promote morality and social cohesion. The authority of lineage elders was recognized, and Neo-Confucian family values were promoted. At the same time, Taizu centralized control over spiritual life, both through the national education system and through new controls over religious activities, a move that in effect placed constraints on the Neo-Confucians' competition.[107] These measures were intended to bring stability to rural society after decades of civil war; they institutionalized the authority of local communities and gave them a certain standing in relationship to local government.

It is also true, however, that Taizu was determined to assert the emperor's supremacy over the bureaucracy. The civil service examination of 1385 asked: "When the empire has the Way, then rites and music and military campaigns will come from the Son of Heaven. When the empire lacks the Way, then rites and music and campaigns and military campaigns will come from the feudal lords." The winning essay celebrated the centralization of authority in the hands of the emperor.[108] I suspect Taizu saw himself as a sage-king who had united politics and morality. In his world there could be no grounds for denying the legitimacy of his rule. "To keep your life depends on the ruler," he announced; "even if you have [life] from your parents, you cannot survive without the ruler."[109] Although some of the stories about Taizu's despotic behavior are later fabrications,[110] there is no doubt that he was deeply suspicious of the bureaucracy and demanded its total compliance. Taizu found much to admire in the beehive and anthill, societies in which all played their roles unquestioningly.[111] He also aspired to tell the populace how to behave, although at the same time he wanted them to take responsibility for themselves.[112]

Taizu was aware that he was contesting Neo-Confucian claims to authority. He recognized that honoring Confucius and Mencius had come to mean honoring the idea that moral authority lay with scholars, and he sought to end offerings to them (but later reinstated them) and ordered 85 passages that he saw as undermining the ruler's authority removed from the *Mencius* (they were reinstated in 1414).[113] He wished to strengthen local society but was unwilling to encourage literati organization outside his institutions.

It seems to me that at least in terms of social policy there were important continuities between the founder's reign and his successor's. Fang Xiaoru was the most famous of the Neo-Confucian literati still active late in the founder's reign. Fang had turned to studying the Way of the Sages and building networks of likeminded men; eventually he joined the court of a son of Taizu in Sichuan. A year before his death, when he was "forty and free from doubts" as Confucius said,[114] Fang published a collection of writings that refuted Taizu's view of his authority but at the same time called for the invigoration of the township (*xiang*), a jurisdiction below the county-government level, in which leaders would be chosen by local consensus and institutions would be locally maintained.[115] Fang was an outspoken proponent of Neo-Confucianism, which he saw as superior to the literary culture of Northern Song intellectuals and the utilitarianism that had appealed to some of his own teachers.[116] The Song dynasty was his model, it was superior to Han and Tang, Fang opined, and just as good as Zhou itself, for during its three hundred years of history moral values truly mattered. Song learning came closest to that of antiquity.[117] For 1,500 years scholars had been unsure about the Way, but Neo-Confucianism had answered their questions.[118] Fang's strategy was to treat the Song dynasty as a historical model for Ming to imitate; it mediated between Ming times and an ideal antiquity, and its philosophers mediated between man and ultimate truth.[119] The prize essays from the metropolitan examination of 1400 addressed the question of whether the emperor is (or was) a sage and how much moral authority an emperor should have. The consensus view stopped short of sagehood but certainly stressed the enormous importance of the ruler, and unity (unity also as the unity of the moral mind possessed by all humanity) emerged as the ultimate value.[120]

Fang refused to accept the Yongle emperor's usurpation; he was executed, together with his lineage.[121] But rather than denying Neo-Confucianism, the new regime launched a series of projects that supported scholars and Neo-Confucianism, in particular through the collection and publication, in 1415, of Neo-Confucian interpretations of the Four Books and Five Classics and Neo-Confucian writings on moral philosophy, the *Great Compendia of [Neo-Confucian Commentaries on] the Five Classics, Four Books, and Nature and Principle*.[122] Zhu Di himself set out to claim the mantle of a sage-king, this time with a treatise from his own hand, it is said, entitled *The Mind Method of Sage Learning*, with its core concepts drawn directly from Zhu Xi's introduction to his commentary on the *Doctrine of the Mean*. Like Emperor Taizu, Zhu Di claimed both the early imperial ideal of rulership—specifically Emperor Taizong of Tang—and the Neo-Confucian model, but to a far greater degree than his father the founder he also granted that authority over learning belonged to the Song masters.[123]

Perhaps this was the point at which Neo-Confucians decided to secure their own position by going along with Ming imperial claims to Neo-Confucian sagehood.[124] But once again the story is more complex than it appears, for just as this was happening some Neo-Confucians set themselves apart, making clear that they would not participate and turning once again to teaching and building up networks among the literati. The most famous example is a man from Jiangxi, home to many leading officials in the early fifteenth century. In philosophical studies, Wu Yubi represents a turn from the Neo-Confucian intellectualism of Zhu Xi to internal reflection and thus points toward the great revival of literati Neo-Confucianism with Wang Yangming at the beginning of the sixteenth century.[125] We can also see Wu as reviving the possibility of taking the Neo-Confucian position as the basis for one's personal identity. In turning away from government service, literary endeavors, and even the production of Neo-Confucian scholarly texts, Wu provided his times with an example of principled independence. In doing this, he greatly alarmed his father, who understood full well that under the current regime his son's refusal to participate in politics could be seen as disloyalty. His father, Wu Pu (1363–1426), placed first in the metropolitan examination of 1400 and had been appointed to the Hanlin Academy by the Jianwen emperor, but he had transferred his loyalty to the Yongle emperor and was director of studies at the Nanjing National University from 1408 until his death.

Wu Yubi kept a diary of his quest for self-transformation. It begins in 1425, right after the Yongle reign, continues through the dynastic crisis that resulted from the Mongols' capture of the emperor in 1449, and ends in 1468 on the eve of his death. The ten-odd entries a year connect his withdrawal to his Neo-Confucianism. He began with two dreams. In the first he saw the two sages, Confucius and King Wen, and asked them about "innate moral knowledge and feeling secure in practice." These two themes—being able to know what is right and being able to act accordingly without generating obstacles for oneself—would occupy Wu in years to come. He also saw a book that appeared to be a genealogy of King Wen; it was still possible for a Ming literatus to imagine joining the lineage of sages and worthies.[126] In his next dream, he saw Zhu Xi and was awed by Zhu's combination of decorum and happiness. His next entry records a nighttime reverie on the widespread suspicion, much discussed at the time, that the second Song emperor, Taizong, had murdered his brother the first emperor on his deathbed in order to claim that he had been chosen as successor.[127] This prompted Wu to reflect that a true king, a sage-king, would not kill a single innocent to gain the empire and on the fact that teaching the ruler about moral rulership requires that the teacher's heart at root be pure "moral conscience."[128] I read these three opening entries as a restatement of the Neo-Confucian position: despite the claims rulers make or others make for them, latter-day rulers are not sages; the authority of the sage-kings was transferred to Confucius as a scholar; Zhu Xi represents this tradition in modern times; and literati can still make a personal connection to the sages and Zhu and continue this tradition in the present. For Wu, Neo-Confucianism was a living tradition; it could not be controlled by the emperor and it was still possible for literati to claim the authority of the sages. Some confirmation is found in an entry from two years later, which argues that the granting to Shun of heaven's mandate and the assignment to Confucius of the eternal role of being the teacher to all rulers were in fact the same thing, even if Confucius did not receive the mandate to rule. Both mandates, to rule and to teach rulers, were responses to the individual's possession of virtue; Wu must therefore seek to fortify his virtue.[129]

Although he was living in a world in which intellectual culture and political power in general had proclaimed their adherence to Neo-Confucianism, Wu Yubi was trying to recover the original transformative power of Neo-Confucianism. He took self-cultivation seriously, he withdrew from the examinations and contemporary political society, and he refused to join in pandering to the imperial house. In all these ways he put himself at odds with the world. At the same time he made clear his wish to join the ranks of King Wen, Confucius, and Zhu Xi.

Wu Yubi was not an intellectual entrepreneur in the manner of Zhu Xi, yet he clearly located himself within literati society as a model for a morally superior literati life. He did, after all, take on the role of teacher, although his teaching was clearly different from those who prepared students for the now Neo-Confucian examinations, and he had students who continued his life of learning and others who went on to official careers. He shared the widespread fifteenth-century interest in genealogies but stressed in poems for friends and inscriptions for the studies, studios, and pavilions that marked their residences and estates that life outside the court was a way of living a life of learning. Finally he made it clear that he was concerned with the state of the nation, submitting a ten-point memorial in 1457, when the emperor sent a special messenger appointing him tutor to the heir apparent (he was recommended for appointment five times between 1446 and 1457 but always declined to serve).

Neo-Confucianism had become an ever-more mainstream phenomenon, supported by the wealth and power of a state that aimed to co-opt it. But exactly at the height of official patronage, we find a well-placed young literatus asserting that in his times it was necessary to make a distinction between politics and morality. When Wu Yubi decided to learn to become a sage, that decision could not be separated from his conclusion that even Song emperors could not have been sages, much less Ming ones.

We can find examples of later rulers who sought to counter this pressure and reassert the claim to be uniting politics and morality, the most famous being the Jiajing emperor (r. 1522–66).[130] But we can also find numerous examples during the course of the Ming dynasty of Neo-Confucians who wrote works defining their view of rulership,[131] took principled stands against the abuse of imperial authority at the expense of their own lives, who created networks among likeminded men, and who turned their attention to using Neo-Confucianism to revive local leadership in their home areas.[132] The practice of "discoursing on learning" that swept the nation in the wake of Wang Yangming systematically mobilized and organized the literati community.[133] And once again, and again unsuccessfully, the court tried to suppress the Neo-Confucian movement, now revitalized by Wang's ideas. In the early seventeenth century, the organization of the literati independently of the political system took the form of new national organizations, with membership lists, meetings, and circulars, which sought both to inspire the literati and to exercise a decisive influence over government.[134]

The three great Qing emperors of the seventeenth and eighteenth centuries claimed to have ended the distinction between politics and morality and the tension between literati and rulers by uniting the "succession of the Way" and political power in their own persons. In fact, they became the paragons of devoted bureaucratic management that the Neo-Confucians had called for, and they were the great defenders of Zhu Xi's Neo-Confucianism against the disturbing developments of late Ming Wang Yangmingism. They defined how they wanted to appear to their officials and the literati in Neo-Confucian terms, but their goal, it has been argued, was to block Neo-Confucian opposition to the imperial will. "The Ch'ing rulers, then, became the unique representatives of both traditions. No independent ground was left for Confucians to oppose political power. The critical function of the Way, which was once exercised by the Sung and Ming Confucians, was thus eliminated."[135] But they also lived in an era when Neo-Confucianism was no longer the vital center of literati thought.

Neo-Confucianism created a new kind of tension between rulers and literati intellectuals, one that strengthened the position of the literati far more than it did that of the emperor. It allowed the literati to see themselves simultaneously as participants in the imperial system and as scholars who stood apart from it, for it provided them with grounds for organizing themselves and taking responsibility for the world around them, whether or not the state wished them to. Their willingness to take this position had much to do with their conviction that morality in the world was not something created by political power but the product of cultivating universal qualities endowed in all human beings alike. We now turn to the grounds for this conviction.

5

Learning

We can restate the Neo-Confucian view of politics as a series of assertions: politics had become distinct from morality, those responsible for
politics needed to accept the correct view of morality, authority over
morality belonged to those who had cultivated it rather than those who
held political authority, and morality could be practiced by anyone independently of government instruction. The term the Neo-Confucians
used in making these assertions was "learning" (*xue*). The distinction
was between learning and politics: politics should be guided by learning,
but authority over learning belonged to those who knew how to do it
correctly, and one did not need a political position in order to engage in
learning and make a difference in society. If we want to understand
what a term like "morality" could have meant for the Neo-Confucians,
we need to ask what they meant by "learning."

Neo-Confucian Learning
as Theory and Practice

In asking what Neo-Confucians meant by learning, it will be useful to
begin by distinguishing what we, as observers on the past, think Neo-
Confucians were actually doing and what the Neo-Confucians claimed
to be doing. Historians are inclined to assume that culture forms the
person, that people internalize what they are taught, that they adopt the

values of the group they wish to belong to, and that the choices that are available to them are defined for them by the society in which they live. To state this in an extreme form: people are blank slates on which society writes its culture, and because people internalize what they are taught, they come to believe the way they behave is somehow natural to themselves.

If we take this view, we would, I suspect, be inclined to view Neo-Confucian philosophy as merely a justification for traditional models of Confucian ethical conduct represented by such doctrines as the Three Bonds (the duties of minister to ruler, son to father, and wife to husband), the Five Relations (ruler-minister, parent-child, husband-wife, older-younger, and friend-friend), and the Five Constant Virtues (humaneness, righteousness, ritual propriety, wisdom, and trustworthiness).[1] In other words, their philosophizing was not meant to show people how to think for themselves but to persuade them to imitate traditional models, on the philosophical grounds that the models were in fact natural to all humans.

One can find evidence to support the view that for Neo-Confucians learning was in fact a process of internalization. Consider Zhu Xi's explanation of the first line of the *Analects* of Confucius, "To learn and rehearse it constantly, is this indeed not a pleasure":

"To learn" (*xue*) means "to emulate" (*xiao*). Human nature is in all cases good, but in becoming aware of this goodness, there are those who lead and those who follow. Those who follow in becoming aware of it must emulate those who lead in becoming aware of it. Only then can they understand the good and return to their original state. . . . Master Cheng said ". . . The student takes it and puts it into practice. Since he rehearses it constantly, what he learns becomes part of him."[2]

This suggests that there is no real need for self-reflection or awareness of one's own moral conscience, and even that the goodness of human nature is irrelevant for the student who emulates the teacher's model. The student who thinks he is becoming aware of his innate goodness is in fact persuading himself to believe in something he was not originally aware of. Moreover, Zhu Xi produced a number of works that contained models students could rehearse, such as his *Elementary Learning*, to train young people in proper behavior, and the *Family Rituals*, a handbook for the performance of rites of passage in family life.[3]

Following the detailed scripts for the ceremonial performances found in the *Family Rituals* is an example of learning as imitation, as the internalization of norms and behaviors dictated by another. There seem to be examples of Neo-Confucians who extended this approach into the realm of social relationships, so that learning might be seen as a process of turning social interactions into ceremonies. At first glance, this appears to be what Rao Lu, a mid-thirteenth-century teacher of local renown, was doing when he explained "investigating things" (*ge wu*), understood as "fully apprehending the coherence of things" (*qiong li*), as the fundamental method of learning.

To investigate things is to fully apprehend moral principles (*daoli*) at exactly the most hidden place; from outside to inside, from crude to refined. Within the inside there is an inside, and there is something even more refined in the refined; layer by layer. For example, a son must be filial, a minister loyal. What is obvious and easy to see is the outside. But the individual terms "filial" and "loyal" cannot exhaust how to be filial and how to be loyal. In the case of filial piety: when at home, to bring reverence to bear; in caring for them [parents], to bring joy to bear; when [they are] sick, to bring concern to bear; in mourning, to bring grief to bear; in offering sacrifices, to bring strictness to bear—all these are subjects inside filial piety. This is what I mean by the inside of it. But as for what is called "at home, to bring reverence to bear"—how should you bring reverence to bear? For example, "when entering and departing and attending on them, to be careful, when ascending and descending and coming and going, to be polite"; to dare not belch or cough; to dare not slouch or lean on something; when cold, to dare not unfurl the robe sleeves; when itching, to dare not scratch—all these are items within the subject of bringing reverence to bear. Thus, to bring reverence to bear when at home is the outside, and the fine details of the items in this subject are the inside, but these are things that are manifested on the outside when maintaining reverence.

As for true reverence, such as [the attentiveness required when] "holding a jade or carrying something full to the brim," [so attentive] that one sees what is formless and hears what is soundless, that is the marrow in the bone of these items. You have to investigate and investigate further, until you get to the point that there is nothing more to investigate, that then is the ultimate point. The same holds for the crude and refined . . . if you see the outside but not the inside, see the crude but do not apprehend the refined, it surely is incomplete, but if you only fully apprehend the inside and ignore the outside, see the refined but ignore the crude, it is also incomplete. It is only "investigating things" when one reaches both outside and inside, refined and crude.[4]

Rao considered a traditional ethical norm, filial piety, and created a detailed, prescriptive catalog of correct behaviors drawn from social expectations and the Classics. But on closer inspection, he was actually arguing that grasping the coherence or principle of filial piety, and presumably any other norm of behavior, means discovering a level of attentive reverence in oneself. The set of behaviors can be described, and description is important, but it is not enough That is why the mental-physical process of investigating things, of learning, is necessary.

Leading Neo-Confucians were adamant in insisting that morality is *not* something fused onto the person from outside and that learning is *not* realized by inculcating models in students. Ethical behavior is not, Cheng Yi contended, something to be attained by training oneself to accord with a model—even if all agree that the model is correct, one still has to discover something in oneself.[5] Zhu Xi—the greatest producer of texts in the history of Neo-Confucianism—took a similar view: relying on the teachings of others creates a greater distance between the student and moral development; the real point of departure lies in the self.[6]

Neo-Confucians certainly did not suppose that people were blank slates, but their position was complicated by the fact that they distinguished between what makes a person what he is and learning as the process by which he becomes aware of what he can become. They supposed that, without intervention, human behavior is largely determined by the individual's unique physical makeup. However, at the same time, they asserted that (1) there are integrated, harmonious, and coherent processes that create and sustain all life; (2) precisely because humans as biological beings are products of these processes, they contain within themselves the principles necessary for an integrated, harmonious, and coherent order; and (3) by becoming conscious of the coherence they possess innately and acting accordingly, they can bring about an integrated, harmonious, and coherent society. In this view, "learning" is the process of realizing that which we possess innately and, thus, of bringing "morality" into being. Zhu Xi explained:

The fact that people have this life means that heaven has given them humaneness, righteousness, ritual propriety, and wisdom as their nature; it has ordered the relations of ruler and minister, father and son; and it has instituted the norms for how things and affairs ought to be. But because his [an individual's] physical constitution has imbalances and his desires for things create blind spots, he may not see his nature clearly, he may upset his relations and thwart his norms yet not know to turn back. It will be learning that sets him on the right course, and then he will be able to set his mind in the right and cultivate his person and establish a basis for instituting harmony in the family and governing the country. This is why people must learn, but how one learns does not in the first place mean memorization and composition, and it is not something that differs according to the degree of one's intelligence or the level of one's social status.[7]

In this instance, learning externalizes what is internal to the human being. Neo-Confucians held that they were identifying things that were real in themselves, which would continue to be so irrespective of what people thought, rather than creating paradigms for understanding reality.

Let us grant that Neo-Confucians assumed there is something real in people that can provide moral guidance and that they thought they had rediscovered the means of giving it expression. Even if others perceive this as a process of internalization, they argued that what is being realized is something that humans possess in reality, although they have been unaware of it for 1,400 years. Learning enables us eventually to experience the perfect fit between the reality of who we are and what we become conscious of. The forms of ethical behavior we find in texts can in fact have an internal basis—the fact that the external models are seen first in texts or in custom does not mean that they are untrue to our real selves. (The Neo-Confucians are not alone in making this argument. Contemporary sociobiological approaches to human ethics also posit something real in humans that has ethical significance.)[8]

Let us suppose that the Neo-Confucians, and the sociobiologists, are right. Even so, as the Neo-Confucians pointed out, humans had not understood this for over a millennium, and a moral society cannot exist unless humans share a correct understanding of both the grounds of morality and the process of its realization. Their argument was not that we naturally behave morally, far from it. Rather, if we learn correctly, we are able to become conscious of the moral guides innate to us as human beings. Realizing morality in the world thus depends on becoming conscious of something in our own persons.

This is where "internalization" does figure, for what simply must be internalized, or believed, is a *theory* about how to understand, cultivate, and realize in practice something that we humans can experience personally because we possess it innately. The modern age depends solely on a proper theoretical understanding and self-consciousness, in contrast to antiquity. Cheng Yi explained the difference:

It was easy for those who learned in antiquity, but it is hard for those who learn today. From the time the ancients entered the elementary school at eight and the greater school at fifteen, there were decorations to nurture their eyes, sounds to nurture their ears, majestic ceremonies to nurture their four limbs, and song and dance to nurture circulation, and moral principle (*yili*) to nurture their minds. Today all [the physical aids to learning] are lost, there is only moral principle to nurture their minds. Must we not make an effort?[9]

Learning in antiquity was a matter of getting people in tune, so to speak, and this could be accomplished by training the body and the senses as well as by articulating norms. By way of analogy, we might say that ancients taught people by immersing them in the language of culture, whereas modern learning proceeds not from immersion—the ancient language is no longer spoken, no longer complete—but from gaining a mental understanding of the universal rules of that language. Modern learning is a matter of thought in the first place rather than training.

This is, I think, also a statement of an extreme position. If the universal rules of language are innate, then it ought to be possible to free language of the burden of centuries of confusing historical usage and speak in a new, rational, and pure language that realizes those universal rules. Why should we be beholden to historical knowledge at all? As opposed as they may have been to being seen as advocating internalizing prescriptions and past models, the Neo-Confucians did not deny the value of historical models and classical precepts—witness Rao Lu's discussion of "investigating things" in the practice of filial piety. Our challenge is to see how they could argue both that learning was about realizing things that were innate or finding something in the self and, at the same time, that it valued historical models and classical precepts.

I think the way out of this conundrum is to recognize that Neo-Confucian learning came with a theory of learning, and this theory gave those who internalized it a ready means of making sense out of the everyday human experience of acquiring knowledge, thinking, feeling, and making choices. It not only told them how to divide up and organize into a coherent whole the various aspects of human experience, but also justified respect for historical models. It allowed them to argue, as we shall see, that their ideas were true to the Classics (and thus deny that they were making it up themselves) and that learning would transform how people as social and political actors behaved.

The Neo-Confucian enterprise of learning could never be divorced from a discussion of how one should learn, or what I would call a discussion of theory. During the Song, Yuan, and Ming periods, Neo-Confucians engaged in what they called *jiang xue*, "discoursing on learning" or "discussing how to learn." Learning would work only if literati learned how to conceive of the natural processes of creation, the history of civilization, and the human condition; memorizing texts and mastering correct models was secondary.

Neo-Confucian theory explained how concepts were interrelated, how the processes they defined worked, and how they could be tested and verified in practice. In the Neo-Confucian case, we generally do not have to infer a theory that "lies behind" the scattered utterances of a thinker, as we must with the Confucius of the *Analects*. This might not appear to be true of the Cheng brothers, who wrote almost no philosophical treatises; analysis of their major concepts has depended largely on records of their lectures left by their disciples.[10] But the Cheng brothers talked with their students about their concepts and how they fit together.

Evidence of the importance of theory abound. One was the appearance of glossaries of key terms, such as Cheng Duanmeng's *Glosses of Terms for Nature and Principle*, which briefly glosses thirty terms,[11] and Chen Chun's more lengthy *Meanings of Terms*.[12] Neo-Confucians gave and published lectures that were systematic accounts of their learning.[13] They used records of speech to compile systematic introductions to the theory of learning and its practice in literati life, such as *Reflections on Things at Hand*.[14] And, beginning with Zhou Dunyi's *Explanation of the Diagram of the Supreme Ultimate*, they used diagrams to show how different concepts were related. In the twelfth century, Li Yuangang explained various Neo-Confucian topics with his *Diagrams of the Sage Enterprise*.[15] In the thirteenth century, the Neo-Confucian teacher Wang Bo put together a series of seventy charts, arguing that diagrams represented the original, preliterary mode of teaching. One of his successors, Xu Qian, took recourse to diagrams to explain to students Zhu Xi's commentaries on the Four Books.[16] Zhu Xi had used sometimes elaborate diagrams, and interpreters of Zhu Xi found that they could set out his philosophy through a series of diagrams.[17] What is important about diagrams is that they focus attention on the *relations* between and among concepts and thus give the student a means of seeing in one glance that many different concepts form a *system* of relationships.

Neo-Confucians used their theory of learning to distinguish themselves from their literati contemporaries and earlier Confucians. We shall see that it also gave them a means of understanding the vocabulary of "traditional ethics" in new ways. But making the issue a theory of learning also led to abstraction: as they set out arguments about the way the cosmos worked, the origin of civilization in antiquity, and the human condition in the present, Neo-Confucians had to talk about matters that were, in their terms, "above form," that were not concrete and visible.

I begin with a set of theories that emerged during the Song period, some of the principal ambiguities and tensions that these theories tried to resolve, and the new perspective on ethics they supported. I turn next to the new curriculum based on these theories, parts of which were officially adopted in Yuan and early Ming, thus becoming required knowledge for all literati. Finally, I take up the revival of theoretical discourse in the Ming period, at a moment when to many Neo-Confucians practice had become a matter of mastering texts and writing about them.

"Heaven-and-Earth," Civilization, and the Human Condition

"HEAVEN-AND-EARTH" AS *QI* AND *LI*

The founding thinkers of Neo-Confucianism argued that true values have their basis in nature itself, the processes by which "heaven-and-earth" give rise to life. At the time, this set them apart from the Ancient Style writers, who based their claims about what the present should value on interpretations of antiquity, the sage-kings, and the Classics, but who no longer believed that there was a necessary connection between heaven-and-earth and the sage-kings' creation of civilization in antiquity. At one level, this meant taking seriously the traditional idea that the cosmos was an organic unity, a unity that included humanity, and finding morally significant regularity and coherence in the spontaneous processes of creation.

The question was how to connect an organic worldview to a way of learning, to make it something more than a general notion that people should value the unity of all things. The first important attempt began with the long-established idea that everything was composed of *qi*. *Qi* was taken to be a combination of matter (condensed solid as in stone, liquid as in water, rarified as in air) and the energy inherent in matter, thus the common translation of *qi* as "material force." As noted in Chapter 4, the movement and quality of *qi* was further understood in terms of two kinds of *qi*, *yin* and *yang*, which were seen as operating in tandem. An example is the cycle of the year, from rising of warm weather (*yang qi*) in spring through its peak in summer to the rising of cold (*yin qi*) in the fall and its peak in winter; or the cycle of day (*yang*) and night (*yin*). The *yin* and *yang* cycle was often combined with the five phases, or agents, of change (water, metal, wood, fire, earth). The five phases could be used to describe the *yin-yang* cycle but also (in the sense of five elements) to classify all things (colors, tastes, directions, grains) into five qualities of *qi*. The old idea of cosmic resonance was based on the assumption that things in a similar *qi* state resonated with one another, as when a string plucked on one lute causes the string tuned to the same note on other lutes to resonate. The "Monthly Ordinances" chapter of the *Book of Rites*, for example, tells the ruler to change his clothes, food, location, and work to stay in harmony with the larger cycle of the year, warning that a failure to do so would upset the course of nature itself— wearing winter colors in the spring, for example, would bring on a late frost. The idea was not to stop change but to ensure that political power accorded with the cycle of change, for if it deviated, nature would go off course, natural disasters would occur, and the dynasty would be destabilized. In cosmic resonance theory, the natural and human realms are interactive.

However, the early Neo-Confucian philosophers did not use the idea of *qi* categories to define appropriate behavior in the style of the "Monthly Ordinances." Zhang Zai, who developed a theory of learning based on a concept of how *qi* operated, asked instead how the individual literatus could, like the sages of antiquity, attune his mind to the unfolding patterns of *yin-yang qi* transformation so that his responses to events would help realize in society the organic harmony inherent in the operation of the heaven-and-earth (the realm of nature). Zhang posited that *qi* exists in two states, an invisible, undifferentiated Great Void and the *qi* that has condensed out of the Great Void to form particular things. In his scheme, when things perish, their *qi* disperses and returns to the Great Void. He further supposed that all people possess this undifferentiated *qi*, in which the patterns and forces leading to the development of an integrated and coherent organism are inherent. Put more simply, the individual is a microcosm of the universe: just as heaven-and-earth has at its core that which gives life, so does the human being. This, he concluded, is what "human nature" has to be, the engine of life and creation itself. However, although all humans possess the exact same engine of life, the physical constitution varies from person to person. By distorting and constraining the expression of the nature, the physical constitution, Zhang argued, produces humans that act out of bias and partiality, and, by stirring their selfish desires, keeps people from realizing their potential to create a harmonious society. People who lead a merely physical existence are at the mercy of things around them. Things stimulate and upset such people, who end up consumed by selfish desire. Their minds are not attuned to their true natures. It follows that "learning" is a process of training the body, so as to gain control over the physical constitution—for example, by the diligent performance of ritual—and by then attuning the mind to the "Great Void" within. The result is a person who, although he lives in a world of selfish, biased people, is himself guided by a mind that instinctively sees the potential for harmonious patterns in daily life. Such a person responds to things so that those patterns are realized and people are brought back on track. This is what it means to be a sage, Zhang concluded, and this is what it means to learn.[18]

Some later thinkers returned to Zhang Zai's ideas about *qi*, but in the late Northern Sung the Cheng brothers gained a wider following. They did not deny that creation involved the constant transformation of *qi*, but they focused on what guided the process. Zhang had used the word *li* to describe those guides, but he had not made it the focus of learning. The Cheng brothers did and, in doing so, gave it new significance. The term *li* had a long history: it appeared in early philosophical texts, in legal writing, in literary criticism, and in some Buddhist schools. In the Neo-Confucian case it has most often been translated as "principle," although for reasons explained below, I have followed Willard

Peterson in adopting the translation "coherence" in many instances. It was used as a descriptive term to refer to how something worked, the logic, reasoning, or coherence of a statement, and the pattern or system of relationships that held the parts together. It was also used as a normative term, meaning the standard according to which something ought to function and which ensured that all the parts would work together.[19] Note that *li* was being used as a term for describing how things worked and as a normative term for identifying how things should work. We today see a clear distinction between the descriptive and the normative, thinking it impossible to generate a statement about what a thing ought to be from a description how that thing is in fact. The next chapter explains how it was possible for Neo-Confucians to combine the two; for the moment it will suffice to say that to speak of the *li* of a thing was also to speak of the way in which it could work successfully, where success meant operating in such a manner that it could function harmoniously as part of a larger, self-sustaining, organic whole.

Li was a term known to every literatus—it was used in the common binome *li-hui* 理會, usually to be translated as "to understand" how something is or ought to be. More significantly, it was used in judging the quality of civil service examination papers. Examiners graded papers on the basis of *wen li* 文理; that is, the literary form (the *wen*) and the understanding of the subject (the *li*). It was possible to have good literary form but get the *li* wrong. Here *li* might be translated as "correct reasoning."[20] In all these cases, *li* is something that the mind grasps; it is not material.

The Cheng brothers and Zhu Xi made three crucial claims (each discussed in greater detail below) that made *li* fundamental to learning.

1. Every single thing (such as a tree) or affair (such as being a child to one's parents) has its *li*, by which they meant that there is a norm or standard for every single thing.

2. It is possible for the mind to see the *li* of something absolutely, with total certainty.

3. All *li* are one *li*.

Thus, in contrast to Zhang Zai, who described the workings of the universe primarily in terms of *qi*, the Chengs and Zhu Xi supposed that what was constant and unalterable were the *li* according to which the process of creation unfolded in the medium of *qi*, which were the same *li* that every thing and every affair that was part of the universe possessed. The Way, the Dao, was simply a term for *li*. In his glossary of Neo-Confucian terms, Chen Chun explained:

[On the Way] The Way is the path . . . the common path for people to walk on. The general meaning of the Way is the *li* people should follow in their daily affairs and human relations. . . . *Li* has no form or shape. Because it is naturally so, it is called Heaven. . . . The term Heaven means *li*. . . . As the *qi* of the single origin spreads out, it brings into being humans, and it brings into being things. There are thus lines and veins; these are the paths that humans and things travel along.

[On *li*] Generally speaking, the Way and *li* are the same thing. . . . Compared with *li*, the Way is broader, but *li* is more substantial. *Li* has the idea of being definite and unchanging. Hence, the Way is that which can be followed forever, and *li* is that which is forever unchanging. How can *li*, which is without physical form or shape, be seen? It is simply the norm for what a thing should be. . . . What a thing should be is simply its being precisely the way it ought to be, nothing more, nothing less.[21]

What is li? To say that every thing and every affair has its norm gets at the main concern of Neo-Confucians: the possibility of knowing how humans should act and how things and affairs should function. But Neo-Confucians also shared the assumption of the times: that it was possible to figure out systems and structural relationships and see the parts in terms of the whole. With this in mind, I think we can understand the Neo-Confucian use of the term *li* in the following manner. All things are made up of *qi*, but their *li* determine how they operate and how they should function. Chen Chun explained: "In the operation of the two *qi* [of *yin* and *yang*], the process of production and reproduction has gone on without cease from time immemorial. It is impossible for there to be nothing but *qi*. There must be something to direct it, and that is *li*. *Li* is in *qi* and acts as its pivot."[22]

First, things have their distinctive structure: the structure of a tree is the interconnectedness of leaf, branch, trunk, and root, in which one part depends on another as branch to root; the structure of the family ties together parent and child in ways that create distinct social roles and practices. Second, things have their distinctive direction and process of development: the tree goes through daily and annual cycles and grows through a certain life span; the interaction between the parent and child changes over time as well. Third, things have their distinctive functions in relation to other things as part of a larger whole: a certain kind of tree plays a certain kind of role in an ecosystem, the wood from a particular tree can be used to make particular kinds of implements; the adult child has a distinctive function to play in relation to a parent, the child-parent relationship has a function in the larger corporation of the family, and the family has a function in the larger web of society. *Li* is of the essence for Neo-Confucians because it provides a way of saying how things should be, but it is also problematic because it involves making choices about how we want to see things: is a tree to be seen as part of an ecosystem or as a source of charcoal for smelting iron? Is the egg destined to be a chicken or to become an omelet? Is the function of human to become a sage or to be a source of labor, a servant to be bought and sold?

Knowledge of *li* is meta-knowledge, that is, it is knowledge about how something is put together, how it develops over time, and what role it should play. Although things are *qi*, in that they have substance, and affairs are *qi*, in that they involve the movement of *qi* in action, it is *li* that orders them. All things and affairs possess *li*; so we can say that all things are alike in possessing *li*, and that the *li* of every thing is alike in that it plays the same role in every thing.

It followed, at least for Cheng and Zhu, that the *li* in a thing was the same as what the ancients had referred to as the "nature" (*xing*) of a thing, that is, the innate and unchanging norms according to which that thing operates. Again Chen Chun:

[On Nature] Nature is *li*. Why is it called nature and not *li*? The reason is that *li* is a general term referring to the *li* common to all things in the world, and nature is *li* in oneself. It is called nature because *li* is received from Heaven and is possessed by the self. The character *xing* 性 consists of two parts, *sheng* 生 [to come or bring into being, to live] and *xin* 忄 [mind]. It is called nature because from birth humans possess *li* complete in their minds.

An illustration of this would be that the totality of the *li* of the plum tree is present right there in the pit and continues to run through the plum tree as it grows. Similarly, the totality of the *li* of the person is present in the fetus. The *li* of the child-parent relationship is also part of the *li* endowed in all humans.

We today might distinguish the natural (the tree) from the cultural (the parent-child relationship): a tree must necessarily develop in a certain way, according to its *li*, otherwise it cannot exist; whereas we would argue that humans create social norms and then choose whether to adhere to them—parents can neglect their children, children can disrespect their parents. The Neo-Confucians deny that such a distinction exists; the *li* of the parent-child relationship is just as real as the *li* of a tree and just as necessary to ongoing life—if infants are neglected, they will die, and the *li* of the parent-child relationship will not have been realized. It is expressed in particular cultural forms for historical reasons, as discussed in the next section, on antiquity. But it is possible for people not to accord with the *li* with which they are endowed—why that is so and what can be done about it are discussed in the succeeding section, on the human condition.

All the principles guiding life and growth in the universe as a whole are right there from the start, just as they are in the plum pit, as the process of creation has unfolded down to the present, and they are in every individual thing that has come into being in the history of the universe. Analytically speaking, *li* is distinct from and prior to *qi*, for the *li* for everything is inherent in the universe even before the things themselves come into being. However, *li* cannot exist apart from *qi*: the *li* of the plum tree is embedded in the pit, and *li* exist in human activities as they take place.

Neo-Confucians further asserted the *unity* of *li* and the *identity* of *li*. The unity of *li* is easier to comprehend. The universe is a single, all-encompassing system, operating according to a single "Way." There is no alternative universe, there is no alternative "way," and no thing and no event can have some alternative *li* that is just as good for us to choose or reject. Thus the *li* of every single thing is part of the *li* of the universe as an integrated system in which all principles are tied together. *Li* is the Neo-Confucians' basis for what scientists would call a "unified field theory" or a "theory of everything."

The identity of *li* means that all *li* are the same *li*. There are two ways of understanding how this is possible. The first is a theoretical supposition that follows from the unity of *li*. Suppose there was a seed that contained all the *li* for the entire unfolding of the universe and everything in it and that every single created thing had that seed. It follows that each person (and each tree) has the *li* for being itself and at the same time the *li* for all other things.

Zhu Xi took from Zhou Dunyi the term "Supreme Ultimate" (Taiji) to refer to the unity of *li* and identity of *li*. Each thing receives the totality of principles, and the differences between things, and among people, are a consequence of what part of that totality they have ready access to. Zhu Xi's analogy was between standing out in the open and seeing all the light and being in a house and seeing only part of the light through a window. Thus humans can see more than horses. So the difference is how much of the totality a thing can gain access to, and this is decided by the *qi* that makes it up.[23] Chen Chun explained:

[On the Supreme Ultimate] The Supreme Ultimate is simply *li*. *Li* is originally circular [i.e., perfect]; therefore the *li* of the Supreme Ultimate is fundamentally undifferentiated. *Li* has no physical shape and no boundary or division. Therefore all things that exist fully obtain the Supreme Ultimate, and the Supreme Ultimate in itself in each and every thing is an undifferentiated whole. Only the *qi* of the human being is correct and penetrating, the human is the most intelligent of all things, for he is able to fully comprehend the undifferentiated in itself. The *qi* of other things is partial and obstructed; they are not as intelligent as the human. So although they have the undifferentiated in itself, they are not able to comprehend it.[24]

The Chengs and Zhu Xi also used the term "heavenly *li*" (*tian li*), translated in the previous chapter as "moral conscience" and "universal coherence" (also translatable as "innate coherence" or "total coherence"), to refer to the endowment of the totality of *li* in the person to which he could turn for moral guidance.

Chen Chun pointed to a second way of understanding the identity of *li*: through cognition. What distinguishes the human being from all other things in the universe is that humans can see more, both because less of the light is blocked to begin with—their *qi* is more transparent—and through learning they widen the window, so to speak, and thus see more than before. The "mind" or "mind-and-heart" is the set of faculties that enables them to see *li*—to see structure, process, and functional relationships. When Neo-Confucians suppose that *li* gives structure, process, and function to all things, they are identifying something that also makes each and every thing coherent and comprehensible. Let us take *li* to stand for the "coherence" every thing inherently possesses; we can then see that the coherence we apprehend in things is the same coherence that every other thing has, and in fact is the character of our own mental process. To put this another way: just as any given thing has its own coherence, the coherence of one thing is the same coherence as that of another; coherence itself does not vary even when each thing has its own coherence. To see the *li* of something is to see its coherence, and that coherence is both there in the thing and in our mind.[25]

Neo-Confucians came to disagree over the implications of this. Those who saw the mind as an aspect of the physical constitution stressed it variability: some people were dim and would see little light unless they worked hard, and some were born bright. For such people, among them Cheng Yi and Zhu Xi, human nature, innate coherence, was the *li* of the mind. The task for the mind was to become aware of its own *li*, of its own nature. For others, among them Lu Jiuyuan and Wang Yangming, the mind was *li* itself, and their focus was on activating it so that it would always respond to things from its own coherence. For both sides, it seems to me, believing that all things possessed coherence and belonged to a larger coherent whole was part of seeing coherence in things and self.

ANTIQUITY AND SAGES

The Neo-Confucian understanding of heaven-and-earth and morality as *li*/coherence is universalistic and ahistorical. It is not true because an authoritative figure proclaimed it to be so or because the Classics spelled it out. As Zhu Xi once explained to the emperor: "You should know that what I say is not a theory (*shuo*) I have made up but the theory of the ancient sages and worthies. And it is not a theory the sages made up but the self-so *li* of heaven's norms and earth's standards. These are some things that even the sages . . . and worthies . . . [of antiquity] could not transgress."[26] Nevertheless, the Neo-Confucians did have to show how their ideas could account for the creation of civilization in antiquity, the role of the "former kings" or "sages" in it, and its later demise. Moreover, they had to explain both the creation of cultural forms and the reason they had authority. In the beginning, they also wanted to answer those who thought that the origins of civilization pointed to very different ways of understanding the grounds for values.

Their explanation is as follows. Civilization began when some men responded coherently to the situations humans lived in at the time and created things that made it possible for humans (who originally competed with the birds and beasts for survival) to live in productive harmony. Whether they were aware of it or not does not matter; they had spontaneous insight into *li* and thus could create things such as agricultural implements and institute affairs such as government and writing that realized the *li* of an integrated social order and made continued life possible. This is what it means to be a sage—to have an innate endowment of *qi* so fully pure and transparent that one's mind encounters no obstruction in illuminating the coherence of things. This is why the ancients thought of sages as men who were "born knowing it." What they created was in no sense "man-made" since it actually gave form to *li*. This was a cumulative process; as the sages added more, they brought into being a coherent, integrated social order in which all people had a role to play and the well-being of all was secured. Not all rulers were sages, of course, but those who were not could continue the rites and institutions of the past until new sage-kings appeared to revise them and add to them. It is not that the first sage-king had a complete blueprint for the future; sages responded to what was happening around them and did what was necessary to attain a state of good order, and in this manner a complete and adequate civilization took shape.[27] Civilization was the working out of the *li* for civilized life, the natural unfolding of the inherent nature of humanity, the realization of humanity's role as participants in the ongoing life of the universe.

In antiquity people depended on imitating the models received from the past and from superiors, but when those in power were not born sages and thus fell prey to selfish desires and ignored past models, they went astray—taking everyone else with them. And thus the Zhou, the last of the Three Dynasties, fell into a decline, but this time no new sage-king appeared. Rather, Confucius, the sage who was not a king, chose to teach and establish the Classics as guides for posterity. It was apparent from the *Analects* and some other texts, Neo-Confucians thought, that Confucius had been trying to help students realize that there was only one solution: scholars had to *learn* how to become sages themselves. They could not rely on the small chance that a ruler would happen to be born a sage. The true teachings of Confucius, about how and why to learn, were ignored, and the learning of the sages was lost until the eleventh century. Nevertheless, the Classics had largely survived, and if literati knew how to read them correctly—if they knew what to read for—then they could cultivate the means to see what the sages saw.

THE HUMAN CONDITION

As we have seen, Neo-Confucians blamed the end of antiquity and the failure of people to realize their innate coherence on the human susceptibility to desire. Heaven-and-earth continued on course, Zhu Xi once explained, but when humanity became consumed by desire, people ceased to resemble heaven-and-earth. Living according to desire—for example, living in a system, as the Neo-Confucians did in their day, that relied on self-interest—is certainly possible, but to do so would be to ignore what is real and universal and in the world's true interest. There could not be and never would be two legitimate paths for anyone hoping to achieve a harmonious world.[28] For the Neo-Confucians, desire was both real and for most people unavoidable, but to try to stop desire by retreating from the world, which they saw as the Buddhist solution, would mean a withdrawal from political and social responsibility and thus defeat their purpose.

Neo-Confucians understood desire as the physical body's instinctive response to external stimulation. The mind is aware of the body, as when one feels thirsty or hungry, and the mind is capable of spontaneously directing the body to act to satisfy physical inclinations. Desire is unavoidable because the physical constitution, with all its senses, constantly interacts with the world around it. This kind of response takes place at the level of *qi* (and for Zhu Xi the mind is constituted of *qi*) without conscious reflection. Here was the legacy of earlier ideas of *qi*, which held that different things constituted of *qi* of the same category attract one another. This view sees external things as stimulating internal reactions in us; for example, we salivate at the sight of food or move to the rhythm of music. The problem with allowing *qi* to guide the person is that each individual has a different *qi*. Spontaneous selfishness varies with the person (each person has his own "physical nature"), and a society based on the satisfaction of desires would soon descend into violent competition for self-satisfaction, as each grabbed for whatever assuaged the thirst of the moment. The traditional solutions for this problem were to try either to avoid external temptation, to train oneself to inhabit the correct models, or to count on rewards and punishments to direct self-interest toward productive ends.

Against these solutions, the Neo-Confucians argued that the mind is aware not only of the physical constitution but also of the coherence, the unity of *li*, that all humans possess innately. Awareness is not guaranteed, because *qi* varies with the individual, making some slow and some quick, some dim and some bright, but the possibility always exists that the mind can catch some glimmer and make a choice between "human desire" and "innate coherence." "There is no definite boundary between human desire and heavenly *li*," Zhu said, but in every situation there is always a real distinction to be made, although it often requires careful attention to see the difference.[29] An example will illustrate the nature of the difference. Zhu asserted that "to eat and drink is heaven's principle; to demand gourmet food is human desire."[30] To feed the body is coherent—it continues life in a state of harmonious functioning—but to demand something fancy is simply to indulge in a sensation or to impress others, it is selfish.

The idea that the individual could learn to respond spontaneously to events because of his awareness of coherence allowed Neo-Confucians to make a distinction between desire (*yu*) and emotional responses (*qing*). Feeling angry or happy about something can, of course, be prompted by mere physical stimulation, but when one responds with anger and joy from an awareness of coherence, by definition the response serves the common good. A person with this awareness does not need to calculate, to think about what means best serve a desired end. Neo-Confucians reserved the term "emotion" (or feeling) for emotional responses filtered through an awareness of coherence. The mind provides the link between one's own internal coherence and emotional responses to the external world. Cultivating an awareness of coherence in the mind is not an obstacle to active engagement with the world. A famous statement of this comes from Cheng Hao, responding to Zhang Zai's complaint that an awareness of external things was upsetting his effort to maintain inward calm. Zhang was making a false distinction between what was internal and external, Cheng argued; the mind's awareness of coherence could be maintained no matter what one was doing. To paraphrase:

The process of creation includes all things without bias or partiality. So, too, the sage: he responds emotionally to things as they actually are without personalizing the matter. Those of us who aspire to be sages through learning should aim to be broadly inclusive yet impartial. When something comes up, we respond spontaneously, in a simple and straightforward way without calculation or hesitation. If you focus instead on trying to block out external temptations and distractions, you will never get to the end of it. . . . When the sage is happy, it is because the things he is dealing with ought to make him feel happy, and when he is angry, it is because those things deserve anger. His emotions are not tied to his own particular biases but to the state of the thing itself.[31]

Attaining this state, in which one responds to things spontaneously and correctly, without preconceived ideas, without calculating, thus involves a substantial transformation of the human condition as it is experienced in practice. "Learning" is this transformation.

Learning as the Solution, Learning as the Problem

The Neo-Confucian program of learning began with its theoretical grounding—the subject with which *Reflections on Things at Hand* begins—and at first it must have been a challenge for students to figure out that common terms such as human nature, mind, and *li*, which had been used for over a millennium, now had to be used with specific meanings and as part of a complex of terms.[32] The very nature of learning itself had changed. As one fourteenth-century observer put it, the great Neo-Confucian discovery was that learning was not a matter of acquiring habits, reciting sayings, and imitating others. Instead: "Knowing the Way is essential to defining learning, and illuminating the mind is essential to engaging in learning."[33] But what did it mean to engage in learning in practice?

Learning combined two kinds of effort. First, one needs to practice seeing the coherence of things outside the self, "extending knowledge by fully apprehending the coherence of things" (or "investigating things"). Second, to see coherence in things external to the self is simultaneously to become aware of that coherence in the self, as the coherence of one's own mind. As Zhu Xi put it: "Once we have understood these *li*, we will find that they are originally inherent in our own nature, not imposed on us from the outside."[34] Precisely because coherence is already present in the mind (human nature being the coherence of the mind), it is possible to see coherence in things in the first place. To illuminate the coherence of something is thus to illuminate the nature of the mind itself, and thus to realize something that is eternally true and unchanging. In theory, true understanding is objective and not a matter of subjective interpretation; it is absolute and not a provisional conclusion subject to revision on the basis of new evidence. With time we may see more, but the validity of what we have already seen is not in doubt. This does not preclude misapprehension in practice, however, and Zhu Xi stressed the corrective role of teachers and friends and of careful reading in order to reduce it.

Seeing coherence as inherent both in things and in the mind created a fundamental tension in the practice of learning, one already apparent with the Cheng brothers, between an "external" and an "internal" approach, even if the Neo-Confucians prided themselves on having "united the internal and external." On one hand, learning could be construed as a cumulative process of "investigating things" to illuminate their coherence, a process meant to gradually expand the mind's awareness of coherence and make its *qi* more transparent, and which promises to make it ever easier to respond to things coherently in daily practice. On the other hand, learning could be seen as attaining and maintaining a state of internal coherence—the state in which the mind realizes its own nature, in Neo-Confucian terms—which promises to enable the person to respond spontaneously to things in a manner true to the coherence of self and things (which are, of course, one and the same). If we begin from the external, then the internal is merely a matter of keeping the mind in the calm, attentive, focused, and impartial state necessary to apprehend coherence. If we begin from the internal, then the external is merely a matter of staying aware of what was happening in the world so that one can respond to it.

Reading provides a ready example of the external, cumulative process of investigating things to see their coherence. Internally, one shuts out distractions, brackets out presuppositions and prejudices, focuses attention on the text at hand, and proceeds to work through the text in an orderly manner. In reading, the goal is to arrive at a coherent understanding of the text; its "meaning" lies in grasping how all the parts necessarily fit together. This may involve consulting other interpretations and points of view, but at a certain moment one "gets it" and the text's coherence becomes apparent. As Zhu put it, one experiences *huoran guantong*, "to comprehend as all connected with total clarity."[35] Seeing the coherence is seeing the associations, correlations, relationships, and links that tie things together, that make the phenomena in question a coherent whole.

The internalist answer to the question Why read? might be that it was good training for the experience of seeing coherence, and since literati were also preparing for the examinations, reading for coherence was close to what they were already doing. An externalist answer might be that since *li* are constant and unchanging, reading the works of the sages, the Classics, provided the best possible means of rapidly accumulating knowledge. Zhu Xi explained:

It is, of course, true that in high antiquity, before there was writing, those who learned had no books to read, so that some people of the better than middling sort could apprehend [coherence] of themselves without depending on reading books. However, ever since the sages and worthies began to do things, the Way has been stored in the Classics in some detail. Even a sage such as Confucius could not have pursued learning apart from them.[36]

Thus, it was not just that reading books was the path of least resistance, it was that certain books contained more of the kind of knowledge that Neo-Confucians sought. But the process could be applied to other aspects of literati learning. As Cheng Yi explained:

Every thing has its coherence, and you must fully apprehend its coherence. There are many methods for fully apprehending coherence. One may read books and elucidate moral coherence. One may discuss past and present figures and distinguish right and wrong. One may respond to affairs and things and arrange them as they should be. All are [means of] apprehending coherence.[37]

The sociopolitical focus and the assumption that, once coherence was illuminated, one had gotten what was important help explain why Neo-Confucians were not, by and large, interested in knowledge about the natural world. Neo-Confucian learning was grounded in a view of the natural order, and Zhu Xi was more interested in the natural world than most, but he used it to confirm the universality of his own position. He was not trying to analyze particular things or categories of things in depth with the aim of arriving at knowledge that others did not possess or adding to the common store of factual knowledge.[38] A fourteenth-century book, originally titled *Collection on Investigating Things*, devotes considerable attention to natural phenomena, but its investigation is explicitly an investigation through quotations of earlier texts rather than through the things themselves.[39] There was at least one doctor and medical theorist who adopted a Neo-Confucian framework, but my impression is that Neo-Confucian thinkers were not themselves writing medical treatises.[40]

Thus the curriculum, and literati concerns, directed the student's interest, but within that context the ancients gained new relevance because they allowed one to see the coherence of one's own ideas and theirs. Consider the following comment by Cheng Yi about the minister-ruler relationship. That relationship has its own coherence, but it can be further broken down into the two roles, each of which has its own perspective, and these two roles can in turn be thought through in terms of different aspects of the relationship. Here Cheng addressed the issue of entering into the relationship in the first place.

A worthy who has no official status should not on his own seek office. If he does, he will never be trusted. This is why the ancients always waited for the ruler to invite them with the utmost respect and in the best manner before they went to serve. This was not because they regarded themselves as important, but because [as Mencius said] "unless the ruler honors virtue and delights in righteousness to this extent, it is not worth having anything to do with him."[41]

This is coherent: the would-be minister who seeks advancement will be suspected of being self-interested and thus will not be trusted by the ruler; the ruler who does not show that he truly wants worthy ministers is not prepared to trust that his ministers will be devoted to their role as impartial advisors and administrators and thus is not worth serving.

The unity of *li* allowed some Neo-Confucians to assert the cumulative nature of learning while holding out the promise that at a certain moment everything would come together into a coherent whole. Having listened to the statement quoted immediately above, a student asked:

"In apprehending the coherence of things, is it necessary to apprehend it thing by thing, or do you just apprehend one thing and then the myriad principles are known?" Cheng's answer is that it is a cumulative process.

How can you then comprehend inclusively? Even [Confucius' best student] Yanzi would not have dared say that if you arrived at only one thing, you would comprehend multitudinous coherences. You must arrive at one item today and another tomorrow; once practice has accumulated, then, as if released, there will be a point at which all is coherently connected.[42]

But the identity of *li* also could mean that seeing the coherence of one thing was the same as seeing the coherence of another. Thus on another occasion Cheng Yi could conclude:

It is not so that one must apprehend [the coherence of] all things under heaven. Just fully apprehend coherence in one instance, and the rest can be inferred by categorical similarity. For example, how to be filial. If you can't apprehend [the coherence] for one thing, then apprehend it with another . . . just as there are a multitude of roads that all lead to the capital, just find one road that leads in and it will do. The reason that one is able to apprehend [coherence] is that all things are coherent, and so every single thing and affair, however minor, has this coherence.[43]

It seems to me that for Cheng Yi the cultivation of internal states and mental attitudes—what he called taking "straightening the internal as the basis"[44]—was in support of the work of apprehending coherence externally. Cheng Hao, however, saw learning as a matter of arriving at a permanent mental state that enabled spontaneous moral action; studying served this end. His explanation of what it means to be truly conscious of humaneness (*ren*, the greatest of all virtues) spoke for the internalist view.

Those who learn must first of all recognize *humaneness*. One who is humane forms one body with things without differentiation. [The other major virtues] righteousness, ritual propriety, wisdom, and trustworthiness are all humaneness. Recognize this coherence and maintain it with integrity and attentiveness. Staying on guard is unnecessary. Exhaustive searching is not necessary. If the mind is lax, then there is a need for being on guard. If the mind is not lax, then what need is there for being on guard? If coherence has not yet been apprehended, then there is a need for exhaustive searching. If it has been preserved, then how could it depend on searching? This Way does not exist as the counterpart of things. It is beyond mere greatness. [With it] the functioning of heaven-and-earth is the functioning of myself. Mencius said: "All things are complete in me." "One must reflect on oneself and have integrity." That is the greatest joy. If you reflect on yourself and do not yet have integrity, then it is as if self and things are two separate things, and in the end you will never unite yourself with them, so how will there be any joy? . . . If you preserve [humaneness], then you will succeed in unifying [self and things].

In my view, the innate ability to know the good and the innate ability to do good have never been lost. But as long as the attitude formed by old habits has not been eliminated, it is necessary to preserve and habituate this attitude [of humaneness]. With time one can overcome old habits. This matter is extremely simple, the only danger is that you will not be able to defend it. Once you are able to embody it and then find joy, there will be no danger of not being able to defend it.[45]

For Cheng Hao, awareness is a kind of oceanic feeling, a joyful sensation of being one with heaven-and-earth and the myriad things. He can step into this state—the capacity for it is inherent in us—and it guarantees that as he spontaneously responds to things, he will be helping them join him in the condition of harmony and equilibrium that is the proper state of self, society, and cosmos.[46]

Although Cheng Yi died twenty years after Cheng Hao, a fair number of his followers resurrected Cheng Hao's line by turning to Buddhist masters, believing that the Chan idea of sudden enlightenment through self-reflection was not at odds with their own pursuit of sagehood.[47] In Zhu Xi's own lifetime, Lu Jiuyuan was the great spokesman for the intuitive apprehension of the unity of coherence and the possibility of activating it through an act of will. Perhaps the appeal of Lu's teachings prompted Zhu Xi to defend even more strongly the cumulative view of learning.[48]

LEARNING HOW TO LEARN
AND THINKING FOR ONESELF

To learn in the Neo-Confucian sense required in the first place learning how to learn, but the theory of learning allowed for different understandings, making theoretical discussion necessary to the Neo-Confucian project. This created a special place for the person who could guide others, the Neo-Confucian teacher and scholar, the "Dao-xue master." His life story featured self-transformation, and his biography was no longer the customary recital of official positions but an account of his teachings and writings.[49]

Learning justified literati participation in public life as critics of those in power locally and nationally and as local activists, whether they had official rank or not. It also strengthened the literati's position in relation to Buddhism, which for centuries had appealed to those serious about morality, who sought to transcend social and political self-interest, and which had been a major source of education, economic infrastructure, public space, and spiritual care in localities across the country. The Neo-Confucians' critique of Buddhism as being self-interested (concerned with one's own salvation rather than helping those in need) may have been disingenuous, and their understanding of Buddhist philosophy, in Zhu Xi's case at least, was shallow. But the idea that all things were composed of *li* and *qi* allowed the Neo-Confucians to claim not only that things were real in themselves (rather than the illusory product of our own desires) but also that their way of learning enabled them to find in things themselves the norms for those things. It also allowed them to grant that the differences in the constitutions of people necessarily had a bearing on the effort of self-cultivation. Finally, their positive evaluation of the emotions, in distinction to selfish desire, allowed them to claim that engagement with the external world was essential to self-cultivation.[50]

Neo-Confucianism made the "mind" central to learning. For Zhu Xi, it was the means by which one became cognizant of coherence in things and in the self, and it was the mind that made it possible to respond to events responsibly.

The mind is a term for the ruler. In both activity and stillness, it is the ruler. It is not that when one is still, it has no function or that there is only a ruler when one is active. The ruler is the inclusive systematizing inside oneself (*hunran ti-tong zi zai qi zhong*). The mind unites the emotions and the nature, [but] it does not form some crude entity together with nature and emotion that cannot be distinguished from them.[51]

For Lu Jiuyuan, the mind in action was coherence itself. But both perspectives meant that learning could no longer be equated with the mastery of the texts of the Classics or the ability to write in a good style, the two things the examination system tested. And although Zhu Xi supposed that Confucius' use of the term "humaneness" (*ren*) was the same as what Zhu meant by "mind," that term was not part of Confucius' vocabulary in the *Analects*. Nor was it the same thing as Mencius' "heart," the dispositions or feelings that Mencius saw as the starting point of morality.[52] As long as moral action had to spring from the mind that was aware of coherence, learning could not be reduced to acting correctly according to some external standard or simply doing things according to the rules of ritual.[53]

But should we suppose, as one authority on Chinese philosophy has forcefully argued, that the effect of Zhu Xi's understanding of learning was to turn people away from thinking for themselves and that "the emphasis for the individual should be on learning to obey, not on judging for himself and then choosing what is good"? Or that "The conclusion is unmistakable. Until the inner master is clear, an individual must also look for a master externally where other authorities exist. The content of what those outer authorities teach is identical to what the inner master would reveal were it clear"?[54] The argument in essence is that since we are not born sages, by definition the ruler within is not clear. However, the current ruler is the contemporary equivalent of the sage rulers of antiquity, all of whose words were expressions of innate coherence. Thus we should accept external authority. To this can be added Zhu Xi's great reluctance to allow that non-sages may vary from the "constant" (*jing*) and exercise their own judgment at variance with the norm (*quan*).[55]

It seems to me that Zhu was consistent in distinguishing imperial rule from the sage rule of antiquity, and in arguing that unless contemporary rulers first became sages, their utterances and behaviors could not claim such authority. However, perhaps there is another possibility: the Neo-Confucians spent so much time talking about how to learn because they were trying to justify a manner of learning that was in practice oriented toward the discovery of rules for everything, rather than learning how to see coherence for themselves in every situation in which they found themselves. Certainly Zhu Xi, in contrast to Lu Jiuyuan, worried greatly that students would jump to conclusions, read their own views into the text, and generally find ways of serving themselves rather than transforming themselves.

So was this kind of learning really "learning for oneself" (*wei ji zhi xue*), as Neo-Confucians claimed? I think it was in fact, but at the same time it is clear that for Zhu Xi the study of texts was a primary form of engaging in learning. In support of the first point, consider the following:

[The *Great Learning* phrase "abide in] the utmost goodness" speaks in terms of the ultimate. Not only are you to understand (*li-hui*) to the ultimate point, you also must act to the ultimate point. For example, [what is referred to in the sentence] "In being the ruler of men he abides in humaneness" is certainly this one thing, humaneness, but humaneness is of many sorts; you have to look at it according to the context. If this matter ought to be thus, then to be thus is humaneness; if that matter ought to be so, then to be so is also humaneness. If you do not understand and are concerned only with sticking to one thing, then you are being one-sided.[56]

In this case, the judgment of virtue depends on seeing it in context rather than sticking to a rigid definition. This is also an example of the Neo-Confucian idea that "*li* is one, but its manifestations are many" (discussed in the following chapter).

My next example comes from the contrast between early imperial and Neo-Confucian understandings of the opening lines of the *Doctrine of the Mean*:

> What heaven ordains is called [human] nature;
> to follow this nature is called the Way;
> cultivation of the Way is called instruction.[57]

The Han and Tang explanations began from the assumption that the process of creation endowed humans with certain moral potentials. They should follow these in action, and by doing so they create models for others to follow. More specifically: the five phases endow people with the five kinds of *qi*, each of which is responsible for a different virtuous behavior (humaneness, righteousness, propriety, wisdom, trustworthiness) when stimulated. This is an instinctive response, but it needs to be "controlled and broadened" in order to produce behaviors worthy of imitation. But people receive these different kinds of *qi* in unequal measure; hence, some are wise and some are foolish, some more humane and some more righteous. Everyone gets something but not in equal amounts. Thus people need models to learn to act properly; ideally the ruler would have a fair measure of all virtues so that he could be the model for others to follow. In short, this view accounted for the appearance of virtuous behavior, but it focused attention on producing and imitating models, not on cultivating the mind.[58] For the Neo-Confucians, however, the Way and human nature were one and the same thing, they were the same coherence, and all people had the totality in equal measure; the task was to cultivate awareness, given the differences in individual physical constitutions. Instruction was a matter not of creating models to imitate but of showing people how to cultivate awareness.[59]

Another example comes from the *Analects*. Confucius tells a disciple: "There is one single thread binding my way together," and the disciple responds: "Yes." The other students ask the disciple what this means; he explains: "The way of the Master consists in loyalty (*zhong*) and reciprocity (*shu*). That is all."[60] I understand this as an implicit appeal to two standards. In the first case, reading "loyalty" as the ethic of a subordinate to a superior, one takes the demands of the superior as the standard of behavior and does one's best to satisfy them; in the second case, reading reciprocity as the ethic of a horizontal relationship, one takes oneself as a standard and does not demand more of others than of oneself. But for Zhu Xi, the sage's mind is, in terms of its substance or structure, "one integrated coherence," which in application or function is expressed variously as the occasion requires. And he saw these two aspects as meaning to fully reveal this mind and its coherence and to extend from the mind outward to other things so that they find their proper place. The cultivation of one's mind has become the center and the grounds for bringing order to the world.[61]

A final example comes from Zhu's explanation of "humaneness" (*ren*), the first of all virtues, which Cheng Hao (quoted above)[62] understood as consciousness stemming from the unity of self and things and had defined as an innate moral guide. Zhu Xi wanted to undo Cheng Hao's view, but he also needed to explain why it was possible to say, as Mencius had, that the four virtues of humaneness, righteousness, propriety, and wisdom were part of human nature, and what it meant to say that human nature is good. Zhu's solution was to treat the ongoing process of creation as the framework within which individual ethical cultivation and practice unfolds. "The mind of heaven-and-earth is to bring things into being," he wrote quoting the Cheng brothers, and it is exactly this "mind" that all things brought into being receive. What is humaneness? It is the virtue of this "mind to bring things into being." Thus "love," which might be considered the application of humaneness in practice, is to be understood as wanting to see that the process of creation is continued. And it is this attitude that gives meaning to all the other virtues—righteousness, propriety, wisdom—which now are seen in terms of their role in continuing life itself.[63] It is this perspective—that the role of the individual is to help ensure that the process of harmonious and integrated creation continues—that must be brought to the study of particular principles and behaviors and in responding to events. The larger process of the cosmos, which in the early imperial period was understood to be best expressed in the social realm by the state system, has now been brought inside the self, and responsibility for its future has shifted to the individual who devotes himself to learning.

However, it is also true that Zhu Xi devoted much of his scholarly life to composing commentaries. His commentaries on the Four Books were both an introduction to the Learning of the Way and texts on which students could practice apprehending coherence. But he warned of getting stuck in the Classics:

Classics have commentaries as a means to comprehend the Classics. Once you have comprehended a Classic, then you need not be concerned with its commentaries. You use the Classics to comprehend coherence. Once coherence is apprehended, then you do not need the Classics. If your thought is stuck in them, then when will you be able to break free and comprehend?[64]

Yet he also said, "All the words of the sages are innate coherence and so-of-themselves," and "All the Six Classics are books of the Three Dynasties. They passed through the [editorial hand] of the sage [Confucius] and are completely heavenly coherence."[65] Why, then, would students ever want to depart from them? Moreover, reading the Classics with the aim of gaining a coherent understanding that spoke to the reader could easily become an end in itself, a challenge that promised a certain degree of satisfaction. As Zhu Xi said, "Your reading will be successful only if you understand the spot where everything interconnects—east and west meet at this pivotal point. Simply dedicate yourself to what you're doing at the moment. Don't think about the past or the future, and you'll naturally get to this point."[66]

As the new curriculum emerged and as the theory of learning was explained ever more systematically, students gained a much clearer idea of what they were looking for and how to tell when they had found it. The Classics became a way of testing one's understanding, rather than things that themselves still had to be understood. Zhu Xi had become nationally influential by the time of his death in 1200. For some, Neo-Confucianism was now in a sense complete: students needed to master the curriculum and practice what they had learned, but the theory of learning and the understanding of heaven-and-earth and humanity that were its foundation had been perfected. In the thirteenth and fourteenth century, some teachers, rather than writing their own commentaries on the Four Books and Five Classics, began to teach the commentaries of Zhu and his students. Some took this a step further and began to write commentaries on the commentaries. Learning continued to be a transformative experience for individuals who encountered the texts or found a Neo-Confucian teacher—we have enough testimony from individuals to know this—but philosophically minded scholars were increasingly working within Zhu Xi's framework.[67] Some saw their mission as holding the various strands of Neo-Confucian thought together—in the Yuan period Wu Cheng, for example, thought of himself as resolving the tension between those who stressed internal cultivation (in the Cheng Hao and Lu Jiuyuan tradition) and those like Zhu Xi who emphasized external knowledge seeking.[68] What I find striking in Wu's case is that his goal was to unify the theory of learning.

When the Neo-Confucian curriculum was mandated for the examination system during the Yuan period, some Neo-Confucians feared that making their teachings into a state-mandated curriculum would turn literati away from practicing what they had learned and thus undercut the goal of moral transformation. Others argued that at last the distinction between true learning and examination learning had disappeared.[69] In fact, the Yuan examination system was extremely limited and not fully supported by those in power; it was not until the Ming that the negative consequences of combining the Learning of the Way with a system for recruiting literati for government service would become clear.

The Revival of Discoursing on Learning During the Ming

During the Song, becoming well acquainted with the Neo-Confucian position was a matter of choice, and more likely than not a decision to adopt the identity of one who would stand apart from the majority of literati and their concerns with passing the examinations, securing office, and improving their social status. It was a time when Neo-Confucians could believe they were transforming themselves by learning to become the first sages for over a millennium and transforming the world by spreading their teachings through schools and shrines, performing rituals, holding lectures, and publishing their texts. They were succeeding in reinterpreting much of the cultural tradition by showing how the Classics, histories, and literature could be understood from a Neo-Confucian perspective. Neo-Confucian literati and retired officials were active in programs aimed at improving the local welfare, at a moment when the court was concerned more with the survival of the dynasty than with transforming society. And in the thirteenth century, they were also making headway in persuading the court to recognize that they represented the learning of the sages. To be a Neo-Confucian was to be an outsider who claimed to belong inside, to be an unorthodox figure who claimed to speak for orthodoxy.

By the mid-1400s, the situation was very different. Now the Neo-Confucian position was something literati had to learn if they hoped to pass the examinations, even if they did not agree. To speak against Neo-Confucianism was to take the minority position and place oneself at odds with the status quo. It seemed that the work of figuring out what the ideas were and how they should be applied had been accomplished; in 1415 the court compiled everything one needed to know in the three great compendia on the Four Books, the Five Classics, and nature and principle. The Neo-Confucians had always claimed that it was possible to know the Way; now they could claim that the Way was known. There is no need to write more, opined Xue Xuan, for Master Zhu has already illuminated the Way; all that is necessary is to put it into practice.[70] In fact, as Xue's own career illustrates, he faced the constant challenge of getting others to see that the Cheng-Zhu system of learning was aimed at transforming the way they acted in daily life, that it was something more than book learning, that they should make it the basis of their own identity. He also wanted to show that the theory of learning was a still unfinished project, that there was more to be said about fundamental concepts.[71]

At this time, standing up for righteousness by criticizing those in power could have terrifying consequences, as purges and executions made clear. Some emperors were claiming to share the Neo-Confucian view of learning and treating it as an ideological pillar of their own authority.[72] Even if one questioned their sincerity, one could agree that Ming social policy was centered on the ideal of a local moral community that had strong Neo-Confucian roots, one that promised stability, welfare, and education and recognized the importance of family and moral conduct in social relations. Literati were expected to help make the system work, not to criticize it or to mobilize themselves to do what they thought was right on their own.[73]

During the latter half of the fifteenth century, in the political turmoil that followed the Mongols' capture of an emperor who led an expedition north of the Great Wall in 1449 and as the economy gradually returned to prosperity, some intellectuals began challenging Neo-Confucian assumptions. But among those who sought to practice Neo-Confucianism in their own lives, we can see a division emerging that would soon lead to a great revival of discoursing on learning and Neo-Confucian activism.

On one side were those who continued to work within Zhu Xi's framework. Zhang Mou, for example, after he was flogged and imprisoned for remonstrating with the emperor for indulging his desires, returned to his native Jinhua prefecture (Wuzhou in Song and Yuan), where for most of the next forty years he devoted himself to mobilizing the local literati to recover their Neo-Confucian heritage and play active roles in local life, all the while defending Zhu Xi's position against those who found it an inadequate guide to learning to be a sage. Zhang built a national reputation through his efforts and eventually was called back to office as the director of the National University in Nanjing.[74]

On the other side was a man whose ideas about learning Zhang Mou objected to: Chen Xianzhang. He began as a brilliant student, passing the provincial examination at only twenty but then failing the metropolitan examinations twice in a row. Rather than seek a low-level office, he went to Jiangxi to study with Wu Yubi. Inspired but still feeling that he had not found his way, he returned home the next year to study on his own. Chen described what happened next:

I searched for it day after day in book after book, neglecting to sleep and eat. I went on this way for many years and still did not apprehend anything. *What I mean by "did not apprehend anything" is that this mind of mine and this coherence* (li) *did not converge and tally with one another.*

Then I forsook the complexities [of apprehending coherence] and sought, through quiet sitting alone, for what was essential within myself. In time I was able to see the substance of my own mind as it wondrously revealed itself, as if it were a material object. Henceforth, in the daily round of social intercourse, in everything I followed my heart's desire, just like a horse guided by bit and bridle. Moreover, in the investigation and realization of the coherence of things and in the examination of the sages' teachings, there was a clue and source for everything, just as water always has a source. Thereupon I gained great self-confidence, and said, "Does not the effort to become a sage lie in just this?"[75]   (Italics added)

Ultimately it took ten years of solitary effort for Chen to reach his realization that making sense of the coherence of things and the Classics depended on seeing the fundamental aspect of his own mind clearly. Instead of apprehending coherence in things and texts as a way of setting the mind in the right, as Zhu Xi had taught, Chen was using his enlightened mind to assimilate and integrate. "I am the Way," he concluded; as long as his mind was open and receptive, it would respond to things spontaneously as they arose, and its response would always be correct. There was no need to copy the ancients or accept authoritative models. A disciple claimed that Chen had made the Cheng brothers irrelevant; he had connected directly with Confucius.[76] Chen's theory of learning, "the learning of apprehending it for and in the self," was meant to engender the kind of literatus whose inner tranquility was not threatened by events in the world: "Whether my lot be wealth and honor or poverty and low station, or I be pressed by barbarians, adversaries, and calamities, none of these circumstances can disturb the mind. This is called apprehending it for and in yourself." Such a man would be "oblivious even to the greatness of Heaven-and-Earth or the transformations of life and death . . . when one examines his writings, one finds that he gives weight to the internal and esteems lightly the external. He advances [to office] reluctantly and withdraws easily. . . . He stands erect, majestically alone."[77] The danger in Chen's position is that being unaffected by the world will lead to disengagement from it. Chen himself did not see that as a danger, and he kept up his political and scholarly connections, tried again to gain office, and gathered disciples of his own.

In retrospect, we can group Chen with a number of people in the fifteenth century who saw themselves as parting ways with the common learning of the times, which in their view allowed the individual to feel he was doing the right thing without having to transform himself. They were concerned with finding something within themselves, whether it was a state of equilibrium, freeing themselves from the obstacles to spontaneously respond to events, or a sense of unity and coherence or of unity with all things. For all of them the possibility of being a moral agent in the world required overcoming their sense that there was a disconnection between the external and the internal.[78]

The focus on the internal state before one engaged in responding to things departed from Zhu Xi in one respect but not in another. Zhu, too, believed that "quiet sitting" is a useful technique for calming the mind and maintaining a receptive impartial state of "inner mental attentiveness." But he did not think one could (as he accused Buddhist meditators of doing) use the mind to look at the mind. Rather, the state of inner calm is paired with illuminating coherence, and it is this process that enables the individual to respond to events coherently.[79] The mind alone is not adequate; it has to become aware of the coherence of the things it is responding to. And yet at the heart of Zhu's claim for human nature is the idea that the great virtues that inform ongoing life and the creation of order in the world are fundamentally already present and accessible to the mind, they are in fact the nature—the coherence—of the mind. Why is it not possible, as Cheng Hao and Lu Jiuyuan had thought, to draw on that kind of awareness in responding to things?

Those who did not think that studying books to see coherence was helping them activate their moral awareness found a spokesman in Wang Yangming. Wang's way of understanding the mind, coherence, and the phenomenal world provided a new theoretical framework for understanding how to learn, but the result, perhaps contrary to Wang's expectations as a rather learned man, was that moral activism came to be more firmly detached from knowledge about things. Wang did not start out with a commitment to Neo-Confucianism. About the time he passed the provincial examinations, he is said to have tried without success to apprehend coherence by observing bamboo for an extended period. The fact that he did not succeed is evidence, I think, that an experiential understanding of Zhu Xi's doctrine of investigating things was not necessary either to passing the examinations or, in Wang's case, to revitalizing the Neo-Confucian mission. Moreover, after that, Wang became involved successively in literary studies, military arts, Daoist physical cultivation techniques, and Buddhist meditation. He passed the examinations in 1499 and entered office. He rose quickly and once at court offered lectures to students. It is said that he told them to make up their minds to become sages, yet it seems that he himself was still searching for the method. It was not until 1508 that, having been exiled to the aboriginal southwest for joining in criticizing the most powerful eunuch of the day, he came to the sudden realization that coherence is not to be sought in things but in one's own mind. Wang's views were not seen as Neo-Confucian at first, but Wang himself soon insisted that he was in fact being true to the sages and the Classics.[80] And although he took direct issue with the contemporary understanding of Zhu's theory of learning, he tried to claim that by the end of his life Zhu himself had reached Wang's own conclusions. In other words, although he did not start out as someone with a Neo-Confucian identity, he ended up claiming with considerable success that he was the successor to Zhu.

Wang stated his basic doctrine as "the mind is *li*." To grant this was to depart from two of the fundamental precepts in the officially sanctioned view: "nature is *li*," and the mind can best be set in the right by investigating things and illuminating their coherence. If mind and coherence are one and the same, then two conclusions follow. First, effort should be directed at activating the mind, and any effort to correct it by appealing to external sources is misplaced. Second, realizing coherence in one's involvement in the world depends on activating the mind; there is no need to acquire knowledge about things or check one's own ideas against the opinions of the sages, the Classics, teachers, or fellow students.

Why was it important to say that "the mind is *li*"?[81] Like Neo-Confucians generally, Wang was committed to basing his ideas about how people can learn to act morally on how humans are inherently constituted, so that moral action can truly be said to come from the self. Distinguishing *li* from the mind, he held, has the opposite effect. We have come to think that the mind and *li* are separate things. And this allows us to claim that we can distinguish between the quality of our actions and the nature of our motivation. Thus, he argued, some of us look at the hegemon lords who had saved the ancient Zhou dynasty and judge their actions as being in accord with *li* because all would agree that saving the Zhou was good under the circumstances, yet at the same time they grant that because those same figures were motivated to act by self-interest, their minds were not informed by a commitment to the common good. Why did this matter? Because if we conclude that it is enough for our actions to be seen as satisfying commonly shared values, we will be free to use this as camouflage for pursuing our own selfish purposes. A world of doubleness, insincerity, and deception will be the result, where people cannot trust others to act for the common good. Just like all Neo-Confucian thinkers before him, Wang demanded that action be motivated by moral commitment. For Wang, the actions of an actor not motivated by self-generated moral purpose could not be regarded as good.[82]

But if one treats the mind as *li* and holds that this is the inherent, natural condition of all humans, what does *li* mean? It can only mean that the unity and oneness of *li* is the original condition of the mind, not that the mind contains a catalogue of all the principles and standards for things out in the world. To say that the sages were born as sages, that they instinctively knew what was good, must mean that they were inherently capable of making moral judgments, not that they innately knew anything about the details of the world in which they lived. But if all people are, without knowing it, in the same state, if all minds are fundamentally unified and coherent, why do people do evil? Because as soon as the mind moves beyond its original state and becomes aware of things, as soon as the will becomes active, a situation is created in which the individual is responding, even if it is only a matter of an emotional response to a perception. This provides the opening for selfish desire; one might end up responding not from the mind in its fundamental aspect but from self-interest.

However, the mind is not a static entity. Precisely because it is fundamentally coherent, it can tell the difference between what is in accord with its original coherence and what is not. Since one can choose to act one way and not another at this point, it is possible to say that the mind is distinguishing between what is good (in the sense that good means to maintain the mind's original coherence) and what is evil (whatever goes against that). The mind's faculty of being able to distinguish between its original state and the intrusion of self-interest, between good and evil, Wang called "innate knowing of the good" (*liang zhi*). He posited that this faculty is something innate to all humans, something intuitive and perfect that cannot be lost or destroyed. It is simply a matter of deciding to activate it and follow it, thus doing what is good and getting rid of what is evil. Toward the end of his life, Wang spelled this out in what came to be known as the "Doctrine of the Four Axioms."

> Having no good and no evil is mind-in-itself.
> Having good and having evil is the activity of the will.
> Innate knowing is knowing the good and evil [in the
>   activity of the will].
> Performing good and getting rid of evil is the rectification
>   of actions.*83

Wang's two most important disciples interpreted this in opposite ways. One saw the axioms as an injunction to think about what is good and what is evil and, having learned to recognize them, to do good and avoid evil. The other began from Wang's starting point: if the mind originally is simply as it is, without any distinctions or divisions, then good and evil are judgments made relative to phenomena (whether they come from outside or arise from the self), they are not real in and of themselves. In which case, rather than trying to distinguish between good and evil, one should simply trust to the mind as something that is beyond good and evil. The whole issue of distinguishing good and evil becomes irrelevant. Wang agreed with both interpretations as being appropriate for different kinds of people.84

Wang's position was very controversial. It disconnected the effort to acquire knowledge about the things out there—the world of texts, history, and government, about which Wang himself knew a great deal—from the transformation of the self into a morally and socially respon-

---

*The "rectification of actions" translates Wang's interpretation of *ge wu*, which Zhu Xi had understood as the "investigation of things" in order to apprehend their coherence.

sible person who extended his knowledge of the good to the things out there. But from Wang's perspective, the crucial issue was to show literati how to conceive of a real basis in the self for responding to things. Action cannot be separated from knowing, Wang argued (against Zhu Xi, who supposed that knowledge precedes action); you cannot know the taste until you try the food, and you cannot think a thought until you think it. This makes sense if, like Wang, we think of things not as static entities but as constantly developing events and activities whose meaning changes as circumstances change, for to deal successfully with such a world we need to learn to respond independently and flexibly, rather than trying to find a rule from another time and place that tells us how to act.[85]

Wang gained a national following during his lifetime, and after his death his teachings were spread, and developed, by generations of followers. By the 1550s intellectuals were taking his ideas more seriously than Zhu Xi's theory of learning, great assemblies were being held at which literati and officials discussed his ideas, and new thinkers were appearing who traveled the land discoursing on their version of learning for all who wished to attend, literati and commoner alike.

This time, however, although Wang's significant letters and conversations were compiled as *Instructions for Practical Living*, the production of texts took second place to inspirational lecturing aimed at persuading the audience that they could find what they needed in their own minds. What gave the new movement so much vitality was that for its proponents talking about the new way of thinking was also a way of practicing it. Discoursing on learning built networks and mobilized literati communities; it was coming to be seen as a way of transforming society through learning, and some of its foremost proponents preferred not to take the government offices for which they had qualified through the examinations. Increasingly these new Neo-Confucians were at odds with those in power, and in 1579 the court tried to close the academies as a way of putting an end to discoursing on learning.

The danger in all this depended on one's point of view. Some who believed that public life was the domain of the literati were put off by the idea that even the barely literate could be sages and teachers. Others continued to believe that there ought to be a real connection between intellectual knowledge about the world and moral awareness. Some saw that those who held that the most important thing was trusting one's own inclinations were undermining the very possibility of shared values, or even a shared theory that had normative implications. And still others tried to organize the literati around the idea that the good mattered, that it had a real foundation in human nature, and that moral effort was more important than spontaneity.[86]

But what was now clear was that a common Neo-Confucian foundation could support two theories of learning that pointed in two different directions, neither of which was entirely satisfactory. By the end of the seventeenth century, large numbers of serious intellectuals had been drawn to modes of learning that did not require Neo-Confucian assumptions.

———

This chapter has argued that the core content of Neo-Confucianism was a theory of how to learn and that understanding how to learn and put what one had learned into practice was the central concern of Neo-Confucian teachers. Whether literati studied Zhu Xi's commentaries on Four Books or Wang Yangming's doctrine of innately knowing the good, the subject of learning was learning itself, and the goal of learning was transforming oneself into a responsible actor in the world. Certain relationships were always present and real, whether the political relationship between ruler and subject or the social relationship between parent and child. But the relationships themselves did not determine action; individuals still had to figure out how to conduct themselves. Let us grant a difference in order to ascertain a common problem. Zhu Xi called for the cumulative acquisition of knowledge by apprehending principle; Wang Yangming for activating the innate ability to know the good. Why did both positions work for literati? If all things and affairs contained principles, then how could one say that one thing was better than another? Zhu Xi's answer—that actions are sometimes in accord with innate coherence and sometimes in accord with selfish desire—leaves open the question (for those who do not believe that innate coherence exists) of what in practice Zhu Xi was trying to accord with. Similarly, if people can innately know the difference between good and evil but the mind in itself is without good or evil, then what is it that the mind draws upon to know? Wang's answer—that the mind's intelligence simply was able to do this—leaves open the question (for those who do not believe this) of what was guiding the mind in making this distinction. I do not doubt that they believed their answers were real, but I would suggest that the viability of their assertions depended on something more. That is the subject of the next chapter.

6

Belief

For Zhu Xi, the *Great Learning* outlined a sequential program that begins with apprehending coherence in things external to the self. But Zhu attached no less importance to the *Doctrine of the Mean*. He thought the two texts are in perfect agreement, although they speak to different issues. The *Mean* focuses on what is internal to the self as the necessary foundation for responding to the world. It opens with three definitions:

> What Heaven imparts to man is called the nature.
> To follow our nature is called the Way.
> Cultivating the Way is called education.*

It then asserts that the Way is integral to daily practice:

> The Way cannot be separated from us for a moment. What can be separated from us is not the Way.

Zhu Xi understood this to mean that since the Way (that is, *li* or coherence) is complete in us as human nature, any departure from the Way

---

*Andrew Plaks translates: "By the term 'nature' we speak of that which is imparted by the ordinance of Heaven; by 'the Way' we mean that path which is in conformance with the intrinsic nature of man and things; and by 'moral instruction' we refer to the process of cultivating man's proper place in the world" (see Plaks, Ta Hsüeh *and* Chung Yung, 25).

and our nature must be due to something that is not true to our moral selves.

The text then distinguishes between two states, equilibrium and harmony. For Zhu, equilibrium is the internal state and harmony its external equivalent. Equilibrium describes the unstirred and unstimulated state of our "nature" (that is, our innate coherence), and harmony the state that results when our emotional responses to stimuli are guided by the nature.

Before the feelings of pleasure, anger, sorrow, and joy are aroused is called equilibrium. When these feeling are aroused and each and all attain due measure and degree, it is called harmony. Equilibrium is the great foundation of the world, and harmony its universal path. When equilibrium and harmony are realized to the highest degree, heaven-and-earth will attain its proper order, and all things will flourish.[1]

Equilibrium is the great foundation, Zhu explained, because the nature is what heaven imparts to man, and it is that from which all coherence under heaven issues. Harmony is the universal path because harmony means to accord with the nature, and it is this path through which all under heaven are to proceed. And when harmony is realized, all things will flourish because we are basically of one body with all things; when our minds are correct, then the mind of heaven-and-earth is correct, and if our *qi* is in accord with that correctness, then the *qi* of heaven-and-earth will accord as well.[2]

The question this chapter addresses is What is it that one is supposed to find in the self and use in responding to the external world? I shall argue that the core of the Neo-Confucian self is belief—a conscious commitment of faith—rather than a philosophical proposition or unarticulated assumption.

The Problem of Judgment and Motivation

The process of learning aims to cultivate an awareness of the coherence (*li*) in things and in the self. Since there is always a *li*, in theory there is always a response that accords with *li* and is coherent. Students thus need to train themselves to apprehend coherence. But acquiring knowledge by reading books, and even by rigorously investigating all the different aspects of a subject until its coherence is fully apprehended—as

Rao Lu illustrated in the case of filial piety—does not solve the problem of acting in a particular context. Events unfold over time, the relationships among the actors change, and meaning can depend on the
situation. Jin Lüxiang (1232–1308), whose followers saw him as a successor to Zhu Xi, put the problem like this.

The virtuous practices of past and present might be soft or hard, square or
straight, pure or harmonious, noninterfering or demanding, but I cannot stick
to a fixed method. I must choose the good and follow it. This is what is called
"choosing what is right." However, the good has no fixed standard. It may be
the very same thing, but if you do it at that time it is right, whereas if you do it
at this time it is wrong. It may be the very same standard, but if you apply it to
this affair it is wrong whereas if you apply it to that affair it is right. This is
what the ancients called "shifting rightness."[3]

For Jin the moral meaning of the response depended on the situation.

Virtue refers to practice. Goodness refers to coherence (*li*). . . . All the virtues
of past and present can be taken as models. But [different times] institute practice differently. One cannot be limited to a fixed model. It all depends on
choosing the good one. Although all the *li* under heaven are good, if one
chooses the mean according to the times, then here, too, one cannot be limited
to a fixed standard.[4]

If Jin could not know the moral choice by consulting external authorities, how was he supposed to know it? The fact that he thought that
everything has coherence did not solve the problem. He could have
said that he needed to think through the coherence of the situation,
seeing the particular instance in an ever-expanding network of connections, until he saw what action would be coherent under the circumstances. But this is not the conclusion he reached. Instead, Jin argued
that the solution lay in maintaining the right mental state: "As for what
the school of the sage called 'always hitting the mean' [in the *Doctrine of
the Mean*], which is how one compares and contrasts, who except
someone with a purely sincere and fixed mind will be able to choose
precisely and be free of error?"[5]

But even if Jin knew the right choice, would he act accordingly? This
was a problem that Wang Yangming thought inevitable when "knowing" was conceived of as a matter of reading books: people might not
translate their knowledge of what they should do into action. This sepa-

ration of knowledge and action worried Zhu Xi as well. His solution was to develop the ability to judge the quality of one's motivation: Is our inclination to act in a certain way motivated by self-interest or by a moral sense? For Zhu Xi, this is something we all can know and feel because the mind is capable of becoming aware of its own moral nature, the innate coherence, *tian li*, that exists in us all alike. For Wang Yangming, this was a matter of "innately knowing the good," *liang zhi*, which all people are capable of. People do not have to try to investigate a dynamic situation to the point they see every connection. Above all, both Zhu and Wang rejected utilitarian thinking; that is, calculating possible outcomes and, having found the most advantageous one, choosing the actions that will achieve the desired result. Instead, both argue that we can appeal to our own innate moral sensibility and know whether our motivation is right; the motivation must be right for the act to be right. Theoretically this is correct, since the innate coherence of the mind is also the coherence of an integrated and harmonious universe. In the words of the *Mean*: when our feelings are aroused and we respond, each and all attain due measure and degree, and harmony prevails.[6]

We can equate Zhu's innate coherence and Wang's innate knowing with what we generally mean by "conscience." We may even be inclined to believe, as Mencius proposed, that all people in past and present have the same conscience, just as all palates prefer the sweet to the bitter. But we need to ask what constituted the "conscience" in the Neo-Confucian case, for it is this that allowed them to differentiate the moral from the self-interested. What constituted it defined their fundamental sense of what the "moral" meant in a positive way, as something more than the mere absence of selfishness. As Wm. Theodore de Bary has put it: "To find the unifying thread, the balanced mean, the underlying value or all-embracing conception remained the fundamental aim of Neo-Confucian teachings."[7]

Unity as Belief

It may at first seem too reductive to say that the Neo-Confucian moral sensibility was a belief in "unity," but unity appeared in different guises in many contexts. There was political *unity*, not so much the centralized bureaucratic system (whose superiority over a decentralized system Neo-Confucians often questioned) but the belief that the men who made up the government could share the same moral commitment rather than represent a coalition of interest groups. There was the belief in the possibility of *consistency* in the theory of learning, that contemporary Neo-Confucians could perfectly rearticulate the ideas of the sages of antiquity, thus establishing the *dao tong*, the "Succession of the Way." There was the *identity* and unity of coherence, *li*, itself. There was the belief in a state of perfect *integrity* or sincerity (*cheng*), in which emotional responses (*qing*) are fully consonant with the innate coherence of "heavenly *li*," and the mind always vanquishes selfish desires and controls the *qi* of the physical constitution. There was the belief in possibility of social *harmony*, in which all find a place in an integrated social organism. There was the idea of a "*single* thread" (*yi guan*) that connects the "root and branch" of ideas or practices into a consistent whole. And there was the antipathy toward modes of learning seen as *zhi li*, "disconnected details presented without a sense for the whole to which they belong,"[8] and all those ways of cultivation, such as Buddhism and Daoism, that Neo-Confucians classed as "different starting points."

Belief in unity served as a mental filter for discerning what was good. Unity was a belief about how the human world ought to be and how the physical world came to be. When faced with a situation that required that one judge one's motivation, that which was right and good was that which the individual sensed most closely fit the goal of maintaining unity, coherence, interconnectedness, continuity, seamlessness, harmony, integrity, wholeness, and constancy. To say that this was a belief is not only to recognize that it was so deeply ingrained that it was beyond question but also to recognize that it provided the individual mind with a way of testing its inclinations at a sensory level; we sense that something is coherent, even if we are not sure we can explain why it is. This is not to deny that "unity" may degrade into uniformity, agreement into imitation, coherence into dogmatism.

The passage by Jin Lüxiang quoted above begins:[9] "Virtue refers to practice. Goodness refers to coherence (*li*). Unity refers to the mind. How we judge things depends simply on [the mind's] being able to be unified (*ke yi*)."* Jin was drawing here on Zhu Xi's explanation of a

---

*The phrase *ke yi* is understood by earlier commentators to mean being able to be "constant," "unchanging," "single-minded," and "certain." I have translated it awkwardly as "being able to be unified" so that its meaning is left open to definition.

passage from a chapter in the *Book of Documents*, "All Shared a Unifying Virtue." The passage in the *Documents* reads:

Virtue has no constant model; it takes as the model having good as its master. The good has no constant master; it is what accords with being able to be unified. Thus the myriad surnames all say, "Great are the King's words." And they further say: "Unified is the King's mind. He can protect the legacy of the Former Kings and support the existence of the populace."[10]

When Zhu Xi was asked: Does this mean to take the good person, whoever that might be, as one's model and teacher rather than one particular person? He responded:

No, Hengqu [Zhang Zai] explained it best with "Virtue takes as its master all the good in the world; the good traces back to the unity of the world." The four phrases [i.e., "Virtue has no constant model; it takes having good as its master. The good has no constant master; it is what accords with being able to be unified."] are in three sections, with each section resembling the others.

Virtue is referred to generally; there is virtue with good outcomes and bad, and thus it must take the good as its master for it to have good outcomes.

What is good is also referred to generally: in this situation it is good, in that it is not; here it is good, there it is not good; yesterday it was not good, today it is good.

It must "accord with being able to be unified" for it to be good. Which is to say, measure the degree of goodness with this [unified] mind. That is why when Zhang Zai said "traces," it was as if [he was saying that] the good was determined by unity. It ought to be that what is good is determined according to unity.

Virtue is spoken of in terms of affairs. The good is spoken of in terms of *li*. Unity is spoken of in terms of the mind. To sum up, the spirit of this chapter resides in the several uses of the character "unity." You need to look at it carefully. Only when this mind is unified will it have constancy without ever changing.[11]

Elsewhere Zhu was asked what the "good" takes as its master. He replied: "It simply takes the *liang xin* [the mind that knows the good] as master."[12] In short, Zhu fell back on the inherent ability of the mind to sort things out, but at the same time the state of mind that is able to judge is said to be in a "unified" state.

We might argue that "unity" as an ideal was such a part of the imperial system and its traditional ideology that it hardly needed justification.

This is true, but the point is that the Neo-Confucians moved it out of the imperial system and into the self. We might also argue that it pervaded Song intellectual culture. This is true as well, but no one had gone so far as to make it the foundation for the mind. And Neo-Confucians made arguments for the unity of the cosmos, human society, doctrine, and the mind with exceptional urgency.

THE UNITY OF THE COSMOS

Neo-Confucians supposed that all creation, "heaven-and-earth and the myriad things," is a coherent, unified whole with a unitary origin and unitary process. Zhang Zai explained this unity with *qi*, which enabled him to assert that all the dualities through which creation operates are at the same time unitary.[13] "Existence and nonexistence, emptiness and substantiality, are all a single thing, not to be able to unify is not to realize the nature."[14] Similarly, in speaking about the all-inclusiveness of the *Change*, Zhu Zhen (1072–1138) held that although "it does not go beyond the duality of *yin* and *yang*, ultimately it is simply unitary. Unity is the root of heaven-and-earth, the start of the myriad things, the source of *yin* and *yang*, of movement and stillness. Thus it is called the Supreme Ultimate. Learning halts at this point."[15] It is precisely "Learning halts at this point" that suggests that arriving at the point of "unity" is arriving at the point where it all depends on faith.

The unity of the cosmos includes human society. In contrast to those contemporaries who denied a necessary connection between the cultural-historical world and heaven-and-earth, Cheng Yi insisted:

How could one understand the way of man but not understand the way of heaven? The Way is one. How could the way of man only be the way of man and the way of heaven only be the way of heaven? The *Mean* says that when one realizes his nature, he is able to realize the nature of others. When he is able to realize the nature of others, he is able to realize the nature of the myriad things. And when he is able to realize the nature of the myriad things, he is able to participate in the transformative and nurturing processes of heaven-and-earth.[16]

For Cheng Yi and Zhu Xi, *li*, the idea of the inherent coherence of a thing, made this unity intelligible. Neo-Confucians used *li* to define crucial terms. What was the "Way"? The way of heaven? Human nature? All were *li*. Moreover, if *li* was one and all things received the unity of *li*, as Zhu Xi asserted, then all things were fundamentally the same. Cheng Yi objected to the common view that a person's "nature" was that person's individual character in order to assert not that all humans were alike but that they were fully integrated into an organic cosmos. For Zhu Xi, this meant that all things equally received the full endowment of innate coherence, the "Supreme Ultimate," but the human kind differed from all other kinds in that it could increase its awareness and thus alter its behavior.

Seeing the world as a coherent and inclusive system, as "one," does not preclude the recognition of difference. The Cheng-Zhu doctrine of "*li* is one but its manifestations are many" (*li yi fen shu*) spoke to this. In terms of the physical universe, this means that although all things possess the same unity of coherence, each thing operates according to its own coherence. In human terms, it means that although all people equally possess the unity of *li*, each person has a particular role in a particular web of relationships and needs to be treated accordingly.

As Zhu Xi's teacher Li Tong (1093–1163) explained: "Do not worry about *li* not being one; the hard part is that the manifestations are many."[17] Not all agreed; for Cheng Hao, Lu Jiuyuan, and Wang Yangming, the unity of *li* was the focus of the mind. "One *li* fills heaven-and-earth," wrote Lu, and elsewhere: "The universe is my mind; my mind is the universe."[18] But for the Zhu Xi school, this doctrine meant it was still necessary to make distinctions. The doctrine of "*li* is one but the manifestations/roles are many," Zhu wrote, was the great challenge in learning. From the perspective of the unity of coherence, one could speak of the conceptive and generative forces (*qian* and *kun*) as father and mother of all creation. However, in terms of actual roles and manifestations, an individual's mother and father were different from the conceptive and generative forces, and yet "what is referred to by 'coherence is unitary' runs through 'the roles are many' and has never been separated from it."[19] Too much seeing things as one led to ignoring the particulars of one's duties, but ignoring the unity of things led to partiality and selfishness. As a contemporary explained, one needed to avoid both treating all fathers as the same as one's own father and focusing selfishly on one's own kin and forsaking one's duties toward others.[20] The mind needed to maintain an awareness of unity even as it responded to each thing in a manner appropriate to that thing.

THE UNITY OF SOCIETY IN ANTIQUITY

Neo-Confucians recognized that they lived in a world in which the unity of *li* was not fully manifest in society. They could explain why this was so in physiological terms—the *qi* with which individuals are endowed varies and makes them more and less susceptible to self-interested responses to external stimulation—and hence they saw transforming the self through learning as the solution. But they were not willing to suppose that this had always been true or that humanity by virtue of its physical existence is fated to create a world of dissonance and struggle. Their insistence that antiquity was a perfectly integrated social order was a statement of faith, it seems to me, rather than a historical argument, for it depended on believing that there was a *real* distinction between antiquity—the time of the sage-kings Yao, Shun, and Yu and the Three Dynasties that followed (Xia, Shang, and Zhou)—and the subsequent empires.

The idea of a perfect society in antiquity was not new, and it had gained new ideological weight when the Ancient Style writers promoted it to justify transforming government into an agent for serving the common interest, giving government a higher purpose than maintaining the dynasty. Neo-Confucians took this further by treating unity as the natural social condition, division as its perversion. The Neo-Confucian primer, *Reflections on Things at Hand*, explains:

In the world, whether it is a case of the country or the family or a case of the myriad things, the reason they are not in harmonious union is that something has set them apart. If they are not set apart, they will be in union. Even in the production of heaven and earth and the completion of all things, only unity can lead to success; whenever unity is not achieved, it is because something has set things apart. When there is separation or cause for hatred between ruler and minister, between father and son, or among relatives or friends, it is usually because some slander or wrong has set them apart. Remove this separation and unify them; they will be in harmony in all respects and, furthermore, will be in proper order.[21]

In antiquity, people were not divided:

In ancient times, from lords and great officers down, every person's position matched his merits. They occupied their positions for life, for they fulfilled their lot. If the position was not up to a person's merit, the ruler would promote him. A scholar would pursue his learning. When his learning was complete, the ruler would send for him. No one manipulated things for himself. Farmers, artisans, and merchants were diligent at their work, and they lived simply. Therefore each person's mind was fixed and settled, and it was possible for the world to be united in one mind. In later generations, from the common people to the great lords, people turn their minds to glory and honor every day. Farmers, artisans, and merchants turn their minds to wealth and extravagance every day. Millions and millions of people, each with his own mind, compete for wealth. The world is thus in great confusion. How can there be unity? It is hard to see how the world can fail to become chaotic.[22]

Selfishness, to see and act from one's own interests rather than the original unity that was the natural state of human society, was the problem. Wang Yangming took the same view.

The essentials of this teaching are what was successively transmitted by Yao, Shun, and Yu, and what is summed up by the saying, "The human mind is precarious, the moral mind is subtle. Have refined discrimination and singleness [of mind] thus to hold fast the mean." Its details were given by Emperor Shun to Xie, namely, "between father and son there should be affection, between ruler and minister there should be righteousness, between husband and wife there should be attention to their separate functions, between old and young there should be a proper order, and between friends there should be faithfulness, and that is all." At the time of Yao, Shun, and the Three Dynasties, teachers taught and students studied only this. At that time people did not have different opinions, nor did families have different practices. Those who practiced the teaching naturally and easily were called sages. . . . People of low station . . . all received this teaching, which was devoted only to the perfection of virtue and conduct. . . .[23]

The task of the school was only to perfect virtue. However, people differed in capacity. Some excelled in ceremonies and music, others in government and educations; and still others in public works and agriculture. Therefore, in accordance with their moral achievement they were sent to school further to refine their abilities. When their virtue recommended them to government positions, they were able to serve in their positions throughout life without change.

Those who employed them desired only to be united with them in one mind and one character to bring peace to the people. They considered whether the individual's ability was suitable, and did not regard a high or low position as important or unimportant, or a busy or leisurely job as good or bad. Those who served also desired only to be united with their superiors in one mind and one character to bring peace to the people. . . . At that time people were harmonious and contented. They regarded one another as belonging to one family. Those with inferior ability were content with their positions as farmers, artisans, or merchants, all diligent in their various occupations, so as mutually to sustain and support the life of one another without any desire for exalted position or competition for external things. . . . For the learning of their mind was pure and clear and had what was requisite to preserve the humanity that made them and all things form one body. Consequently their spirit ran through and permeated all and their will prevailed and reached everywhere. There was no distinction between self and other, or between self and things. It is like the body of a person. The eyes see, the ears hear, the hands hold, and the feet walk, all fulfilling the functions of one body. The reason the learning [of the sage] can easily be achieved and the ability easily perfected is precisely that the fundamentals of the doctrine consist only in recovering what is common to our original minds, and are not concerned with any specific knowledge or skill.[24]

Antiquity thus served as a point of reference for thinking about the meaning of unity in practice. Neo-Confucians derided those who would judge the value of an act by its consequences. To adopt such a utilitarian strategy, they warned, was to make profit and advantage the measure of morality. To act from moral motivation was to act in accord with one's true nature and original mind; there was no need to worry about the outcome, for antiquity showed that the outcome would be a world of harmony and order. This was supported in philosophical terms as well.

THE UNITY OF DOCTRINE

The correctness of Neo-Confucian doctrine rested on a scientific claim and a historical claim. The scientific claim is that Neo-Confucians had a correct understanding of how the human as a biological being is integrated into the physical universe. The historical claim is that the doctrine they had rediscovered is in fact the way of learning of Confucius, Mencius, and the ancient sages. The Neo-Confucian commentaries and writings were vital to ensuring that the doctrine would continue to be understood correctly: they explain how the doctrine fits the human condition, they show that it is continuous with the thinking of Confucius, and they provide a means for transmitting the correct way of learning.

Zhu Xi's preface to his commentary on the *Mean* addresses all these issues but makes a particularly important claim about the unity of doctrine.[25] When Wang Yangming said, in the passage quoted above, that "the essentials of this teaching are what was successively transmitted by Yao, Shun, and Yu," he was following Zhu's preface. Zhu began with the purpose of the text—to preserve a record of how to learn the Way—but then shifted to the very first articulations of Learning of the Way in high antiquity.

Preface to the *Doctrine of the Mean by Chapter and Verse*

Why was the *Mean* written? [Confucius' grandson] Master Zisi wrote it because he was worried lest the transmission of the Learning of the Way (*dao xue*) be lost. The transmission of the Succession of the Way (*dao tong*) should have had its beginning when the divine sages of antiquity continued the work of Heaven and established the ultimate standard. As for this appearing in the Classics—there is [the phrase]

> Hold fast to the mean.[26]

which is what Yao gave to Shun. And

> The human mind is precarious.
> The moral mind is subtle.
> Have refined discrimination and singleness.
> Thus to hold fast to the mean.[27]

which is what Shun gave to Yu. Yao's one utterance is complete and all-inclusive, but Shun added three more in order to show that Yao's words can be fulfilled only in this way.

The term "Succession of the Way," used for the first time in this passage, would come to stand for the lineage of those who understood the Way correctly and thus had authority over values. Zhu's argument, which he took up again later in his preface, is that the single phrase "Hold fast to the mean" is an adequate statement of doctrine and that the use of four phrases is simply an elaboration that explains how to do it. He then clarified what his readers should understand this to mean.

I shall try to explain: the mind as the pure intelligence and consciousness is one and only one. But that I think there is a difference between the human mind (*ren xin*) and the moral mind (*dao xin*) is because the human mind comes into being from the personal particularity of physical form and *qi*, whereas the moral mind has its source in the correctness of the nature and destiny [endowed in all humans], and it is on this account that as consciousnesses they are different. Consequently, the human mind is in a precarious position [liable to evil] and is not secure, and the moral mind is subtle and not easily seen. However, all humans have this physical form, and therefore even the most intelligent necessarily possesses the human mind. And they all have this nature, and therefore even the most ignorant necessarily possesses the moral mind. The two minds are mixed in the space of a square inch [in the heart]. If we do not know how to manage them, what is precarious will become even more precarious and what is subtle will become even more subtle, and the impartiality of innate coherence (*tian li*) cannot in the end overcome the selfishness of human desires. Refined discrimination means to discriminate between the two so that they do not get mixed up, and singleness means to hold to the correctness of the original mind and not depart from it. If one devotes himself to this task without the slightest interruption, making sure that the moral mind is always the master of one's person and the human mind will obey it every time, then what is precarious will become secure and what is subtle will become manifest, and in tranquility and in action, in speech and in deed, one will be free of the error of going too far or not far enough.

Zhu's account of the single mind that has two sources of consciousness does not depend on the sages to be true. It is how the mind works universally; the enigmatic four sentences can be understood in terms of this reality. The physical constitution is particular to the individual, and thus people have different desires. However, all people possess a moral nature, "innate coherence," the totality of the *li* of the cosmos as an organic whole, and the goal of learning is to be able to sense this and ensure that its inclinations trump desires that arise from the physical constitution. However, this universalistic claim is combined with a historical one:

Yao, Shun, and Yu were great sages of the world, and to hand down the empire was a great affair of the world. If, when the great sages of the world undertook this great affair of the world, their repeated admonitions consisted of only so many words, then how could there be a *li* of the world that improved on them?

Given that those who created the empire in the first place took this doctrine as the key for ruling, we, too, should take this doctrine as authoritative. Zhu then asserted that this one idea was continued by sage rulers and ministers thereafter. Confucius stands apart. He was not a significant political figure, yet his accomplishment surpasses that of the first sages because he not only understood learning when others did not but also made it possible for others to understand it.

From this point on, one sage passed it on to another. King Tang [r. 1751–1739 B.C.?], King Wen [r. 1171–1122 B.C.], and King Wu [r. 1121–1116 B.C.] as sovereigns, and Gao Yao, Yi Yin, Fu Yue, the Duke of Zhou [d. 1094 B.C.], and Duke Shao [d. 1056 B.C.]* as ministers, all thanks to this continued the transmission of the tradition of the Way. As for our Master [Confucius], although he did not gain the official position he deserved, in the way he continued the past sages and enlightened future generations, his accomplishment was superior to that of Yao and Shun.† However, few understood him in his time. Only what was handed down by Yan Hui and Zeng Can apprehended the main line. But when it went to the Confucius' grandson Zisi, he was already at a distance from the sage and heterodox doctrines had arisen.

Zhu next developed his argument about the precarious state of this learning. Of all Confucius' disciples, only two got it right; moreover, by the generation of his grandson, the author of the *Mean*, divergent points of view had emerged. Zhu explained how Zisi went about writing the book.

Zisi feared that the further away from Confucius, the more the true account would be lost. So he found a basis in the ideas that had been passed down since Yao and Shun, verified them with what he had heard from his father and teacher, deducing one from the other, and wrote this book to instruct those who would learn in future generations. He feared for it deeply, and so he spoke about it pointedly; he thought about it far-reachingly, and so he explained it in detail. When he said [in the opening lines] "what heaven endows" and "following our nature," he was talking about the moral mind. When he said "choose the good and hold fast to it,"‡ he was talking about refined discernment and singleness [of mind]. And when he said "the superior man hits the mean at all times,"[28] he was talking about holding fast to the mean. He lived in an age more than a thousand years later, but what he said did not differ

---

*Gao Yao was a minister of Shun. Yi Yin helped Tang found the Shang dynasty. Fu Yue was a minister of Gaozong of Shang. The Duke of Zhou and Duke Shao were ministers of King Cheng of Zhou.

†Zhu is citing *Mencius* 2A2.

‡*Zhongyong*, sec. 20.

from the originals in any way but tallied with them perfectly. He made selections from various works of past sages. In bringing out the main principles and revealing the subtle points, no other work is as clear and as thorough as his.

Having argued that the *Mean* is in full agreement with the original doctrine, Zhu proceeded to argue that the works of Mencius are also simply a further elaboration of the original teaching. However, the transmission ended with Mencius and other teachings flourished, thus leading to a world in which Buddhists and Daoists could dominate thinking about morality.

After this, it was further transmitted, and there was Mencius. He was able to elaborate on and clarify this book and to continue the tradition of past sages, but with his death its transmission was lost. Consequently, our Way was consigned merely to words and writings. Heterodox doctrines arose with increasing novelty and strength to the point that when people like the Buddhists and Daoists emerged, the more their doctrines approached coherence, the more they violated its authentic form.

This brought Zhu to the eleventh century and the Cheng brothers; their ideas are a clarification of Zisi's work, which is in turn an elaboration of the original learning.

Fortunately, this book had not been lost. When the Masters Cheng, the two brothers, appeared, they had something to look into in order to continue the thread that had not been transmitted for a thousand years and had something to rely on in order to reproach the wrong that seemed to be the right of the two schools [of Buddhism and Daoism]. The contribution of Zisi was great, but were it not for the Cheng brothers, it would be impossible to understand his mind from his words. Unfortunately the Cheng brothers' explanations were lost. What Shi [Dun] compiled just came from the sayings recorded by pupils.[29] Thus, although the fundamental ideas were clear, the subtle words were not well explained.

The Chengs departed the world without leaving behind their specific explanations of the *Mean* as a text. This situation created an opening for their students, who unfortunately began to lose the main line and drift into Buddhism and Daoism. This set the stage for Zhu Xi.

As to the explanations their pupils did themselves, although they were detailed and comprehensive and offered many new interpretations, in some cases they violated their teachers' tenets and fell into the fallacies of Daoism and Buddhism. I read them at an early age and was skeptical. After some years of repeated pondering, one day I seemed suddenly to be able to understand its essential points. Thereupon I put the various interpretations together and arrived at a common ground. Thereupon I finished the *Mean in Chapters and Verses* in one chapter as the final version to offer to later scholars for their appraisal. Later, with one or two like-minded friends, I edited Shi Dun's compilation, deleting the overlapping and confused material, and entitled it *Abbreviated Collection*.[30] I further wrote down my discussions and my arguments for accepting or rejecting various interpretations to constitute my *Questions and Answers on the Mean* as an appendix. As a result, how the fundamental ideas of the *Mean* in their outline and details form a coordinated system are expressed briefly or fully as the case calls for and are presented in their major and minor aspects; in addition, the agreements and disagreements of the several interpretations and their merits and demerits can now be clarified and elucidated, and their meanings may now be fully understood. Although I dare not foolishly make any proposals about [who has shared in] the Succession of the Way, perhaps the beginning scholar may find something in this work. If so, it can be a help to those who want to travel far and scale the heights.

Thus, Zhu claimed, he had produced a text true not only to the Chengs but also to Mencius, Zisi, Confucius, and the founding sages that articulates the Learning of the Way in a manner appropriate for his day.

The unity, the restored continuity, of the Learning of the Way through millennia of change is the theme here. It is one that both had an appeal and generated questions. Why, asked a student of Wang Yangming, if "innately knowing the good is unitary," did different sages find different principles when they interpreted texts (in this case the *Book of Change*)? Wang's answer allows more leeway for difference than Zhu Xi might have liked, "How could these sages be confined to a single rigid pattern?" but he was no less committed to the idea that there was a single foundation for all the sages: "So long as they all sincerely proceeded from innate knowledge, what harm is there in each one's explaining it in his own way. . . . If all are the same in innately knowing the good, there is no harm in their being different here and there."[31] Wang's approach to the four-phrase doctrine differed more in nuance than in substance from Zhu's. He saw the moral mind as the original mind, with the human mind being that state the mind enters when desires start to intrude; thus, he called for people to recover their original mind by activating their innate ability to know the good.[32]

Much of Zhu Xi's intellectual career was devoted to shaping the legacy of the Northern Song moral philosophers into a consistent and coherent body of doctrine. He edited their works, produced a history of the school, and disputed other interpretations. There was an attempt, not successful, to get Zhu and Lu Jiuyuan, who himself had a significant following, to resolve their differences.[33] After Zhu's death, Lu's followers continued to promote his more intuitionist approach, and at least one observer, sympathetic to Zhu, thought that scholars were ignoring moral conduct in favor of abstract reflection on the ultimate coherence of things.[34]

Some have argued that we should not read the great doctrinal split between Zhu Xi and Wang Yangming that emerged in the sixteenth century back into earlier periods and have suggested that there was not such a sharp distinction between a Zhu Xi school and a Lu Jiuyuan school, both of which were concerned with the "learning of the mind."[35] There is much to this, but the potential challenge Lu Jiuyuan's views posed to Zhu Xi's was a real concern for Neo-Confucians well before Wang Yangming. Cheng Hao's opinions represented as much of a challenge, although that seems to have been largely overlooked at the time. It seems to me that the issue was a perceived need to assert the unity of Neo-Confucian doctrine, and that there was a desire to believe that any apparent contradictions could be resolved. This is evident in the work of Wu Cheng during the Yuan period, and it reappeared in 1489, well before Wang Yangming emerged as an intellectual force, when Cheng Minzheng (ca. 1445–ca. 1500) annotated the letters between Zhu Xi and Lu Jiuyuan in order to demonstrate that their initial disagreements were eventually resolved. He titled his work *The Way Is One Collection*.[36]

Wang Yangming shared this concern with the unity and continuity of doctrine. "If [my] doctrine of pulling up the root and stopping up the source does not clearly prevail in the world, people who are learning to become sages will be increasingly numerous, and their task increasingly difficult. They will then degenerate into animals and barbarians and still think this degeneration is the way to learn to become a sage."[37] And he tried to demonstrate that his position was perfectly congruent with Zhu Xi's by writing *Conclusions Reached by Master Zhu Late in Life*. As Wang Yangmingism spread and antagonistic Zhu and Wang camps emerged, anthologies seeking to mediate between the two or demonstrate the correctness of one side rather than the other began appearing.[38] The idea that there could only be one true doctrine was a necessary part of Neo-Confucianism; I am inclined to think that once different understandings of learning came to be seen as incompatible, Neo-Confucianism lost much of its authority.

THE UNITY OF THE MIND

The final aspect of the Neo-Confucian belief in unity has to do with learning to experience and maintain a mental state of unity. This is related to the mental experience of coherence, the moment of seeing how everything one has understood is connected together in a seamless whole, as if on a single thread;[39] it is the moment at which the mind, when its *li* meets with the *li* in things, grasps that all *li* are one *li*.[40] As Zhu Xi described it, the experience of total coherence is the product of cumulative effort.

After exerting himself for a long time, the student will one day achieve a wide and far-ranging integration (*tong* [also "penetration"]). Then the internal and external and the refined and coarse [aspects] of all things will be apprehended, and the mind, in its total substance and great functioning, will illuminate everything.[41]

However, unity as a mental state needs to be maintained whether we know a little or a lot. In that sense, it is not a goal to be worked toward but a state that has to be found and maintained as we learn, for it frees us of bias and enables us to see things clearly. As a state of internal equilibrium, it is the platform for making a decision about how to respond to things. In a state of unity, the mind is its own measure: it can tell whether it is being upset or divided. A response that arises in the mind and threatens to distort its impartiality or upset its equilibrium can be sensed, and this will be a sign that personal desire is intruding. In short, anything that threatens the mind's unified state can be classed as something that does not accord with innate coherence as the foundation of the mind.

Zhou Dunyi explained how to become a sage through learning with this statement:

The essential way is [for the mind] to be unified. What is unified has no desire. If it has no desire, then, when tranquil, it is vacuous and, when active, it is straightforward. When it is tranquil and vacuous, then it clearly illuminates; when it clearly illuminates, then it comprehends. When it is active and straightforward, then it is impartial; when it is impartial, then it is inclusive. To illuminate and comprehend and to be impartial and be inclusive—that comes very close [to perfection].[42]

If we assume with Zhou that the universe is in a state of organic wholeness and that the mind is originally attuned to this state, then desire is whatever distracts the contemplative mind, preventing it from illuminating and comprehending what is taking place around it, and thus keeping the active mind from seeing things impartially and responding appropriately.

Over the centuries, there was much debate over what the state of mind being sought was and how it could be experienced and maintained (or recovered). It seems to me that there is a distinction to be made between seeing a unified mental state as a means to impartial understanding and seeing it as something of fundamental moral significance. Cheng Yi and Zhu Xi, for example, took the term *jing*, traditionally meaning to show respect through behavior, and made it a term for a mental state: "[use] *jing* to straighten the internal, righteousness to square the external."[43] Translated as "inner mental attentiveness" or "seriousness,"[44] *jing* stands for the effort to keep one's attention focused. Here an equation of *jing* with unity simply means concentrating on "one" thing at any given moment and not letting the mind become distracted. This follows Cheng Yi's statement: "To concentrate on *yi* [one, unity] is what is meant by *jing*; not getting away is what is meant by *yi* [one, state of unity]."[45] This did have larger implications. Keeping the mind focused and undistracted was seen as essential to apprehending coherence and thus enabling a spontaneous coherent response.[46] *Cheng*, traditionally something like "sincerity," meant to be true to the mind's intimation of the good; that is, for the mind to be one with its innate coherence.[47] Cheng Yi also said: "To concentrate on *yi* [one thing] is what is meant by *jing*. *Yi* [the state of unity] is what is meant by *cheng*."[48]

The stronger reading understood *jing* as keeping the mind focused on "unity" itself and that a state of *jing* is attained by concentrating on unity. Zhang Shi, although relying on the first statement by Cheng Yi, held that there was a direct connection between concentrating on unity and being "humane" (*ren*) in the sense of being fully moral. The Way sustains the process of creation, Zhang argued, and humans, who are endowed with a nature that is in full accord with the Way, sustain the Way by realizing that nature through moral behavior. The danger is that we will be distracted and thus undermine the process of creation. This is why we must concentrate on unity. Anyone who nourishes this sense of unity always, without distraction, is on the path to realizing unity.[49] In other words, to ensure that the unified process of creation continues, one must keep the mind focused on unity itself. A belief in unity becomes the filter of correct ideas and inclinations.

This view fit well with the belief, shared by all sides, that unity was a particularly important and meaningful mental experience, not unlike the Chan sense of enlightenment. Yang Jian (1141–1226), who did much to systematize and spread Lu Jiuyuan's teachings, once described how in thinking about an admonition to reflect on himself, "suddenly I was aware of the emptiness in which there was no inside or out and no divisions, in which heaven, earth, and humanity and the myriad things, myriad transformations, and myriad affairs and the illuminated and the hidden, existence and nonexistence, were comprehended in a single, seamless body."[50] From this perspective, differentiating between things could be seen as a threat to maintaining a unified—that is, moral— attitude, as when Yang's fellow disciple explained that one needed to think about the ruler and the populace as a single body, for to be guided by their difference in social status would destroy the unity of the mind.[51]

During the Ming period, it became increasingly common to understand "concentrating on unity" as meaning keeping the mind in a unified state. Zhan Ruoshui, for example, objected that concentrating on one thing, as Zhu Xi preferred, is in fact destructive of the unity of the mind; keeping the mind unified means not letting any one thing impinge on it.[52] "Unity is the *li* of the mind," wrote Wang Shu (1416– 1508).[53] For Chen Xianzhang, coherence lies in the mind, it is its irreducible unitary source; keeping the mind vacuous (in the positive sense of open and totally receptive) and unified is essential, for otherwise we risk reducing the unity of the Way to what we learn through language and experience. The piecemeal quality of all perception and the fragmentary nature of all texts and language can never, however, capture the unity that is inherent in the mind. To respond to things morally is to respond from a state of mental unity.[54]

In emphasizing that "*li* is one but its manifestations are many" and "concentrating on one thing," Zhu Xi was trying to thwart those who thought that maintaining a mental sensation of unity or oneness would free them from having to pay attention to the particulars of things and circumstances. We do not have to look far to find the source of Zhu's concern within the Neo-Confucian camp. Cheng Hao had asserted:

Those who learn must first of all understand the nature of humanity (*ren*). The man of humanity *forms one body with all things without any differentiation.* Righteousness, propriety, wisdom, and faithfulness are all humanity.

One's duty is to understand this principle and preserve this humanity with *cheng* and *jing*—that is all. There is no need for caution and control. Nor is there any need for exhaustive search. Caution is necessary when one is mentally negligent, but if one is not negligent, what is the necessity of caution? Exhaustive search is necessary when one has not understood principle, but if one preserves humanity long enough, it will automatically dawn on him. Why should he have to depend on exhaustive search?[55]   (Italics added)

Having assumed the unity of creation, the existence of the innate coherence (*tian li*) guiding creation, as an organic whole in the self, Cheng Hao is content, it seems to me, to assert that anyone who truly maintains this belief in the unity of all things will practice humaneness and all the other virtues will fall into place just as the limbs coordinate with the entire body. To be immoral—to be selfish—is to divide, to lose that sense of unity, and to treat one part as more worthy than another.[56] Yang Shi had adopted the ideas that the unity of self with the myriad things defined humanity and that humanity was simply love for all; in response, Zhu Xi objected that "unity is not the reality that makes humanity a substance"; that is, it is not a state of consciousness.[57]

Nevertheless, Cheng Hao's view found repeated support among those in Song, Yuan, and Ming who emphasized the fundamental importance of the unity of *li* and the ability of the mind to respond to things from an awareness of one's unity with heaven-and-earth and the myriad things.[58] Even Hu Juren, who agreed that some people, such as Chen Xianzhang, were practicing "being one with heaven-and-earth and the myriad things" at the expense of "investigating things," argued that one needs only to investigate things and apprehend their coherence at the very first stage of learning, just enough to persuade oneself that things are in fact coherent. After that, one needs only *jing*, because the unity of *li* is, after all, in the mind.[59] "Concentrating on unity" was, I suggest, about maintaining belief.

This suggests that what Jin Lüxiang meant by the "pure and sincere mind" being able to make the right choice, what Zhu Xi meant by the moral mind of the "mind of the way," and what the Chengs and others meant by *tian li*, innate coherence, was nothing other than a belief in unity that had been cultivated to the point that it was not apparent to oneself that it was a belief at all.

This applies to Wang Yangming as well. In his "Inquiry on the *Great Learning*," Wang argued that what Zhu Xi had taken to be progressive, sequential steps were in fact simultaneously occurring activities described from different perspectives. But for this to work—and Wang had a cogent explanation for why this should work—we have to grant his initial premise:

The great man regards heaven-and-earth and the myriad things as one body. He regards the world as one family and the country as one person. As for those who make a cleavage between objects and distinguish between the self and others, they are small men. That the great man can regard heaven-and-earth and the myriad things as one body is not because he deliberately wants to do so, but because it is natural to the humane nature of his mind to do so. Forming one body with heaven-and-earth and the myriad things is not only true of the great man. Even the mind of the small man is no different. Only he himself makes it small.[60]

The sense of being one with all things is, in Wang's view, natural to the human mind. To "manifest the clear character," "love the people," and "abide in the highest good" are nothing more than the expressions of this sensibility in practice. And it is precisely this ethic that is articulated in practice by "innately knowing the good." Wang put forward the same premise in one of his most famous statements of what it means to be morally engaged with society, "Pulling up the Root and Stopping up the Source."

The mind of a sage regards heaven-and-earth and the myriad things as one body. He looks upon all the people of the world, whether inside or outside his family, or whether far or near, but all with blood and breath, as his brothers and children. He wants to secure, preserve, educate, and nourish all of them, so as to fulfill his desire to form one body with all things. Now the mind of everybody is at first not different from that of the sage. Only because it is obstructed by selfishness and blocked by material desires, what was originally great becomes small and what originally comprehensive becomes obstructed. Everyone has his own selfish view, to the point where some regard their father, son, and brothers as enemies. The Sage worried over this. He therefore extended the humanity that made him form one body with heaven-and-earth and all things to teach the world, so as to enable the people to overcome their selfishness, remove their obstruction, and recover that which is common to the substance of the minds of all men.

The essentials of this teaching are what was successively transmitted by Yao, Shun, and Yu, and what is summed up by the saying, "The human mind is precarious, the mind of the Way is subtle. Have refined discrimination and unity [of mind] thus to hold fast the mean."[61]

Although Zhu and Wang differed in many respects, they shared the same beliefs that humans are part of a single organic whole and that the goal of learning is to enable the individual to realize this so that he may participate in the realization of this unity in human society. They also shared the same fear that selfishness—that is, to act from a position in which the interests of the self rather than unity motivate behavior—will make this impossible. And they shared the view that this problem had a solution, namely, that humans must learn to rely on their own minds, minds that, as we have seen, must be focused on unity in the first place.

⸺

The belief in unity—of the cosmos as an organic system, of antiquity as an integrated social order, of doctrine as universal and unchanging, and of the mind's experience of oneness—was at odds with the world in which Neo-Confucians lived. The alternative moral orders of Buddhism and Daoism continued to flourish, literati opinion was never fully persuaded of the validity of Neo-Confucian views, foreign powers invaded and conquered, natural disasters struck, literati reinterpreted doctrine, and, from the emperor on down, the minds of men lost the battle with selfish desire. A belief in unity went together with an understanding that the world in which Neo-Confucians lived was very different.

Yet this fundamental tension between how the world was and how it ought to be gave Neo-Confucians a common purpose. To restore an integrated order in the present, they had to begin by recognizing that the world in its present state was not good enough. The all-encompassing hierarchical order of the early imperial system, justified as the human counterpart to heaven-and-earth, had once claimed to be the realization of unity in practice. If that had not been entirely true in fact, it had been maintained symbolically through ritual and writing. But the Neo-Confucians shifted the focus of a belief in unity away from the imperial system and into the mind as something individuals embodied and could act on. They had internalized the classical idea of empire.

Once the very idea of empire had been internalized, it was no longer necessary to maintain the fiction that the political order was the only possible way to achieve integration, harmony, continuity, and unity. It was not that government was incapable of serving this great purpose, if the right men led it, but that in practice it was not doing so and was unlikely to do so under present circumstances. And thus to make a difference, Neo-Confucians had to persuade others to share their cause, and they had to find ways of acting for the common good on their own. This leads us to the Neo-Confucianism as a movement in society.

7

Society

It might seem paradoxical that people who believed that unity was the ultimate test of all that was right and good would create a tension between themselves and the political-social order by claiming that the ultimate source of moral authority lay outside politics, history, and culture but was accessible to men who engaged in true learning. As literati (*shi*), they were part of the national social and political elite; government service was their prerogative, and their status as the national elite depended on the survival of the political system. Moreover, their ideal world was free of tension, paradox, contradiction, and ambivalence; it did not need Neo-Confucians. In the world of the sage-kings, all were bound together in a single community, there was no disjunction between how people should live and how they did live, and the political, economic, social, and cultural orders were one and the same.

But there is no paradox. Neo-Confucians recognized that those in power were not sages, and the literati acted out of self-interest. Emperors were sometimes tyrants, and literati were sometimes people who had to be warned, as one Neo-Confucian put it, "not to murder themselves through cleverness, murder others through government, murder their descendants through examination studies, and murder the future through learning."[1] Setting the world right depended on the people who shared responsibility for it choosing to pursue true learning and to act accordingly.

In Southern Song and Yuan, and then again in the second half of the Ming period, Neo-Confucians set out to persuade literati to become sages by creating a distinctive program of literati education, offering them an alternative model for the family, and encouraging them to lead voluntary institutions to improve conditions in local society. They were to be the vanguard, the "first to become aware" (*xian juezhe*), who would be a model for others and would lead them in bringing about what I shall call "self-supervising moral communities." Maintaining the distinctiveness of their endeavors—relative to both government and religious institutions—was crucial to their mission. In distinguishing what they were doing from the alternatives, they were asking literati to make what they saw as the fundamental moral choice in life: between "righteousness" (*yi*) and "profit" (*li*), between self-seeking and being true to their moral nature. That is, joining in Neo-Confucian endeavors was supposed to be different from pursuing power and wealth, from going along with the status quo in politics and society; it was a chance to act on the basis of personal moral motivation rather than for an ulterior, self-interested purpose. I shall call this a commitment to "voluntarism" and use that term to describe actions seen as being motivated by a commitment to "righteousness." The voluntary institutions that marked Neo-Confucian programs for education, family, and local society often were labeled as *yi*—for example, a granary for lending grain to those in need was called an *yi cang*—a term sometimes translated as "charitable" or "community." Voluntarism was morally significant as long as there was a significant distance between what the Neo-Confucians saw as morally responsible behavior and socially acceptable and legally mandated behavior; we shall see that in the early Ming this distance was greatly diminished when an unprecedented program of social legislation mandated the institution of self-supervising moral communities.

There were "pure" Neo-Confucians and there were more accommodating ones, but by and large they maintained the kind of distinctiveness that accompanies seeing oneself as a righteous minority in a corrupt world. However, the pure among them did not imitate the Buddhists and try to create communities that divorced their members from the demands of political power, society, and the economy; and the accommodating saw themselves as getting the system to adopt their program rather than as accepting the system's demands on them.

The attempt to maintain distinctiveness led to ambivalence on both sides. Neo-Confucians could have doubts about the political, cultural, social, and economic orders of the day, but they still had to take them into account, and for their part government and local elites had to decide how far to accommodate Neo-Confucian activities. During the thirteenth century, the Neo-Confucians had great success in advancing their program among literati and at court. Zhu Xi died in 1200, in the middle of the court's proscription of the Learning of the Way as a "false learning," one requirement of which was that examination candidates certify that they were not adherents. Yet in 1212 the court allowed state schools to make available to students Zhu Xi's commentaries on the *Analects* and the *Mencius*, and finally in 1241 it granted the request to remove Wang Anshi from the Confucian Temple and install Zhu Xi, the Cheng brothers, Zhou Dunyi, and Zhang Zai.[2] In the sixteenth century, the court would similarly resist and then give in to requests that Wang Yangming be included in the Temple.[3] However, honoring Neo-Confucians in the Confucian Temple did not mean that the court listened when Neo-Confucians submitted memorials, lectured at the Classics Mat, or served as imperial tutors, and reading Neo-Confucian texts for the civil service examinations did not mean the literati accepted the claims those texts advanced. Nevertheless, state recognition and the end to persecution were signs of the Neo-Confucians' increasing success in persuading the literati public of the importance of their cause.

Creating a Choice in Literati Learning in Song and Yuan

During the course of the Northern Song period, the pool of men who could call themselves *shi*, literati, by virtue of their education for the examinations expanded. The expansion culminated under the New Policies with an unprecedented investment in a national school system, including a system of schools internally organized into three grades that extended down to the county level, changes in the content of the examinations, and the creation of a national curriculum that would be taught in the schools and tested in the examinations. At one point in the early twelfth century, almost 200,000 men were registered at the schools. The expansion of opportunity, together with a doubling in the size of the bureaucracy, pulled rich and powerful local families into education. At the same time, a variety of new economic institutions and social organizations increased the government's role in local society at the expense of those same families, giving them an added incentive to join the ranks of literati, the one status the state recognized and privileged as the pool from which it drew its officials. Among the tangible rewards for investment in an examination education were tax relief for registered students, contact with local officials, protection from the demands of clerks and lawsuits, and social connections with other leading local families.[4]

In Southern Song, the bureaucracy shrank by half to about 20,000 civil officials, the school system lost its monopoly on examination education, and the government reduced spending on local education, but the numbers of those pursuing a literati education continued to increase. This made it ever more unlikely that a literatus would pass the examinations or hold office—less than a third of Zhu Xi's 500-some students are known to have held office[5]—but it created careers for literati as teachers and a market for their books. There must have been far more men working as teachers, as household tutors, lineage school instructors, and private academy lecturers than there were active civil officials.[6]

The state educational system was closely tied to the examination system; from an institutional perspective, it was a means of recruiting officials. Each county and prefecture in Southern Song was limited to a single official school. Applicants entered the county school by passing a test. Once admitted, they were provided with instruction and lodging and could test for admission to the prefectural school. The prefectural school held examinations that qualified students for the next higher level: the Ministry of Rites examination during the Song and the provincial examination thereafter. Passing the triennial Ministry examination guaranteed that one would pass the palace examination, receive a *jinshi* degree, and be given official rank (during the Ming provincial graduates could also gain a post). The number of stipended places in a school was quite limited, hundreds for prefectural schools and tens for county schools.[7] The Ming dynasty initially set the quotas for the number of certified (and stipended) students (*shengyuan*) at forty for the prefecture, thirty for the subprefecture (*zhou*), and twenty for the county (*xian*), but within twenty years it began to enlarge the quotas and eventually allowed students to be certified (and thus eligible to take higher examinations) without receiving a stipend. It did not, however, expand the number of *jinshi* degrees.[8] The number of certified students was far less than the number of people who wished to participate in the examinations. In Southern Song, students could sit for the qualifying examinations without being stipended students, and by the mid-thirteenth century 400,000 were participating in the examination cycle; perhaps five times as many had a similar education.[9] By late Ming, there may have been 500,000 certified students, but perhaps ten times as many were seeking certification.[10] It is certainly possible that 10 percent of the male population from Southern Song on had some degree of literati education.

From a Neo-Confucian perspective, this demand for teachers and schools, which exceeded what the government could supply, was both an opportunity and a challenge. This large potential audience was concerned more with examinations and literati status than with moral cultivation. Neo-Confucian rhetoric contrasted the Learning of the Way with the kind of studies found in the government schools. Neo-Confucian learning, they claimed, represented what Confucius had called "learning for oneself" (*wei ji zhi xue*), whereas examination education was merely "learning for others" (*wei ren zhi xue*). Learning for oneself meant becoming aware of one's innate coherence and realizing it in practice, whereas examination education merely trained literati to satisfy others' criteria.[11] The idea that education ought to develop a person's potential was widely shared—it was also a goal of New Policies education—but Neo-Confucians raised the ante, proposing that literati ought to aim at nothing less than sagehood and saving the world. As Cheng Hao had explained to the emperor in his day: "The essential training should be the way of choosing the good and cultivating the self until the whole world is transformed and brought to perfection, so that all people from the ordinary person on up can becomes sages."[12] Zhu Xi called on his audience, many of whom came from families that aspired to *shi* status, to go beyond their social aspirations to higher moral goals: "Those who learned in antiquity began by acting as literati and ended by acting as sages. That is to say, if they knew how to act as literati, then they knew how to act as sages. Those who act as literati today are many, but I have not yet heard of any who have attained sagehood."[13]

Positioning themselves outside the examinations and state schools allowed the Neo-Confucians to argue that the choice was between self-seeking and a commitment to morality. Forty years after Zhu's death, when state schools were beginning to acknowledge the importance of the Learning of the Way, this rhetoric was still common. The contrast, a Neo-Confucian teacher argued, was between public education and private education. The school system was meant to prepare the literati for government service; it served "literati who, seeking to get ahead and be employed, begin by entering the school, and thus schools became the path of fame and profit." But those who wanted to realize "the substance of moral principles . . . depend on teachers who discourse privately."[14]

There was some truth to this claim. Government schools did teach to the examinations. There were annual, monthly, and weekly tests, and no matter what the content of the examinations, passing them required composing works in specific literary genres in fairly well defined styles. The sheer number of candidates pushed examiners to rely on the most objective criteria possible—it was easier to fail candidates for a mistake in composition than for the quality of their ideas, the sincerity of their purpose, or the degree of their effort. In Southern Song, a candidate for the *jinshi* degree could opt to be tested on his literary skills—a regulated verse poem, a rhapsody, a prose essay, and treatises on public policy or scholarship—and his knowledge of the Classics as instituted under the New Policies (but without requiring the New Policies commentaries) with essays on the meaning of passages from the Classics, a prose essay, and treatises on policy or scholarship. When the examinations were reinstated in 1315, and in the Ming, all candidates were required to write essays on passages from the Four Books and a Classic of choice, compositions in various literary forms, and treatises on policy or scholarship. By the end of the fifteenth century, the essays on the Four Books had to be written in the form of the rigorously structured "eight-legged essay."[15]

But the claim that the only choice was between a morally responsible education with private Neo-Confucian teachers and examination training in a state school obscured the diversity in education and thought in

Southern Song. Literati could find private teachers and schools that offered both examination training and intellectually engaging (but not
Neo-Confucian) curricula. Consider, for example, the situation in Wuzhou (modern Jinhua) in central Zhejiang, which became a leading center of Neo-Confucian learning thanks to Lü Zuqian, who compiled the
Neo-Confucian primer *Reflections on Things at Hand* with Zhu Xi and had
gathered students at his residence when he was not serving in government. There (and elsewhere) private publishers offered new editions of
the writings of Su Shi and his family, works that provided not only
models for literary composition useful in the examination but also the
essentials of their way of thinking about government, the Way, and
sagehood. Their popularity, even among Zhu Xi's allies, prompted Zhu
both to criticize his friends for thinking one could write like Su Shi
without thinking like him and to compose his own polemic against Su
Shi and his brother for their Buddhist and Daoist tendencies.[16]

Wuzhou was also home to Chen Liang (1143–94), who gained a reputation as a teacher and writer well before passing the examinations in
1193, the year before his death. Chen admired the Ancient Style writers
of Northern Song, but his fame lay in advocacy of a historical approach
to statecraft in opposition to Zhu Xi's idealization of antiquity and focus on personal morality. The leading statecraft scholar of the day, Ye
Shi (1150–1223) from nearby Wenzhou, had also taught in Wuzhou and
had a large following there; although Ye had been listed as a proponent
of False Learning in 1198, he and Zhu Xi had already parted ways.[17]

Wuzhou was one of the most successful prefectures in the country
in the examinations, taking about ten *jinshi* degrees at every sitting by
the end of the twelfth century, and one of the most competitive.[18] It
owed much of its success to the proliferation of private schools funded
by wealthy families. Some of these were influenced by Neo-Confucian
teachings. For example, Guo Qinzhi (1128–before 1190) founded the
Stone Grotto Academy (Shidong shuyuan) in the 1160s. Guo himself
had once studied with the Neo-Confucian Zhang Jiucheng (1092–1159),
and his sons became followers of Zhu Xi. Stone Grotto remained active for at least thirty years and was visited by a number of luminaries:
the famous writer Lu You, the classicist Tang Zhongyou (1136–88)
(himself from Wuzhou), and the statecraft scholars Chen Fuliang (1137–
1203) and Ye Shi from Wenzhou.[19] But others were clearly not associ-

ated with either Neo-Confucianism or Ye Shi's statecraft school. Tang Zhongyou had returned to Wuzhou in 1182, his career but not (yet) his reputation destroyed by Zhu Xi's memorials charging him with immoral conduct and malfeasance as prefect of Taizhou. He was a scholar of "broad learning" (*bo xue*), producing books on the Classics, statecraft, geography, astronomy, poetic composition, and history. On his return, Tang had begun teaching, but he soon moved, with over one hundred of his students, to neighboring Dongyang county to accept a position as the headmaster of the Antian Community School (Antian yi shu), an academy with a library and endowment established by the wealthy Wu Wenbing in 1174. There he succeeded Xu Ji, who had studied with the Hanlin Academician Zhu Zhen, a proponent of numerological studies of the *Book of Change* and of synthesizing Cheng Yi's philosophy with Han through Tang thought. Xu himself was famous for being able to write Ancient Style prose in the style of Ouyang Xiu and Zeng Gong. Tang was in turn succeeded by Fu Yin (1148–1215), who never held office. Fu published a book on the "Tribute of Yu," an early geographical text, and compiled an encyclopedia that became the foundation for the *Investigation of the Multitude of Books* by Zhang Ruyu (*jinshi* 1196), another local headmaster.[20] These teachers and schools were intellectually eclectic and prepared students for the examination, but they were also centers of broad learning.

Zhu Xi's concern to maintain the distinctiveness of the Learning of the Way and to keep it from being treated as merely one strand in the variegated weave of intellectual culture is evident in his efforts to keep Lü Zuqian in line. Lü came from the most illustrious ministerial family of Northern Song; his forebears included chief councilors and high officials and supporters and students of the Cheng brothers. His branch had fled the north and been provided housing by the Wuzhou government. Given his pedigree, his support for Zhu Xi's teachings was particularly welcome. Lü created a formal association of his students in the late 1160s and early 1170s,[21] and after Lü's death his supporters persuaded local officials to build a shrine to him, which, some thirty years later, became the Lize Academy.[22] Lü worked to ensure that the Neo-Confucian message was heard. He arranged with Zhu Xi to have a bookseller ship at least one hundred copies of the *Essential Meanings of the Analects* for local purchase[23] and found a local donor to sponsor the republication of Zhou Dunyi's *Tongshu* and Cheng Yi's *Commentary on the Change*.[24] In all this Lü was an exemplary Neo-Confucian, but he had also passed a special examination for men of great literary talent and, at imperial command, had compiled the most important anthology of Northern Song writing, now known as the *Mirror of Song Literature*. More to the point, it is clear that Lü recruited students by offering to prepare them for the examinations. In devoting time to literary learning and examination teaching, Lü crossed a line that some Neo-Confucians did not think he should cross. Zhang Shi wrote to Lü and Zhu objecting.[25] Zhu Xi objected as well and took Lü to task for the kinds of "nonsense" (i.e., books printed for examination education) being printed in Wuzhou. Lü Zuqian defended himself:

> You say that examination learning is of no value for perfecting the self and perfecting things. However, in the past in Jinhua, one studied alone without anyone with whom to discuss things and improve oneself. Were I to get rid of examination training, the local literati would feel cut off. They would have no reason to be in contact with one another. Thus I offer the opportunity of examination training to get them to come. Then, from among them I choose those of promise and talk to them. Recently a good many have been turning in our direction. Since last fall I have offered one class [for the examinations] every ten days, just to keep them. But when it comes to what one ought to discuss about engaging in learning, I do the right thing.[26]

Lü apparently did not think he could compete unless he helped students prepare for the examinations. Zhu would later deny that Lü was a true Neo-Confucian, arguing that fundamentally he had a historical point of view rather than thinking in terms of the constant verities of the Classics, but Lü agreed that spreading the Learning of the Way required an alternative curriculum.[27]

A NEW CURRICULUM

We can, I think, best understand Zhu Xi's leadership in creating a comprehensive curriculum as an effort to show that the Learning of the Way was adequate for all areas of literati learning. In doing so, however, he was competing less with the examination training offered at the state schools and more with the successful but eclectic private schools and academies. The core of this new curriculum was the modern texts that laid out the new way of thinking: the editions Zhu and his allies produced, with commentaries, of the writings and oral teachings of Zhou Dunyi, Zhang Zai, and the Cheng brothers. The texts of the Northern Song masters, together with editions of Zhu Xi's conversations and his own collected writings, defined a new set of Confucian philosophers. Just as important was the creation of a new set of Classics, the Four Books. For the *Analects* and the *Mencius*, Zhu cited over thirty other authorities (but mainly the Cheng brothers and their followers), and he wrote carefully worked-out commentaries on the *Doctrine of the Mean* and the *Great Learning*, transforming these two texts into primary vehicles for Neo-Confucian doctrine.[28] In contrast to the Five Classics, the Four Books explicitly address issues of personal cultivation. In Zhu Xi's hands, they became the vehicle for a coherent philosophy, clearly distinct from earlier interpretations, and evidence for his claim that the Learning of the Way was the learning of the sages of antiquity.[29]

Zhu did not neglect the traditional Five Classics. With some reservations, he accepted Hu Anguo's commentary on the *Spring and Autumn Annals*, which applied Cheng Yi's philosophy to the interpretation of the one major Classic excluded from the New Policies curriculum. Zhu himself wrote two works on the *Book of Change*: the *Introduction to the Study of the Change for Beginners* and the *Original Meaning of the Zhou Change*.[30] At Zhu Xi's behest, Cai Shen (1167–1230) produced his *Collected Commentary on the Book of Documents*.[31] Zhu began and his students finished an exhaustive study of a ritual classic rejected by the New Policies curriculum, *The Comprehensive Explication of the Classic of Ceremonies and Rites and Its Commentaries*.[32] And he produced the *Collected Commentaries on the Book of Odes*.[33]

Zhu took on history as well. He produced a sort of intellectual history of the Cheng school[34] and a collection of biographies of Northern Song statesmen, which his grandson extended into Southern Song.[35] With the *Digest of the Comprehensive Mirror for Aid in Government*, Zhu and his students transformed Sima Guang's great chronological history, the *Comprehensive Mirror for Aid in Government*, from a work intended to show that history revealed the necessary principles for ordering the state into one meant to train students in passing moral judgment on individual political behavior.[36] Nor did Zhu neglect literature. He composed a collected commentary on the *Songs of Chu*, a foundational text of the literary tradition, and a critical edition and commentary on Han Yu's literary collection, a foundational text for writing in the Ancient Style.[37]

Zhu Xi also organized the compilation of two other works that would be of signal importance because they spoke to the question of how to learn and act. The *Elementary Learning* (*Xiao xue*), a work intended to guide the instruction of younger students, used quotations from the Classics, histories, Song Neo-Confucian texts, and other works to set out the moral purpose of education; its realization in the Five Relationships (in the order parent-child, ruler-minister, husband-wife, elder-younger, and friend-friend); and the fundamental importance of taking oneself seriously as a moral actor in society ("reverencing oneself," or *jing shen*) through the cultivation of the mind, comportment, dress, and eating.[38] *Reflections on Things at Hand*, consisting of quotations from the oral teachings and writings of the Cheng brothers, Zhang Zai, and Zhou Dunyi, was arranged to show how the first Neo-Confucians thought about cosmology, learning and self-cultivation, the family, serving (or not) in government, government and institutions, teaching, Buddhism and Daoism, and the sages and worthies of antiquity and the Song.[39] Some Neo-Confucians thought students should read these two works before taking up the Four Books.[40]

From the perspective of all that was being published in the Song, the texts coming from Zhu and his school were merely some among many. Zhu was well aware of this. He once drew up a proposal for a reform of the school and examinations systems that called for a comprehensive study of the Classics (with multiple commentaries), histories, philosophers, and literature, one that did not privilege his own school, although we may be sure that Zhu did not think they fundamentally challenged his position; but he never submitted it.[41] We can also find examples of individuals of comparable breadth of learning (such as Tang Zhongyou and Lü Zuqian). Yet no other scholar combined breadth with such philosophical coherence; the result is that Zhu's corpus of historical, philosophical, canonical, and literary works served as a carefully conceived intellectual agenda.

Some Neo-Confucian teachers would later contend that Zhu Xi had put together a body of work that made further writings unnecessary; students simply needed to engage the program of learning and self-cultivation. In practice, however, this corpus provided a foundation for writing and publishing ever more commentaries, reading notes, records of oral teaching, philosophical tracts, letters, collected writings, primers, biographies, and anthologies. It provided a framework for later scholars to produce works that contributed to the Neo-Confucian discourse on learning, rather than offering an alternative to it, and it created communities of readers and commentators with shared knowledge of a body of texts, a common vocabulary, and common issues to dispute. Studying the texts became a way of being a good Neo-Confucian, as Sun Yingshi (1154–1206), an admirer of both Zhu and Lu Jiuyuan, wrote: "Classical studies has become the means of apprehending coherence, realizing the moral nature, establishing the Way, and completing virtue."[42]

THE ACADEMIES

Creating a curriculum went together with creating places where literati would devote themselves to learning it. This was the academy (*shuyuan*). The later imperial academy originated in the proliferation of private schools in the south. Some were funded by wealthy families to prepare lineage members for the examinations; the more ambitious might hire a teacher of some reputation and welcome outsiders. Some were created by the teachers themselves—retired officials or local scholars—and were presumably funded by the students, who might come from distant prefectures, as was the case with Zhu Xi's students. Academies were not at first necessarily committed to a particular curriculum, although the teachers might well have particular intellectual interests. They increased the opportunity for a higher-quality education, they provided an intellectual center for the local literati elite, and they gave the donors considerable prestige.[43]

Neo-Confucians soon began to see the academy as a place where they could transmit their learning, particularly at a time when it was still excluded from discussion in government schools. It allowed them to control membership and to install a curriculum and practice a method of teaching that served their pedagogical aims. But because their founders distinguished them from the state schools and from examination education, Neo-Confucian academies also represented a choice to pursue learning for the sake of oneself. For some, this was part of their attraction, and their students were known to draw attention to that difference by walking, talking, and dressing in a style of their own.[44] Some

Neo-Confucian academies created rules for student conduct, telling them, among other things, how to sit (stay erect, do not splay or cross the legs), how to listen (without staring or cocking the ear), how to dress (simply and cleanly, always keeping the head and feet covered), how to eat (plainly and only at appointed times, wine only at festivals), how to write (square style only, no cursive script), how to address others (as elder or older brother, according to their birth order, rather than using other status terms), how to use their free time (lute-playing, archery, or pitchpot, but not chess), and how to treat the servants (firmly but kindly).[45] The sense that they were different from others was made clear in the desire, at least on the part of the teachers, to show that Neo-Confucian students were self-disciplined and not self-indulgent, were upright and not slack, were austere and not profligate, and were focused on the moment rather than cunningly planning for future advantage. This, and the desire to preserve their distinctiveness, added weight to the Neo-Confucians' conviction that they alone were capable of transforming society.[46]

But what was a Neo-Confucian academy supposed to accomplish? Zhu Xi's proclamation for the White Deer Grotto Academy in Nankang, Jiangxi, which he rebuilt in 1180, long after it had fallen into ruin, became the most influential guideline:

The sages and worthies of antiquity taught people to pursue learning with one intent only, that was to make students understand the meaning of moral coherence (*yili*) through discussion, so that they could cultivate their own persons and then extend it to others. The sages and worthies did not wish them merely to engage in memorizing texts or in composing poetry and essays as a means of gaining fame or seeking office. . . . If you understand what ought to be so on the basis of coherence and accept responsibility yourself for making it be so, then you will not depend on others setting up rules and prohibitions for you to hold fast to. In recent times, regulations have been instituted in schools, and students have been treated in a shallow manner. This method of making regulations does not at all conform with the intentions of the ancients. . . . Rather, I have selected all the essential principles that the sages and worthies have used in teaching people how to pursue learning . . . follow them, take personal responsibility for their observance. . . . If you do otherwise or reject what I have said, then the regulations others speak of will have to take over.[47]

Using short quotations from Confucian texts, Zhu defined the essential principles of how to pursue learning as a combination of subject, method, and practice. The subject should be the Five Relationships: "for those who engage in learning, they are all they need to learn." The method was to "apprehend coherence" through a sequence of "study, inquiry, pondering, and making distinctions." And practice was to go from personal cultivation (be sincere in word and deed, curb anger and lust, and correct errors) to handling affairs (be guided by moral coherence not personal advantage), to dealing with others (do not do to others what you would not have them do to you; if you fail in practice, seek the cause in yourself).[48]

For later times, the significance of the White Deer Grotto Academy lay in the idea that literati could form a community to devote themselves to learning as a process of personal cultivation, that they could be guided by the principles of the endeavor rather than the rules and punishments common to the state schools (although Zhu was willing to bring them to bear if his advice was not followed), and that by doing so they were establishing a viable alternative to examination education. Students should be there because they had chosen to be there.

But Zhu Xi was not simply rebuilding a place that had once been an academy about which little was known. Although he certainly encouraged government school students to see learning by his lights, he chose not to improve or add to the local state schools, something that was well within his power to do, for Zhu Xi was in Nankang as the prefect, responsible for three poor counties. By Zhu's own testimony, Nankang did not have a particularly strong literati community or large numbers of examination candidates. In fact, in discussions with students elsewhere, Zhu had made it clear that he opposed using government money to strengthen prefectural and county state schools as real centers of learning (for example, by restoring the graded school system of the New Policies era), on the grounds that it would be too expensive given the large demand. This was, as he knew, a departure from the Cheng brothers, who thought students should be supported by a state school system.[49] But Zhu did want two things from the government, and his position as prefect empowered him to force the issue. First, he wanted the court to recognize the legitimacy of what he was doing—by explicitly allowing it and by giving gifts of books and an official signboard, written preferably by the emperor himself. Second, he wanted the court to agree to what he had already done: he had used government officials, funds, land, and corvée labor to carry out the building project in addition to contributions of cash and land from the local literati elite. This created a precedent that would give his allies in government license to establish Neo-Confucian academies using government resources wherever they served. But the court did not agree (until after Zhu had accepted a new post in Zhejiang), even when Zhu insisted that it agree or he be allowed to quit his post and assume the position of headmaster.[50]

In short, what Zhu had in mind was the state's acceptance of the co-existence of a Neo-Confucian counterpart to its network of prefectural and county schools, an alternative that would be controlled by Neo-Confucian teachers and supported by local elites but able to tap the state's resources without becoming responsible for preparing students for the examinations. The White Deer Grotto Academy was successful when Zhu was there, and it was a magnet for scholars in the region, although its buildings had an uneven history and were not consistently maintained in good repair until the Ming dynasty. State recognition and support would encourage students to attend, and Zhu himself demanded that the local students who had passed the prefectural qualifying exams spend the summer there before they went to the capital for the next examination.

The Neo-Confucian academies built after Zhu Xi's death and after the removal of the proscription of Neo-Confucianism as False Learning continued the pattern set by White Deer Grotto of maintaining ideological control over the academy and its curriculum, raising support from local elites, and asking for recognition from the court and financial aid from local government. Some were extensions of a local shrine to Neo-Confucian masters, an endeavor Zhu Xi himself had encouraged. Although not all were devoted to Neo-Confucianism and more were built than the court was willing to recognize or local government to support, increasingly Neo-Confucians in government used their influence and resources to found academies that would coexist with the local government school. By the end of Song, literati and officials who saw themselves as part of the Neo-Confucian movement had founded perhaps sixty academies on this model.[51] An example is the great "Illumined Way" (Ming dao) Academy in Jiankang prefecture (modern Nanjing), which commemorated Cheng Hao and was officially recognized in 1256. It had an endowment of 4,900 *mou* of fields spread over five counties.

The prefectural government gave it 5,000 strings of cash a month (it had received 100,000 strings annually at one point) to cover the salaries and allowances of instructors and attendants, the stipends and allowances of the students, and support for descendants of Cheng Hao.[52]

When in 1264 the court ordered that all academy headmasters be officially commissioned (although this seems to have applied only to the directors of officially recognized academies), it gave official sanction to the idea of a dual system. One such headmaster, Ouyang Shoudao, celebrated this event but made the point that the position of headmaster should be reserved for men of "pure scholarship": even if they had official status, they should be men who were interested more in learning than in an official career, for although the academies helped career-oriented literati, they also made a place for those literati who did not wish to become part of government.[53]

Government support for academies was resumed in the south less than twenty years after it was conquered and absorbed into the Mongols' Yuan dynasty in 1279. Legislation formally protected academies from encroachment and gave special recognition to those who privately founded academies, but it also ordered that the state school system be expanded down to the elementary-school level. The government soon resumed responsibility for appointing and salarying the headmasters and endowed academies with land rents. Well before the examinations, now based on the Neo-Confucian Four Books, were reinstated in 1315, Neo-Confucian learning had become the dominant strain in literati learning in the south and Zhu Xi and other Neo-Confucian masters had been enshrined in the academies.[54]

What did government support in late Song and Yuan imply? Some argue that when the academies and Zhu Xi's Neo-Confucianism received government sponsorship, and when the position of headmaster became a way of entering the regular bureaucracy, the academies became part of the governing apparatus, thus losing the independence that had initially characterized them.[55] An examination of the actual academies and headmasters shows that the opposite was the case: government schools were increasingly influenced by the academies and the Neo-Confucian curriculum.[56] The history of academies in Yuan was continuous with developments that Zhu Xi himself had initiated. Table 7.1 shows that, with the exception of Fujian, the growth of academies in

Table 7.1
Academies Established in Selected Song, Yuan, Ming, and Qing Provinces

Province	Zhu Xi disciples	Founded by officials				Founded by families				Unknown				Totals				Provincial total
		S	Y	M	Q	S	Y	M	Q	S	Y	M	Q	S	Y	M	Q	
Jiangxi	79	26	8	79	122	179	81	188	128	19	5	20	73	224	94	287	323	928
Zhejiang	80	16	6	75	144	125	24	88	152	15	19	36	99	156	49	199	395	799
Fujian	164	13	3	76	129	38	3	18	19	14	5	13	14	65	11	107	162	345
Hunan	14	13	3	55	133	41	15	34	91	16	3	13	52	70	21	102	276	469
Guangdong	4	12	3	103	203	19	4	42	131	8	3	11	8	39	10	156	342	547
Jiangsu	7	6	2	46	71	16	4	7	23	7	0	13	21	29	6	66	115	216
Sichuan	7	7	3	40	202	16	0	11	77	8	2	12	104	31	5	63	383	482
Anhui	15	4	2	63	69	12	10	23	18	4	3	13	8	20	15	99	95	229
Henan	1	9	3	86	210	8	7	15	27	3	2	11	39	20	12	112	276	420
All provinces	108	108	51	972	2,190	502	181	507	935	101	63	220	721	697	298	1,699	3,868	

ABBREVIATIONS: S, Song; Y, Yuan; M, Ming; Q, Qing.

SOURCES: Chen Guija and Deng Hongbo, *Zhongguo shuyuan zhidu yanjiu*, 354–59; data on academies founded by Zhu Xi's disciples—Chen Rongjie, *Zhuzi menren*, 11. For a listing of the names, locations, and founders of over 450 Song-period academies, see Wu Wanju, *Song dai shu yuan yu Song dai xue shu zhi guan xi*, {QB} 299–338.

Yuan took place in exactly those places where they had been most popular in Song and where Zhu Xi had disciples. (The table includes figures for the most academy-rich provinces; it does not distinguish between the Northern and Southern Song periods because few foundings can be dated to Northern Song.)

During the last century of Song, Neo-Confucianism was a success. Over half the Song academies were founded during this period.[57] More and more successful examination candidates were using Neo-Confucian ideas in writing their papers and citing Zhu Xi as an authority.[58] Moreover, about two-thirds of the examiners in Southern Song came from the provinces with large numbers of Neo-Confucians, Jiangxi, Liangzhe (modern Zhejiang and parts of Anhui and Jiangsu), and Fujian.[59] But success also brought criticism. There were those who attacked the Neo-Confucians for being too exclusive, for denigrating great figures from the past who were different, and for failing to give due attention to literature and statecraft.[60] But there were those who argued that Neo-Confucians were including literature and statecraft, but on their own terms.[61] There were those, such as Zhu Xi's son-in-law Huang Gan, who thought that the "succession of the Way" should be limited to one person in an age, as well as those who asserted, successfully, that there could be a plurality of successions.[62] There were those who thought that any criticism of the Neo-Confucian masters ought to be expurgated from received texts,[63] and those who thought that Neo-Confucians had become so caught up in book learning that they had lost sight of the mind.[64] Yet such criticism was a recognition that more and more literati were willing to listen to the Neo-Confucian message. One account, meant to disparage the late Song Neo-Confucians, stands as evidence that, even as they succeeded, Neo-Confucian literati maintained their distinctiveness.

They read only the Four Books, *Reflections on Things at Hand, Comprehending the Book of Change, Diagram of the Supreme Ultimate, Eastern and Western Inscriptions*, and the "records of speech." They pretended that their learning was setting the mind in the right, cultivating the self, governing the country, and bringing tranquility to the world. Therefore they took the following slogan as their guide: "Be the ultimate standard for the populace, establish the mind of heaven-and-earth, inaugurate great peace for a myriad generations, and continue the lost learning of the former sages." When they served as prefects and intendants, they always established academies and shrines to the various worthies of their school or published and wrote commentaries on the Four Books and compiled "records of speech" in excess. Then they were called "worthies" and could gain great fame and a fat salary. The examination compositions of the literati would always quote [their writings], and then they would take high-ranking degrees and become famous. . . . With that, everyone began to imitate them, and when there was the slightest criticism of them, the faction classed [the critics] as morally inferior. Even the ruler could not dispute them, so strong was their influence.[65]

When discussions began in Yuan about restoring the examinations, some Neo-Confucians opposed not only restoring traditional literary examinations testing poetry but also examining candidates on the Four Books and Zhu Xi's commentaries.[66] But others celebrated the fusion. Cheng Duanli's *Daily Schedule of Study in the Cheng Family School*, an elaborate and influential curriculum for elementary and higher education, aimed to integrate fully Zhu Xi's White Deer Grotto Academy exhortations with examination education while still keeping the school private.[67]

An Alternative for the
Family in Song and Yuan

Just as the Neo-Confucians created an alternative model for literati learning—by establishing their difference from the status quo, by recruiting literati to their way of doing things, and then by asking that government recognize and support their efforts—so, too, did they offer a model for the family that drew on yet departed from the status quo. And just as their approach to schooling largely ignored state education and private religious education, their view of the family largely ignored its relations to the state and religion.

From the state's perspective and, as far as we can tell, from society's perspective, the family (the *jia*) was an economic and ritual corporation based on the idea of kinship. The father and sons held the family property until the death of the father, at which point it was normally divided equally among the sons. Legally, each property-holding unit was a household (a *hu*) led by the registered head of household. The state held the household responsible for paying the tax on its land and assessed its other obligations based on the household's total wealth. Although the government traditionally praised families that did not divide their property and fissure into separate households, in practice its revenues benefited from an increase in the number of independent households. As a ritual unit, the family included the members of those households linked by kinship, with kinship defined by mourning obligations, which in theory extended over five generations. The counterpart of the obligation to mourn and make sacrificial offerings to one's ancestors was the obligation to secure an heir for oneself, so that the line of those making offerings would be continued. Beginning in the eleventh century, there was renewal of interest in how kinship ties should be maintained over time. Eventually, new forms of genealogy appeared, and a new way of leaving property to descendants emerged: the charitable estate, a land endowment whose income was intended to help family members or descendants forever. Both genealogies and charitable estates encouraged families to maintain kinship ties beyond the five generations required by mourning rituals. The spread of lineages (*zu*), taken most simply as a social group created by maintaining kinship ties among the descendants of a common founding ancestor beyond the mourning grades, dates from the Song period.

The division of property created enormous problems for the family whose wealth was based on land. Sons could see their father's or grandfather's borrowing as a threat to their inheritance. A married son who died before his father needed an heir to inherit his share, perhaps a nephew but perhaps someone from his wife's family, whose loyalty would be suspect. The division of property was an engine of downward social mobility; it guaranteed that each household would have less than the previous generation. This was particularly true for literati families, because they had far more sons (four or five) than the average household (one).[68] A twelfth-century manual of advice for well-to-do families, Yuan Cai's (ca. 1140–ca. 1190) *Precepts for Social Life*, bases its arguments for ethical norms on the family's economic interests,[69] and legal cases from the Southern Song show that family members most commonly sued one another for economic reasons. Religious specialists came into play in the ritual side of family life, particularly in the ceremonies that dealt with illness, death, and the departed: shamans evicted the spirits thought responsible for illness, Buddhist monks oversaw cremations and funerals, and Daoists performed various rites. This, too, was an economic relationship, in the sense that families dealt with the unseen forces in the realm of the ghosts-and-spirits by purchasing the services of religious specialists with the theoretical knowledge of that realm and practical techniques for mediating between the living and the dead.

The Neo-Confucians had little to say about the family as a legal or economic entity, the primary concerns of the state. Instead, they focused on the family as a kinship-based ritual unit that could serve as the basic building block of local society. Some eleventh-century thinkers had thought about ritual in broad theoretical terms, as the model for an orderly and harmonious world and as an all-encompassing body of practices that could be used to orchestrate all aspects of life, and as a noncoercive Confucian means for weaning the population from its centuries-old involvement with Buddhism and Daoism. Ritual was also addressed in the particular: under the New Policies, rituals for the emperor, the imperial clan, officials, and commoners were promulgated. Some scholars set their hand to drawing up ritual guides for family life, Sima Guang being a famous example.[70]

From the start Neo-Confucians had argued that ritual had to be understood not simply as ceremonies but as a social means of giving expression to coherence (*li*). As Zhang Zai put it: "In my view ritual is coherence. You must first learn to apprehend coherence; ritual is then the means by which you put into practice what is right [according to coherence]. If you understand coherence, then you can institute rituals, but rituals come after coherence."[71] Zhang, Cheng Yi, and Zhu Xi saw themselves as having the understanding necessary to institute rituals for family life in particular. In doing so, they were primarily drawing up coherent systems, although they saw these as both commensurate with what could be found in the Classics and relevant to current practices.

In one respect, they did call for the return to an ancient form that was quite at odds with current practice: the institution of the descent-line heir system (*zong*), in which the eldest son of the deceased had the exclusive right to officiate at ancestral rites. This was a system meant to ensure family continuity over the generations rather than to perpetuate the power of the family elders or the authority of those members who held official rank.[72] In fact, Zhang Zai and Cheng Yi favored the descent-line system not only for ritual but also for the inheritance of property, in the belief that primogeniture would help great families avoid splitting the estate and eventual declining but would create a body of hereditary official families.[73] That idea was not adopted by Zhu Xi and his school.

Zhu Xi and his students produced the most influential ritual manual in the later imperial period, the text known as *Master Zhu's Family Rituals*. The *Family Rituals* adapted Sima Guang's family rites (which Zhu found too difficult) and incorporated Cheng's descent-line system for the performance of ancestral rites.[74] Just as the Neo-Confucian academy was an alternative to the state school, the *Family Rituals* was an alternative to the state-mandated ritual program. The New Policies government had issued a comprehensive manual of rites, the *Zhenghe Reign Period New Ceremonies for the Five Categories of Rites* (*Zhenghe wu li xin yi*). Although largely devoted to imperial ceremony, it included separate liturgies for the marriage, capping, and funerals rites of ranked officials and, for the first time, of commoners. However, it limited ancestral temples to ranked officials.[75] At the very start of his career, Zhu proposed a reworking of the *Zhenghe Rites* to allow it to be put into practice not only at local government ceremonies but also by "the families of *shidafu* and commoners" in local society; he also suggested "local literati (*shiren*) who like ritual" be appointed to guide others in their practice.[76] Ultimately, however, he created his own alternative with the *Family Rituals*.[77] For those literati who chose to pursue the Learning of the Way, it was also a guide, something they could bring home to their own families; if they could not persuade their elders to adopt it, they could impose it on their own descendants.

The *Family Rituals* details the performance of the capping and pinning ceremonies marking the transition to adulthood for young men and young women, weddings, funerals, and seasonal and ancestral sacrifices. But its import goes beyond the conduct of these rituals, as Zhu Xi explained in his introduction:

All ritual has its basis and its forms. In terms of its application in the family, the maintenance of status distinctions and the substance of love and respect are its basis; ceremonial displays and the specifications for cappings, weddings, funerals, and ancestral rites are its forms. The basis is the constant "substance" for the daily "functions" of the household and thus must be cultivated every day. All its forms are means by which the course of human existence is regulated.[78]

The "general principles" begins with the proper structure of the offering hall each house is to have but goes beyond this to describe in detail the garments to be worn and the relations and practices to take place in the household—economic (e.g., sons and daughters-in-law are not to hold private property), social (how to behave in relations with parents), cultural (elementary education), and in all ways moral. The rites are not limited to one household; other members of the descent group have to be brought into the picture.

Who is the *Family Rituals* for? The text makes it clear that, in contrast to tradition, it is not reserved to families holding official rank. Rather, it is addressed to the *junzi*, the moral man, that is, the man who acts from a commitment to righteousness rather than out of self-interest. But it is also clear that these are rites for literati families—literate people with servants and enough land to set some of it aside as an endowment to maintain the rites and offerings. It seems to me that, taken as a whole, the *Family Rituals* is the Neo-Confucian answer to the question "What should the 'family' be?" just as their curriculum and academy answered the question of what a learned person should be. It fit with the increasing popularity of the idea that a literati family should maintain itself as a common descent group, as a lineage of people descended from a common ancestor who would maintain a certain degree of kinship solidarity over many generations.[79] And it fit with the "charitable estates" (*yi zhuang*) some literati families were creating to aid poor members, to help kin keep up appearances as literati in their conduct of weddings, funerals, and other communal rites, to support a lineage school, and to help kin travel to the examinations.[80]

Not all families agreed that the fundamental expression of family and kinship required instituting a coherent body of ritual practices as defined by a normative text rather than local custom. Nor did they necessarily think of the family as a ritual entity in the first place. Yuan Cai's *Precepts for Social Life* probably is more representative of elite views of the family. For Yuan, writing as a local official, a family was made up of people who acted out of self-interest; he argued that they should try to be more cooperative, harmonious, and law-abiding by appealing to utility.[81] Nor did they agree that they should exclude Buddhist and Daoist specialists from services that would mediate between the living and the realm of the ghosts-and-sprits. Implementation of the *Family Rituals* could not have been easy at first, for the Buddhist conduct of funerary rites and the practice of cremation were pervasive, and the *Family Rituals* was quite specific in rejecting the employment of Buddhist rites. Still, committed Neo-Confucians in the twelfth and thirteenth centuries began adopting the new program.[82]

The *Family Rituals* became the new foundation for a tradition of ritual manuals. Zhu's text was frequently republished, and later Neo-Confucians published commentaries on it and produced their own revisions. By the Ming, it had gained a certain official imprimatur and was used by the government in issuing its own guides. Yet in Ming times, the idea that the descent line should proceed through the oldest son was dropped.[83] This change is instructive, for it highlights the expansion of Neo-Confucian focus from the family as the ritual unit to the lineage. This can be illustrated with the charitable estate. When a family—the *jia* as the unit that held property—took part of its holdings and created an estate for the lineage, the *zu*, it supposed that all members of the lineage to which the family belonged or that all the descendants of the donating family within the lineage would receive benefit. In other words, the lineage included descendants of all sons, including those outside a given individual's five mourning grades, in contrast to the descent-line system Zhu Xi had advocated.

Essential to the existence of a lineage was the genealogy. Literati lineages had already been compiling genealogies, something we do not find in the *Family Rituals*, but in the Yuan period Neo-Confucians began to promote genealogy compilation—and thus lineage creation—as part of the program of activities aimed at ensuring that the families that made up a lineage would be moral actors in society. Their prefaces celebrated genealogies as an essential means of maintaining ritual order among the families within the lineage and, thus, as essential for the lineage to function as the foundation for social harmony in the community.[84] For example, in 1346 the Wuzhou Neo-Confucian Lü Pu wrote:

Heaven creates this people, and thus there are clans. Although descendants multiply and procreate without cease, in the beginning it was one person and one allotment of *qi*. Although the *qi* divided and thus there are distinctions in the degree of kinship and attachment, still, from the perspective of the beginning, there is just this one *qi*, and all are descended from it. They are not different. And if perchance the centered, harmonious *qi* is in this one branch, then how could the rich and noble not care about their poor and humble [kin], or the wise not care about the foolish. Thus descent lines are recorded, and the genealogy is written, all in order to tie them together and have them share both the good and the ill. Thus one treats a lineage like one family and those of the same *qi* as one body, giving full expression to the idea of treating kin as kin. This is how the lineage shows caring, and this is why a genealogy is good for the clan. But when there is a decline and people of the same *qi* see one another as strangers, then they lose interest in genealogy.[85]

The great Fuzhou (Jiangxi) scholar Wei Su (1303–72), wrote in his preface for this genealogy:

However, Mencius said, "The centered cultivate the noncentered, and the talented cultivate the nontalented, [that is why people are happy to have worthy fathers and elder brothers]." Today the history (*shu*) of one family cannot help being different from the history (*shi*) of one country. With a large population, the country must have strict laws for rewarding good and punishing evil. But with the multitude of a single family . . . one can lead them by setting an example of rectitude, one instructs them with the teaching of the sages and worthies, of classics and commentaries. One develops the innate ability of their hearts to examine their own behavior. Thus every person will act like a moral person and literatus. And those who are not innately capable [will be corrected by fathers and brothers], for whether [one is born] wise and foolish is decided by heaven. Lü descendants should think about Pu's intention in writing this and make an effort to be better, and they will see their goodness recorded in the genealogy.[86]

A clear statement of how this enterprise would help transform society comes from Fang Xiaoru in his preface to a genealogy of his teacher Song Lian's lineage:

Literati without office can transform society by harmonizing their lineages (*mu zu*). How is it that we can transform such a large world by harmonizing our lineages? All people want to harmonize their lineages; the problem is they do not know how to do it correctly. If we go first, then who will not follow us, and when all lineages are harmonized, then who in the world will join in evil? If the evil cannot take license, then perfect order is but a step away.

There are three ways to harmonize the lineage: do a genealogy to connect the lineage, visit the grave of the first resident ancestor to bind the hearts [of members], and strengthen the rites of kinship to nurture kindness to others. . . .

When all three are practiced, then even the literatus can transform others, how much more so one with [an official] position. Changing all society's customs is not difficult, how much less something as near at hand to one as the community and village. What is near ought to be easy to do, and those with position ought to be easy to transform. That they do not do it and that those with position are not transformed is because few know what they ought to do. If you know what to do and have a position, how could people not look up to you?[87]

The primary goal of constructing the family and lineage as a ritual entity was to make it a moral entity operating in a social context. A family's survival had much to do with its property and power, and its biological continuity depended on sexual activity, but the point of treating it as a ritual construction was, I think, not so much to pretend that these did not exist as to establish an alternative basis for thinking about why the family mattered and how it should act. From the perspective of wedding ritual, the bride's transformation into wife and the groom's into husband subsumed their transformation into male and female sexual partners.[88] Similarly, acquiring an heir was important economically, but treating this in terms of rites and moral duty shifted the focus from property to ritual effectiveness.*

The ritual primacy Neo-Confucians placed on family and lineage led to a reconsideration of the relationship of the wife to the husband's family. In common Song elite practice, wives owned and controlled the dowry they brought with them into marriage, returned to their natal families following divorce or the death of the husband, decided on whether and whom to appoint as heir to the husband's estate should he die childless, and remarried. Against this, Neo-Confucians promoted the idea that the wife should fully become part of her husband's family. A truly virtuous wife did not have property of her own (and neither did junior males) but would donate her dowry to the husband's family; she viewed her husband's family rather than her natal family as her family; and she remained chaste after her husband's death.[89] In addition, Neo-Confucians agitated against the institutionalized role of women—such

---

*As Anne Waltner (*Getting an Heir*, 70–74) notes, Neo-Confucians could take two positions. One held that since an heir adopted from a different surname was of different *qi*, he would not be able to summon the ancestors of his adopting family in performing sacrifices. The other held that sincerity of feeling could overcome the difference in *qi*.

as courtesans—as sexual partners for males outside the ritual family context.[90]

The absorption of wives into the husband's family and the promotion of widow chastity gained the force of law only in the Yuan dynasty. When the government sought to ensure that households (and the service obligations they owed) would be continued and applied to Chinese subjects the Mongols' rule of continuing households through levirate marriage, widow chastity became grounds for a legal exception. It was at this point that women lost the right to take dowry property with them out of a marriage, and the widow either remained with the husband's family as a chaste widow or allowed them rather than her natal family to remarry her. Even before levirate marriage was outlawed for Chinese in 1330, the promotion of chaste widowhood had become part of state policy. Households with chaste widows could be granted official insignia and an exemption from corvée labor in recognition of their virtue. These policies were adopted into Ming law as well.[91] In addition, following earlier Neo-Confucian opposition to literati involvement with courtesans, the early Ming closed the entertainment quarters to literati.[92]

Neo-Confucians tended to place themselves in opposition to what they presumed to be the customary behavior of literati families, but they chose their issues carefully. Some matters they apparently let pass unremarked, such as the custom of binding women's feet that was then spreading among elite families.[93] When they did focus on an issue, such as widow chastity in literati families, and were able to gain state support for their views, they had some influence over social practice. But what was intended and what eventually emerged were not the same thing. Initially the point of widow chastity was binding the wife to the patrilineal family permanently, her "loyalty" to her deceased husband was the equivalent of the minister's loyalty to his ruler. The moral imperative was the maintenance of unity and continuity. This did not mean, of course, that the binding was happy and successful. The recompense to the husband's family for continued support of the widow was cultural: the local government's recognition of a family's chaste widow became a mark of an upstanding family. The celebration of a widow's suicide in defense of chastity and continued widowhood in late Ming seems to be rather different: a somewhat non-Neo-Confucian appreciation of the wife's passionate devotion rather than ritual duty. The more extreme phenomenon in the eighteenth century of suicide by women in the face of perceived threats to their chastity has been seen as yet another phenomenon, having to do with a state-sponsored shift from family and loyalty to a somewhat atomistic ethical personhood.[94]

The family that lived by Neo-Confucian principles would establish harmony among kin, maintain continuity with the ancestors, educate its offspring, succor those in need, promote the spiritual and material welfare of the neighborhood with like-minded families of different surnames, and work together with local officials. It would, over time, become a lineage, rather than a set of households held together by mourning rituals. As their genealogies proclaimed, these lineages were both a model for an integrated social order and a concrete step toward its realization. The genealogy-based lineage was, I think, a way of maintaining multigenerational continuity among households despite the division of property that took place when the head of the household died. From this perspective, families that tried to create strictly regulated multigenerational family communes—in which multiple households held their property in common, maintained their own schools, and succeeded in placing members in office—were an anachronism. However, they were a time-honored ideal. Although they could be associated with Neo-Confucianism as the current definition of Confucian tradition, I am not sure they fit well.[95] A famous, and much studied, example was the Zheng family of Pujiang in Wuzhou prefecture.[96] Such a multigenerational communal family was hard to maintain over the long term, even when large number of kin continued to reside in the same area. Sons often decided to divide the family estate, and when there were disputes over property, the family had no legal power to prevent members from going to court.[97] For most the lineage was a much more fluid arrangement, a loose corporation that sometimes had considerable authority and sometimes not, a network of associated people who often saw it as useful insurance in times of stress and a resource for taking advantage of opportunities.[98] Moreover, it was possible to object in principle to efforts to create a communal family. In imitation of the Zhengs, a member of the Huang family tried to persuade his kin to form a communal family after they had already divided the property: they would own all their houses in common, all their fields would be under a single registration, their movable property would be stored together, tools would be overseen by one authority, and their servants would treat them all as masters. The Neo-Confucian objection was simple: this kind of unity depended on military discipline, which in turn depended on the ability to reward and above all punish. But this was not true unity, for true unity depended on each individual realizing the values that were common to all minds and developing integrity and sincerity in practice to influence others.[99] Or, we might say, it required that the members choose to participate.

Literati Voluntarism and
Community in Song and Yuan

"Official households"—literati households with a member with official rank—could expect the local government to supply them with attendants and transportation, deliver their salaries, free them from most tax obligations, and excuse them from appearing in court. And their descendants could try to inherit some of these privileges.[100] Families without office who wanted to identify with the literati families in their locale certainly needed to acquire a literati education, but they needed to establish relationships with their peers, through marriage alliances, for example, and demonstrate their support for local enterprises that benefited the community, by supporting education, religion, relief, and local self-defense.[101] But the behavior of local elites, literati and officials, could also be destructive; some used their stronger financial position to drive poor farmers into debt and acquire their land, to bribe local clerks into taking their land off the tax registers, and to ruin their enemies through litigation.[102]

This was the context in which twelfth-century Neo-Confucians worked not only to persuade literati to learn the Way and reform their families but also to make a difference in local society. The Neo-Confucians worked in the first place to create communities of literati who shared their vision and would work together to provide local leadership. To some extent, they were inventing the idea of a local literati community. Recall that Lü Zuqian had justified offering examination preparation as well as teaching the Way on the grounds that "were I to get rid of examination training, the local literati would feel cut off. They would have no reason to be in contact with one another."[103]

But, once again, there were already alternatives. The state had systems that organized the population for the purposes of extracting goods and services, systems that in theory made no allowance for elites that mediated between state and society. Households were registered and ranked according to relative wealth in order to assess their obligation to provide service and certain taxes, and land was measured and registered in order to assess its proportion of the local land tax quota. In return for this, the state tried to provide relief when harvests failed, protection against banditry, punishment of criminality, and access to the courts to settle disputes. There were also organizations, Buddhist monasteries mainly, that were privately supported and created communities of lay people and encouraged charity. Monasteries populated the landscape in far greater numbers than any government installations. Local records attest to the founding of over 400 monasteries of various sizes in Wuzhou prefecture alone by 1200 (and another 300 between 1200 and 1480).[104] In some places, the numbers were much higher, Jianning prefecture in Fujian is said to have had 912 monasteries by the middle of the eleventh century. Where there were monasteries, there were lay organizations, which not only arranged religious services but also pooled money to help participants in need, particularly for funerals.[105] Literati also participated in these associations and, as wealthy families, could be expected to contribute to the founding and repair of monasteries and temples. Localities had their local gods, as well as associations that supported them and sought their protection. More important, during the twelfth century some local deities were transformed into regional gods with networks of temples spreading across prefectural boundaries.[106] Although some officials attacked as "profane" those local cults not formally recognized by the government as "orthodox," it is clear that literati families also participated in them.[107]

In short, religious activities to serve the interests of the participants and to protect the locality already existed in the space between the family and local government. They were not ignored by the government— local officials themselves maintained shrines for official offerings—and certainly in the eyes of their followers these deities had powers that local officials could rarely match.[108] Zhu Xi argued that what people took for "ghosts-and-spirits" were emanations of *qi* rather than beings with intelligence and will, but some Neo-Confucians still became involved in cults.[109] The increasing commercialization of the economy, which linked villages to periodic markets and markets to permanent market towns, created another network between local government and the family, and helped generate the wealth available to be invested in religious life and Neo-Confucian projects.

Organized teaching, particularly at Neo-Confucian academies, brought together sympathetic literati who might have once worked in relative isolation. The academies provided venues for Neo-Confucian lecturers and made it possible for teachers to build reputations as Neo-Confucian leaders. They taught students a new social mode of learning, in which discussion of issues with one another and the teacher had greater intellectual importance than memorizing texts and composing examination essays. They instituted rituals and taught participants how to conduct them. They supported literati, some of whom had traveled from other prefectures and provinces, providing them with room and board. Academies defined belonging on the basis of a shared commitment to a way of learning, not on the basis of rank or wealth, yet they gave literati a chance to establish bonds with Neo-Confucians who had become officials. In short, they created translocal networks of like-minded literati who were engaged in a common program of learning and in discussions of shared problems.[110] Academies created social networks, which in turn provided new grounds for establishing marriage ties; indeed, there is evidence that by the end of the Southern Song some saw being a Neo-Confucian rather than an official as a criterion of social value in choosing marriage partners.[111]

A different but related Neo-Confucian community-building institution was the "shrine for successors to the Way." Zhu Xi had promoted their founding during his lifetime, and in the early thirteenth century they spread to most Southern Song prefectures. These shrines, initially devoted to Zhou Dunyi and the Cheng brothers, celebrated the eleventh-century masters' repossession of the Way lost after Mencius. They thus challenged the account of Confucianism found in the Confucian temples associated with the state schools, which contained a variety of early and later figures (including Wang Anshi until 1241) who in Neo-Confucian eyes had not understood true learning. Not only that, but in contrast to shrines built to celebrate scholars with some connection to the locality, these shrines were national; local literati built them in places that the early masters had never visited as a testament to their own commitment to the Way. As Zhu Xi pointed out, the transmitters represented the possibility of achieving influence and fame by virtue of one's learning, rather than office and power.[112] Shrines thus made the connection between a national movement and the local place. They brought local literati into a more direct connection with the founders: they could see their portraits, read their works, and discuss their significance. And they could add to them, either by building another shrine to local Neo-Confucians or by placing their own local masters together with the founders.[113]

A third Neo-Confucian institution, the "local" or "community" compact (*xiang yue*), was a fellowship that members formally joined with the purpose of encouraging themselves to moral behavior. Lü Dajun (1031–82), a student of Zhang Zai, first developed it, probably as part of Zhang's efforts to formulate a model for the organization of local society inspired by the well-field system of the *Rites of Zhou*. As such, it was an alternative to the New Policies' *bao jia* system in that it was a voluntary, self-imposed system of communal self-regulation rather than something imposed on society through legal sanctions. But it was also an alternative to the religious societies of the laity. Lü Zuqian had organized a fellowship for students as men of "common resolve" (*tongzhi*). As he revised them over a few years, Lü's rules grew from a set of strictures about how students were to behave at school into a formal compact that defined the way in which registered members were to relate to one another.[114] Lü's version contributed to the most enduring model of the community compact, Zhu Xi's revision of Lü Dajun's text, which he instituted at the White Deer Grotto Academy.[115]

The compact took place through monthly meetings, which began with a formal ceremony to worship Confucius and then turned to the recital and discussion of the compact itself. Having reminded themselves of what they had agreed to regard as good and bad conduct, members then presented accounts of their own deeds, which, after discussion and evaluation, would be duly registered. The record of good deeds would be read aloud, and the record of bad deeds circulated for silent reading. Then, they would share a meal, after which they would join in entertainment, physical recreation, or discussion of other matters. The fellowship was meant to be a compact among local (*xiang*) literati, who were to be seated by age. There were two exceptions to this: "nonliterati (*shi*) sorts" in attendance were not formally seated, and those local men who were high-ranking officials were seated as special guests rather than by age.

The compact created lateral bonds of obligation between members that extended outside the meeting. They were expected to maintain the rules of decorum based on distinctions of age when associating with other members in daily life, to ensure that their families were represented at funerals and weddings in the families of other members, and to aid other members when formally notified by lending what they had, property, tools, vehicles, and servants. Not to do these things constituted faults, and those who would not change their ways were to be excluded from the compact.

Together with academies and shrines, Song compacts created a Neo-Confucian literati community by drawing members from different families. They were not envisioned as organizing all the people living in a village or all the members of the families involved. In addition, it was up to the members to agree on the forms of good and bad behavior they would maintain. Zhu Xi's version is fairly elaborate in defining what constituted good in terms of family life, work and associations outside the family, and responsibilities for aiding others. Perhaps more interesting, it also recognized behavioral faults that members were to avoid: drunken quarreling, gambling, dishonesty, bullying, and various forms of self-aggrandizement and self-glorification. It supposed that in practice consistent moral behavior by elites at the local level depended on their forming a self-supervising community devoted to that purpose.

The fourth element involved various forms of organized economic support. This was controversial. Not all Neo-Confucians thought literati should become involved in creating community institutions that went beyond the family.[116] Some did want to find ways of working together, as when former students of an academy agreed among themselves not to take advantage of the poor harvest to speculate profitably in grain, but saw this as a private agreement among like-minded men rather than an institutional commitment.[117] And some literati were generally opposed to the idea that local literati should encroach on the responsibilities of government. Chen Liang wrote to Zhu Xi that he was not willing to participate in such activities: "In living in my locality, I have never once gotten involved in affairs outside the family, not even in those that with my means I could easily undertake, which the customs of the day regard as eminently good and which the Confucians (*ru*) commonly practice: community granaries, help in fulfilling service obligations, relief, and such matters."[118]

In some instances, the goal was to benefit the literati community exclusively. Some locales established charitable or "righteous" estates, inspired by lineage charitable estates, to provide financial aid for marriages and funerals to poor literati families (but perhaps more often to the impoverished descendants of officials). Officials created some of these, using government land, but the wealthy were exhorted to contribute as well.[119] But others were meant to benefit a larger public. "Public-spirited literati who care about righteousness" (*gongxin haoyi zhi shi*) led projects that a single family could not manage alone yet local officials were not prepared to undertake, as happened in the case of irrigation projects, a vital concern in rice agriculture.[120] Even in urban areas, where merchants and craftsmen had guilds and had direct contact with officials, locally initiated action tended to come from literati.[121] Neo-Confucian literati also took the initiative in creating compacts among local families to manage labor service obligations fairly. Called "righteous" or community service (*yi yi*), they appeared in Wuzhou in the middle of the twelfth century, and local officials elsewhere soon began to promote similar enterprises. Households would agree to make regular contributions, or donate fields for land endowments, to defray the costs of those households who, in rotation, were obliged to provide onerous and expensive services such as managing tax collection. The workings of these charitable foundations and compacts varied from place to place and changed over time. They were used for other purposes as well: for example, as a source of poor relief. They were common by the end of Song and continued to be promoted during Yuan.[122] It was also Wuzhou Neo-Confucian literati during Yuan who undertook on their own initiative, for the sake of "righteousness," a countywide revision of the tax rolls to ensure equity among the elite.[123]

The most famous economic institution was Zhu Xi's "community granary" (*she cang*) or "righteous granary" (*yi cang*). At first some Neo-Confucians argued that this was too similar to the Green Sprouts program of the New Policies and thus opened the way to a return to coercive state intervention in local affairs. The New Policies had transformed the Ever Normal Granary system, which bought and sold grain in an effort to stabilize prices and provide relief, into a system for providing credit to farmers. At the same time, they had attempted to limit the acquisition of land by the wealthy (as well as mandating support for the indigent aged and orphaned young and broadening educational opportunity). Some conservative opponents had argued that the state should stick to its administrative responsibilities and avoid efforts to transform society. Some Neo-Confucians had a far more radical vision—a return to the well-field system of antiquity in which land would be equitably distributed and virtuous local elites would teach and manage—although Zhu Xi was not persuaded that restoration of the well-field system was possible.[124] In Southern Song, the government no longer sought to provide rural credit, but it continued its efforts at price stabilization through the Ever Normal Granaries in the administrative seats and maintained a system of granaries to provide poor relief and famine relief. Neither of these worked particularly well. They were part of the official apparatus and suffered from inflexibility, neglect, and malfeasance. Nor was exhorting rich families to charity greatly effective.[125]

The goal of Zhu Xi's community granary was to create, from a donation of capital by local government or leading families, a self-sustaining means of providing relatively low-interest loans to farmers. He had already been involved in such a venture in Fujian, and in 1181, while serving as the Ever Normal Granary commissioner for eastern Zhejiang, he successfully proposed a general model to the court. Leading local families could petition the local government to establish a community granary. They would borrow the capital for it in grain from the Ever Normal Granary or contribute it themselves, charge 20 percent interest and, once they had built up sufficient capital and repaid the initial loan, reduce their charges to an administrative fee. Depending on the customs and conditions of the place, other models could be proposed. What made this different from what the government was doing, in particular from the much denigrated Green Sprouts program of the New Policies, was that it was voluntary: the initiative had to come from leading literati families, who would be responsible for its maintenance (although the local government would check the books).[126] As Zhu explained in an inscription for one such granary in Wuzhou: "The original intention in establishing the Green Sprouts policy was not bad, but it gave [farmers] money rather than grain, it was located in the county seat rather than in the local community, it was administered by officials rather than local morally committed literati, and it was put into effect to increase revenue rather than out of feelings of concern, loyalty, and benefit."[127]

For Neo-Confucians, the community granary was a practical manifestation of what it meant to act in accord with the unity of principle and the fundamental impulse of heaven-and-earth to continue the process of life.[128] It proved particularly popular once the ban on Zhu's learning was lifted: charitable granaries are known in sixty late Southern Song counties, with some counties having over ten granaries.[129] However, what began as a market-based mechanism to support the weakest members of the rural economy, often became a charity institution that drew resources from endowment fields given by government and provided relief and support for the indigent (particularly foundlings); others replicated the Ever Normal Granaries, buying grain cheap and selling dear; and they began to rely more on local government management.[130] The community granary came to be seen as useful to local government priorities, but powerful families also saw it as a state-sanctioned way of increasing their role in the local economy to their own advantage.[131]

———

From the twelfth century on, the dissemination and elaboration of the Neo-Confucian curriculum, the founding of academies, the establishment of shrines, the institution of compacts, and founding of community estates and granaries began to happen in place after place in the south. It seems to me that the status of those taking the initiative—whether they were active or retired officials or local literati—is less important than the fact that these were voluntary institutions that involved individuals, families, and literati communities. Moreover, they were seen as a set of related activities. I will illustrate this with two examples.

The first case is from the moment when Neo-Confucians were just beginning to see how they could make connections between personal transformation and community and involves members of the Pan family in Jinhua county in Wuzhou prefecture. Their activities were entirely local, they did not achieve national fame, and they had only limited success in bringing the rest of the lineage with them.[132] Pan Jingxian (1134–

90) founded a community granary in the early 1180s modeled after Zhu Xi's proposal for a community granary; he intended it to be the first in a series of nine.[133] The granary was the culmination of over a decade of increasingly greater involvement with Neo-Confucians on the part of Pan and some of his kin. Pan Jingxian's daughter was married to Zhu Xi's son, and his brother Pan Jingliang married Lü Zuqian's daughter.[134] At Pan Jingxian's request, Zhang Shi did the calligraphy for the grave inscription for their father, Pan Haogu (1101–70), and Lü Zuqian wrote the "record of conduct" for Pan Haogu's brother.[135] Prior to this, Pan Jingxian, who had received the *jinshi* degree in 1163 with Lü Zuqian but would decline every office he was offered, had built a combination grave site, retirement villa, self-cultivation center, library, and lecture hall several miles outside the Jinhua county seat, endowing it with about fifteen acres of fields to support visitors. Zhu Xi named it for him as Ke'an (i.e., "One May [Die in the Evening if He Has Heard the Way in the Morning] Retreat").[136] At the time Zhu had been corresponding with Pan and other members of his family about the superiority of the Learning of the Way.[137] Some of the Pans may have joined the compact Lü Zuqian established for his students.

Pan Jingxian had been so precocious that at age nine he was brought to the capital for the memorization and calligraphy examination given child prodigies. Lü Zuqian had turned him away from examination studies toward the Learning of the Way, and he devoted the rest of his life—and a good bit of his family's wealth—to establishing himself as an intellectual presence among literati and as a leader of the local community. His younger brother, Pan Jingyu (*jinshi* 1190), became a student of Lü Zuqian and corresponded with Zhu Xi as well. It was Lü Zuqian who persuaded Pan to adopt the Neo-Confucian mourning ritual on his father's death.[138] Pan wanted to live a pure life, he was a model of frugality and was interested in Buddhist spirituality, but he also sought social engagement. Zhu Xi's letters to Pan explain that self-cultivation is a continuous process, in which thinking about texts is more effective than reciting them, and requires the practice of inner mental attentiveness. Zhu's letters to Pan Jingyu discuss self-cultivation as constant self-regulation; it is not about achieving liberation by overcoming some ultimate desire. Zhu warned that reading history is of limited usefulness as a means of transforming oneself. It is precisely because literati want to read and know a lot that they fail to think profoundly about the moral coherence in the words of the sages and thus they may wrongly conclude that "our" learning is merely empty words and that Buddhism offers substantial means of self-improvement. He cautioned Pan Jingyu that studying masters of prose such as Su Shi is morally and intellectually suspect and lamented that literati would rather read prose essays than study the Four Books. He urged him not to think that "something as crude as power and fame" is actually the way the world works; rather, he must make a clear distinction between good men and bad and cooperate with the good. The Pan brothers' interest in moral cultivation stands in contrast to the behavior of some of their relatives. Pan Jinggui (1127–after 1201) had ties to the anti-Neo-Confucian Qin Gui party and was forced to retire from office after being repeatedly attacked as vicious, conniving, and corrupt.[139] Pan Jingkui was dismissed from a vice-prefectship in 1190 for arbitrariness and extorting property from religious establishments. Pan Jinglian was removed from a prefectship for corruption in 1208.[140]

My second illustration comes from the time when Neo-Confucians were ascendant and able to use their positions in office to promote their learning and activities. Huang Gan (1152–1221) was Zhu Xi's most loyal student, and later his son-in-law and biographer. He did not try to enter government until 1195, petitioning the new emperor for a post at Zhu's urging, and at first was given a very low level appointment. He went on to hold a series of county and prefectural appointments with great success and refused positions at court. He also promoted the idea that Zhu had in fact received the "succession of the Way" and worked assiduously to see that Zhu's views were transmitted accurately, becoming a famous teacher himself.[141] Both as a literatus and as an official, he promoted the establishment of shrines, schools, and community granaries. Like other Neo-Confucian officials, he often cited coherence when judging legal cases rather than the letter of the law itself, and in some cases he followed coherence at the expense of the law.[142] As a judge and as a teacher, he promoted the idea that a wife should be fully a member of her husband's family, that a widow should remain chaste, and that her dowry should be treated as her husband's property.[143] He developed a network of Neo-Confucian local officials who supported local literati initiatives. Huang had a vision of literati bringing about harmony in society through their behavior as individuals, family members, scholars, local activists, and officials. They would resolve conflicts through moral suasion, practice the rites, engage in Neo-Confucian learning, and provide relief to the distressed.[144]

From Voluntarism to Legislation: The Ming Founding

During Southern Song and Yuan, Neo-Confucians promoted their program for learning and spiritual cultivation, family unity, community formation, and doing good, and they established shrines, academies, publishing ventures, ancestral halls, compacts, and granaries to put their ideas into practice. The program was national—Neo-Confucian literati read the same texts, performed similar rituals, and created similar institutions—but it worked only when groups of literati in particular localities chose to do something about it. As the voluntary endeavor of local literati, it stood in contrast to state-mandated systems. They acted because they thought it right to do so, not because they were legally required to do so; they were acting from moral innate coherence, listening to the promptings of the "mind of the Way," which existed in every person, rather than from a desire to secure advantage or avoid punishment. Yet, as the work of a social and political elite that saw itself as responsible for government and society, it also stood in contrast to religious endeavors to create communities that distanced themselves from government and family. It was a program the literati could undertake themselves without having to forgo participation in all the political, cultural, economic, and social activities that were part of elite life. And, Neo-Confucians could point out, the state had thrice tried to suppress them and thrice failed. From the Neo-Confucian perspective, it was the state that depended on Neo-Confucianism, not Neo-Confucianism on the state.[145] Nevertheless, some serious Neo-Confucians did become officials, and as officials they often used the power of their position to promote their programs and institutions. And, as we have seen with academies, granaries, and public charitable estates, they often actively sought not only government recognition of their activities but also government funding. The point was to secure government support for voluntary literati leadership in local society.

And yet, from the founding of the Ming dynasty in 1368 until the late fifteenth century, Neo-Confucian voluntarism largely disappeared from local society. The most apparent reason for this is the economic downturn that began with the civil wars of the mid-fourteenth century. Dramatic population losses in parts of the southeast and the north had a devastating impact on the commercial economy. In retrospect, we can also see that the policies of the early Ming government, which were aimed first and foremost at social stability, probably hindered a return to economic growth.[146] One indicator of this was a sharp decline in academies during the first century of Ming rule; although the overall totals for the Ming are impressive, most foundings occurred in the sixteenth century.[147] Academies, whether they were Neo-Confucian in orientation or not, depended on the existence of surplus wealth at the local level, held either by wealthy families or by the local government.

The disappearance of local voluntarism did not mean that fewer people were learning Neo-Confucian ideas. The re-establishment of the examination system as the primary means of recruiting literati for government service combined with the adoption of the Neo-Confucian curriculum ensured that the Ming political elite was far better versed in this learning than its Yuan predecessor. Already in late Yuan, a consensus had been emerging—even among literati interested more in literary, historical, and statecraft learning—that the Neo-Confucian view of human nature and self-cultivation was the correct way to think about personal morality.[148] A thirteenth-century encyclopedia illustrates this when it speaks of "using Cheng to transform the mind and using Su [Shi] to transform learning" and accepts Zhu Xi as the modern counterpart to Confucius: just as Confucius had defined the Classics, so Zhu had defined the commentary on the Classics.[149] Moreover, some early Ming literati, such as Wu Yubi and Chen Xianzhang, saw the Neo-Confucian position as a way of life and devoted much of their lives to personal cultivation, but did not undertake community projects (although Wu lent his support to genealogy writing) apart from private teaching.[150]

Perhaps the bloody purges of the early Ming—which involved accusations and executions at the local level—made literati cautious about joining any project outside the family for fear of provoking others to bring charges against them. It may also be true, as one scholar has argued, that late Yuan Neo-Confucians had concluded that only a strong, even autocratic, ruler could end the corruption, misgovernment, and social disjunction of the mid-fourteenth century and had put their faith not in local efforts but in central leadership.[151] However, I think if we look beyond the autocratic relationship between the Ming founder and the bureaucracy to the relationship between government and society, we see that in the quest for social stability in an impoverished land after decades of war, Neo-Confucianism played a central role, not by inspiring literati activists but by providing a model for a new social order.

Early Ming social policy translated the Neo-Confucian vision of the self-supervising moral community into legislation aimed at making it universal and obligatory. A surprising number of the founder's early scholarly advisers, such as Song Lian, came from Wuzhou, where they had been involved with Neo-Confucian teachers and academies, genealogy compilation, communal families, and fiscal reforms. But these same men had also concluded that their efforts to combine mutual aid, moral learning, and elite leadership needed to be written into law.[152] Fang Xiaoru, although less well connected to the founder himself, was Song Lian's best student and articulated a vision of local society as a self-supervising community.[153] Song, Fang, and others were advocates of lineage formation and genealogy writing and held that lineage institutions, which in Southern Song had been considered appropriate only for official and literati families, could be spread to all families.[154] Zhu Yuanzhang, the Ming founder, had seen Neo-Confucian voluntary activities at work during his rise to the emperorship; he once described the Zheng commune in Pujiang in Wuzhou as an example of the ideal communitarian society of antiquity, of the *Da tong*. Despite the family's run-ins with the law, he continued to acknowledge it as a model and show it unusual favor.[155]

Voluntarism ceased because the literati and local government could not pay for it, but the social goals of that voluntarism were given substance in a system of both pre-existing institutions and innovations intended to transform local society into self-supervising moral communities. The components of the new system were the tax captaincy (*liang zhang*) system, which made wealthy households responsible for transporting tax grain from their area to its destination; the village tithing (*li jia*) system, which organized households in groups of 110, with each of the ten wealthiest (as measured by landholdings and number of adult males) leading a tithing of ten households with the post of village head (*li zhang*) rotating among them, for the purposes of tax collection, security, mutual aid, and moral improvement; the community school (*she xue*) system, which ordered moral instruction for all male youth; the elders (*lao ren*) system, which granted to several elders in each rural community juridical powers to be exercised independently of county (*xian*) officials and clerical staff; and the relief granary (*yubei cang*) system, which allowed for a high degree of community self-management. These were accompanied by nationally distributed documents that, among other things, explained how the systems were to operate and set forth the vision that justified them: the three "Grand Injunctions" (*Da gao*) and the "Placard of Instructions to the People" (*Jiao min bang wen*). These documents had the force of law and were expected to be made known to the entire population; the placard in particular was devoted to the self-supervising local community, and it gave unprecedented juridical authority to the local elders and village heads. In addition to the practical work these systems performed—the collection and delivery of taxes and the implementation of local justice—the village tithings were also ritual associations. Each community scheduled offerings at its own altar to the Soils and Grains, for which responsibility rotated among members and at which they renewed their pledge to the community compact with the "Oath to Restrain the Strong and Support the Weak." There were also new community rites, similar to those held at the city god temples in county seats, at which an oath was taken as well. Buddhist and Daoist religious specialists were excluded from these rites. At the semiannual community drinking ceremony, the elders and village heads would recognize the virtuous and the miscreants, and their names would be displayed at the county pavilions devoted either to honoring the virtuous or to recording the names of wrongdoers among the local population.[156]

As other scholars have seen, early Ming social policy had to do more with social integration (and the mobilization of resources) than with mere control over the population.[157] It was the product of a court that saw "rural rectification as a positive solution."[158] In contrast to New Policies social legislation, in which local government managed local social and economic institutions, Zhu Yuanzhang's goal was to insulate

the local community and its institutions from local government interference and make it possible for communities to supervise themselves.
In this, the early Ming social program is much closer in spirit and content to Zhu Xi's "Placard of Encouragement and Instruction"[159] than
to the New Policies approach to improving local society through official activism and bureaucratic entrepreneurship. But it was a legislated
program; it did not depend on literati voluntarism.

Where did the literati fit into an order that described the community
leaders as "good commoners" (*liang min*)? The answer, I think, is twofold. First, the restoration of state schools, recruitment of students
through recommendation, and resurrection of the examination system
provided literati families with an institutional means to maintain their
identity. "Literati students" (*shi zi*) were also given the right to wear distinctive clothing in 1391, and the exemption from labor service given to
official households and retired officials was eventually extended to students.[160] Second, the rural order depended on management by well-to-
do and literate families. Zhu Yuanzhang envisioned an order that would
include everyone, but it was not an egalitarian order. His policies demanded that hierarchical distinctions, both in terms of age and wealth,
be clearly recognized, and they required those with age, wealth, and
learning to provide local leadership.[161] The tax captains were drawn
from the largest (in terms of household size and landholdings) households in the area. They wore clothing reserved for officials and literati,
were eligible for appointment to office, maintained the lifestyle of Song
and Yuan literati, and pursued literary accomplishment and the Learning of the Way.[162] In Wuzhou the Zheng family of Pujiang held a tax
captaincy, even after a member was executed on a charge of falsely recording family landholdings.[163] The village heads were drawn from the
richest households in the village and expected to be literate. Several factors made it likely that the heads and elders included senior members of
literati lineages: one effect of the spread of lineage formation in Southern Song and Yuan in the southeast was an increase in the number of
people who could claim kinship with officials; ever larger numbers of
families without histories of official service began to form lineages; and
Ming law supported lineage formation.[164] We would expect that some
branches of these lineages educated some sons—villages were allowed

to set up community schools even after it was no longer obligatory, and incentives were offered for studying the Grand Injunctions.[165]

In short, the early Ming institutionalized the Neo-Confucian program. Moral self-cultivation was central to state education. Much of the Neo-Confucian model of the family was adopted, but now with the idea that it would apply to all families. Regular exhortations of the populace to behave morally were instituted.[166] In Song and Yuan, literati voluntarism had accomplished things in places where there were many literati families with wealth to contribute, but it had not been effective uniformly across the south. Now, families certainly had less money to spend, but the community programs the Neo-Confucians favored were mandated and no longer required voluntary expenditures.*

The Great Revival and the Return of Voluntarism

The re-emergence of local literati communities facilitated the revival of Neo-Confucian voluntarism in the sixteenth century. The revival combined a new wave of Neo-Confucian "discoursing on learning" with the re-establishment of earlier community institutions. It took place as the economy was recovering and elite families were growing rich once again, giving them the means to contribute. The history of the Lu family, one of the greatest literati and official lineages in Dongyang county in Wuzhou (now Jinhua prefecture) in Ming and Qing illustrates this. As tax captains under the Ming founder, four members had lost their lives in the mass of executions resulting from the "blank receipts" tax cases.[167] By the end of the fifteenth century, family members were organizing community efforts to equalize the tax burden, providing relief, lending without interest from their granary, and repairing roads and bridges.[168] The decline of the village institutions legislated in the early Ming created a space for such voluntary initiatives: the tax system, with its collection of goods in kind and its complicated and expensive delivery system, did not fit a

---

*Did the early Ming government have an alternative? Could it, for example, have sought social stability by adopting measures conducive to the regeneration of private wealth? This was the approach Southern Song and Yuan statecraft thinkers had taken to transforming society. We need to ask whether these voices were still to be heard in early Ming and, if they were, what the objections were to a strategy of favoring "profit" over "righteousness."

commercializing economy; the village tithing system and labor service systems were too inflexible to accommodate change; and local government had curtailed the independence of elders and village heads. In some places, Neo-Confucians devoted themselves to learning and reviving local traditions of learning and community action rather than pursuing careers in government. Zhang Mou, after being cashiered in 1478 for criticizing the emperor's behavior, returned home to devote the next decades to teaching Zhu Xi's learning, which he defended against the criticism of Chen Xianzhang, and organizing literati in his native Jinhua (formerly Wuzhou) prefecture, reviving academies and shrines, and calling on local literati to return to the models set by their Song and Yuan predecessors. By doing so, he gained national fame and returned briefly to high office as the chancellor of the National University at the Southern Capital.[169]

Within a generation Zhang Mou was no longer exceptional. After Wang Yangming suppressed the rebellion of the Prince of Ning in Jiangxi in 1519, he sought to restore social harmony by instituting the "community compact," and he "discoursed on learning" before audiences that numbered in the hundreds. Zhan Ruoshui, a student of Chen Xianzhang, held a series of high offices at the Southern Capital in 1505–40 and also directed the National University for a time. After he retired to Guangdong in 1540, he founded thirty-six academies and is said to have had over 4,000 students.[170] Zhan Ruoshui urged students to participate in examinations (it is striking that Zhan found it necessary to insist that students had an obligation to participate) and warned them against the dangers of either the one-sided pursuit of "fragmentary" learning (i.e., Zhu Xi as he saw it) or self-absorption (Wang Yangming). But Zhan also asserted that, of the Five Relations, the bond between friends was of greatest importance (rather than the parent-child or the ruler-minister relationship) and saw the academy as a place in which literati would reside for limited periods to train themselves in "realizing innate coherence (*tian li*) wherever they may be in whatever they are doing."[171] All these men were frequently at odds with those in power in government and dismayed at the state of the world; some of their best-known followers chose to spend much of their lives teaching and lecturing.

The restoration of academies responded to the demand for literati education and, at least on the part of many teachers, an interest in taking self-cultivation seriously rather than in merely preparing for the examinations. When Zhu Xi's White Deer Grotto Academy was restored in 1465 and Wu Yubi's student Hu Juren accepted the invitation to serve as headmaster, his first precept was "Set a true direction and establish the will."[172] Some academies offered a broad curriculum that went well beyond the Neo-Confucian. The Hongdao Academy, founded in 1480, expected students to study the Four Books and Five Classics, the *Family Rituals*, Ancient Style prose and Tang poetry, examination essay composition, statecraft, military texts, water conservancy, and famine relief as well as recording their merits and demerits in behavior and practicing archery and the lute.[173]

The reinvigoration of the complex of earlier activities—academies and lectures, compacts among participants, and shrines to past masters —is illustrated by developments in Ji'an prefecture in Jiangxi in the years following Wang Yangming's service there in 1516–20.[174] Wang thought highly of academies and recognized their value as a vehicle apart from the state school system for encouraging literati to practice morality.[175] As one of his disciples wrote:

Now we again establish academies separate from the [state] schools. . . . We know that the establishment of schools was [begun] long ago. That length of time has made schools [familiar and] commonplace. Being commonplace, [what they do] is considered trifling. Being considered trifling has resulted in neglect. With neglect, the way of learning has become lax.

The establishment of academies is recent. Recentness is newness. Newness makes for attentiveness. Attentiveness makes for determination. With determination, the way of learning will be practiced. What is being done now is of the first order in establishing government and education.[176]

Wang's lectures were moving affairs, and while in Jiangxi he tried to lecture every day. Six years later when an official gave a series of philosophical lectures at the county school and drew large numbers, some of those who had heard Wang before formed the Time Misers' Association. Members were to meet five days a month with the purpose of helping one another maintain their resolve to practice the innate knowing of the good. Their organization replicated Zhu Xi's community compact, with rituals, mutual evaluations, records of good and bad deeds, and formal agreements to abide by the compact, their contract with one another. The association held together, admitting new members, for at least thirty years.[177] Ten years after establishing the group, they built an academy, with the support of local officials, retired officials, and literati who advocated Wang Yangming's views. This set a precedent, and almost immediately others built three new academies. After that came the Association of the Four Localities and then an annual meeting for like-minded literati from all five counties in Ji'an. Funds were raised for a Transmitting the Mind Hall (Chuanxin tang) and a shrine to Wang Yangming and four of his Jiangxi disciples. In the 1570s, the annual meeting hall became the Meeting Hall of the Nine Counties (Jiu yi hui guan). Out of this process came an extraordinary blossoming of academies, about 100 in Ji'an and two neighboring prefectures. The degree of support is evident in a donor list for a local academy from 1592: 574 donors, of whom only 44 percent ranked as officials. The same pattern unfolded elsewhere as Neo-Confucian literati and officials founded associations to announce their shared commitment (often called "common resolve associations," *tongzhi hui*) and built academies.[178]

It might seem contradictory that one of the consequences of the spread of Wang Yangming learning was the formation of highly structured and formal associations. Wang and the lecturers that followed him were interested less in producing curricula than in speaking directly to an audience and motivating them to activate the innate ability of their own minds. The emotional catharsis of a meeting—Wang recommended motivational activities such as group singing[179]—was meant to inspire individuals to act. But perhaps we should see this as a kind of compensation: precisely because learning was not seen as a matter of progressing through a structured curriculum, those who committed themselves to it sought other structured ways to form communities.

Wang Yangming's ideas were disseminated by disciples who traveled through the southern provinces discoursing on learning. "Lecture (or discourse) assemblies" (*jiang hui*) were also held at the capital in 1553–54, and thousands attended. The movement was sustained by a new generation of lecturers, men who had never met Wang himself. Luo Rufang (1515–88), it is said, could open the hearts of his listeners, and they did not have to be particularly well educated to grasp the message; 40,000–50,000 people attended one such gathering, and "hollerers" were employed to amplify his lecture.[180] The political implications of this were not lost on the powerful grand secretary Zhang Juzheng

(1525–82), who ordered the closing of academies in 1579 in order to end literati agitation against the court. In Zhang's model of the proper order of things, the interests of the state were paramount, its institutions were the basis for public order, and it was the opinions of its officials that mattered.[181]

The suppression was short-lived. Soon after Zhang's death, Wang Yangming was officially enshrined in the Confucian temple and recognized as a "true Confucian."[182] Wang's message was controversial, but its dissemination drove critics to hold lecture assemblies of their own. At the start of the seventeenth century, proponents of "innate knowing" dismayed by the overly idiosyncratic, self-absorbed, and emotional tendencies of some followers of Wang's learning set out to create a national organization that would bring together literati and officials who believed that being moral required both an act of will and constant effort. The Donglin Academy—which had lecture assemblies, membership lists, compacts, and publications—gained a regional following in the southeast and national fame as it sought not only to redirect intellectual culture and literati opinion but also to place its members in government and reform politics. It was suppressed in 1625, twenty-two years after its founding, and six of its leading members died in prison.[183] There is no Song or Yuan parallel for this kind of literati organization.

This was not the only change from pre-Ming traditions. The Neo-Confucian revival was not exclusively for literati. Audiences for Neo-Confucian teachers were not limited to literati, and there were exceptional cases of charismatic Neo-Confucian lecturers who were themselves barely literate.[184] When Neo-Confucians promoted kinship organization, as they did with various revisions of Zhu Xi's *Family Rituals* and their own family instructions,[185] they were addressing a society in which lineages and genealogies had become commonplace and were no longer confined to the literati. He Xinyin (1517–79), who tried to persuade his lineage to transform itself into a communal family, had a notion of family that extended to seeing all under heaven as one family. This, together with his belief in the fundamental importance of the relation between friends before all other relations, suggests that it was the communitarian aspect of family life rather than hierarchies of age and gender that interested him most.[186] There was also a new interest in celebrating women as moral exemplars—not simply because they remained chaste in widowhood, something the government formally recognized, but because they were willing to die in order to defend their moral commitment to chastity.[187]

The leadership of community activities to improve the lives of the common people also broke with Song and Yuan precedents. The lines between literati and others, particularly merchants, were still apparent, but new associations made a point of crossing those lines. Moreover, there was an interest not only in benefiting the people but also in getting them to see themselves as moral actors with responsibility for one another.

This change is evident in the use of the community compact. In Song and Yuan, members of literati families had created compacts across kinship lines as associations for putting Neo-Confucian learning into daily practice. Now the community compact was also seen as an instrument for organizing the common people of a locale in an inclusive fashion at a time when the legislated forms of community had lost their vitality and efficacy. Similarly, proposals for community granaries envisioned them as being stocked and maintained by groups of families rather than by well-to-do literati families on behalf of the poor.[188] The most famous community compact text was by Wang Yangming, written for villagers who had been restored to commoner status after being caught up in the Prince of Ning's rebellion.[189] Its purpose was to create a community by having them enter into a compact under self-chosen leaders, which would help them maintain the intention to do good henceforth. They were to build a hall, pay dues, resolve conflicts, defend themselves against extortion by local government personnel, pay their taxes, farm their fields, conduct marriages and funerals properly, prevent foreclosures on land by creditors, and hold elaborately choreographed meetings at which their good and bad deeds would be registered. A number of Wang's followers worked to institute community compacts in Jiangxi and elsewhere.[190]

Of particular note was the appearance of societies, with dues and membership lists, devoted to the moral improvement of the members and to charity toward others.[191] The first "benevolent societies" (*tong shan hui*) were founded by committed Neo-Confucians engaged in the whole range of local activities discussed here and sympathetic to Wang Yangming. Yang Dongming (1548–1624), from Henan, founded one of the first benevolent societies; it used its funds to aid in road and bridge repair and help defray the costs of funerals. He also founded a granary to equalize the price of grain, arranged farmland for the poor, established a community school, engaged in dike repair, revived the community drinking ceremony for local elders, and founded an association for improving literati education.[192] Gao Panlong, a director of the Donglin Academy, was similarly involved in all forms of local activism, as was his close follower Chen Longzheng (1585–1645). Gao's benevolent society continued to meet until 1671, long after his death. His lectures for the society did not deal with learning in Zhu Xi's sense but with the importance of family virtues as a bottom-up solution to transforming society. Family virtues in this case meant the Six Maxims proclaimed by the Ming founder (which were in fact taken directly from Zhu Xi's placard exhorting the common people to community moral self-supervision). Chen also made the point that the charitable institutions such societies were to create should be differentiated from both the aid the state offered the poor and the activities of Buddhist monasteries. Once again literati voluntarism as a cross-lineage activity was being offered as an alternative to state institutions and religious endeavors, but Chen also hoped to avoid the politicization that had engulfed the academies.[193]

The new inclusiveness of late Ming literati voluntarism had roots in the early Ming social legislation. The idea that all should be involved, with the better-off leading the way, had come to be part of how Ming Neo-Confucians understood their mission in social terms. However, by the end of the sixteenth century, it had become clear that moral cultivation movements, community building, and local activism were no longer the province of Neo-Confucians alone. To some extent, this was a matter of religious competitors asserting their own roles. The Buddhist monk Zhuhong (1535–1615), for example, created lay societies devoted to releasing life as a means of individual transformation.[194] Christian missionaries established their own community organizations for personal cultivation and doing good.[195] The Three Teachings Are One movement of Lin Zhao'en (1517–98) set up its own self-cultivation halls, letting participants choose between Buddhist, Daoist, and Confucian modes, and even had its own unique clothing.[196]

Establishing a link between cultivating personal morality and acting with social responsibility could be accomplished in a manner that was at odds with Neo-Confucian philosophy. This is evident in the increasingly popular ledgers of merit and demerit, which spelled out good and bad deeds appropriate to different social groups.[197] Yuan Huang (1533–1606), a persuasive advocate of the use of such ledgers, argued that they were efficacious as a means of getting what one wanted, such as passing examinations and having sons, and to argue this he appealed not to Neo-Confucian theory but to the idea that for every deed there was an inevitable recompense. Yuan shared the view of many in the Wang Yangming school that individuals by their own actions determined their own fate, but he turned Neo-Confucianism on its head, for his reason to do good was that it was to one's own advantage. Neo-Confucians continued to believe that moral action was moral precisely because it was motivated by an appeal to innate coherence or one's innate ability to know the good, not by thoughts of gain. Objections by leading Neo-Confucians did not, however, diminish the popularity of the ledgers.[198]

It was not only religious movements that challenged the centrality of Neo-Confucianism to voluntary efforts to create moral communities. Among the secular literati, some were turning back to what made literati different from the rest of the population and what made Confucians different from religious specialists: their traditions of scholarship and their role as officials and aspirants to office. Lü Kun (1536–1618) from Henan is an example of someone deeply interested in serving the public good by improving local welfare, public education, and moral improvement. But he was not a Neo-Confucian idealist when it came to self-cultivation: he sought to correct his faults in what has been called a "fact-centered approach" rather than by seeking something within himself that would enable him to be free of faults. In thinking of ways in which local elites could work together with local government to help local society, he gave greater weight to local officials.[199] This turn away from moral idealism and toward statecraft is nowhere more evident than in the successor to the Donglin Academy: the Restoration Society (Fu she), founded in 1629. It also aspired to change national life, but its 2,000–3,000 registered members had lost much of the Neo-Confucian conviction that being a moral person was the fundamental solution to the ills of the age and had instead turned their attention to practical institutional means of solving problems in local society and national politics.[200] Those scholars at the end of the Ming, who would later be seen as the first generation of the new style of literati scholarship known as "Evidential Learning," were attuned more to the Restoration Society than to the Donglin Academy, for they had largely abandoned the Neo-Confucian view that the goal of learning was sagehood and instead sought ways of knowing that did not depend on the Neo-Confucian belief in unity.

AFTERWORD

China's History and
Neo-Confucianism

In thinking about the larger role Neo-Confucianism played in China's history, I am concerned less with the question of whether it supported autocracy in politics and orthodoxy in thought than with how it was related to the larger changes in state and society that emerged during the Tang-Song transition. I see it as an *alternative* solution to the breakdown of the early imperial order as a political, social, economic, and cultural system. I call it an alternative solution because in the Northern Song *the* solution was the New Policies. The New Policies was the ultimate realization of the Ancient Style project that was first articulated in the late eighth century and gained general currency in the eleventh. Namely, (1) that the *shi* as the national elite could through learning gain a systematic understanding of the construction of civilization in antiquity as represented in the Confucian Classics; (2) that with this understanding as their guide, they could produce a new style of literary and cultural engagement that would demonstrate how they planned to set the world aright and the quality of their commitment and their ability to do so; (3) that having proven themselves through their writing, they could take power at court; and (4) that at court they could reform the activities and institutions of government so as to transform society into an integrated social order and improve the lives of all. The New Policies not only accepted the realities of the social and economic changes that had been taking place—the disappearance of the great clan oligarchy, the commercialization of economic life and private landownership, the growth of the south, the binding of *shi* status to education—but also furthered them. Wang Anshi's great insight was that by accepting the changes that were taking place, rather than trying to halt them as some of his opponents demanded, both the government and the economy could expand and grow. A larger, stronger, and wealthier government did not mean, as conservatives with their zero-sum view of the economy thought, that the populace had to become poorer. But the New Policies did involve greater intervention in the economy, in society, and in culture in ways that challenged the dominance of powerful local families. The New Policies regime intervened in large-scale commerce and the provision of rural credit, it organized rural householders into a system that in principle was under the command of local government, and it instituted a national curriculum and school system. These policies worked against the immediate interests of wealthy merchants and landowners, but they also offered the powerful the chance to become *shi*, to see themselves as members of the national elite, and to compete for office.

The first Neo-Confucians (Zhou Dunyi, Zhang Zai, the Cheng brothers, and their followers) were part of the conservative opposition to the New Policies. They differed in some ways from other opponents: they thought that ethical conduct was a more important indicator of personal worth than were literary accomplishment and learning; they were not interested in the lessons of history because the verities they sought transcended history; and they looked for the natural philosophical grounds for the learning of the ancient sages rather than taking the texts of the Classics as a sufficient foundation. Some favored decentralization and local *shi* leadership, but they came from families with histories of officeholding and saw themselves as part of a national political elite that should ideally be hereditary.

It was not until the Southern Song period that Neo-Confucianism as learning and social practice came to be seen as the foremost alternative to the New Policies solution. It succeeded by cultivating an audience among the *shi*, the literati, by which I mean anyone who was pursuing the education that marked men as literati. Zhu Xi, its leading intellect and organizer, recognized that he was speaking to those who were "being shi" (*wei shi zhe*), not just those who were "being officials" (*wei guan zhe*). Building on the philosophical doctrines of his predecessors and borrowing from and revising the views of his allies, he formulated a theory of learning that applied equally to the emperor and the literatus. His formulation placed the grounds of moral authority and responsibility in the individual, but its realization required a serious program of self-transformation. It was not the prerogative of the court and the government to tell men who cultivated themselves how to behave. Literati could be part of the national elite at an intellectual level through learning, and they could put their learning into practice by taking responsibility in local society. They could transform their families, they could create local communities of like-minded literati, and they could use their resources to create voluntary institutions for the improvement of local conditions. Unity, in all its many meanings, depended primarily on them and secondarily on government.

With the exception of the early Neo-Confucians, eleventh-century thinkers had been political thinkers, in that they assumed that changing the way government operated in relation to society was the goal of learning. In contrast, the Neo-Confucian alternative that emerged in Southern Song envisioned a government that would do less in local society and local literati who would voluntarily take it on themselves to do more. It was a model that gained adherents in the prosperous regions of the south among the many well-to-do families with money to spend on education and community work. And it spread during a period when those families who did have members in office were finding new ways of ensuring that some of their descendants would serve as well, when the examination system was becoming less fair and producing a smaller proportion of officeholders than in Northern Song, and when the bureaucracy was becoming less of a meritocracy based on education—trends that continued into the Yuan period.

But was it really Neo-Confucianism that was creating this model, or was it social and political conditions? In general, local elites did not want the government to interfere in land tenure and commerce, they wanted taxes reduced and tax revenues spent locally, and they were taking initiatives on their own to improve access to education and local conditions. At the same time, the government was often preoccupied with national defense. Neo-Confucians were responding to conditions with ideas that worked for literati—however we may define them, "lo-cal elites" were people who called themselves *shi*—and Neo-Confucians saw the potential of private educational institutions. Most important, by the end of the twelfth century, a coherent Neo-Confucian program for literati learning and social transformation under voluntary literati lead-ership was in place. They were the ones who justified local activism by binding it to a totalizing theory of life and self and by tying local social responsibility to elite privilege. The fact is that theirs was the program that spread, over the court's opposition, until the court was compelled to recognize their claim to authority over learning and values.

In this book, I have not dwelt on an alternative to the Neo-Confucian approach that emerged in Southern Song: the "statecraft" approach ad-vanced by thinkers such as Zhu Xi's contemporary Ye Shi. Statecraft thinkers were concerned with how the state could, in addition to main-taining national defense, increase the country's material welfare by facili-tating the growth of the private economy. Despite the appeal of their views in economically advanced regions, statecraft thinkers were political theorists rather than the organizers of a social movement that spoke to the literati as a national elite without prospects of government service.[1]

What were the consequences of the spread of Neo-Confucianism among local literati? As local voluntarism gained importance, the value of service in government as a means of realizing ideals declined. Gov-ernment service did not become less rewarding in a material sense—it still gave officials financial privileges and legal immunities—but there was now a way of pursuing ideals and serving the common good out-side government. It is striking that after the Song and before the eigh-teenth century the government rarely tried to provide adequate official salaries; it apparently assumed that officials would seek to profit from their posts, making government service a profitable calling but not a morally high one. What clearly is the case is that the court rarely again tried—and when it did, it failed—to overhaul its institutions so that the state apparatus became the active agent in transforming society in the manner of the New Policies of the Northern Song. In a sense, the Northern Song criticism of imperial government, that it was concerned with its own preservation rather than the common good, applied once more, but it applied in a context in which literati were doing things out-side government that they had not been doing in Northern Song. When

Neo-Confucians did serve in government, they supported the spread of Neo-Confucian learning and local voluntarism rather than trying to expand the state's role at the expense of local elites. This had implications for what it meant to be an official—rather than asking what the government could do, Neo-Confucians focused increasingly on how officials behaved as people and the kind of personal models they were creating; ideally they were to persuade people to take responsibility for themselves. It seems to me that the consequences were the personalization and moralization of politics. But authority over national ideology and "Confucian values" did not return to the court, and when the occasional Ming emperor tried to claim such authority, the claim was contested.

At first glance the Ming founding appears to have been a return to the model of activist state that intervened in society, culture, and the economy. Certainly the Ming founder's social policies, by translating into law the Neo-Confucian vision of society as composed of self-supervising local communities with a shared morality, were a concerted intervention in society. But they were not, I would argue, a return to governmental activism in the New Policies manner, nor did they tie government activities to an expanding commercial economy. The Ming founder's goals were to keep government to the minimum and certainly to keep it from interfering in and harming the local community. And, if Fang Xiaoru's extant writings are a reliable indicator, this was also to be a policy goal of the founder's grandson, the Jianwen emperor. Whether the juridical powers of local leaders survived the Yongle reign is open to question. Although the Yongle emperor officially patronized Neo-Confucian ideology, it is not clear that the usurping emperor, whose power base was on the northern border, shared the Neo-Confucian social vision. But the disappearance of voluntarism lasted only a century. As the community systems began to break down—I suspect as a result of inflexibility in the face of population growth and the return of commercialization, the investment of private wealth in securing literati status through education, and the reluctance of elite families with officeholders and examination candidates to play their assigned roles in local systems—literati voluntarism led by Neo-Confucian activists returned.

Those who study middle-period history are frequently struck by how many of the phenomena of that period reappear in the late Ming: commercialization, ideological ferment, local elite (often called "gentry") activism, and divisions between the court and literati in and out of office. Yet late Ming voluntarism, like much of late Ming Neo-Confucian discoursing on learning, is different from that of Song and Yuan. Above all it is more inclusive. I think this difference owes much to the inclusive social legislation of early Ming and suspect that Wang Yangmingism was successful not only because it reinvigorated individual moral effort and offered new literati ways of becoming involved in public life but also because it tapped into the ideals that lay behind early Ming policy. In Song the literati were the target, and voluntary community institutions meant that literati families were in charge of doing good. But in late Ming, the audience for Neo-Confucian learning, particularly for Wang Yangming's teachings, included nonliterati. Some community compacts tried to include all the families in a community and not just representatives of literati families, and societies devoted to going good for the local community included people of means who were not literati. An interpretation of Neo-Confucian doctrine that stressed moral motivation at the expense of acquiring knowledge and proposed that the mind was capable of providing moral guidance by an act of will rather than through the cumulative cultivation of awareness fit a time that saw social responsibility as the duty of people from all backgrounds.

In late Ming, the Neo-Confucian model of a limited government with local voluntarism was adopted by other local religious and secular organizations. It seems to me that the degree of organizational activity in late Ming—of academies, associations, and benevolent societies, and the longevity of the organizations created—goes beyond Song and Yuan precedents. I can at most speculate as to why this was so. These new organizations (even when they had dues and membership lists) look a lot more like multinodal social networks than, for example, hierarchically structured organizations or proselytizing movements. In the Song case, the role of Zhu Xi in transforming Neo-Confucian learning into a social movement and the role of Zhu's writings in defining correct ideas after his death provided an ideological center and touchstone. The reliance on social networks rather than a shared ideology in late Ming goes together with the obvious breakdown in intellectual unity among Neo-Confucians in the decades after Wang Yangming, the increasing relativism among literati intellectuals, and the willingness of

some to identify with different ideological positions simultaneously—
for example, Neo-Confucianism and Christianity.

The Neo-Confucian model of limited government with voluntary communal leadership survived both the Qing conquest and Neo-Confucianism's loss of the center of elite intellectual culture, although it seems to me that local leadership in the early Qing lacked the ideological inspiration of its Ming predecessors. In the late seventeenth and early eighteenth centuries, the Qing emperor claimed he had at last truly united legitimate political authority and moral authority (or "legitimate succession" in politics, *zheng tong*, and "succession to the Way" in morality, *dao tong*).[2] However, he did not try to restore early Ming social legislation; he did not change the model of limited government and local elite leadership. Qing imperial policy did, however, retain the Four Books and Zhu Xi's commentaries as important subjects tested in the examination system, and thus it ensured that the empire's educated elite would continue to be conversant with Zhu Xi's explanation of why social morality was grounded in the individual, even when literati intellectual culture was moving away from philosophy.

Accounting for the rise of Evidential Learning goes beyond the scope of this study, but I would suggest that it was discontinuous with Neo-Confucianism in important respects. The turn toward the disciplined study of the physical world, antiquity, history, the Classics, and all sorts of texts did not proceed on Neo-Confucian premises. It was not part of a program of learning that advanced the student toward sagehood, it did not reveal the learning of the sages, it did not cultivate awareness of innate coherence or innate knowing of the good. It seems to me that it proceeded without assuming that there was an innate coherence to things that scholars should seek to apprehend. In short, the search for meaning was not premised on a belief in unity, and a sense of illuminating the coherence of a subject in the mind was not the goal of learning. Rather, Evidential Learning as an enterprise avoided the assumption that there was a necessary coherence to things and asked instead what meaning and knowledge could be under those circumstances. The answer was that knowledge consisted of reaching factual conclusions that added to knowledge, conclusions that were not at first apparent but emerged from the careful study of the evidence.[3] I suspect that there is an important difference between this and empirical studies in Europe in the same era, where the idea of discovering the inherent coherence of the world provided grounds for breaking with traditional authority. In China the inherent value of coherence and unity had become suspect.

Yet as an intellectual movement among the literati Evidential Learning had some things in common with Neo-Confucianism. Although the supporters of Evidential Learning defined learning differently, they supposed that learning was the means of intellectual discipline and cultivation for the literati. After an initial period in which history, literature, the natural world, and mathematics were also subjects of inquiry, Evidential Learning scholars focused increasingly on the Classics and antiquity and produced a new, but very different, tradition of commentaries. China's antiquity still mattered, not as the source of moral knowledge for those seeking sagehood, but as both the pre-eminent testing ground for the method of learning and the object of cumulative research. Finally, much like their Neo-Confucian predecessors, they asserted the independence of intellectual life from political power while seeking support and recognition from the bureaucracy and the court.

When I first began to learn about China's history, "Confucianism" was taught as a purely historical subject, a part of a past that had been cast aside, despite the efforts of some twentieth-century thinkers to establish it as a part of a Chinese tradition of philosophy. Although the twentieth century saw the greatest degree of state intervention in all aspects of life since the New Policies, I am convinced that Confucianism is much more than a historical subject; it remains a resource for thinking about the present. The general Confucian interest in how the social system, government, economy, and culture can be made to further human community and welfare speaks to China today, as does the Neo-Confucian concern with the autonomy and responsibility of the individual. The irrelevance of Communist Party ideology, the corruption of the bureaucratic apparatus, participation in a shared world order, and the extraordinary growth in private wealth have opened the way for a new search for a shared intellectual foundation. But who is the audience for a new formulation of learning that will address these concerns? And what shape, under current circumstances, might that formulation take as ideology and social practice?

Reference Matter

Notes

For complete author names, titles, and publication data for works cited here in short form, see the Bibliography, pp. 319–51.

Chapter 1

1. Three recent studies survey the historiography and interpretation of the transformation of China's political, economic, social, and cultural life from Tang to Song. For a discussion of the formative role of Japanese scholarly debates, see von Glahn, "Imagining Pre-modern China," which locates Song in world-historical perspective. See also Bol, "Tang Song bianxing de fansi." For an important discussion of central issues in conceptualizing change, particularly useful for its discussion of recent scholarship in China, see Liu Liyan, "He wei 'Tang Song bianges'?"

2. Tao, *Two Sons of Heaven*, 77–78.

3. Mote, *Imperial China*, 117.

4. Hansen, *The Open Empire*, 269.

5. Although from the perspective of Jin, and some Song, writers, Song had failed to live up to its obligations to aid Jin in the campaign against Liao.

6. The best survey history of the northern states is Mote, *Imperial China*, 2–91, 168–288.

7. For an argument that paintings depicting foreign tributaries give way to "ethnographic" paintings of Liao people as different, see Leung, "The Frontier Imaginary in the Song Dynasty"; and idem, "'Felt yurts neatly arrayed.'"

8. Holcombe, "Immigrants and Strangers."

9. Tuotuo, *Jin shi*, 73.

10. From his announcement on taking the throne, in Qian Bocheng et al., *Quan Ming wen*, 1.2.

11. See the various announcements to rulers of Japan, Turfan, and other states in ibid., 1.22, 3–4, 324, 347.

12. Bol, "Seeking Common Ground."

13. Tillman, "Confucianism in the Chin."

14. Dong Guodong, *Zhongguo renkou shi: Sui Tang Wudai shiqi*, 198–99; Wu Songdi, *Zhongguo renkou shi: Liao Song Jin Yuan shiqi*, 122–35.

15. For a discussion of the visible evidence for state-administered land tenure systems in the north but not the south, see Leeming, "Official Landscapes in Traditional China."

16. Liu Liyan, "He wei 'Tang Song biange'?" cites Qi Xia on private ownership. My understanding of economic development is drawn largely from McDermott and Shiba, "Economic Change During the Song."

17. Hartwell, "Demographic, Political, and Social Transformation of China."

18. Farmer, *Early Ming Government*.

19. So, *Prosperity, Region, and Institutions in Maritime China*.

20. Bol, "Government, Society, and State," 167.

21. For a survey of technological changes, see Elvin, *The Pattern of the Chinese Past*, 113–99.

22. Yang Weisheng et al., *Liang Song wenhua shi yanjiu*, 269, citing work by You Xiuling 游修齡.

23. McDermott and Shiba, "Economic Change During the Song."

24. Ge Jinfang, *Song Liao Xia Jin jingji yanxi*, 141–43.

25. Hartwell, "Markets, Technology, and the Structure of Enterprise," 37.

26. McDermott and Shiba, "Economic Change During the Song."

27. I take the terms "tributary" and "petty-capitalist" modes of production from Gates, *China's Motor*. Gates does not differentiate between them in regional terms.

28. Shiba Yoshinobu, *Sōdai Kōnan keizaishi no kenkyū*, chaps. 1–4.

29. Liu Guanglin, "Wrestling for Power," app. D.

30. G. William Skinner ("Introduction") points out that the centrally appointed bureaucracy and the total number of counties and prefectures did not grow with the population, which increased from 100 million at the end of the eleventh century to 450 million by the end of the nineteenth.

31. Bol, "Reconceptualizing the Nation in Southern Song."

32. For this contrast between Chang'an and Kaifeng and the transformation of cities, see Heng, *Cities of Aristocrats and Bureaucrats*.

33. Ibid., 189–90.

34. Shiba Yoshinobu, "Sōdai no toshika wo kangaeru."

35. My understanding of the Song economy and fiscal policy owes much to Liu Guanglin, "Wrestling for Power."

36. Ouyang Xiu and Song Qi, *Xin Tang shu*, 54.1386, 1389; Du You, *Tong dian*, 204.

37. Gao Congming, *Songdai huobi yu huobi liutong yanjiu*, 103.

38. Hartwell, "Markets, Technology, and the Structure of Enterprise," 29–31.

39. For a discussion of the development of monetary policy from the Song on, see von Glahn, *Fountain of Fortune*.

40. Gao Congming, *Songdai huobi yu huobi liutong yanjiu*, 295; Guo Zhengzhong, *Liang Song chengxiang shangpin huobi jingji kaolue*, 349, citing Quan Hansheng, gives 45 million strings.

41. Guo Zhengzhong, *Liang Song chengxiang shangpin huobi jingji kaolue*, 224–28.

42. Ibid., 229–301. Cf. Shiba Yoshinobu, "Sōdai no toshika wo kangaeru."

43. Liang Gengyao, *Songdai shehui jingji shi lunji*, 510, 346.

44. For an account of the tea and horse trade with Inner Asia, see Paul Smith, *Taxing Heaven's Storehouse*.

45. Sun Hongsheng, *Tang Song chaye jingji*, 64–65, 69; totals calculated by Liu Guanglin.

46. Guan Lüquan, *Songdai Guangzhou de haiwai maoyi*.

47. These two views are taken, respectively, by Clark, *Community, Trade and Networks*; and So, *Prosperity, Region, and Institutions in Maritime China*.

48. McDermott and Shiba, "Economic Change During the Song."

49. In adopting this view, I follow Shiba and Elvin, rather than Bao and Miyazawa. See Bao Weimin, "'Songdai jingji geming lun' fansi"; Elvin, *The Pattern of the Chinese Past*; Miyazawa Tomoyuki, *Sōdai Chūgoku no kokka to keizai*; Yoshinobu Shiba, *Commerce and Society in Sung China*; idem, "Urbanization and the Development of Markets"; and idem, *Sōdai Kōnan keizaishi no kenkyū*.

50. Liu Guanglin, "Wrestling for Power."

51. Ye Xiaoxin, *Zhongguo fa zhi shi*, 205–6, 12–14, 21–27, 40–41. I thank Guanglin Liu for these references.

52. McDermott and Shiba, "Economic Change During the Song."

53. Chaffee, *The Thorny Gates of Learning in Sung China*, 39–40; for a discussion, see Bol, "The Examination System and the *Shih*."

54. These issues extend into Ming and Qing as well. See, e.g., Danjō Hiroshi, "Ming Qing xiangshen lun"; Miyazawa Tomoyuki, "Songdai dizhu yu nongmin de zhuwenti"; Mori Masao, "Sōdai iko no shitaifu to chiiki shakai"; Tanigawa Michio, "Problems Concerning the Japanese Periodization of Chinese History"; and idem, "Zhongguo shehui gouzao de tezhi yu shidafu de wenti."

55. Miyazaki Ichisada, "Sōdai no shifu."

56. The Marxist periodization was first sketched out by Maeda Naonori 前田直典 in 1948 and, after his death in 1949, developed by Ishimoda Tadashi 石母田正. Ishimoda drew on Sutō Yoshiyuki's 周藤吉之 work on Song and Yuan land tenure; see Teraji Jun, "Nihon ni okeru Sōshi kenkyū no kichō" for a discussion of these figures and their political attitudes. This view of the Tang and Song also drew on Niida Noboru's 仁井田陞 legal studies. Some of the major statements of the "Tokyo school" view of later imperial history are translated in Grove and Daniels, *State and Society in China*. For an overview of debates between the Kyoto and Tokyo interpretations, see von Glahn, "Imagining Pre-modern China."

57. Yao Yingting, "Shilun lixue de xingcheng."

58. Some of the works that have contributed to this view are: Bossler, *Powerful Relations*; Chaffee, *The Thorny Gates of Learning in Sung China*; Ebrey, *The Aristocratic Families of Early Imperial China*; idem, *Family and Property in Sung China*; Hartwell, "Demographic, Political, and Social Transformation of China"; Hymes, *Statesmen and Gentlemen*; Johnson, "The Last Years of a Great Clan"; and idem, *The Medieval Chinese Oligarchy*. For a synthetic account, see Bol, *"This Culture of Ours,"* chap. 2, "The Transformation of the *Shih*."

59. Bol, *"This Culture of Ours,"* 43–45.

60. Sima Guang, *Sima Wenzheng gong chuan jia ji*, 40.517.

61. Chaffee, *The Thorny Gates of Learning in Sung China*, 95–115.

62. James T. C. Liu, "The Sung Views on the Control of Government Clerks."

63. Kondō Kazunari, "Sai Kyō no kakyo, gakkō seisaku."

64. Lu You, *Lu Fangweng quanji*, 21.124.

65. Quoted in Chen Wenyi, *You guanxue dao shuyuan*, 361.

66. Chen Liang, *Chen Liang ji*, 34.457.

67. Bol, "Zhang Ruyu, the *Qunshu kaosuo*, and Diversity in Intellectual Culture."

68. Bol, "Local History and Family in Past and Present."

69. This is, in essence, the argument advanced in Bossler, *Powerful Relations*.

70. This is the case set out by Hymes, *Statesmen and Gentlemen*.

71. I.e., Pan Jingliang; see Lü Zujian, *Donglai Lü shi ji*, app. 1.1a–8a. On northern refugee families, see Wu Songdi, *Beifang yimin yu Nan Song shehui bianqian*.

72. Zheng Qiao 鄭樵, introduction to the treatise on clans and lineages in the *Tong zhi* 通志.

73. Oh Kuemsung, *Mindai shakai keizaishi kenkyū*.

74. School enrollments are cited by Ge Shengzhong, *Danyang ji*, 1.2b–4b. For an authoritative account of changes in educational institutions under

Huizong, see Yuan Zheng, *Songdai jiaoyu*, 120–51. Kondō Kazunari ("Sai Kyō no kakyo, gakkō seisaku") argues that the expansion of schools and tax breaks contributed directly to the expansion of the *shi*. For a challenge to Oh Keumsung's position, see Takahashi Yoshirō, "Sōdai no shijin mibun ni tsuite."

75. Chaffee, *The Thorny Gates of Learning in Sung China*, 136–37.

76. Liang Gengyao, *Songdai shehui jingji shi lunji*, 626–29.

77. Bol, "The Examination System and the *Shih*."

78. Chia, *Printing for Profit*.

79. Wang Shuizhao, *Songdai wenxue tonglun*, 46–47.

80. Zhu Chuanyu, *Songdai xinwen shi*, chaps. 1–4.

81. De Weerdt, "Byways in the Imperial Chinese Information Order."

82. Based on the records collected in Hu Zongmao, *Jinhua jingji zhi*.

83. The increased use of the protection privilege and less competitive qualifying examinations for official offspring resulted in what John Chaffee has called a "failure of fairness"; see *The Thorny Gates of Learning in Sung China*.

84. This is one of the many insights in Liu Liyan, "He wei 'Tang Song biange'?"

Chapter 2

1. Fan Zhongyan, *Fan Wenzheng gong quanji*, 5.9b, "On the Values of Emperors and Kings."

2. Ouyang Xiu, *Ouyang Xiu quanji* (1961), waiji 9.411–13.

3. Hon, *The Yijing and Chinese Politics*, 60.

4. I follow the numbers of degrees given in Chaffee, *The Thorny Gates of Learning in Sung China*.

5. Wei Zheng and Linghu Defen, *Sui shu*, 32.903.

6. This was the "Insight into the Classics" (*ming jing*) field, which differed from the Tang memorization track of the same name. For the legislation, see Xu Song, *Song huiyao jigao*, xuanju 3.33a–34a.

7. For the contents of the examinations in all fields, the Five Dynasties models, and the earliest changes, see Jin Zhongshu, "Bei Song keju zhidu yanjiu, I," 2–12; and idem, "Bei Song keju zhidu yanjiu, xu," 105–6.

8. Hong Mai (*Rong zhai sui bi*, 3.31) noted that early Sung candidates did not always understand the point of the assigned theme or recognize its original context (they were allowed to ask the examiner) and in some cases brought books with them into the hall. This is confirmed by an edict from 1005; see Xu Song, *Song huiyao jigao*, xuanju 1.7b–8a. Ye Mengde (*Shilin yan yu*, 8.3a–b) noted that eventually the passages from the histories and Classics that provided the themes were printed and distributed to candidates beforehand. Both Ye and Hong were speaking of the palace examination.

9. Fumoto Yasutaka, *Hoku Sō ni okeru Jugaku no tenkai*, 33, quoting Ye Mengde.

10. Ma Duanlin, *Wenxian tongkao*, 35.322a.

11. Xu Xuan, *Xu Qisheng ji*, 23.230.

12. Tian Xi, *Xian ping ji*, 2.9b.

13. The idea was usually used with reference to Sima Qian's (ca. 145–ca. 85 B.C.) assertion that the Zhou dynasty valued *wen*, Shang loyalty or reverence, and Xia native substance. Ouyang Xiu wrote one of the several examination questions on the subject; see *Ouyang Xiu quanji* (1986), 528. See also Liu Chang's (1019–68) essay, "The Three Eras Shared a Common Way," in Liu Chang, *Gongshi ji*, 38.10a. Both men were questioning whether *wen* alone was enough.

14. *Analects* 9.5.

15. Ma Duanlin, *Wenxian tongkao*, 38.357c.

16. *Song huiyao: xuanju* 7.5b–6a. For a table of palace themes from the beginning of the dynasty through the 1060s, see Jin Zhongshu, "Bei Song keju zhidu yanjiu, xu," 142–48. The rhapsody theme was taken from the Pi hexagram in the *Book of Change*.

17. Yao Xuan, *Tang wen cui*, preface 1a.

18. Zhang Yong, *Guai yai ji*, 10.11a; reply to a student's query on *wen*.

19. Ouyang Xiu, *Ouyang Xiu quanji* (1961), 17.124.

20. Su Shi, *Su Dongpo ji*, 4.12.8.52–53.

21. Su Che, *Longchuan lue zhi*, bie zhi 1.11a–b.

22. This and the following section appear in greater detail in Bol, "When Antiquity Mattered."

23. Wang Anshi, *Linchuan xiansheng wenji*, 67.711–12.

24. Cheng Yi identified this in his 1059 essay "What Learning Was It That Yanzi Loved?" (Cheng Hao and Cheng Yi, *Er Cheng ji*, Yichuan ji 8.577–78).

25. This reader-centric approach to the Classics is evident in the commentaries of Liu Chang, who was also fascinated by the *Spring and Autumn Annals*. See the discussion by Inaba Ichiro in Hervouet, *A Sung Bibliography*, 49.

26. Su Xun, *Jiayou ji*, 6.1a–10a.

27. Ouyang Xiu, *Shi ben yi*, 14.7a–9a.

28. Bol, "The Sung Context," 26–42.

29. Su Xun, *Jiayou ji*, 6.1a–2b.

30. Ouyang Xiu, *Ouyang Xiu quanji* (1961), waiji 16.481–82.

31. Cai Xiang, *Cai Xiang quanji*, 424, 557–58.

32. Li Gou, *Li Gou ji*, 5–23. See also Su Che, *Luan Cheng ji*, 1268–69.

33. For a discussion, see Bol, *"This Culture of Ours,"* 195–96.

34. See Ouyang Xiu's three-part essay "On Fundamentals," in *Ouyang Xiu quanji* (1961), waiji 9.411–13, jushi ji 17.121–24; and Zhang Fangping, *Le quan ji*,

86–88 ("Li yue lun"), 92 ("Jian su"), 110–12 ("Shihuo lun"), 275–78 ("Lun shuaiqian muyi shi").

35. Asim, "Aspects of the Perception of Zhou Ideals in the Song Dynasty."

36. See, e.g., their writings for the decree examination of 1061: Su Shi, *Su Dongpo ji*, 6.18.6.45–48 (three-part essay on *Zhongyong*); and Su Che, *Luan Cheng ji*, 386–89 (cover letter).

37. Wang Anshi, *Linchuan xiansheng wenji*, 47–48 (letter to Zu Zezhi), 181 (cover memorial for the commentary on the "Hongfan"), 242–43 ("Jiu bian er shang fa ke yan").

38. Ibid., 181 (cover memorial for the *Zi shuo*).

39. An important exception to this is the Buddhist monk Qisong (1007–71), who argued for the compatibility of Buddhist theory and cosmic resonance theory. For the history of cosmic resonance theory and its fate in Northern Song, see Skonicki, "Cosmos, State and Society."

40. Wang Anshi, *Linchuan xiansheng wenji*, 47–48 (letter to Zu Zezhi), 240–41.

41. Ibid., 181.

42. Bol, "Wang Anshi and the *Zhou li*."

43. Wang Anshi, *Linchuan xiansheng wenji*, 39.410.

44. Zeng Gong, *Zeng Gong ji*, 433–36.

45. Bol, *"This Culture of Ours,"* 235–36.

46. Ibid., 282–93; for greater detail, see Bol, "Su Shih and Culture." For a discussion on the importance of principle (*li*) in Su Shi's literary thought, see Fuller, *The Road to East Slope*, chap. 1.

47. Kasoff, *The Thought of Chang Tsai*, chap. 3.

48. Ibid., chap. 4.

49. Bol, *"This Culture of Ours,"* 306–27.

50. Graham, *Two Chinese Philosophers*, 44–58.

51. James T. C. Liu, *Ou-yang Hsiu*, 96–98.

52. Bol, "Su Shih and Culture," 78–81.

53. For a comparative discussion of the role of *qing* in Tang and Song, see Virág, "That Which Encompasses the Myriad Cares."

54. See, e.g., the account of the inheritability of moral quality in Tang epitaphs in Bossler, *Powerful Relations*.

55. For a study of the factional politics of the period, see Luo Jiaxiang, *Bei Song dangzheng yanjiu*.

56. Wang Anshi, *Linchuan xiansheng wenji*, 39.410–23.

57. Ibid., 73.779.

58. Ibid., 66.707.

59. Zeng Gong, *Zeng Gong ji*, 12.197–98.

60. For surveys of the New Policies, see Bol, *"This Culture of Ours,"* chaps. 6–7; Higashi Ichio, *Ō Anseki shinpō no kenkyū*; James T. C. Liu, *Reform in Sung China*; and Ye Tan, *Da bian fa*.

61. Paul Smith, *Taxing Heaven's Storehouse.*

62. Bol, "Examinations and Orthodoxies," 32–46.

63. Wang Anshi, *Linchuan xiansheng wenji*, 67.714.

64. Ibid., 84.880.

65. Shen Liao, *Yunchao bian*, 8.73b–74a.

66. Cheng Hao and Cheng Yi, *Er Cheng ji*, Yichuan ji 11.643.

Chapter 3

1. For a history of the term "Neo-Confucianism," see de Bary, *The Liberal Tradition in China*, 3–4. Hoyt Tillman has objected to the use of this term and also to the view of Neo-Confucianism he associates with de Bary; see Tillman, "A New Direction in Confucian Scholarship"; and de Bary, "The Uses of Neo-Confucianism: A Response to Professor Tillman." I think, for a study that crosses the centuries, using an outsider's term creates less confusion than adopting one term from within the tradition. On terminology in Chinese, see Zhu Hanmin, *Song Ming lixue tonglun*, 40–43.

2. Yao Mingda, *Cheng Yichuan nianpu*, 47; Cheng Hao and Cheng Yi, *Er Cheng ji*, Yichuan wen 8.580.

3. Cheng Hao and Cheng Yi, *Er Cheng ji*, yishu 6.95; cf. yishu 18.187.

4. Gardner, *Zhu Xi's Reading of the* Analects.

5. For a very good recent history of Confucianism as an unfolding tradition, see Berthrong, *Transformations of the Confucian Way*.

6. My use of these issues as a way of making some general distinctions in thought owes much to Mencius' distinction between the doctrines of others and what he took to be the Confucian position, and to Peterson, "Squares and Circles."

7. Tsuchida Kenjirō, "Shakai to shisō."

8. For a discussion of this process, see Thomas Wilson, *Genealogy of the Way*. To a large extent, as the case of Mou Zongsan illustrates, modern Confucian philosophers proceed in the same manner.

9. Cheng Hao and Cheng Yi, *Er Cheng ji*, Yichuan ji 11.640. Elaborated translation.

10. *Li*, translated as "principle," is a fundamental philosophical term for the Chengs. My reasons for adopting "coherence" are discussed in a later chapter.

11. Cheng Hao and Cheng Yi, *Er Cheng ji*, Yichuan ji 11.638. For Cheng, *dao* and *li* are equivalent.

12. Zhu Xi, *Yi Luo yuan yuan lu*.

13. For a refutation of the primacy granted Zhou Dunyi, see Graham, *Two Chinese Philosophers*, 152–75. For Zhou's text, the "Explanation of the Diagram of the Taiji," as Zhu understood it, see Wing-tsit Chan, *A Source Book in Chinese Philosophy*, 463–65. For an alternative rendering that aims to be true to Zhou, see Joseph Adler's translation in de Bary and Bloom, *Sources of Chinese Tradition*, 672–76.

14. Birdwhistell, *Transition to Neo-Confucianism*; Wyatt, *The Recluse of Loyang*. For a somewhat different reading of Shao Yong's ideas, see Bol, "Reconceptualizing the Order of Things."

15. Kasoff, *The Thought of Chang Tsai*.

16. For a social-historical account of the establishment of Neo-Confucianism in Fujian, see Kojima Tsuyoshi, "Fukken nanbu no meizoku to Shushigaku no fukyū."

17. See, e.g., Selover, *Hsieh Liang-tso and the* Analects *of Confucius*. Dong Yu-zheng (*Zhongguo lixue dacidian*, 115–16) argues that Yin Tun's lack of influence was a result of his being too loyal to the letter of Cheng Yi's teachings.

18. Borrell, "*Ko-wu* or *Kung-an?*"

19. Bol, "Chu Hsi's Redefinition of Literati Learning."

20. See the conference volume edited by Chaffee and de Bary, *Neo-Confucian Education*. See also Wing-tsit Chan, *Chu Hsi and Neo Confucianism*; idem, *Chu Hsi: New Studies*; and Zhu Xi, *Learning to Be a Sage*. For an account of Zhu Xi's response to other views within the Neo-Confucian camp, see Tillman, *Confucian Discourse and Chu Hsi's Ascendancy*.

21. My view of Lu owes much to Foster, "Differentiating Rightness from Profit."

22. On Wu Cheng's synthesis, see Gedalecia, "Wu Ch'eng's Approach to Internal Self-Cultivation and External Knowledge-Seeking." For others in the fourteenth century who accepted Lu, see Mabuchi Masaya, "Gen Minsho seiri-gaku no ichi somen." For a Ming effort to combine Lu and Zhu, see Cheng Minzheng, *Dao yi bian*.

23. For an analysis of the ban, see Schirokauer, "Neo-Confucians Under Attack."

24. De Weerdt, "The Composition of Examination Standards."

25. On the political goals of the court in recognizing Neo-Confucianism, see James T. C. Liu, "How Did a Neo-Confucian School Become the State Orthodoxy?"

26. Cheng Duanli, *Wei zhai ji*, 5.1b.

27. On the clustering of Southern Song (and later) Neo-Confucian leaders in Fujian, Zhejiang, and Jiangxi, see He Yousen, "Liang Song xuefeng de dili fenbu." Of the 511 known disciples of Zhu Xi, the largest concentrations were

in Fujian (171), Zhejiang (76), and Jiangxi (81) (Liu Shuxun, *Minxue yuanliu*, 511–80). Liu's work supplements the 467 disciples counted by Wing-tsit Chan (*Zhuzi menren*, 128).

28. Cai Fanglu, *Songdai Sichuan lixue yanjiu.*

29. Bol, "Seeking Common Ground."

30. Xiao Qiqing, "Yuandai de ruhu" (Yao Dali, "Yuanchao keju zhidu").

31. For an account of Neo-Confucianism in the north, see Tillman, "Confucianism in the Chin"; and Miura Shūichi, *Chūgoku shingaku no ryōsen*, 47–99. Tillman demonstrates, *contra* the traditional view, that the spread of Daoxue preceded the Mongols' capture of the Song scholar Zhao Fu in 1235, although Zhao did play an important intellectual role in the early Mongol period; see Yao Dali, "Jinmo Yuanchu lixue zai beifang de chuanbo." On Jin intellectual culture, see also Bol, "Chao Ping-wen."

32. For a survey of the establishment of Neo-Confucianism in Yuan, see Wing-tsit Chan, "Chu Hsi and Yuan Neo-Confucianism." See also de Bary, *Neo-Confucian Orthodoxy*, 35–60, esp. for Xu Heng.

33. This very important conclusion is arrived at through a detailed comparison of southern and northern literati careers and ideology by Wen-Yi Chen, "Networks, Communities, and Identities."

34. Wu Cheng is the subject of Gedalecia, *The Philosophy of Wu Ch'eng*, and idem, *A Solitary Crane in a Spring Grove*. Xu Qian of Jinhua is an example of a teacher who stayed home; see Meng Peiyuan, *Lixue de yanbian*, 251–59.

35. On Song loyalism, see Jay, *A Change in Dynasties*. Some have found the loyalty of literati officials to Yuan disconcerting; see, e.g., Qian Mu, "Du Mingchu kaiguo zhuchen shi wen ji."

36. Dardess, *Confucianism and Autocracy.*

37. Danjō Hiroshi, *Minchō sensei shihai no shiteki kōzō*, pts. 1 and 2.

38. This is how I read the evidence in Andrew, "Zhu Yuanzhang and the Great Warnings"; George Jer-lang Chang, "Local Control in the Early Ming"; and Farmer, *Zhu Yuanzhang and Early Ming Social Legislation.*

39. Fang's importance is recognized by both Dardess, *Confucianism and Autocracy*, 264–89; and Danjō, *Minchō sensei shihai no shiteki kōzō*, pt. 3. See also Ditmanson, "Contesting Authority"; Ji Xiuzhu, *Mingchu daru Fang Xiaoru yanjiu*; and Mote, "Fang Hsiao-ju."

40. Lin Qingzhang, "*Wujing daquan* zhi xiuzuan."

41. See, e.g., Elman, "Where Is King Ch'eng"; and idem, "The Formation of 'Dao Learning' as Imperial Ideology."

42. Wing-tsit Chan, "The Ch'eng-Chu School of Early Ming," 45.

43. See the revisionist study of Xue and his northern school by Koh, "East of the River and Beyond." For Xue's view of Xu Heng and his lack of a sense

of local tradition, see ibid., pp. 57–64. Another northern Neo-Confucian was Cao Duan (1376–1434) from Henan, who taught in Shanxi.

44. Fifteenth-century intellectual culture awaits a thorough study; for an overview, see Chu Hung-lam, "Intellectual Trends in the Fifteenth Century."

45. Wang Tingxiang is one such case; see Ong, "The Principles Are Many."

46. For a discussion of the reasons why that decline can be traced to early Ming social and economic policies, see von Glahn, "Ming Taizu *ex Nihilo?*"

47. For the case of Wuzhou/Jinhua in Zhejiang, see Bol, "Culture, Society, and Neo-Confucianism."

48. Wang Yangming, *Wang Yangming quanji*, 230.

49. For a study of the Donglin's criticism of the court and the court's suppression of the Donglin, see Dardess, *Blood and History in China.*

50. Chu Hung-lam, "The Debate over Recognition of Wang Yang-ming."

51. This view of empire and culture in history goes back to the earliest texts; see the discussion of the *Book of Odes* in Saussy, *Problem of the Chinese Aesthetic,* 151. It dominated the early Tang view of history; see Bol, *"This Culture of Ours,"* 76–107.

52. Neo-Confucians were aware of the earlier view of history as cycles of the rise and fall of empires; see Schirokauer, "Chu Hsi's Sense of History," 214. The idea of an ideological rupture between antiquity and imperial history was first spelled out by Han Yu and adopted in the cause of political reform in the mid-eleventh century. The Neo-Confucians adopted the model but denied Han Yu a place in it.

53. Breisach, *Historiography.*

54. Quoted in Wang Shuizhao, *Songdai wenxue tonglun*, 4, 46.

55. See Zhu's introduction to his commentary on the *Doctrine of the Mean*, in Zhu Xi, *Sishu zhangju jizhu.*

56. A recent example is Qi Xia, *Songxue de fazhan he yanbian*, 140–88.

57. For example, in the importance of individual insight for both Chan Buddhism and Han Yu; see Yu Ying-shih, "Intellectual Breakthroughs in the T'ang-Sung Transition."

58. Zanning and Zhiyuan are examples of this; see Welter, "A Buddhist Response to the Confucian Revival," 36–47. Qisong, although an accomplished writer in the Ancient Style, was strongly critical of Ancient Style ideological claims.

59. The following works are representative of this view: Ge Zhaoguang, *Qi shiji zhi shijiu shiji Zhongguo de zhishi*; Guan Changlong, *Liang Song daoxue mingyun de lishi kaocha*; Li Huarui, *Wang Anshi bianfa yanjiu shi*; Tsuchida Kenjirō, *Dōgaku no keisei*; Yu Yingshi, *Zhu Xi de lishi shijie*; Zhu Hanmin, *Song Ming lixue tonglun*; and Xu Hongxing, *Sixiang di zhuanxing.*

60. Wang himself wrote commentaries on sutras and defended treating su-tras as one would the Confucian Classics, and during the New Policies period the use of Buddhist and Daoist concepts was accepted in the examinations. For Wang's openness to Buddhism and the Neo-Confucian criticism of him for this, see Jiang Yibin, *Songdai ru shi tiaohe lun ji paifo lun zhi yanjiu*. Huizong, the last of the New Policies emperors, gave unprecedented support to Daoism in society and in the examinations; see Ebrey, "Art and Taoism in the Court of Song Huizong"; and Bol, "Whither the Emperor?" 127. For Su Shi, see Grant, *Mount Lu Revisited*.

61. Borrell, "*Ko-wu* or *Kung-an?*"

62. See, e.g., Chi-chiang Huang, "Elite and Clergy in Northern Song Hang-zhou."

63. Halperin, *Out of the Cloister*.

64. Tsuchida Kenjirō, *Dōgaku no keisei*, chapter on Huayan; Peterson, "Con-fucian Learning in Late Ming Thought," 721–23, on Wang Ji.

65. Wing-tsit Chan, in Etienne Balazs and Yves Hervouet, *A Sung Bibliogra-phy*, 44; Gardner, *Chu Hsi and the* Ta Hsueh. Zhu's commentaries on the *Ana-lects* and the *Mencius* cited the views of as many as 56 other scholars, principally the Cheng brothers and their followers.

66. Han Xiuli et al., *Sishu yu xiandai wenhua*.

67. Qiu Jun, *Daxue yanyi bu*.

68. The *Lanxi County Gazetteer* (*Lanxi xianzhi*) edited by Zhang Mou is an example.

69. Zhu Xi and Lü Zuqian, *Reflections on Things at Hand*; Wang Yang-ming, *Instructions for Practical Living*.

70. Chen Chun, *Neo-Confucian Terms Explained*.

71. Lackner, "Die 'Verplanung' des Denkens am Beispiel der *T'u*."

72. Fuller, "Aesthetics and Meaning in Experience."

73. Han Jingtai, *Lixue wenhua yu wenxue sichao*; Ma Jigao, *Song Ming lixue yu wenxue*; Pan Liyong, *Zhuzi lixue meixue*.

74. Song Lian, *Song Lian quanji*, 52.1356. For a further discussion, see Bol, "Examinations and Orthodoxies," 48–56.

75. Zheng Yu, *Shishan xiansheng wenji*, preface to his own literary collection. Elaborated translation.

76. The dualism Zheng Yu objected to is found earlier and later. A passage in an examination compendium (preface 1245) speaks of using Cheng Yi to transform the mind and Su Shi to transform learning; see Liu Dake, *Bi shui qun ying dai wen hui yuan*, 44.6b–7a. I thank Hilde De Weerdt for this reference. For a call to unify the *wen* of Tang Ancient Style writing with the *dao* of Cheng and Zhu, see Fang Xiaoru, *Xunzhi zhai ji* (SKQS), 14.31b.

77. This is shown most clearly by Tillman, *Confucian Discourse and Chu Hsi's Ascendancy*.

78. "Sō-Mingaku kenkyū bunken mokuroku" 宋明學研究文獻目錄, in Uno Tetsuto et al., *Yōmeigaku binran*; Charles Fu and Wing-tsit Chan, *Guide to Chinese Philosophy*; Hirotsune Jinsei, *Gen Min Shindai shisō kenkyū bunken mokuroku*; Lin Qingzhang et al., *Zhuzi xue yanjiu shumu*; and Wu Yining, *Zhu Xi ji Song Yuan Ming lixue*.

79. Yao Xinzhong, *An Introduction to Confucianism*.

80. Feng Dawen, *Song Ming xin ruxue luelun*; Jiang Guozhu and Zhu Kuiju, *Zhongguo renxing lun shi*; Uno Tetsuto, *Shina tetsugakushi*; Yamanoi Yū, *Min Shin shisōshi no kenkyū*; Zhang Liwen, *Dao*; idem, *Li*; idem, *Qi*; and idem, *Xin*.

81. Berthrong, *Transformations of the Confucian Way*; Chen Lai, *Song Ming lixue*; Hou Wailu et al., *Song Ming lixue shi*; Okada Takehiko, *Sō Min tetsugaku no honshitsu*.

82. De Bary, *Neo-Confucian Orthodoxy*; idem, *The Message of the Mind*.

83. Thomas Wilson, *Genealogy of the Way*.

84. Yamanoi Yū, *Min Shin shisōshi no kenkyū*, 5–14.

85. Chen Zhengfu and He Zhijing, "Shilun Cheng Zhu lixue de tedian."

86. Chung Tsai-chun, *The Development of the Concepts of Heaven and of Man in the Philosophy of Chu Hsi*; Yu Ying-shih, "Intellectual Breakthroughs in the T'ang-Sung Transition."

Chapter 4

1. This translation largely follows Gardner, *Chu Hsi and the Ta Hsueh*, 88–94. I have changed Gardner's "empire" to "world," "state" to "country," "household" to "family," and "principle" to "coherence" and have added the auxiliary verb "may" to references to person, household, country, and world.

2. See, e.g., James T. C. Liu, *China Turning Inward*.

3. See, e.g., the attack on Liu Qingzhi discussed in Yu Yingshi, *Zhu Xi de lishi shijie*, 2: 118–31.

4. Yu Yingshi has made the case for this view in breadth and depth; see ibid., 2: 60–68, 182–86.

5. Fu Zhengyuan, *The Autocratic Tradition and Chinese Politics*, 58; quoting Arthur Wright in the second instance.

6. The idea that Song brought an increase in autocracy was used by Naitō Konan (1866–1934) and especially Miyazaki Ichisada (1901–95) to explain why the "modern" tendencies in Song were not realized. For this and a general account of Naitō and Miyazaki, see Miyakawa Hisayuki, "An Outline of the Naitô Hypothesis." For the formation of Naitō's account of the Tang-Song transition, see Fogel, *Politics and Sinology*, 168–210. Note also Miyazaki Ichisada,

Tōyōteki no kinsei; idem, "Introduction," in Saeki Tomi, *Sōshi shokkan shi sakuin*, 1–57; and Tonami Mamoru, *Tōdai seiji shakaishi kenkyū*. In "Sōdai no shifu," Miyazaki Ichisada argued that the *shidafu* were caught between selfless subjection and the venal pursuit of their economic interests, thus opening the way to autocratic rule; he did not think it was possible to know if Neo-Confucianism provided a way out of this.

7. Chang Hao, "The Intellectual Heritage of the Confucian Ideal of *Ching-shih*," 72–91.

8. Lee, "Academies," 135.

9. Munro, *Images of Human Nature*, 155–91.

10. De Bary, *The Trouble with Confucianism*, 23.

11. A particularly important example is the intellectual historian Shimada Kenji; see his "Sōgaku no tenkai," 440–43. For a discussion of views of Neo-Confucianism in regard to this and other issues in Japanese scholarship in the 1950s, see Yamanoi Yū, *Min Shin shisōshi no kenkyū*, 4–14.

12. For the European case, and the shift from monarchs who ruled by divine right to the Enlightenment monarchs, see Monod, *The Power of Kings*.

13. Jaeyoon Song ("Shifting Paradigms in Theories of Government," chaps. 5–6) shows that there was a major shift in political thought from Northern Song to Southern Song, from the view that the prefecture-county system was an irreversible historical development to the view that a decentralized system based on feudal (*fengjian*) principles was superior. Southern Song Neo-Confucians generally shared this view.

14. Cheng Gongxu, *Cang zhou chen fou bian*, 14.1a. This phrase, from the "Li yun" chapter (9.20) of the *Book of Rites*, is cited in various Song commentaries on the Classics and, most appropriately, in explications of Zhang Zai's "Western Inscription."

15. From the official Tang preface to the *Book of Change* in Ruan Yuan, *Shisan jing zhushu*, Prefaces to the *Book of Change*.

16. Li Shimin, "Di fan," 6.

17. *The T'ang Code*, 2.138–52.

18. Wei Zheng and Linghu Defen, *Sui shu*, 32.903.

19. Lewis, *Writing and Authority in Early China*.

20. Twitchett, *The Writing of Official History Under the T'ang*.

21. Liu Yi, "Songdai huangling zhidu yanjiu."

22. Arthur F. Wright, "Propaganda and Persuasion."

23. Tao, *Two Sons of Heaven*.

24. As Zhu Xi explained, natural disasters were the result of changes in *yin* and *yang*: "The sage-kings of antiquity on meeting disaster were frightened,

they cultivated their virtue and rectified affairs, and thus they were able to change disaster into good fortune" (*Zhu Xi ji*, 14.566–67).

25. To be sure, officials kept submitting reports of portents, and the government duly recorded them, but occasionally it tried to restrict submissions; see Yang Shiwen, "Ruiyi lilun yu Songdai zhengzhi." My understanding of the political use of portents and cosmic resonance theory owes much to Skonicki, "Cosmos, State and Society."

26. Bol, "Government, Society, and State," 160–78.

27. This is a central theme in Xiao-bin Ji, *Politics and Conservatism in Northern Song China*.

28. Liu Jingzhen, *Bei Song qianqi huangdi he tamen de quanli*. Like Wang Ruilai (see below), Liu sees a change with the third emperor, Zhenzong. Liu argues, however, that this was not an institutional change but a failure of personality: Zhenzong lacked the personal qualities necessary to function as an autocrat and contented himself with symbols and let ministers and the empress gain power. Renzong, the fourth emperor, increased his power by acting as the arbiter between scholar-official factions. It seems to me that we should distinguish institutional centralization from autocracy and the institutionalization of autocratic rulership from efforts by particular emperors to maintain power vis-à-vis the outer court.

29. Teraji Jun, "Sōdai seijishi kenkyū hōhō shiron."

30. Kondō Kazunari, "Sōdai shidaifu seiji no tokushoku"; Cheng Minsheng, "Lun Songdai shidafu zhengzhi." Cheng points out that literati officials generally did constrain the emperor.

31. Wang Ruilai, *Sōdai no kōtei kenri to shidaifu seiji*, 493–512. See also idem, "Lun Songdai huangquan" and "Lun Songdai xianggquan."

32. For an argument that this was the case in granting court recognition to local gods, see Sue Takashi, "The Shock of the Year Hsuan-ho 2."

33. Liu Jingzhen, *Bei Song qianqi huangdi he tamen de quanli*, 193–204.

34. Xu Song, *Song huiyao jigao*, xuanju 7.31b.

35. Ebrey, "Art and Taoism in the Court of Song Huizong"; Bol, "Whither the Emperor?"

36. Xu Song, *Song huiyao jigao*, xuanju 7.36b.

37. Ibid., 8.1a. Wang Anshi's commentaries on the Classics were attacked but not forbidden in early Southern Song. In 1138 the court explicitly rejected a proposal to rely exclusively on Wang's texts and decided instead to allow scholars to use traditional commentaries and their own opinion in essays on the Classics. Even Qin Gui, associated to some extent with Wang's learning and attacked by the followers of Cheng Yi's teaching, agreed both that Wang's failing was his desire that others agree with his own opinion and that literati

need not stick to one view. See Yuan Zheng, *Songdai jiaoyu*, 273–80. For Gaozong's opposition to portents, see Yang Shiwen, "Ruiyi lilun yu Songdai zhengzhi," 75.

38. Bol, *"This Culture of Ours,"* 157–66.

39. See Chapter 3, p. 84, for a translation of this passage.

40. See, e.g., Ouyang Xiu's argument that the imperial age distinguished governance from instruction, without taking the latter seriously, in Bol, *"This Culture of Ours,"* 195–97.

41. De Bary, "Chen Te-hsiu and Statecraft," 352–53.

42. Wood, *Limits to Autocracy*, 111–19.

43. For translations and an analysis of Zhu Xi's defense of this proposition against Chen Liang, who argued that antiquity and imperial times were continuous, see Tillman, *Utilitarian Confucianism*, 153–68.

44. Both the Duke of Zhou and Tang Taizong had murdered brothers, but, Zhu Xi argued, the Duke's action was a case of varying from the standard and he remained a sage, whereas Taizong acted from self-interest; see Wei Cheng-t'ung, "Chu Hsi on the Standard and the Expedient," 265.

45. Van Ess, "The Compilation of the Works of the Ch'eng Brothers."

46. Hou Wailu et al., *Song Ming lixue shi*, 246–67.

47. *Mencius* 2B9.

48. *Analects* 9.5.

49. Citing Sima Qian's *Shiji* (p. 3297).

50. Paraphrasing "Preface," Hu Anguo, *Chunqiu Hu shi zhuan*. Hu's commentary is also discussed in Wood, *Limits to Autocracy*, 123–31; and Hou Wailu et al., *Song Ming lixue shi*, 224–47.

51. Kong Yingda, "Chunqiu zhengyi."

52. Cheng Hao and Cheng Yi, *Er Cheng ji*, Yichuan ji 8.578, "What Learning Was It That Yanzi Loved?"

53. Zhu Xi, *Zhuzi yulei*, 82.2155. However, Zhu was not fully satisfied with Hu's interpretation and doubted that it was possible to infer the intent of Confucius in every instance; see ibid., 82.2144, 2147, 2154, 2155.

54. De Bary, *Neo-Confucian Orthodoxy*, 3–13. Yu Yingshi (*Zhu Xi de lishi shijie*, 1: 32–67) argues that Zhu Xi's preface to the *Doctrine of the Mean* did not in fact grant that non-rulers could be part of the *dao tong*. However, Yu allows that others, including Zhu's son-in law Huang Gan, read the text as meaning exactly this.

55. Li Xinchuan, *Dao ming lu*, preface 1a.

56. Yang Weizhen 楊維楨, "Sanshi zhengtong bian" 三史正統辨, discussed in Davis, "Historiography as Politics."

57. Wood, *Limits to Autocracy*, 119–29; Hou Wailu et al., *Song Ming lixue shi*, 228–41; Su Yuezong, "Cong 'zun wang rang yi.'"

58. Zhu Xi, *Zhu Xi ji*, 11.439, from 1162.

59. For example, Fan Zuyu (1041–98), an ally of Cheng Yi and Sima Guang, discussed in de Bary, *Neo-Confucian Orthodoxy*, 98–131.

60. Zhu Xi, *Zhu Xi ji*, 12.490, from 1189.

61. Munro, *Images of Human Nature*, 155–91.

62. Chun-chieh Huang, "Imperial Rulership in Cultural History," 196–200.

63. Schirokauer, "Chu Hsi's Political Thought," 140–45.

64. Zhu Xi, *Zhu Xi ji*, 13.514, from 1181.

65. The *Book of Documents*, "Counsels of Yu the Great." For a discussion of this passage, see Chapter 6.

66. Zhu Xi, *Zhu Xi ji*, 11.440–41, from 1162.

67. Ibid., 13.506, from 1163.

68. Ibid., 11.456, from 1180. Cf. 12.490–91, from 1189, on "discoursing on learning to set the mind right."

69. Ibid., 11.462, from 1181.

70. Ibid., 15.572–96.

71. Ibid. 11.437–49, from 1162; 11.450–58, from 1180; 13.514–17, from 1181; 11.460–87, from 1188; and 12.489–500, from 1189. For a summary of his major points, see Schirokauer, "Chu Hsi's Political Thought." Zhu's views of the political ruler as a key part of the governmental system generally echo Sima Guang's views.

72. Zhu Xi, *Zhu Xi ji*, 11.485–86. Cited in Schirokauer, "Chu Hsi's Political Thought."

73. Zhu Xi, *Shijing zhuan*, preface; trans. in Lynn, "Chu Hsi as Literary Theorist and Critic," 344–46.

74. Zhu Xi, *Sishu zhangju jizhu*, preface to the *Daxue*; trans. in Gardner, *Chu Hsi and the* Ta Hsueh, 77–86.

75. Cheng Hao and Cheng Yi, *Er Cheng ji*, Yishu 15.162–63.

76. Zhu Xi, *Zhu Xi ji*, 72.3743–48.

77. Zhen Dexiu, *Daxue yanyi*, preface. For a discussion of this text and Zhen's thought, see de Bary, *Neo-Confucian Orthodoxy*, 98–131; and idem, "Chen Te-hsiu and Statecraft."

78. Zhen Dexiu, *Daxue yanyi*.

79. De Bary, *Neo-Confucian Orthodoxy*, 126; on Neo-Confucianism under the Mongols, cf. ibid., 22–60. Traditionally the transmission of Neo-Confucianism to the north is attributed to Zhao Fu; see Hou Wailu et al., *Song Ming lixue shi*, 687. In fact this was a more gradual process and began somewhat earlier; see Tillman, "Confucianism in the Chin."

80. Chu Ping-tzu, "Tradition Building and Cultural Competition," 97–134.

81. See, e.g., the memorial from Shi Kangnian, submitted after the funeral for Zhu Xi, in Qiao Chuan et al., *Qingyuan dangjin*, 30a–b. I thank Min Byoung-hee for this reference.

82. Schirokauer, "Neo-Confucians Under Attack."

83. Lü Zuqian, *Donglai Lü taishi wenji*, bieji 5.

84. For Xu Heng in the north, see Ditmanson, "Contesting Authority," 101–4, 112–18. For Wu Cheng in Jiangxi, see Gedalecia, "Wu Ch'eng and the Perpetuation of the Classical Heritage in the Yuan." For the several Jinhua masters in the southeast, who did not hold office, see Bol, "Culture, Society, and Neo-Confucianism."

85. Zhu Xi, *Zhu Xi ji*, 44.2118; trans., slightly modified, from Min, "The Republic of the Mind."

86. Wei Liaoweng, *Heshan ji*, 101.3b–7a.

87. On the circulation of political documents, see De Weerdt, "Byways in the Imperial Chinese Information Order."

88. See, e.g., Su Xun's criticism of the well-field system in Hatch, "Su Hsun's Pragmatic Statecraft."

89. Ong, "Men of Letters Within the Passes," pp. 93–100.

90. Zhang Zai, *Zhang Zai ji*, 62–63, "Zheng meng" 17; trans. Wing-tsit Chan, *A Source Book in Chinese Philosophy*, 497–98.

91. Ching, "Neo-Confucian Utopian Theories and Political Ethics," 1–12; Xiao Gongquan, *Zhongguo zhengzhi sixiang shi*, 511–14.

92. Zhu Xi, *Zhuzi yulei*, 108.2679–86; idem, *Zhu Xi ji*, 68.2596–99; Tillman, *Ch'en Liang on Public Interest and the Law*, 49–54; Ching, "Neo-Confucian Utopian Theories and Political Ethics," 15–19.

93. Zhu Xi, *Zhuzi yulei*, 108.2681; Schirokauer, "Chu Hsi's Sense of History," 216–17.

94. Xiao Gongquan, *Zhongguo zhengzhi sixiang shi*, 512–24.

95. Zhu Xi, *Zhu Xi ji*, 13.512–24, from 1181.

96. Peng Fei 彭飛, preface to Lü Zuqian, *Lidai zhidu xiangshuo*.

97. For a description of Qiu's work and responses to it, see Chu Hung-lam, "Ch'iu Chun's *Ta-hsueh yen-i pu*."

98. This view runs through a guide for families written by a twelfth-century local official; see Ebrey, *Family and Property in Sung China*.

99. See the discussion of the situation in well-documented Huizhou in Song and Yuan in Nakajima Gakushō, *Mindai kyōson no funsō to chitsujo*, 66–148.

100. I am indebted to a manuscript by Thomas P. Massey, "Chu Yuan-chang, the Hu-Lan Cases, and Early Ming Confucianism." Much of the bloodshed took place at the local level where the purge was used to settle old scores.

101. This comparison is developed in Andrew and Rapp, *Autocracy and China's Rebel Founding Emperors.*

102. Dardess, *Confucianism and Autocracy*, 255–56.

103. Danjō Hiroshi, *Minchō sensei shihai no shiteki kōzō*, chap. 4.

104. Elman, *A Cultural History of Civil Examinations*, 68–70.

105. Dardess, *Confucianism and Autocracy*, 195–242; Zhu Yuanzhang 朱元璋, "Yuzhi dagao" 御製大誥, in *Mingchao kaiguo wenxian*, 1.4b–5b.

106. Farmer, *Zhu Yuanzhang and Early Ming Social Legislation.*

107. For the educational system in early Ming, see Schneewind, *Community Schools and the State in Ming China.* For the effort to control local cults, see Hamashima Atsutoshi, "The City God Temples."

108. Citing *Analects* 16.2. On the examination of 1385, see Lin Qingzhang, "*Wujing daquan* zhi xiuzuan," 377–81.

109. Zhu Yuanzhang, "Yuzhi dagao," 3rd collection, in *Mingchao kaiguo wenxian*, 40b–42b.

110. Hok-lam Chan, "Ming T'ai-tsu's Manipulation of Letters."

111. Dardess, *Confucianism and Autocracy*, 193–97, 225.

112. Ibid., 199, 221–22, 50; Farmer, *Zhu Yuanzhang and Early Ming Social Legislation*, 101–10.

113. Huang Chin-hsing, "The Cultural Politics of Autocracy," 283–89.

114. *Analects* 2.4.

115. Dardess, *Confucianism and Autocracy*, 264–87; Mote, "Fang Hsiao-ju," in Goodrich and Fang, *Dictionary of Ming Biography*, 427–33.

116. Fang Xiaoru, *Xun zhi zhai ji* (1996), 14.438.

117. Ibid., 12.358–59, 12.64–65, 14.438.

118. Ibid., 18.539. Xue Xuan made a similar claim: since Zhu Xi had clarified the Way, there was no need to keep writing about it, and literati should instead turn to practicing it; see Julia Ching, "Hsueh Hsuan" in Goodrich and Fang, *Dictionary of Ming Biography*, 616–19.

119. Fang Xiaoru, *Xun zhi zhai ji* (1996), 6.169–70.

120. The questions and answers are in Taiwan xuesheng shuju, *Mingdai dengkelu huibian*, vol. 1. Note the contrast to 1385, when a question unambiguously called for candidates to celebrate the total authority of the ruler; cited in Lin Qingzhang, "*Wujing daquan* zhi xiuzuan," 377–81.

121. Elman, "Where Is King Ch'eng."

122. Lin Qingzhang, "*Wujing daquan* zhi xiuzuan."

123. Li Zhuoran, "Zhi guo zhi dao"; Zhu Di, *Shengxue xinfa.* For a summary of the contents and a positive assessment of Zhu Di's Neo-Confucian commitment, see Hok Lam Chan, "The Chien-wen, Yung-lo, Hung-hsi, and Hsüan-te reigns," 218–21.

124. Elman, *A Cultural History of Civil Examinations*, 69–119.

125. For an account of early Ming Neo-Confucianism and an assessment of scholarship on the period, see Wing-tsit Chan, "The Ch'eng-Chu School of Early Ming." For Wu Yubi in particular, see Wilhelm, "On Ming Orthodoxy." My introduction to Wu was through Kelleher, *Personal Reflections on the Pursuit of Sagehood*. I have also benefited from Hou Wailu et al., *Song Ming lixue shi*; and Rong Zhaozu, *Mingdai sixiang shi*.

126. Wu Yubi, *Kangzhai ji*, 11.1a.

127. For fifteenth-century skepticism about the morality of the Song founders, see Chu Hung-lam, "Intellectual Trends in the Fifteenth Century."

128. Wu Yubi, *Kangzhai ji*, 11.1a.

129. Ibid., 11.10b.

130. Huang Chin-hsing, "The Cultural Politics of Autocracy"; Fisher, *The Chosen One*; and Chu Hung-lam, Review of Carney T. Fisher, *The Chosen One*.

131. Chu Hung-lam, "Ming ru Zhan Ruoshui."

132. Bol, "Culture, Society, and Neo-Confucianism," 269–80; Hauf, "The Community Covenant."

133. Peterson, "Confucian Learning in Late Ming Thought," 738.

134. Busch, "The Tung-lin Shu-yuan"; Atwell, "From Education to Politics."

135. Huang Chin-hsing, *The Price of Having a Sage-Emperor*, 19.

Chapter 5

1. For a discussion of these Han dynasty doctrines and their place in Neo-Confucianism, see Kwang-Ching Liu, "Socioethics as Orthodoxy" and Liu's introduction to the volume.

2. Translation from Gardner, *Zhu Xi's Reading of the* Analects, 31.

3. Ebrey, *Chu Hsi's Family Rituals*; Kelleher, "Back to Basics."

4. Hou Wailu et al., *Song Ming lixue shi*, 728–29; from Rao Lu, *Rao Shuangfeng jiangyi juan* 2, quoting the "Nei ze" and "Ji yi" chapters of the *Book of Rites*.

5. Bol, "Cheng Yi as a Literatus," 180.

6. Zhu Xi, *Zhu Xi ji*, 40.1865, reply to He Shujing.

7. Ibid., 14.546, memorial from 1194.

8. See, e.g., two popular statements of the sociobiological position: Pinker, *The Blank Slate*; and Edward O. Wilson, *Consilience*. In an essay entitled "The Biological Basis of Confucian Ethics: Or, A Reason Why Confucianism Has Endured for So Long," Donald Munro argues that the biological is the basis for Chinese ethicists' contributing to the international discourse on values; see *A Chinese Ethics for the New Century*, 47–59.

9. Cheng Hao and Cheng Yi, *Er Cheng ji*, yishu 21A, 268.

10. Graham, *Two Chinese Philosophers*.

11. Cheng Duanmeng, *Cheng Mengzhai xingli zixun.*

12. Chen Chun, *Beixi ziyi;* idem, *Neo-Confucian Terms Explained.*

13. Examples include Chen Chun's Yanling Lecture, translated in *Neo-Confucian Terms Explained*, 177–86; and Zhu Xi's Lecture at Yushan, in *Zhu Xi ji*, 74.3895.

14. Zhu Xi and Lü Zuqian, *Reflections on Things at Hand.*

15. Li Yuangang, *Shengmen shiye tu.*

16. Wang Bo, *Yan ji tu*, is a Ming reconstruction but includes original charts; see Cheng Yuanmin, *Wang Bo zhi shengping yu xueshu*, 284–91. For Xu Qian's charts, recorded from his lectures by his students, see Xu Qian, *Du Sishu congshuo.*

17. Wing-tsit Chan, *Chu Hsi: New Studies*, 276–88.

18. Kasoff, *The Thought of Chang Tsai*, chaps. 2–4.

19. The classic study of the history of the term is Wing-tsit Chan, "The Evolution of the Neo-Confucian Concept *Li* as Principle." In *Songdai li gainian zhi kaizhan*, Deng Keming gives particular attention to the multiplicity of Northern Song usages but argues that it came to have much of the meaning of "law" (*fa*).

20. *Li* is used about 70 times in documents relating to examination papers in Xu Song, *Song huiyao jigao*, Harvard online edition.

21. Chen Chun, *Beixi ziyi*, 38, 41–42; trans. (modified) from idem, *Neo-Confucian Terms Explained*, 105–6, 12.

22. Chen Chun, *Beixi ziyi*, 6; trans. (modified) from idem, *Neo-Confucian Terms Explained*, 38.

23. Ivanhoe, *Confucian Moral Self-Cultivation*, 47–48; Chung Tsai-chun, *The Development of the Concepts of Heaven and of Man*, 228–33.

24. Chen Chun, *Beixi ziyi*, 72; trans. (modified) from idem, *Neo-Confucian Terms Explained*, 191.

25. This discussion of *li*, and the understanding of it "coherence" specifically, owes much to Peterson, "Another Look at *Li*."

26. Zhu Xi, *Zhu Xi ji*, 11.485–86, memorial from 1188.

27. Bol, *"This Culture of Ours,"* 306–11.

28. Chung Tsai-chun, *The Development of the Concepts of Heaven and of Man*, 212.

29. Zhu Xi, *Zhuzi yulei*, 13.224.

30. Ibid.

31. Cheng Hao and Cheng Yi, *Er Cheng ji*, wenji 4.460–61. For a complete translation, see Wing-tsit Chan, *A Source Book in Chinese Philosophy*, 525–26.

32. The confusion of terminology in what he called "the learning of moral principles" was the subject of an early thirteenth-century examination question; see Chen Qiqing, *Yun chuang j*, 7.3b–4a.

33. Su Boheng, *Su Pingzhong wenji*, 4.35b, preface to the "Explanation of the Diagram of the Learning of the Mind."

34. Cited in Yü Ying-shih, "Morality and Knowledge in Chu Hsi's Philosophical System," 239.

35. For translations of Zhu's comments on how to read in order to see principle, see Zhu Xi, *Learning to Be a Sage*, 128–62.

36. Zhu Xi, *Zhu Xi ji*, 43.2012. Cf. Yü Ying-shih, "Morality and Knowledge in Chu Hsi's Philosophical System," 246–47.

37. Cheng Hao and Cheng Yi, *Er Cheng ji*, yishu 18.188. Wing-tsit Chan translated this somewhat differently; in *A Source Book in Chinese Philosophy*, 560–61. I prefer Graham's translation in *Two Chinese Philosophers*, 76. Cf. yishu 18.193, 19.247.

38. Yung Sik Kim, *The Natural Philosophy of Chu Hsi*, 320–23. Kim also notes: "The *li* of an object or phenomena is not a simple idea or principle that can provide an explanation or an understanding of the object or the phenomenon at a level more fundamental than the object or the phenomenon itself" (p. 25). Cf. Graham, *Two Chinese Philosophers*, 79.

39. Zhang Jiushao, *Lixue leibian*. The author later changed the title after it was objected that his coverage was too narrow to justify the more inclusive term "investigation of things."

40. Furth, "The Physician as Philosopher of the Way."

41. Zhu Xi and Lü Zuqian, *Jin si lu*, 7.1a; trans. (modified) from Zhu Xi and Lü Zuqian, *Reflections on Things at Hand*, 183.

42. Cheng Hao and Cheng Yi, *Er Cheng ji*, yishu 18.188. Chan translated this somewhat differently in *A Source Book in Chinese Philosophy*, 560–61. Cf. note 37 above. Cf. yishu 18.193, 19.247.

43. Cheng Hao and Cheng Yi, *Er Cheng ji*, yishu 15.157; cf. 15.152, 17.175.

44. Ibid., yishu 15.149.

45. Ibid., yishu 2A.16–17; trans. (modified) from Wing-tsit Chan, *A Source Book in Chinese Philosophy*, 523–24.

46. Graham, *Two Chinese Philosophers*, 96–107, 127–30.

47. For a case study of this phenomenon, see Borrell, "*Ko-wu* or *Kung-an?*"

48. On Lu in relation to Zhu, see Tillman, *Confucian Discourse and Chu Hsi's Ascendancy*, 187–230.

49. For a discussion of autobiographical self-reflection by Neo-Confucians, see Pei-yi Wu, *The Confucian's Progress*; and idem, "Self-Examination and Confession of Sins in Traditional China." Here I have in mind the biographies of Neo-Confucian teachers written by their students and friends.

50. Charles Wei-hsun Fu, "Chu Hsi on Buddhism."

51. Zhu Xi, *Zhuzi yulei*, 5.94.

52. Gardner, *Zhu Xi's Reading of the* Analects, 79; Bloom, "Three Visions of *Jen*," 23–33.

53. Wm. Theodore de Bary has written extensively on this point; see his *Neo-Confucian Orthodoxy*; *The Message of the Mind*; and *Learning for Oneself*.

54. Munro makes this case in a chapter entitled "The Ruler and Ruled: Authoritarian Teachers and Personal Discovery" in *Images of Human Nature*, 155–91, citing 72, 63.

55. Wei Cheng-t'ung, "Chu Hsi on the Standard and the Expedient." Wei does not, it seems to me, reach the same conclusions as Munro.

56. Zhu Xi, *Zhuzi yulei*, 14.270–71.

57. Translation following Gardner, "Confucian Commentary and Chinese Intellectual History," 403.

58. Zheng Xuan and Kong Yingda, *Li ji zhengyi*; *Zhong yong*, 52.19a; for a discussion, see Gardner, "Confucian Commentary and Chinese Intellectual History," 403.

59. Zhu Xi, *Sishu zhangju jizhu*, 20–21; trans. (modified) from Chan, *A Source Book in Chinese Philosophy*, 98.

60. *Analects* 4.15. D. C. Lau translates: "The way of the Master consists in doing one's best (*zhong*) and in using oneself as measure to gauge others (*shu*). That is all" (*Confucius: The Analects*, 74).

61. Zhu Xi, *Sishu zhangju jizhu*, Lunyu jiju, 47–48. For a discussion of Zhu's understanding of this passage, see Makeham, *Transmitters and Creators*, chap. 8, "The Rhetoric and Reality of Learning to Be a Sage." Note that the He Yan commentary, still current in Song, understands this passage as follows "The Master's way simply uses the one pattern / principle of *zhong* and *shu* to unite the patterns / principle of all affairs under heaven." It explains *zhong* as "realizing the centered mind" and *shu* as "taking oneself as the measure of things" (He Yan et al., *Song ben Lunyu zhushu*, 2.13b).

62. See pp. 176–77.

63. Zhu Xi, *Zhu Xi ji*, 67.3542–44; for a translation, see Wing-tsit Chan, *A Source Book in Chinese Philosophy*, 466. For a discussion of Mencius', Cheng Hao's, and Zhu's understanding of *ren*, see Bloom, "Three Visions of *Jen*."

64. Zhu Xi, *Zhuzi yulei*, 11.192.

65. Ibid., 11.179, 190.

66. Translated in Zhu Xi, *Learning to Be a Sage*, 131.

67. An example of this kind of attitude is the "Four Jinhua Masters"; see Hou Wailu et al., *Song Ming lixue shi*, 645–75. See also Bol, "Examinations and Orthodoxies," 46–57.

68. Gedalecia, "Wu Ch'eng and the Perpetuation of the Classical Heritage in the Yuan." For broad study of Yuan intellectual culture, see Miura Shūichi, *Chūgoku shingaku no ryōsen.*

69. Bol, "Examinations and Orthodoxies," 47.

70. Cze-tong Song and Julia Ching, "Hsüeh Hsüan," 617.

71. See, e.g., his letters to students in Xue Xuan, *Xue Jingxuan ji*, 1.2a–4a, 10b–19a. For his discussion of philosophical topics, see Chen Lai, *Song Ming lixue*, 206–16.

72. Elman, "The Formation of 'Dao Learning' as Imperial Ideology."

73. For another view of how the early Ming context set the stage for a shift away from Cheng-Zhu thought, see Wing-tsit Chan, "The Ch'eng-Chu School of Early Ming," 45.

74. Bol, "Culture, Society, and Neo-Confucianism," 278–80; Dimberg and Ching, "Chang Mou."

75. Trans. (slightly modified) from Jen Yu-wen, "Ch'en Hsien-chang's Philosophy of the Natural," 57.

76. Ibid., 64, 70–74.

77. Quoted in ibid., 82.

78. My understanding of this period owes much to Youngmin Kim, "Redefining the Self's Relation to the World."

79. Zhu Xi, *Zhu Xi ji*, 67.3540.

80. Wing-tsit Chan, "Wang Shou-jen," 1409–10. On Wang's enlightenment, see Wei-ming Tu, *Neo-Confucian Thought in Action.*

81. In what follows I am drawing on Youngmin Kim, "Redefining the Self's Relation to the World," 68–114.

82. Ibid., 75–66; Wang Yangming, *Instructions for Practical Living*, 251–52.

83. Translated by Peterson, "Confucian Learning in Late Ming Thought," 719. Wing-tsit Chan translates: "In the original substance of the mind there is no distinction between good and evil. When the will is active, however, such distinction exists. The faculty of innate knowledge is to know good and evil. The investigation of things is to know good and remove evil" (Wang Yangming, *Instructions for Practical Living*, 244).

84. See the discussion in Peterson, "Confucian Learning in Late Ming Thought," 719–22.

85. Youngmin Kim, "Redefining the Self's Relation to the World," 93–112.

86. For the post–Wang Yangming period, see Peterson, "Confucian Learning in Late Ming Thought," 723–69.

Chapter 6

1. *Zhong yong* 1, trans. Wing-tsit Chan, *A Source Book in Chinese Philosophy*, 98.

2. Zhu Xi's interpretation, following Zhu Xi, *Sishu zhangju jizhu*, 20–21.

3. Jin Lüxiang, *Zizhi tongjian qianbian*, *juan* 4. I owe this reference to Lee Tsong-han.

4. Ibid.

5. Ibid.

6. The polarity between utility and Zhu Xi's moral motivation is developed in Tillman, *Utilitarian Confucianism*. For a somewhat different solution to the problems addressed here, see Graham, "What Was New in the Ch'eng-Chu Theory of Human Nature."

7. De Bary, *Neo-Confucian Orthodoxy*, 216.

8. This gloss is from Metzger, *Escape from Predicament*, 14.

9. Jin Lüxiang, *Zizhi tongjian qianbian*, *juan* 4.

10. Ruan Yuan, *Shisan jing zhushu: fu jiaokan ji*, *Shang shu* sec. 121, "Xian you yi de."

11. Zhu Xi, *Zhuzi yulei*, 2033.

12. Ibid., 2263.

13. "Zheng meng," sec. 1, in Zhang Zai, *Zhang Zai ji*, 8–9.

14. "Zheng meng," sec. 17, in ibid., 63.

15. Zhu Zhen, *Hanshang yi zhuan*, author's preface.

16. Cheng Hao and Cheng Yi, *Er Cheng ji*, yishu 16.182.

17. For a discussion of Zhu Xi's understanding of *li yi fen shu*, see Wing-tsit Chan, *Chu Hsi: New Studies*, 297–300. For the history of interpretation, including Li Tong's statement, see Dong Yuzheng, *Zhongguo lixue dacidian*, 506–7.

18. Lu Jiuyuan, *Lu Jiuyuan ji*, 12.161, 36.483.

19. Zhu Xi, *Zhu Xi ji*, 37.1655–56.

20. Chen Liang, *Chen Liang ji*, 23.260–61.

21. Zhu Xi and Lü Zuqian, *Reflections on Things at Hand*, 207 (VIII.8).

22. Trans. (slightly modified) from ibid., 206 (VIII.5).

23. Translated in Wang Yangming, *Instructions for Practical Living*, 118–19. For the Chinese text, I have used Wang Yangming, *Wang Yangming Chuan xi lu xiangzhu jiping*.

24. Wang Yangming, *Instructions for Practical Living*, 119–21.

25. Zhu Xi, *Sishu zhangju jizhu*, 17–19. I have largely adopted Wing-tsit Chan's draft translation for Irene Bloom and Peter Bol, eds., *Sources of Song Neo-Confucianism* (forthcoming). See also de Bary, *The Message of the Mind*, 28–29. For a close reading of the preface, see Yu Yingshi, *Zhu Xi de lishi shijie*, 37–67.

26. *Analects* 20.1.

27. *Book of History*, "Counsels of Great Yü," sec. 15. For a lengthy discussion of Zhu Xi's use of these lines, see Elman, "Philosophy Vs. Philology."

28. Ibid., sec. 2.

29. Shi Dun (*jinshi* 1145), *Zhongyong jijie* (Collected explanations of the *Doctrine of the Mean*).

30. Found as a two-chapter abridged compilation of commentaries in the *Zhuzi yishu*.

31. Wang Yangming, *Instructions for Practical Living*, 230.

32. Ibid., 16–17.

33. For a study of Zhu's disputes with contemporaries, see Tillman, *Confucian Discourse and Chu Hsi's Ascendancy*.

34. Huang Zhen, *Huang shi ri chao*, *juan* 82, "Fuzhou xinwei dongzhi jiangyi."

35. De Bary, *Neo-Confucian Orthodoxy*; idem, *The Message of the Mind*; Huang Zhen, *Huang shi ri chao*. For an argument that this is a Yuan-period development, see Miura Shūichi, *Chūgoku shingaku no ryōsen*.

36. Cheng Minzheng, *Dao yi bian*.

37. Wang Yangming, *Wang Yangming quanji*, 118, sec. 142.

38. Thomas Wilson, *Genealogy of the Way*.

39. Wang Wei, *Wang Zhongwen gong ji*, 14.296–97, "Explanation of *Ru*."

40. The Yongle-period Neo-Confucian Xue Xuan was one among many to say this; quoted in Wing-tsit Chan, "The Ch'eng-Chu School of Early Ming," 35.

41. Zhu Xi, *Sishu zhangju jizhu*, Daxue 8; trans. (modified) based on the discussion in Wing-tsit Chan, *Chu Hsi: New Studies*, 305.

42. *Tong shu*, sec. 20, in Zhou Dunyi, *Zhou Lianxi xiansheng quanji*; see also Wing-tsit Chan, *A Source Book in Chinese Philosophy*, 473.

43. Used by Cheng Yi; from the Kun hexagram in the *Book of Change*.

44. See the discussion of *jing* in Chen Chun, *Beixi ziyi*, 32–36; and idem, *Neo-Confucian Terms Explained*, 97–103. I find Daniel Gardner's "inner mental attentiveness" more informative than Wing-tsit Chan's "seriousness."

45. Chen Chun, *Beixi ziyi*, 35; idem, *Neo-Confucian Terms Explained*, 100.

46. Zhu Xi discussed the concept of *jing* and "concentrating on unity/one thing" frequently; see, e.g., *Zhuzi yulei*, 6.92, 6.103, 12.206–8, 17.371; and *Zhu Xi ji*, 47.2275.

47. See Zhu Xi's discussion of the term *cheng* in the *Great Learning* and the *Mean* in Zhu Xi, *Sishu zhangju jizhu*, 5, 36.

48. Zhu Xi, *Zhuzi yulei*, 6.103.

49. Zhang Shi, *Nanxuan ji*, 36.9a–b.

50. Quoted in Chen Lai, *Song Ming lixue*, 193.

51. Quoted in Hou Wailu et al., *Song Ming lixue shi*, 601.

52. Zhan Ruoshui, *Xin lun*, 1a.

53. Wang Shu, *Shiqu yi jian*, 2.4b.

54. Chen Xianzhang, *Chen Xianzhang ji*, 57, 131, 217.

55 Cheng Hao, "On Understanding Humanity"; trans. (modified) from Wing-tsit Chan, *A Source Book in Chinese Philosophy*, 523.

56. See also Graham, *Two Chinese Philosophers*, 97.

57. Wing-tsit Chan, *A Source Book in Chinese Philosophy*, 595; Bloom, "Three Visions of *Jen*," 23–33.

58. Lu Jiuyuan is the most famous Song example. For a little-known Yuan-period example, see Song Lian's biography of Chen Qiao, in *Song Lian quanji*, 400.

59. Hu Juren, *Juye lu*, 17; discussed in Youngmin Kim, "Redefining the Self's Relation to the World," 60–67.

60. From Wang Yangming, "Inquiry on the *Great Learning*," in idem, *Instructions for Practical Living*, 272.

61. Wang Yangming, *Instructions for Practical Living*, 118–19.

Chapter 7

1. Wang Wei, *Huachuan zhi ci*, 8a–b. For a similar Southern Song statement, see Wu Zeng, *Nenggai zhai manlu*, 18.503.

2. Schirokauer, "Neo-Confucians Under Attack"; Thomas Wilson, *Genealogy of the Way*, 39–47.

3. Chu Hung-lam, "The Debate over Recognition of Wang Yang-ming."

4. Prior to the New Policies some called for equating *shi* status with examination literacy, but the resistance to greater access is illustrated by the mid-eleventh-century rule that to enter the prefectural school the student had to be recommended by two men who had already passed the prefectural examination; see Zhou Yuwen, *Songdai de zhou xian xue*, 167.

5. Wing-tsit Chan, *Zhuzi menren*, 15.

6. Drawing on the account of the role of education in defining the literati and providing literati careers in Chen Wenyi, *You guanxue dao shuyuan*, 294–337.

7. Zhou Yuwen, *Songdai de zhou xian xue*, 169–72, 189–200; Meskill, *Academies in Ming China*, 23–24.

8. Hucker, "Ming Government," 31.

9. As calculated on the basis of the quotas set for each prefecture and the passing ratio, see Chaffee, "Education and Examinations in Sung Society," 48, 59. For a discussion of the implications of these figures, see Bol, "The Examination System and the Shih."

10. Peterson, "Confucian Learning in Late Ming Thought," 714–15.

11. Bol, "Chu Hsi's Redefinition of Literati Learning," 151, 156–60.

12. Cited and discussed in de Bary, "Chu Hsi's Aims as an Educator," 192–93.

13. Zhu Xi, *Zhu Xi ji*, 74.3873.

14. From an inscription for a school shrine in Yanzhou by Shi Shaozhang. Shi was from a well-established literati family but made his career as a teacher until passing the examinations in 1253, when he was in his fifties. He wrote this on behalf of the prefect in 1235 to argue that it was good that a shrine to Neo-Confucians was being built in the government school but that the tension was inherent (see Wu Shidao, *Jing xiang lu*, 11.11b–12a).

15. For the Song examinations, see Zhou Yuwen, *Songdai de zhou xian xue*, 173–216; and Lee, *Education in Traditional China*, 381–82. On the dual-track system in Southern Song, see Xu Song, *Song huiyao jigao*, xuanju, 4.31a–34b, 5.1b–2a, 5.24a–26b. On the Yuan and Ming systems, see Elman, *A Cultural History of Civil Examinations*, 35, 41–42, 387–99.

16. For Su Shi's importance, particularly in examination education, see Bol, "Reading Su Shi in Southern Song Wuzhou"; and Tanaka Masaki, "So shi sho-kugaku kō." For Zhu Xi's attack on Su, see Bol, "Chu Hsi's Redefinition of Literati Learning." For a case study of the attention given Su by local literati, see Bol, "Intellectual Culture in Wuzhou ca. 1200."

17. For a discussion of the writings of the statecraft scholars, see Zhou Mengjiang, *Ye Shi yu Yongjia xuepai*. On Chen Liang, see Tillman, *Ch'en Liang on Public Interest and the Law*; and idem, *Utilitarian Confucianism*. On Ye Shi and other statecraft scholars as an alternative to Neo-Confucianism, see Chu Ping-tzu, "Tradition Building and Cultural Competition," 326–442; and Bol, "Reconceptualizing the Nation in Southern Song."

18. Wuzhou was allowed to send fourteen to the metropolitan examination after 1125; see Wang Maode and Wu Xiangxiang, *Jinhua fu zhi*, 18.12a–15b, 46b, 52b. Chaffee (*The Thorny Gates of Learning in Sung China*, 125) identifies Wu, Wen, and Tai as the three prefectures assigned 1/200 pass ratios; according to Zhu Xi, it was also one of four eastern Zhejiang prefectures that relied greatly on the National University examination in addition to the normal avoidance exams. When the number of degrees exceeded the quota for prefectural graduates (e.g., seventeen degrees in 1190), we can conclude that many Wuzhou men qualified in this manner.

19. Ye Shi's inscription from 1198 recounts the history of the academy; see *Ye Shi ji*, 9.154–56. A commemorative volume prepared by a descendant in 1677 contains an inscription from 1172 and texts from visitors; see Guo Fu, *Shi dong yi fang*.

20. For the history of these schools, teachers, and books, see Bol, "Zhang Ruyu, the *Qunshu kaosuo*, and Diversity in Intellectual Culture."

21. The chronology of Lü's career indicates that he met students in various places in the prefectural seat and at his sometimes residence at the family burial ground at Mingzhao Mountain in Wuyi county. See *Nianpu*, in Lü Zuqian, *Donglai Lü taishi wenji*, appendix 1a–8a. For Lü's rules for his students from 1168, 1169, 1170, and 1173, see ibid., bieji 5. This fellowship of what Lü called *tongzhi* was selected from among the many students who went to Lü for examination training; see ibid., 7.6b.

22. See the inscription for the shrine to Lü built in 1208 in Lou Yao, *Gong kui ji*, 55.760–62; see Yuan Fu, *Meng zhai ji*, 30.11a–12a, for the establishment of the Donglai Academy in 1237.

23. Lü Zuqian, *Donglai Lü taishi wenji*, bieji 8.9b.

24. Ibid., bieji 7.6a.

25. Zhang Shi, *Nanxuan ji*, 25.6b; cf. 22.4a.

26. Lü Zuqian, *Donglai Lü taishi wenji*, bieji 7.6b. Lü also apologized to Zhu Xi for having chosen pieces of writing to help students training for the examination; see ibid., bieji 8.3a. For a comparative discussion of Zhu and Lü's approach to teaching and examinations, see Ichiki Tsuyuhiko, *Shu Ki monjin shūdan keisei no kenkyū*, 396–429.

27. See Zhu Xi, *Zhuzi yulei*, 121.2939, 122.49–58.

28. Balazs and Hervouet, *A Sung Bibliography*, 44.

29. As shown by Gardner, *Chu Hsi and the* Ta Hsueh; and idem, *Zhu Xi's Reading of the* Analects.

30. Zhu Xi, *Yi xue qi meng*; idem, *Zhou yi ben yi*; idem, *Introduction to the Study of the* Classic of Change.

31. Cai Shen, *Shu ji zhuan*.

32. Zhu Xi et al., *Yili jing zhuan tongjie*.

33. Zhu Xi, *Shi ji zhuan*.

34. Zhu Xi, *Yi Luo yuan yuan lu*.

35. Zhu Xi and Li Youwu, *Song ming chen yan xing lu*.

36. Zhu Xi, *Zizhi tongjian gangmu*.

37. Zhu Xi, *Chu ci ji zhu*; idem, *Changli xiansheng ji kaoyi*.

38. Kelleher, "Back to Basics."

39. Zhu Xi and Lü Zuqian, *Reflections on Things at Hand*.

40. Chu Ron-Guey, "Pluralism in the Chu Hsi School," 1257–65.

41. The curriculum in the proposal is discussed in de Bary, *The Liberal Tradition in China*, 40–42.

42. Sun Yingshi, *Zhuhu ji*, 9.4b–5b.

43. Walton, *Academies and Society in Southern Song China*, chaps. 3–5.

44. Chaffee, "Chu Hsi in Nan-k'ang," 426. Lu You (*Lao xue an biji*, 9.8b) noted that some Neo-Confucians were defensive about this.

45. Cheng Duanmeng, *Cheng Mengzhai xingli zixun*; for a translation, see Meskill, *Academies in Ming China*, 52–55. Wing-tsit Chan ("Chu Hsi and the Academies," 398) thinks that these rules were meant for elementary schools but came to be incorporated into academy charters. Lü Zuqian, whose compacts with students have been noted, included similar rules.

46. See comments to this effect by Ye Shi, *Ye Shi ji*, 27.554, 29.92, 29.607. I thank Chu Ping-tu for these references.

47. Zhu Xi, *Zhu Xi ji*, 74.3894; trans. (modified) from de Bary and Bloom, *Sources of Chinese Tradition*, 1: 741–42.

48. Zhu Xi, *Zhu Xi ji*, 74.3893.

49. For Zhu's view, see *Zhuzi yulei*, 109.4288. On the Chengs' view, see Zhu Xi and Lü Zuqian, *Reflections on Things at Hand*, 264–65.

50. Chaffee, "Chu Hsi in Nan-k'ang."

51. For a listing, see Wu Wanju, *Songdai shuyuan yu Songdai xueshu zhi guanxi*, 247–50. For Zhu Xi's involvement with academies, including the White Deer Grotto, see Wing-tsit Chan, "Chu Hsi and the Academies."

52. For a discussion of these developments, see Walton, *Academies and Society in Southern Song China*, 54–86, 215–18.

53. Meskill, *Academies in Ming China*, 14–16.

54. Xu Zi, *Yuandai shuyuan yanjiu*, 44–51, chaps. 4, 5, 7.

55. Ibid., 174–82.

56. Chen Wenyi, *You guanxue dao shuyuan*, 183–92.

57. Ibid., 156–57.

58. Already in the 1220s and 1230s, the departmental and National University examinations papers were being impacted; see De Weerdt, *Competition over Content*, 331–45.

59. Oka Motoshi, "Nansō ki kakyo no shikan o meguru chiikisei," 233–74.

60. See the preface to Yu Wenbao, *Chui jian lu waiji*. Some Neo-Confucians thought that literature and politics did fall outside Neo-Confucianism; see the three chapters on "Li xue" in Liu Xun, *Yin ju tong yi*. For a defense of Neo-Confucian exclusiveness from the literary critique, see Lü Pu, *Zhu xi gao*, 2.3a–6a. For a Neo-Confucian explanation of how literature can be included, see Li Qiqing, *Wenzhang jingyi*, items 1, 92, 95, 99. For an analysis of the difference between a Neo-Confucian understanding of aesthetic experience and a traditional literary position, see Fuller, "Aesthetics and Meaning in Experience." For a survey of the tensions between Neo-Confucian and literary endeavors, see Ma Jigao, *Song Ming lixue yu wenxue*. For a Neo-Confucian attempt to justify acquiring broad factual knowledge but as an enterprise separate from discoursing on learning and fathoming coherence, see the compiler's preface to Zhu Mu, *Gujin shiwen leiju*.

61. On the need to combine statecraft and the Learning of the Way, see Peng Fei's preface to Lü Zuqian, *Lidai zhidu xiangshuo*. For an anthology of belles lettres based on Neo-Confucian principles, see Zhen Dexiu, *Wenzhang zhengzong*.

62. Chu Ron-Guey, "Pluralism in the Chu Hsi School," 1265–67. In Yuan, there were at least three lineages (at the capital in the north, in Jiangxi, and in Zhejiang) that claimed to be carrying on the transmission of the Way; see Wing-tsit Chan, "Chu Hsi and Yuan Neo-Confucianism," 197–201.

63. See Cheng Rongxiu's 1333 preface to Li Xinchuan, *Dao ming lu* (1981).

64. This is how I read Wen Jiweng's 1273 inscription for an academy (translated in Walton, *Academies and Society in Southern Song China*, 69).

65. Zhou Mi, *Gui xin za zhi*, 169. Zhou Mi in this instance was quoting another source; for a discussion of Zhou's attitude toward Daoxue and the hostility toward his views in the Ming, see Ishida Hajime, "Shū Mitsu to Dōgaku."

66. Yao Dali, "Yuanchao keju zhidu."

67. Cheng Duanli, *Cheng shi jiashu dushu fennian richeng*. For a discussion of this text, see de Bary, "Chu Hsi's Aims as an Educator," 212–15; for a partial translation, see de Bary and Bloom, *Sources of Chinese Tradition*, 816–19.

68. Taking the number of brothers listed on the examination lists of 1148 and 1256 as representative of literati families at the time; for a discussion, see Chaffee, "Status, Family and Locale."

69. Ebrey, *Family and Property in Sung China*.

70. Ebrey, *Confucianism and Family Rituals in Imperial China*, 45–56.

71. Zhang Zai, *Zhang Zai ji*, yulu 3.326–27.

72. Ebrey, *Chu Hsi's Family Rituals*, xiv–xxii; idem, *Confucianism and Family Rituals in Imperial China*, 56–61.

73. Birge, *Women, Property, and Confucian Reaction*, 144–45.

74. On the difficulty of practicing Sima's liturgies, see Zhu Xi, *Zhuzi yulei*, 2266–67, 2294–95.

75. Zheng Juzhong, *Zhenghe wu li xinyi*. For these rites, see *juan* 178–79, 183–220; for the family ancestral temple, see *juan* 135.

76. Zhu Xi, *Zhu Xi ji*, 69.3628–30; dated to 1148–49.

77. For Zhu's comments on the *Zhenghe Rites*, see Zhu Xi, *Zhuzi yulei*, 2266–67, 2294–95. He drew on its essentials for the ceremony at the opening of an academy (ibid., 2295).

78. For an insightful analysis of the wedding ritual that shows how that rite could give substance to such views, see de Pee, "The Ritual and Sexual Bodies of the Groom and the Bride." Translation (modified) from Ebrey, *Chu Hsi's Family Rituals*, 3, following 184.

79. Ebrey, "The Early Stages in the Development of Descent Group Organization."

80. Walton, "Charitable Estates as an Aspect of Statecraft."

81. Translated in Ebrey, *Family and Property in Sung China.*

82. Ebrey, "Cremation in Sung China." Huang Gan is one example of someone who put both wedding and funeral rites into practice; see Kondō Kazunari, "Sōdai no shidaifu to shakai," 410.

83. Ebrey, *Chu Hsi's Family Rituals*, xxiv.

84. Bol, "Local History and Family in Past and Present"; Hymes, "Marriage, Descent Groups, and the Localist Strategy."

85. Lü Pu preface from 1346, in *Taiping Lü shi zongpu.*

86. Wei Su preface from 1350, in ibid., citing *Mencius* 4B.7. Although this preface does not appear in Wei Su's collection, Wei was the author of numerous prefaces to genealogies.

87. Fang Xiaoru, *Xunzhi zhai ji* (1996), 13.414.

88. De Pee, "The Ritual and Sexual Bodies of the Groom and the Bride," 86–90.

89. Birge, *Women, Property, and Confucian Reaction*, 143–99.

90. Bossler, "Shifting Identities," 33–37.

91. Birge, "Women and Confucianism from Song to Ming," 227–39.

92. Bossler, "Shifting Identities," 33–37.

93. Ebrey, *The Inner Quarters*, 37–43.

94. My understanding of the shifts in the nature of chastity are based on Theiss, *Disgraceful Matters*; see the summary at 26–27.

95. For example, the Wang family of Huizhou had created a multigenerational communal family when it first established itself, then in the eleventh century broke into several branches (to the advantage of some over others). In the thirteenth century, these branches attempted to restore kinship ties by creating a genealogy-based lineage rather than a family commune. See Nakajima Gakushō, "Ruise dōkyo kara sōzoku keisei e."

96. Dardess, "The Cheng Communal Family"; Langlois, "Authority in Family Legislation"; Li Xiaolong, "Yimen da jiating de fenbu"; Qi Xia, "Song Yuan shiqi Puyang Zhengshi jiazu."

97. Kawamura Yasushi, "Sōdai 'hō kyōdōtai' shokō."

98. Endō Takatoshi, "Sōdai ni okeru dōzoku nettowāku ni keisei"; Sangren, "Traditional Chinese Corporations."

99. "Inscription for One Mind Hall," in Su Boheng, *Su Pingzhong wenji*, 7.9b–12b.

100. McKnight, "Fiscal Privileges and the Social Order in Sung China."

101. My understanding of the formation of local elites is from Hymes, *Statesmen and Gentlemen*.

102. For the differences between official households and literati households in local society, see Liang Gengyao, *Songdai shehui jingji shi lunji*, 2: 474–536. Liang sees these problems as being more acute with the families of serving and retired officials than with literati households without close kin in office.

103. See note 26 to this chapter.

104. This figure is based *Chongxiu Jinhua fu zhi*, 13.10a–54b.

105. Von Glahn, "Chu Hsi's Community Granary in Theory and Practice," 246–48.

106. Hansen, *Changing Gods in Medieval China*, 128–59.

107. Kojima Tsuyoshi, "Seishi to inshi."

108. Boltz, "Not by the Seal of Office Alone." Numerous examples of the ways in which spirits were involved in the lives of officials, elites, and non-elite elements are found in the translations from Hong Mai's *Yi Jian zhi* and from a saints cult's collection of miracle stories in Hymes, *Way and Byway*.

109. Gardner, "Ghosts and Spirits in the Sung Neo-Confucian World."

110. Walton, *Academies and Society in Southern Song China*, chap. 5.

111. Bossler, *Powerful Relations*, 174–75.

112. Zhu Xi, *Zhu Xi ji*, 79.4094–96.

113. Neskar, "Shrines to Local Former Worthies"; idem, *The Politics of Prayer*.

114. For Lü's rules for his students see note 21 to this chapter.

115. For a discussion of the Lü and Zhu compacts, see Übelhör, "The Community Compact." For the original text, see Zhu Xi, *Zhu Xi ji*, 74.3903–12. For an abbreviated translation, see de Bary and Bloom, *Sources of Chinese Tradition*, 1: 751–54.

116. For example, Lu Jiuyuan; see Hymes, "Lu Chiu-yuan, Academies, and the Problem of the Local Community."

117. Funerary biography for Guo Cheng, in Lü Zuqian, *Donglai Lü taishi wenji*, 13.4a.

118. Chen Liang, *Chen Liang ji*, 28.339; noted in Tillman, *Ch'en Liang on Public Interest and the Law*, 55.

119. Walton, "Charitable Estates as an Aspect of Statecraft," 267–70.

120. For this and a discussion of the emergence of "mediating society" in the Southern Song, see Shiba Yoshinobu, "Nan Sō ni okeru 'chūkan ryōiki' shakai no tōjō," 188–92.

121. Maemura Yoshiyuki, "Goseichin no naibu kōzō."

122. Wang Deyi, "Nan Song yi yi kao," 260; McKnight, *Village and Bureaucracy in Southern Sung China*, 158–70; Gao Shulin, *Yuandai fuyi zhidu yanjiu*, esp. 106–11 for Yuan.

123. This example comes from Wuzhou in Zhejiang; see Dardess, "Confucianism, Local Reform, and Centralization." For a discussion of local elite leadership in such activities in Huizhou in late Southern Song and Yuan, see Nakajima Gakushō, *Mindai kyōson no funsō to chitsujo*, 66–148.

124. On the radical vision, see Ching, "Neo-Confucian Utopian Theories and Political Ethics." For Zhu Xi, see Tillman, *Ch'en Liang on Public Interest and the Law*, 49–55.

125. Von Glahn, "Chu Hsi's Community Granary in Theory and Practice," 229–33.

126. Ibid., 221–27, 234–41.

127. Zhu Xi, *Zhu Xi ji*, 79.4115–17.

128. Liang Gengyao, *Songdai shehui jingji shi lunji*, 2: 427–73. For Huang Gan's interpretation of the community granary in terms of Neo-Confucian philosophy, see ibid., 431–32.

129. For a listing of 63 granaries, 61 of which were founded between 1182 and 1271, see ibid., 2: 447–53.

130. Ibid., 456–67.

131. Toda Hiroshi, "Kō Shin no Kōtokugun shasō kaikaku."

132. This account is based on Bol, "Intellectual Culture in Wuzhou ca. 1200."

133. See Zhu Xi's funerary biography for Pan in *Zhu Xi ji*, 93.4731–34. See von Glahn, "Chu Hsi's Community Granary in Theory and Practice," 229–33.

134. Zhu Xi, *Zhu Xi ji*, 93.4731–34; Lü Zuqian, *Donglai Lü taishi wenji*, 4.9b.

135. Lü Zuqian, *Donglai Lü taishi wenji*, 12.7a–9a, bieji 10.16a.

136. The name alludes to *Analects* 4.8. For the retreat, see the inscription in Han Yuanji, *Nanjian jia yi gao*, 15.31a–34a.

137. For this correspondence, see Zhu Xi, *Zhu Xi ji*, 46.2232–42.

138. Lü Zuqian, *Donglai Lü taishi wenji*, 12.7a–9a, bieji 10.13b–17a.

139. Xu Song, *Song huiyao jigao*, fangyu 4.21a, zhiguan 74.11b; Tuotuo, *Song shi*, 393.12001, 404.12225.

140. Xu Song, *Song huiyao jigao*, zhiguan 75.36a, 74.11b.

141. Balazs and Hervouet, *A Sung Bibliography*, 450–54.

142. Aoki Atsushi, "Sung Legal Culture." Aoki points out that in practice a judgment that appealed to high principles would usually still have been based on a legal brief. For the case of Huang Gan, see Birge, *Women, Property, and Confucian Reaction*, 185–96.

143. Birge, *Women, Property, and Confucian Reaction*, 185–96.

144. Kondō Kazunari, "Sōdai no shidaifu to shakai."

145. This argument is set forth in the author's preface to Li Xinchuan, *Dao ming lu* (1981).

146. See the discussion in von Glahn, "Ming Taizu *ex Nihilo*?"

147. Meskill, *Academies in Ming China*, 23–24, 28. Citing Cao Songye's 1929 studies, Meskill notes that for the first century of Ming rule the rate of academy restorations, repairs, and foundings was less than one a year on average. This increased to three a year in 1460–1500. The vast majority of Ming academies were founded during the last 150 years of the dynasty and expanded to include Henan in north China and Guangdong in the far south.

148. Bol, "Examinations and Orthodoxies."

149. Liu Dake, *Bishui qunying daiwen huiyuan*, 44.6b, 45.7a–b. I thank Hilde De Weerdt for these references.

150. Fang Xiaoru (*Xunzhi zhai ji* [1983], 14.316) also argued against compartmentalization.

151. This case is made in greatest depth in Dardess, *Confucianism and Autocracy*.

152. For their turn toward legal solutions, see Langlois, "Political Thought in Chin-hua"; and Dardess, *Confucianism and Autocracy*, 224–50, 278–87.

153. Dardess, *Confucianism and Autocracy*, 266–78, 278–83.

154. Dardess, "The Cheng Communal Family," 48–52. As Michael Szonyi has shown in *Practicing Kinship*, fifteenth-century lineages were no longer exclusive to the literati.

155. Dardess, "The Cheng Communal Family," 39–45. In 1393, Zhu called all Zheng men over thirty to the capital to be considered for appointment.

156. This is mainly based on the detailed and systematic discussion of these and other institutions in George Jer-lang Chang, "Local Control in the Early Ming." For a chronological account of village policies institution, see Schneewind, "Visions and Revisions." For the entire range of early Ming legislation and a full translation of the placard and other documents, see Farmer, *Zhu Yuanzhang and Early Ming Social Legislation*. On the relief granary, see Hoshi Ayao, *Chūgoku shakai fukushi seisakushi no kenkyū*, chap. 4. I thank Chen Song for alerting me to this item. For community rites, see Taylor, "Official and Popular Religion," 144–48.

157. I draw this conclusion from Heijdra, "The Socio-economic Development of Rural China."

158. This conclusion is reached by Anita Marie Andrew in her study of the Grand Injunctions, "Zhu Yuanzhang and the Great Warnings," 208.

159. Zhu Xi, *Zhu Xi ji*, 100.5100–102; for a translation, see de Bary and Bloom, *Sources of Chinese Tradition*, 749–51.

160. Oh Kuemsung, *Mindai shakai keizaishi kenkyū*, 21–27.

161. Farmer (*Zhu Yuanzhang and Early Ming Social Legislation*, 39, 83–84) points out that hierarchical distinctions pervaded early Ming social policy.

162. Oyama Masaaki, *Min Shin shakai keizaishi kenkyū*.

163. Dardess, "The Cheng Communal Family," 39–42.

164. Although on paper the village tithing system was based on groups of 110 households, the case that it largely corresponded to natural villages is compelling; see Brook, "The Spatial Structure of Ming Local Administration"; and George Jer-lang Chang, "Local Control in the Early Ming," 115–26.

165. George Jer-lang Chang, "Local Control in the Early Ming," 147–55.

166. Farmer, "Social Order in Early Ming China."

167. Detailed in the biographies of Lu Daoqing and Ms Jia Guang in *Yaxi Lu shi jiacheng*, 205–6. For a discussion of the Neo-Confucian revival in Wuzhou, see Bol, "Culture, Society, and Neo-Confucianism."

168. Biography of Lu Rong, in Lu Ge, *He ting bian lun*, houlu 5/1a–5b.

169. Bol, "Culture, Society, and Neo-Confucianism," 273–89.

170. Peterson, "Confucian Learning in Late Ming Thought," 707.

171. A number of Zhan's rules are translated in Meskill, *Academies in Ming China*, 102–7.

172. Ibid., 56–57.

173. Ibid., 57–61.

174. The Jiangxi case, and the important role literati lineages played, is explored in a number of works: in detail in Hauf, "The Jiangyou Group." See also Lu Miaw-fen, "Practice as Knowledge"; idem, *Yangming xue shiren shequn*; and Zhang Yixi, *Shequn, jiazu yu Wang xue de xiangli shijian*.

175. Meskill, *Academies in Ming China*, 81–84.

176. Translated in ibid., 92–93.

177. Ibid., 119–22.

178. Ibid., 87–91, 118, 122, 127.

179. Ibid., 107.

180. Joanna F. Handlin Smith, *Action in Late Ming Thought*, 42.

181. Peterson, "Confucian Learning in Late Ming Thought," 727–42.

182. Chu Hung-lam, "The Debate over Recognition of Wang Yang-ming."

183. Peterson, "Confucian Learning in Late Ming Thought," 754–66. On the workings of the Donglin Academy, see Busch, "The Tung-lin Shu-yuan." For its politics, see Ray Huang, "The Hung-wu Reign," 536–44.

184. Wang Gen and Yan Jun (1504–96) are the two best-known examples; see Peterson, "Confucian Learning in Late Ming Thought."

185. Ebrey, *Confucianism and Family Rituals in Imperial China*; Lee, *Education in Traditional China*, 506–7.

186. Peterson, "Confucian Learning in Late Ming Thought," 735–37.

187. Carlitz, "Shrines, Governing-Class Identity, and the Cult of Widow Fidelity."

188. Heijdra, "The Socio-economic Development of Rural China," 486–91.

189. Translated in Wang Yangming, *Instructions for Practical Living*, 298–309.

190. Hauf, "The Community Covenant."

191. The most important discussions of these societies are Joanna F. Handlin Smith, "Benevolent Societies"; and Fuma Susumu, *Chūgoku zenkai zendō shi kenkyū*.

192. Joanna F. Handlin Smith, *Action in Late Ming Thought*, 65–83.

193. Joanna F. Handlin Smith, "Benevolent Societies," 310–20.

194. For Zhuhong, see Chün-fang Yü, *The Renewal of Buddhism in China*.

195. Farmer, *Zhu Yuanzhang and Early Ming Social Legislation*; Zürcher, "Christian Social Action in Late Ming Times"; idem, "Confucian and Christian Religiosity in Late Ming China."

196. For Lin's movement, see Berling, *The Syncretic Religion of Lin Chao-en*.

197. For an example, see Sakai Tadao, "Confucianism and Popular Educational Works," 345–62.

198. Brokaw, *The Ledgers of Merit and Demerit*, 95–156.

199. Joanna F. Handlin Smith, *Action in Late Ming Thought*, chaps. 5–8.

200. Atwell, "From Education to Politics."

Afterword

1. See, e.g., Bol, "Reconceptualizing the Nation in Southern Song"; Lo, *The Life and Thought of Yeh Shih*; Jaeyoon Song, "Shifting Paradigms in Theories of Government"; Zhang Yide, *Ye Shi pingzhuan*; and Zhou Mengjiang, *Ye Shi yu Yongjia xuepai*.

2. Huang Chin-hsing, *The Price of Having a Sage-Emperor*.

3. For a more elaborate statement on the turn away from Neo-Confucianism in learning, see Bol, "Looking to Wang Shizhen."

Bibliography

Andrew, Anita Marie. "Zhu Yuanzhang and the Great Warnings (*Yuzhi Da Gao*): Autocracy and Rural Reform in the Early Ming." Ph.D. diss., University of Minnesota, 1991.

Andrew, Anita M[arie], and John A. Rapp. *Autocracy and China's Rebel Founding Emperors: Comparing Chairman Mao and Ming Taizu*. Lanham, MD: Rowan & Littlefield Publishers, 2000.

Aoki Atsushi. "Sung Legal Culture: An Analysis of the Application of Laws by Judges in the Ch'ing-Ming *Chi* [集]." Special Issue: New Directions in the Study of Sung History. *Acta Asiatica* 84 (2003): 61–79.

Asim, Ina. "Aspects of the Perception of Zhou Ideals in the Song Dynasty (960–1279)." In *Die Gegenwart des Altertums: Formen und Funktionen des Altertumsbezugs in den Hochkulturen der Alten Welt*, ed. Dieter Kuhn and Helga Stahl. Heidelberg: Edition Forum, 2001, 459–80.

Atwell, William S. "From Education to Politics: The Fu She." In *The Unfolding of Neo-Confucianism*, ed. Wm. Theodore de Bary and Conference on Seventeenth Century Chinese Thought. New York: Columbia University Press, 1975, 333–68.

Balazs, Etienne, and Yves Hervouet. *A Sung Bibliography / Bibliographie des Sung*. Hong Kong: Chinese University Press, 1978.

Bao Weimin 包伟民. *Songdai difang caizheng shi yanjiu* 宋代地方財政史研究. Shanghai: Shanghai guji chubanshe, 2001.

———. "'Songdai jingji geming lun' fansi" '宋代經濟革命論'反思. *Guoji hanxue* 國際漢學 7 (1999): 111–34.

Berling, Judith A. *The Syncretic Religion of Lin Chao-en*. Neo-Confucian Studies. New York: Columbia University Press, 1980.

Berthrong, John H. *Transformations of the Confucian Way*. Boulder, CO: Westview Press, 1998.

Birdwhistell, Anne D. *Transition to Neo-Confucianism: Shao Yung on Knowledge and Symbols of Reality*. Stanford: Stanford University Press, 1989.

Birge, Bettine. "Women and Confucianism from Song to Ming: The Institutionalization of Patrilineality." In *The Song-Yuan-Ming Transition in Chinese History*, ed. Paul Jakov Smith and Richard von Glahn. Cambridge: Harvard University Asia Center, 2003, 212–40.

———. *Women, Property, and Confucian Reaction in Sung and Yüan China (960–1368)*. Cambridge: Cambridge University Press, 2002.

Bloom, Irene. "Three Visions of Jen." In *Meeting of Minds: Intellectual and Religious Interaction in East Asian Traditions of Thought*, ed. Irene Bloom and Joshua A. Fogel. New York: Columbia University Press, 1997, 8–42.

Bol, Peter K. "Chao Ping-wen (1159–1232): Foundations of Literati Learning." *China Under Jurchen Rule: Essays in Chin Intellectual and Cultural History*, ed. Hoyt C. Tillman and Stephen West. Albany: SUNY, 1995, 115–44.

———. "Cheng Yi as a Literatus." In *The Power of Culture*, ed. Willard Peterson, Kao Yu-kung, and Andrew Plaks. Hong Kong: Chinese University of Hong Kong Press, 1994, 172–94.

———. "Chu Hsi's Redefinition of Literati Learning." In *Neo-Confucian Education: The Formative Stage*, ed. Wm. Theodore de Bary and John Chaffee. Berkeley: University of California Press, 1989, 151–87.

———. "Examinations and Orthodoxies: 1070 and 1313 Compared." In *Culture and the State in Chinese History*, ed. Theodore Huters, R. Bin Wong, and Pauline Yu. Stanford: Stanford University Press, 1997, 29–57.

———. "The Examination System and the *Shih*." *Asia Major*, 3d ser., 3, no. 2 (1990): 149–71.

———. "Government, Society, and State: On the Political Visions of Ssu-ma Kuang (1019–1086) and Wang An-shih (1021–1086)." In *Ordering the World: Approaches to State and Society in Sung Dynasty China*, ed. Robert Hymes and Conrad Schirokauer. Berkeley: University of California Press, 1993, 128–92.

———. "Intellectual Culture in Wuzhou ca. 1200: Finding a Place for Pan Zimu and the *Complete Source for Composition*." In *Proceedings of the Second Symposium on Sung History*. Taibei, 1996, 788–38.

———. "Local History and Family in Past and Present." In *The New and the Multiple: Sung Senses of the Past*, ed. Thomas H. C. Lee. Hong Kong: Chinese University Press, 2004, 307–48.

———. "Looking to Wang Shizhen: Hu Yinglin (1551–1602) and Late Ming Alternatives to Neo-Confucian Learning." *Ming Studies*, no. 53 (2006): 99–137.

———. "Neo-Confucianism and Local Society, Twelfth to Sixteenth Century: A Case Study." *The Song-Yuan-Ming Transition in Chinese History*, ed. Paul Jakov Smith and Richard von Glahn. Cambridge: Harvard University Asia Center, 2003, 241–83.

———. "Reading Su Shi in Southern Song Wuzhou." *East Asian Library Journal* 8, no. 2 (1998): 69–102.

———. "Reconceptualizing the Nation in Southern Song: Some Implications of Ye Shi's Statecraft Learning." In *Thought, Political Power, and Social Forces*, ed. Ko-wu Huang. Taibei: Institute of Modern History, Academia Sinica, 2002, 33–64.

———. "Reconceptualizing the Order of Things in Northern and Southern Sung." In *Cambridge History of China*, vol. 5, pt. 2, ed. John Chaffee. Cambridge: Cambridge University Press, forthcoming.

———. "Seeking Common Ground: Han Literati Under Jurchen Rule." *Harvard Journal of Asiatic Studies* 47, no. 2 (1987): 461–538.

———. "The Sung Context: From Ou-yang Hsiu to Chu Hsi." In *Sung Dynasty Uses of the* I Ching, ed. Kidder Smith, Jr., Joseph Adler, Peter Bol, and Don J. Wyatt. Princeton: Princeton University Press, 1990, 26–55.

———. "Su Shih and Culture." In *Sung Dynasty Uses of the* I Ching, ed. Kidder Smith, Jr., Joseph Adler, Peter Bol, and Don J. Wyatt. Princeton: Princeton University Press, 1990, 56–99.

——— (Bao Bide 包弼德). "Tang Song bianxing de fansi: yi sixiang de bianhua wei zhu" 唐宋變型的反思: 以思想的變化爲主. *Zhongguo xueshu* 中國學術 1, no. 3 (2000): 63–87.

———. *"This Culture of Ours": Intellectual Transitions in T'ang and Sung China*. Stanford: Stanford University Press, 1992.

———. "Wang Anshi and the *Zhou li*." Paper presented at the conference Premodern East Asian Statecraft in Comparative Context: The *Rituals of Zhou* [*Zhouli* 周禮] in Chinese and East Asian History. Princeton University, 2006.

———. "When Antiquity Mattered." In *Perceptions of Antiquity in Chinese Civilization*, ed. Dieter Kuhn and Helga Stahl. Heidelberg: Edition Forum, 2008, 209–36.

———. "Whither the Emperor? Emperor Huizong, the New Policies, and the Tang-Song Transition." *Journal of Song and Yuan Studies*, no. 31 (2001): 103–34.

———. "Zhang Ruyu, the *Qunshu kaosuo*, and Diversity in Intellectual Culture: Evidence from Dongyang County in Wuzhou." In *Qingzhu Deng Guangming jiaoshou jiushi huadan lunwenji* 慶祝鄧廣銘教授九十華誕論文集. Shijia-zhuang: Hebei jiaoyu chubanshe, 1997, 644–73.

Boltz, Judith Magee. "Not by the Seal of Office Alone: New Weapons in the Battle with the Supernatural." In *Religion and Society in T'ang and Sung China*, ed. Patricia Buckley Ebrey and Peter N. Gregory. Honolulu: University of Hawai'i Press, 1993, 241–305.

Borrell, Ari. "*Ko-wu* or *Kung-an*? Practice, Realization, and Teaching in the Thought of Chang Chiu-ch'eng." In *Buddhism in the Sung*, ed. Peter Gregory and Daniel A. Getz, Jr. Honolulu: University of Hawai'i Press, 1999, 62–108.

Bossler, Beverley. *Powerful Relations: Kinship, Status, and the State in Sung China (960–1279)*. Cambridge: Harvard University, Council on East Asian Studies, 1997.

———. "Shifting Identities: Courtesans and Literati in Song China." *Harvard Journal of Asiatic Studies* 62, no. 1 (2002): 5–38.

Breisach, Ernst. *Historiography: Ancient, Medieval, and Modern*. Chicago: University of Chicago Press, 1983.

Brokaw, Cynthia. *The Ledgers of Merit and Demerit: Social Change and Moral Order in Late Ming China*. Princeton: Princeton University Press, 1991.

Brook, Timothy. "The Spatial Structure of Ming Local Administration." *Late Imperial China* 6, no. 1 (1985): 1–55.

Busch, Heinrich. "The Tung-lin Shu-yuan and Its Political and Philosophical Significance." *Monumenta Serica* 14 (1955): 1–163.

Cai Fanglu 蔡方鹿. *Songdai Sichuan lixue yanjiu* 宋代四川理学研究. Beijing: Xianzhuang shuju, 2003.

Cai Shen 蔡沈. *Shu ji zhuan* 書集傳. Taibei: Xin wenfeng chuban, 1984.

Cai Xiang 蔡襄. *Cai Xiang quanji* 蔡襄全集. Fuzhou: Renmin chubanshe, 1999.

Carlitz, Katherine. "Shrines, Governing-Class Identity, and the Cult of Widow Fidelity in Mid-Ming Jiangnan." *Journal of Asian Studies* 56, no. 3 (1997): 612–40.

Chaffee, John W. "Chu Hsi in Nan-k'ang: Tao-hsüeh and the Politics of Education." In *Neo-Confucian Education: The Formative Stage*, ed. Wm. Theodore de Bary and John Chaffee. Berkeley: University of California Press, 1989, 414–31.

———. "Education and Examinations in Sung Society (960–1279)." Ph.D. diss., University of Chicago, 1979.

———. "Status, Family and Locale: An Analysis of Examination Lists from Sung China." In *Ryū Shiken hakushi shōju kinen Sōdaishi kenkyū ronshū* 劉子健博士頌壽紀念宋史研究論集, ed. Kinugawa Tsuyoshi 依川強. Kyoto: Dōhōsha, 1989, 341–56.

―――. *The Thorny Gates of Learning in Sung China: A Social History of Examinations*. Cambridge: Cambridge University Press, 1985.

Chaffee, John, and Wm. Theodore de Bary, eds. *Neo-Confucian Education: The Formative Stage*. New York: Columbia University Press, 1989.

Chan, Hok Lam. "The Chien-wen, Yung-lo, Hung-hsi, and Hsüan-te Reigns, 1399–1435." In *The Cambridge History of China*, vol. 7, *The Ming Dynasty, 1368–1644*, ed. Frederick W. Mote and Denis Twitchett. Cambridge: Cambridge University Press, 1988, 182–304.

―――. "Ming T'ai-tsu's Manipulation of Letters: Myth and Reality of Literary Persecution." *Journal of Asian History* 29, no. 1 (1995): 1–60.

Chan, Wing-tsit (Chen Rongjie 陳榮捷). "The Ch'eng-Chu School of Early Ming." *Self and Society in Ming Thought*, ed. Wm. Theodore de Bary. New York: Columbia University Press, 1970, 29–52.

―――. "Chu Hsi and the Academies." In *Neo-Confucian Education: The Formative Stage*, ed. Wm. Theodore de Bary and John Chaffee. Berkeley: University of California Press, 1989, 389–413.

―――. "Chu Hsi and Yuan Neo-Confucianism." In *Yuan Thought: Chinese Thought and Religion Under the Mongols*, ed. Hok-lam Chan and Wm. Theodore de Bary. New York: Columbia University Press, 1982, 197–232.

―――. *Chu Hsi: New Studies*. Honolulu: University of Hawai'i Press, 1984.

―――. "The Evolution of the Neo-Confucian Concept *Li* as Principle." *Tsing-hua Journal of Chinese Studies*, n.s. 4, no. 2 (1964): 123–47.

―――. "Wang Shou-jen." In *Dictionary of Ming Biography, 1368–1644*, ed. L. Carrington Goodrich and Chao-ying Fang. New York: Columbia University Press, 1976, 1408–16.

―――. *Zhuzi menren* 朱子門人. Taibei: Taiwan xuesheng shuju, 1982.

Chan, Wing-tsit, comp. and trans. *A Source Book in Chinese Philosophy*. Princeton: Princeton University Press, 1963.

Chan, Wing-tsit, ed. *Chu Hsi and Neo-Confucianism*. Honolulu: University of Hawai'i Press, 1986.

Chang, George Jer-lang. "Local Control in the Early Ming (1368–1398)." Ph.D. diss., University of Minnesota, 1978.

Chang Hao. "The Intellectual Heritage of the Confucian Ideal of *Ching-shih*." In *Confucian Traditions in East Asian Modernity: Moral Education and Economic Culture in Japan and the Four Mini-dragons*, ed. Tu Weiming. Cambridge: Harvard University Press, 1996, 72–91.

Chen Chun 陳淳. *Beixi ziyi* 北溪字義. Beijing: Zhonghua shuju, 1983.

――― (Ch'en Ch'un). *Neo-Confucian Terms Explained: The Pei-hsi tzu-i*. Trans. Wing-tsit Chan. New York: Columbia University Press, 1986.

Chen Gujia 陈谷嘉 and Deng Hongbo 邓洪波. *Zhongguo shuyuan zhidu yanjiu* 中国书院制度研究. Hangzhou: Zhejiang jiaoyu chubanshe, 1997.

Chen Lai 陳來. *Song Ming lixue* 宋明理學. Taibei: Hongye chuban, 1994.

Chen Liang 陳亮. *Chen Liang ji* 陳亮集. Ed. Deng Guangming 鄧廣銘. Beijing: Zhonghua shuju, 1987.

Chen Qiqing 陳耆卿. *Yun chuang ji* 筼窗集. Yingyin Wenyuange Siku quanshu. Taibei: Taiwan Shangwu yinshuguan, 1983.

Chen, Wen-Yi (Chen Wenyi 陳雯怡). "Networks, Communities, and Identities: On the Discursive Practices of Yuan Literati." Ph.D. diss., Harvard University, 2007.

——. *You guanxue dao shuyuan: cong zhidu yu linian de hudong kan Songdai jiaoyu de yanbian* 由官學到書院: 從制度與理念的互動看宋代教育的演變. Taibei: Lianjing chuban shiye, 2004.

Chen Xianzhang 陳獻章. *Chen Xianzhang ji* 陳獻章集. Beijing: Zhonghua shuju, 1987.

Chen Zhengfu 陳正夫 and He Zhijing 何植靖. "Shilun Cheng Zhu lixue de tedian, lishi diwei he lishi zuoyong" 試論程朱理學的特點歷史地位和歷史作用. In *Lun Song Ming lixue* 論宋明理學, ed. Zhongguo zhexue shi xuehui 中國哲學史學會 and Zhejiang sheng shehui kexue yanjiu suo 浙江省社會科學研究所. Hangzhou: Zhejiang renmin chubanshe, 1983, 314–27.

Cheng Duanli 程端禮. *Cheng shi jiashu dushu fennian richeng* 程氏家塾讀書分年日程. Annot. Jiang Hanchun 江漢椿. Hefei: Huangshan shushe, 1992.

———. *Wei zhai ji* 畏齋集. Yingyin Wenyuange Siku quanshu. Taibei: Taiwan Shangwu yinshuguan.

Cheng Duanmeng 程端蒙. *Cheng Mengzhai xingli zixun* 程蒙齋性理字訓. Siku quanshu cunmu congshu. Ji'nan: Qi Lu shushe chubanshe, 1997.

Cheng Gongxu 程公許. *Cangzhou chen fou bian* 滄洲塵缶編. Yingyin Wenyuange Siku quanshu. Taibei: Taiwan Shangwu yinshuguan, 1983.

Cheng Hao 程顥 and Cheng Yi 程頤. *Er Cheng ji* 二程集. Ed. Wang Xiaoyu 王孝魚. Beijing: Zhonghua shuju, 1981.

Cheng Minsheng 程民生. "Lun Songdai shidafu zhengzhi dui huangquan de xianzhi" 論宋代士大夫政治對皇權的限制. In *Songshi yanjiu lunwen ji* 宋史研究論文集. Ningxia: Ningxia renmin chubanshe, 1993.

Cheng Minzheng 程敏政. *Dao yi bian* 道一編. Siku quanshu cunmu congshu. Ji'nan: Qi Lu shushe chubanshe, 1997.

Cheng Yuanmin 程元敏. *Wang Bo zhi shengping yu xueshu* 王柏之生平與學術. 2 vols. Taibei: Xuehai chubanshe, 1975.

Chia, Lucille. *Printing for Profit: The Commercial Publishers of Jianyang, Fujian (11th–17th centuries)*. Harvard-Yenching Institute Monograph Series 56. Cambridge: Harvard University Asia Center, 2002.

Ching, Julia. "Neo-Confucian Utopian Theories and Political Ethics." *Monumenta Serica* 30 (1972–73): 1–56.

Chongxiu Jinhua fu zhi 重修金華府志. 1480.

Chu Hung-lam (Zhu Honglin 朱鴻林). "Ch'iu Chun's *Ta-hsueh yen-i pu* and Its Influence in the Sixteenth and Seventeenth Centuries." *Ming Studies*, no. 22 (1986): 1–32.

———. "The Debate over Recognition of Wang Yang-ming." *Harvard Journal of Asiatic Studies* 48, no. 1 (1988): 47–79.

———. "Intellectual Trends in the Fifteenth Century." *Ming Studies* 27 (1989): 1–33.

———. "Ming ru Zhan Ruoshui zhuan dixue yongshu 'Sheng xue ge wu tong' de zhengzhi beijing yu neirong tese" 明儒湛若水撰帝學用書 "聖學格物通" 的政治背景與內容特色. *Zhongyang yanjiu yuan Lishi yuyan yanjiu suo jikan* 中央研究院歷史語言研究所集刊 62, no. 3 (1993): 495–530.

———. Review of Carney T. Fisher, *The Chosen One: Succession and Adoption in the Court of the Ming Shizong*. *Harvard Journal of Asiatic Studies* 54, no. 1 (1994): 266–77.

Chu Ping-tzu. "Tradition Building and Cultural Competition in Southern Song China (1160–1220): The Way, the Learning, and the Texts." Ph.D. diss., Harvard University, 1998.

Chu Ron-Guey. "Pluralism in the Chu Hsi School: Disputes Between Li Fang-tzu and Huang Kan." In *Guoji Zhuzixue huiyi lunwenji* 國際朱子學會議論文集, ed. Zhong Caijun 鍾彩鈞. Taibei: Zhongyang yanjiu yuan, Zhongguo wen zhe yanjiu suo choubei chu 中央研究院中國文哲研究所籌備處, 1993, 1235–70.

Chung Tsai-chun. *The Development of the Concepts of Heaven and of Man in the Philosophy of Chu Hsi*. Taibei: Academia Sinica, Institute of Chinese Literature and Philosophy, 1993.

Clark, Hugh. *Community, Trade and Networks: Southern Fujian Province from the Third to the Thirteenth Century*. Cambridge: Cambridge University Press, 1991.

Confucius: The Analects. Trans. D. C. Lau. Harmondsworth, Eng.: Penguin, 1979.

Danjō Hiroshi 檀上寬. *Minchō sensei shihai no shiteki kōzō* 明朝專制支配の史的構造. Tokyo: Kyūko shoin, 1995.

———. "Ming Qing xiangshen lun" 明清鄉紳論. *Riben xuezhe yanjiu Zhongguo shi lunzhu xuanyi* 日本學者研究中國史論著選譯. Beijing: Zhonghua shuju, 1993, 2: 453–83.

Dardess, John W. *Blood and History in China: The Donglin Faction and Its Repression, 1620–1627*. Honolulu: University of Hawai'i Press, 2002.

———. "The Cheng Communal Family: Social Organization and Neo-Confucianism in Yuan and Early Ming China." *Harvard Journal of Asiatic Studies* 34 (1974): 7–52.

———. *Confucianism and Autocracy: Professional Elites in the Founding of the Ming Dynasty.* Berkeley: University of California Press, 1983.

———. "Confucianism, Local Reform, and Centralization in Late Yuan Chekiang, 1342–1359." In *Yuan Thought: Chinese Thought and Religion Under the Mongols*, ed. Hok-lam Chan and Wm. Theodore de Bary. New York: Columbia University Press, 1982, 327–74.

Davis, Richard L. "Historiography as Politics in Yang Wei-chen's Polemic on Legitimate Succession." *T'oung Pao* 69, no. 1–3 (1983): 33–72.

de Bary, Wm. Theodore. "Chen Te-hsiu and Statecraft." In *Ordering the World: Approaches to State and Society in Sung Dynasty China*, ed. Robert Hymes and Conrad Schirokauer. Berkeley: University of California Press, 1993, 349–79.

———. "Chu Hsi's Aims as an Educator." In *Neo-Confucian Education: The Formative Stage*, ed. Wm. Theodore de Bary and John W. Chaffee. Berkeley: University of California Press, 1989, 186–218.

———. *Learning for Oneself.* Columbia University Press, 1991.

———. *The Liberal Tradition in China.* New York: Columbia University Press, 1983.

———. *The Message of the Mind in Neo-Confucianism.* New York: Columbia University Press, 1989.

———. *Neo-Confucian Orthodoxy and the Learning of the Mind-and-Heart.* New York: Columbia University Press, 1981.

———. *The Trouble with Confucianism.* Cambridge: Harvard University Press, 1991.

———. "The Uses of Neo-Confucianism: A Response to Professor Tillman." *Philosophy East and West* 43, no. 3 (1993): 541–55.

de Bary, Wm. Theodore, and Irene Bloom, eds. *Sources of Chinese Tradition*, vol. 1. New York: Columbia University Press, 1999.

de Pee, Christian. "The Ritual and Sexual Bodies of the Groom and the Bride in Ritual Manuals of the Sung Dynasty (Eleventh Through Thirteenth Centuries)." In *Chinese Women in the Imperial Past: New Perspectives*, ed. Harriet T. Zurndorfer. Leiden and Boston: Brill, 1999, 53–100.

De Weerdt, Hilde Godelieve Dominique. "Byways in the Imperial Chinese Information Order: The Dissemination and Commercial Publication of State Documents." *Harvard Journal of Asiatic Studies* 66, no. 1 (2006): 145–88.

———. *Competition over Content: Negotiating Standards for the Civil Service Examinations in Imperial China (1127–1279).* Cambridge: Harvard University Asia Center, 2007.

————. "The Composition of Examination Standards: Daoxue and Southern Song Dynasty Examination Culture." Ph.D. diss., Harvard University, 1998.

Deng Keming 鄧克銘. *Songdai li gainian zhi kaizhan* 宋代理概念之開展. Taibei: Wen jin chubanshe, 1993.

Dimberg, Ronald G., and Julia Ching. "Chang Mou." In *Dictionary of Ming Biography, 1368–1644*, ed. L. Carrington Goodrich and Chao-ying Fang. New York: Columbia University Press, 1976, 96–97.

Ditmanson, Peter. "Contesting Authority: Intellectual Lineages and the Chinese Imperial Court from the 12th to the 15th Centuries." Ph.D. diss., Harvard University, 1999.

Dong Guodong 凍國棟. *Zhongguo renkou shi: Sui Tang Wudai shiqi* 中國人口史: 隋唐五代時期. Zhongguo renkou shi 中國人口史, ed. Ge Jianxiong 葛劍雄. Shanghai: Fudan daxue chubanshe, 2002.

Dong Yuzheng 董玉整. *Zhongguo lixue dacidian* 中国理学大辞典. Guangzhou: Ji'nan daxue chubanshe 暨南大学出版社, 1995.

Du You 杜佑. *Tong dian* 通典. Beijing: Zhonghua shuju, 1984.

Ebrey, Patricia Buckley. *The Aristocratic Families of Early Imperial China: A Case Study of the Po-Ling Ts'ui Family*. Cambridge: Cambridge University Press, 1978.

————. "Art and Taoism in the Court of Song Huizong." In Stephen Little et al., *Taoism and the Arts of China*. Berkeley: University of California Press, 2000, 101–18.

————. *Confucianism and Family Rituals in Imperial China: A Social History of Writing About Rites*. 1991.

————. "Cremation in Sung China." *American Historical Review* 95, no. 2 (1990): 406–28.

————. "The Early Stages in the Development of Descent Group Organization." In *Kinship Organization in Late Imperial China*, ed. Patricia Buckley Ebrey and James L. Watson. Berkeley: University of California Press, 1986, 16–61.

————. *Family and Property in Sung China: Yuan Ts'ai's Precepts for Social Life*. Princeton: Princeton University Press, 1984.

————. *The Inner Quarters: Marriage and the Lives of Women in the Sung Period*. Berkeley: University of California Press, 1993.

Ebrey, Patricia Buckley, ed. *Chu Hsi's Family Rituals: A Twelfth-Century Chinese Manual for the Performance of Cappings, Weddings, Funerals, and Ancestral Rites*. Princeton: Princeton University Press, 1991.

Elman, Benjamin A. *A Cultural History of Civil Examinations in Late Imperial China*. Berkeley: University of California Press, 2000.

————. "The Formation of 'Dao Learning' as Imperial Ideology During the Early Ming Period." In *Culture and the State in Chinese History: Conventions, Ac-*

commodations, and Critiques, ed. Theodore Huters, R. Bin Wong, and Pauline Yu. Stanford: Stanford University Press, 1997, 58–83.

———. "Philosophy Vs. Philology: The *Jen Hsin Tao Hsin* Debate." *T'oung Pao* 69, no. 4–5 (1983): 175–222.

———. "Where Is King Ch'eng." *T'oung Pao* 79 (1993): 23–68.

Elvin, Mark. *The Pattern of the Chinese Past*. Stanford: Stanford University Press, 1973.

Endō Takatoshi 遠藤隆俊. "Sōdai ni okeru dōzoku nettowāku ni keisei: Han Chūen to Han Chūon" 宋代における同族ネットワークの形成—范仲淹と范仲溫. In *Sōdai shakai no nettowāku* 宋代社会のネットワーク, ed. Sōdaishi kenkyūkai 宋代史研究会. Tokyo: Kyūko shoin, 1998, 77–118.

Fan Zhongyan 范仲淹. *Fan Wenzheng gong quanji* 范文正公全集. Sibu congkan chubian. Shanghai: Shangwu yinshuguan, 1929.

Fang Xiaoru 方孝孺. *Xunzhi zhai ji* 遜志齋集. Guoxue jiben congshu, 1983.

———. *Xunzhi zhai ji* 遜志齋集. Wenyuange Siku quanshu. Taibei: Taiwan Shangwu yinshuguan, 1983.

———. *Xunzhi zhai ji* 遜志齋集. Ningbo: Ningbo chubanshe, 1996.

Farmer, Edward L. *Early Ming Government: The Evolution of Dual Capitals*. Cambridge: East Asian Research Center, Harvard University, 1976.

———. "Social Order in Early Ming China: Some Norms Codified in the Hungwu Period." In *Law and the State in Traditional East Asia: Six Studies on the Sources of East Asian Law*, ed. Brian E. McKnight. Honolulu: University of Hawai'i Press, 1987, 1–36.

———. *Zhu Yuanzhang and Early Ming Social Legislation: The Reordering of Chinese Society Following the Era of Mongol Rule*. Leiden: Brill, 1995.

Feng Dawen 冯达文. *Song Ming xin ruxue luelun* 宋明新儒学略论. [Canton]: Guangdong renmin chubanshe, 1997.

Fisher, Carney T. *The Chosen One: Succession and Adoption in the Court of Ming Shizong*. Sydney: Allen and Unwin, 1990.

Fogel, Joshua A. *Politics and Sinology: The Case of Naito Konan (1866–1934)*. Cambridge: Council on East Asian Studies, Harvard University, 1984.

Foster, Robert Wallace. "Differentiating Rightness from Profit: The Life and Thought of Lu Jiuyuan (1139–1193)." Ph.D. diss., Harvard University, 1997.

Fu, Charles Wei-hsun. "Chu Hsi on Buddhism." In *Chu Hsi and Neo-Confucianism*, ed. Wing-tsit Chan. Honolulu: University of Hawai'i Press, 1986, 377–407.

Fu, Charles Wei-hsun, and Wing-tsit Chan. *Guide to Chinese Philosophy*. Boston: G. K. Hall, 1978.

Fu Zhengyuan. *The Autocratic Tradition and Chinese Politics*. Cambridge: Cambridge University Press, 1993.

Fuller, Michael A. "Aesthetics and Meaning in Experience: A Theoretical Perspective on Zhu Xi's Revision of Song Dynasty Views of Poetry." *Harvard Journal of Asiatic Studies* 65, no. 2 (2005): 311–56.

———. *The Road to East Slope: The Development of Su Shih's Poetic Voice.* Stanford: Stanford University Press, 1990.

Fuma Susumu 夫馬進. *Chūgoku zenkai zendō shi kenkyū* 中国善会善堂史研究. Kyoto: Dōhōsha, 1997.

Fumoto Yasutaka 麓保孝. *Hoku Sō ni okeru Jugaku no tenkai* 北宋に於ける儒學の展開. Tokyo: Shoseki bunbutsu ryūtsūkai, 1967.

Furth, Charlotte. "The Physician as Philosopher of the Way: Zhu Zhenheng (1282–1358)." *Harvard Journal of Asiatic Studies* 66, no. 2 (2006): 423–60.

Gao Congming 高聰明. *Songdai huobi yu huobi liutong yanjiu* 宋代貨幣與貨幣流通研究. Baoding: Hebei daxue chubanshe, 1999.

Gao Shulin 高樹林. *Yuandai fuyi zhidu yanjiu* 元代賦役制度研究. Song shi yanjiu congshu. Baoding: Hebei daxue chubanshe, 1997.

Gardner, Daniel K. *Chu Hsi and the* Ta Hsueh: *Neo-Confucian Reflections on the Confucian Canon.* Cambridge: Council on East Asian Studies, Harvard University, 1986.

———. "Confucian Commentary and Chinese Intellectual History." *Journal of Asian Studies* 57, no. 2 (1998): 397–422.

———. "Ghosts and Spirits in the Sung Neo-Confucian World: Chu Hsi on *kuei-shen.*" *Journal of the American Oriental Society* 115, no. 4 (1995): 598–611.

———. *Zhu Xi's Reading of the* Analects: *Canon, Commentary, and the Classical Tradition.* New York: Columbia University Press, 2003.

Gates, Hill. *China's Motor: A Thousand Years of Petty Capitalism.* Ithaca: Cornell University Press, 1996.

Ge Jinfang 葛金芳. *Song Liao Xia Jin jingji yanxi* 宋遼夏金經濟研析. Wuhan: Wuhan chubanshe, 1991.

Ge Shengzhong 葛勝仲. *Danyang ji* 丹陽集. Yingyin Wenyuange Siku quanshu. Taibei: Taiwan Shangwu yinshuguan.

Ge Zhaoguang 葛兆光. *Qi shiji zhi shijiu shiji Zhongguo de zhishi, sixiang yu xinyang* 七世纪至十九世纪中国的知识、思想与信仰. Shanghai: Fudan daxue chubanshe 复旦大学出版社, 2000.

Gedalecia, David. *The Philosophy of Wu Ch'eng: A Neo-Confucian of the Yuan Dynasty.* Bloomington: Research Institute for Inner Asian Studies, Indiana University, 1999.

———. *A Solitary Crane in a Spring Grove: The Confucian Scholar Wu Ch'eng in Mongol China.* Wiesbaden: Harrassowitz Verlag, 2000.

———. "Wu Ch'eng and the Perpetuation of the Classical Heritage in the Yuan." *China Under Mongol Rule*, ed. John D. Langlois, Jr. Princeton: Princeton University Press, 1981, 186–211.

———. "Wu Ch'eng's Approach to Internal Self-Cultivation and External Knowledge-Seeking." In *Yuan Thought: Chinese Thought and Religion Under the Mongols*, ed. Hok-lam Chan and Wm. Theodore de Bary. New York: Columbia University Press, 1982, 279–326.

Goodrich, L. Carrington, and Chao-ying Fang, eds. *Dictionary of Ming Biography, 1368–1644*. New York: Columbia University Press, 1976.

Graham, A. C. *Two Chinese Philosophers: The Metaphysics of the Brothers Cheng*. La Salle, IL: Open Court, 1992 [1958].

———. "What Was New in the Ch'eng-Chu Theory of Human Nature?" In *Chu Hsi and Neo-Confucianism*, ed. Wing-tsit Chan. Honolulu: University of Hawai'i Press, 1986, 138–57.

Grant, Beata. *Mount Lu Revisited: Buddhism in the Life and Writings of Su Shih*. Honolulu: University of Hawai'i Press, 1995.

Grove, Linda, and Christopher Daniels, eds. *State and Society in China: Japanese Perspectives on Ming-Qing Social Economic History*. Tokyo: University of Tokyo Press, 1984.

Guan Changlong 关长龙. *Liang Song daoxue mingyun de lishi kaocha* 两宋道学命运的历史考察. Shanghai: Xuelin chubanshe, 2001.

Guan Lüquan 關履權. *Songdai Guangzhou de haiwai maoyi* 宋代廣州的海外貿易. Guangdong: Guangdong renmin chubanshe, 1994.

Guo Fu 郭鈇. *Shi dong yi fang* 石洞遺芳. Jinhua congshu. N.p.: Hu shi Tuibu zhai 胡氏退補齋, 1862.

Guo Zhengzhong 郭正忠. *Liang Song chengxiang shangpin huobi jingji kaolue* 两宋城乡商品货币经济考略. Beijing: Jingji guanli chubanshe, 1997.

Halperin, Mark. *Out of the Cloister: Lay Perspectives on Buddhism in Sung China, 960–1279*. Cambridge: Harvard University Asia Center, 2006.

Hamashima Atsutoshi. "The City God Temples (*chenghuangmiao*) of Chiangnan in the Ming and Qing Dynasties." *Memoirs of the Research Department of the Toyo Bunko* 50 (1992).

Han Jingtai 韓經太. *Lixue wenhua yu wenxue sichao* 理學文化與文學思潮. Beijing: Zhonghua shuju, 1997.

Han Xiuli 韓秀麗 et al. *Sishu yu xiandai wenhua* 四書與現代文化. Zhuzi baijia yu xiandai wenhua congshu. Beijing: Zhongguo guangbo dianshi chubanshe, 1998.

Han Yuanji 韓元吉. *Nanjian jia yi gao* 南澗甲乙稿. Yingyin Wenyuange Siku quanshu. Taibei: Taiwan Shangwu yinshuguan, 1983.

Hansen, Valerie. *Changing Gods in Medieval China, 1127–1276.* Princeton: Princeton University Press, 1990.

———. *The Open Empire: A History of China to 1600.* New York: Norton, 2000.

Hartwell, Robert M. "Demographic, Political, and Social Transformation of China, 750–1550." *Harvard Journal of Asiatic Studies* 42, no. 2 (1982): 365–442.

———. "Markets, Technology, and the Structure of Enterprise in the Development of the Eleventh-Century Chinese Iron and Steel Industry." *Journal of Economic History* 26 (1966): 29–58.

Hatch, George. "Su Hsun's Pragmatic Statecraft." In *Ordering the World: Approaches to State and Society in Sung Dynasty China*, ed. Robert Hymes and Conrad Schirokauer. Berkeley: University of California Press, 1993, 59–75.

Hauf, Kandice J. "The Community Covenant in Sixteenth Century Ji'an Prefecture, Jiangxi." *Late Imperial China* 17, no. 2 (1996): 1–50.

———. "The Jiangyou Group: Culture and Society in Sixteenth-Century China." Ph.D. diss., Yale University, 1987.

He Yan 何晏, Xing Bing 邢昺, and Lu Deming 陸德明. *Song ben Lunyu zhushu* 宋本論語註疏. Shanghai: Shangwu yinshuguan, 1929.

He Yousen 何佑森. "Liang Song xuefeng de dili fenbu" 兩宋學風的地理分布. *Xinya xuebao* 新亞學報 1, no. 1 (1955): 331–79.

Heijdra, Martin. "The Socio-economic Development of Rural China During the Ming." In *The Cambridge History of China*, vol. 8, pt. 2, *The Ming Dynasty, 1368–1644*, ed. Denis Twitchett and F. W. Mote. Cambridge: Cambridge University Press, 1998, 417–578.

Heng, Chye Kiang. *Cities of Aristocrats and Bureaucrats: The Development of Medieval Chinese Cities.* Honolulu: University of Hawai'i Press, 1999.

Higashi Ichio 東一夫. *Ō Anseki shinpō no kenkyū* 王安石新法の研究. Tokyo: Kazama shobō, 1970.

Hirotsune Jinsei 廣常人世. *Gen Min Shindai shisō kenkyū bunken mokuroku* 元明清代思想研究文献目録. Tokyo: The author, 1967.

Holcombe, Charles. "Immigrants and Strangers: From Cosmopolitanism to Confucian Universalism in Tang China." *Tang Studies* 20/21 (2002–3): 71–112.

Hon, Tze-Ki. *The Yijing and Chinese Politics: Classical Commentary and Literati Activism in the Northern Song Period, 960–1127.* Albany: State University of New York Press, 2005.

Hong Mai 洪邁. *Rong zhai sui bi* 容齋隨筆. Shanghai: Shanghai guji chubanshe, 1978.

Hoshi Ayao 星斌夫. *Chūgoku shakai fukushi seisakushi no kenkyū: Shindai no shinsaisō o chūshin ni* 中国社会福祉政策史の研究: 清代の賑済倉を中心に. Tokyo: Yamakawa shuppansha, 1988.

Hou Wailu 侯外庐, Qiu Hansheng 邱汉生, and Zhang Qizhi 张岂之. *Song Ming lixue shi* 宋明理学史. Beijing: Renmin chubanshe, 1984.

Hu Anguo 胡安國. *Chunqiu Hu shi zhuan* 春秋胡氏傳. Sibu congkan. Shanghai: Shangwu yinshuguan, 1934.

Hu Juren 胡居仁. *Juye lu* 居業錄. Congshu jicheng. Shanghai: Shangwu yinshuguan, 1936.

Hu Zongmao 胡宗楙. *Jinhua jingji zhi* 金華經籍志. N.p.: Mengxuan lou, 1926.

Huang, Chi-chiang. "Elite and Clergy in Northern Song Hangzhou: A Convergence of Interest." In *Buddhism in the Sung*, ed. Peter Gregory and Daniel A. Getz, Jr. Honolulu: University of Hawai'i Press, 1999, 295–339.

Huang Chin-hsing (Huang Chin-shing). "The Cultural Politics of Autocracy: The Confucius Temple and Ming Despotism, 1368–1530." In *On Sacred Grounds: Culture, Society, Politics and the Formation of the Cult of Confucius*, ed. Thomas A. Wilson. Cambridge: Harvard University Asia Center, 2002, 267–96.

———. *The Price of Having a Sage-Emperor: The Unity of Politics and Culture*. Occasional Paper and Monograph Series no. 10. Singapore: Institute of East Asian Philosophies, 1987.

Huang, Chun-chieh. "Imperial Rulership in Cultural History: Chu Hsi's Interpretation." In *Imperial Rulership and Cultural Change in Traditional China*, ed. Frederick P. Brandauer and Chun-chieh Huang. Seattle: University of Washington Press, 1994, 188–205.

Huang, Ray. "The Hung-wu Reign, 1369–1398." In *The Cambridge History of China*, vol. 7, pt. 1, *The Ming Dynasty, 1368–1644*, ed. Denis Twitchett and Frederick W. Mote. Cambridge: Cambridge University Press, 1988, 511–84.

Huang Zhen 黃震. *Huang shi ri chao* 黃氏日抄. Yingyin Wenyuange Siku quanshu. Taibei: Taiwan Shangwu yinshuguan, 1983.

Hucker, Charles O. "Ming Government." In *The Cambridge History of China*, vol. 8, pt. 2, *The Ming Dynasty, 1368–1644*, ed. Denis Twitchett and Frederick W. Mote. Cambridge: Cambridge University Press, 1998, 9–105.

Hymes, Robert P. "Lu Chiu-yuan, Academies, and the Problem of the Local Community." In *Neo-Confucian Education: The Formative Stage*, ed. Wm. Theodore de Bary and John Chaffee. Berkeley: University of California Press, 1989, 432–56.

———. "Marriage, Descent Groups, and the Localist Strategy in Sung and Yuan Fu-chou." In *Kinship Organization in Late Imperial China, 1000–1940*, ed. Patricia Buckley Ebrey and James L. Watson. Berkeley: University of California Press, 1986, 95–136.

———. *Statesmen and Gentlemen: The Elite of Fu-Chou, Chiang-Hsi, in Northern and Southern Sung*. Cambridge: Cambridge University Press, 1986.

———. *Way and Byway: Taoism, Local Religion, and Models of Divinity in Sung and Modern China.* Berkeley: University of California Press, 2001.

Ichiki Tsuyuhiko 市来津由彦. *Shu Ki monjin shūdan keisei no kenkyū* 朱熹門人集團形成の研究. Tōyōgaku sōsho. Tokyo: Sōbunsha, 2002.

Ishida Hajime 石田肇. "Shū Mitsu to Dōgaku" 周密と道學. *Tōyōshi kenkyū* 東洋史研究 49, no. 2 (1990): 249–71 (25–47).

Ivanhoe, Philip J. *Confucian Moral Self-Cultivation.* New York: Peter Lang, 1993.

Jay, Jennifer W. *A Change in Dynasties: Loyalism in Thirteenth-Century China.* Bellingham: Western Washington University, 1992.

Jen Yu-wen. "Ch'en Hsien-chang's Philosophy of the Natural." In *Self and Society in Ming Thought*, ed. Wm. Theodore de Bary and Conference on Ming Thought. New York: Columbia University Press, 1970, 53–92.

Ji, Xiao-bin. *Politics and Conservatism in Northern Song China: The Career and Thought of Sima Guang (1019–1086).* Hong Kong: Chinese University Press, 2005.

Ji Xiuzhu 姬秀珠. *Mingchu daru Fang Xiaoru yanjiu* 明初大儒方孝孺研究. Taibei: Wenshizhe chubanshe, 1991.

Jiang Guozhu 姜國柱 and Zhu Kuiju 朱葵菊. *Zhongguo renxing lun shi* 中國人性論史. Zhengzhou: Henan renmin chubanshe, 1997.

Jiang Yibin 蔣義斌. *Songdai ru shi tiaohe lun ji paifou lun zhi yanjiu* 宋代儒釋調和論及排佛論之研究. Taibei: Taiwan Shangwu yinshuguan, 1988.

Jin Lüxiang 金履祥. *Zizhi tongjian qianbian* 資治通鑑前編. Yingyin Wenyuange Siku quanshu. Taibei: Taiwan Shangwu yinshuguan 臺灣商務印書館, 1983.

Jin Zhongshu 金中樞. "Bei Song keju zhidu yanjiu, I" 北宋科舉制度研究 I. In *Song shi yanjiu ji* 宋史研究集, vol. 11. Taibei: Guoli bianyi guan, 1979, 1–72.

———. "Bei Song keju zhidu yanjiu, xu" 北宋科舉制度研究續. In *Song shi yanjiu ji* 宋史研究集, vol. 13. Taibei: Guoli bianyi guan, 1981, 61–189.

Johnson, David. "The Last Years of a Great Clan: The Li Family of Chao Chun in Late T'ang and Early Sung." *Harvard Journal of Asiatic Studies* 37, no. 1 (1977): 5–102.

———. *The Medieval Chinese Oligarchy.* Boulder, CO: Westview Press, 1977.

Kasoff, Ira. *The Thought of Chang Tsai.* Cambridge: Cambridge University Press, 1984.

Kawamura Yasushi 川村康. "Sōdai 'hō kyōdōtai' shokō" 宋代「法共同體」初考. In *Sōdai shakai no nettowāku* 宋代社会のネットワーク, ed. Sōdaishi kenkyūkai 宋代史研究会. Tokyo: Kyūko shoin, 1998, 119–50.

Kelleher, M. Theresa. "Back to Basics: Chu Hsi's *Elementary Learning (Hsiao-hsüeh)*." In *Neo-Confucian Education: The Formative Stage*, ed. Wm. Theodore de Bary and John W. Chaffee. Berkeley: University of California Press, 1989, 219–51.

———. *Personal Reflections on the Pursuit of Sagehood: An Interplay of Darkness and Light in the Journal of Wu Yu-pi*. New York: Regional Seminar in Neo-Confucian Studies, Columbia University, 1980.

Kim, Youngmin. "Redefining the Self's Relation to the World: A Study of Mid-Ming Neo-Confucian Discourse." Ph.D. diss., Harvard, 2002.

Kim, Yung Sik. *The Natural Philosophy of Chu Hsi (1130–1200)*. Philadelphia: American Philosophical Society, 2000.

Koh, Khee Heong. "East of the River and Beyond: A Study of Xue Xuan (1389–1464) and the Hedong School." Ph.D. diss., Columbia University, 2006.

Kojima Tsuyoshi 小島毅. "Fukken nanbu no meizoku to Shushigaku no fukyū" 福建南部の名族と朱子學の普及. In *Sōdai no chishikijin: shisō, seido, chiiki shakai* 宋代の知識人：思想・制度・地域社会, ed. Sōdaishi kenkyūkai 宋代史研究会. Tokyo: Kyūko shoin, 1993, 227–55.

———. "Seishi to inshi: Fukken no chihōshi ni okeru kijutsu to ronri" 正祠と淫祠：福建の地方誌におねる記述と論理. *Tōyō bunka kenkyūjo kiyō* 東洋文化研究所 114 (1991): 87–213.

Kondō Kazunari 近藤一成. "Sai Kyō no kakyo, gakkō seisaku" 蔡京の科舉, 學校政策. *Tōyōshi kenkyū* 東洋史研究 53, no. 1 (1994): 24–49.

———. "Sōdai no shidaifu to shakai — Kō Kan ni okeru rei no sekai to hango no sekai" 宋代の士大夫と社會—黃榦における禮の世界と判語の世界. In *Sō Gen jidaishi no kihon mondai* 宋元時代史の基本問題, ed. Satake Yasuhiko 佐竹靖彦 et al. Tokyo: Kyūko shoin, 1996, 389–424.

———. "Sōdai shidaifu seiji no tokushoku" 宋代士大夫政治の特色. In *Chūka no bunretsu to saisei, san–jūsan seiki* 中華の分裂と再生, 三—十三世紀, vol. 9. Iwanami kōza sekai rekishi. Tokyo: Iwanami shoten, 1999, 305–26.

Kong Yingda 孔穎達. "Chunqiu zhengyi" 春秋正義. In *Shisan jing zhushu* 十三經注疏, ed. Ruan Yuan 阮元. Beijing: Zhonghua shuju, 1980.

Lackner, Michael. "Die 'Verplanung' des Denkens am Beispiel der T'u." In *Lebenswelt und Weltanschauung im frühneuzeitlichen China*, ed. Helwig Schmidt-Glintzer. Stuttgart: Franz Steiner Verlag, 1990, 133–56.

Langlois, John D., Jr. "Authority in Family Legislation: The Cheng Family Rules (*Cheng-shih kuei-fan*)." In *State and Law in East Asia: Festschrift Karl Bünger*, ed. Dieter Eikemeir and Herbert Franke. Wiesbaden: Harrassowitz, 1981, 272–99.

———. "Political Thought in Chin-hua Under Mongol Rule." *China Under Mongol Rule*, ed. idem. Princeton: Princeton University Press, 1981, 137–85.

Lee, Thomas H. C. "Academies: Official Sponsorship and Suppression." In *Imperial Rulership and Cultural Change in Traditional China*, ed. Frederick P. Brandauer and Chun-chieh Huang. Seattle: Washington University Press, 1994, 117–243.

———. *Education in Traditional China, a History*. Leiden: Brill, 2000.

Leeming, Frank. "Official Landscapes in Traditional China." *Journal of the Economic and Social History of the Orient* 23, pt. I-II (1980): 153–204.

Leung, Irene S. "'Felt yurts neatly arrayed, large tents huddle close': Visualizing the Frontier in the Northern Song Dynasty (960–1127)." In *Political Frontiers, Ethnic Boundaries, and Human Geographies in Chinese History*, ed. Nicola Di Cosmo and Don J. Wyatt. London: RoutledgeCurzon, 2003, 192–219.

———. "The Frontier Imaginary in the Song Dynasty (960–1279): Revisiting Cai Yan's 'Barbarian Captivity' and Return." Ph.D. diss., University of Michigan, 2000.

Lewis, Mark Edward. *Writing and Authority in Early China*. Albany: SUNY Press, 1999.

Li Gou 李覯. *Li Gou ji* 李覯集. Beijing: Zhonghua shuju, 1981.

Li Huarui 李華瑞. *Wang Anshi bianfa yanjiu shi* 王安石變法研究史. Beijing: Renmin chubanshe, 2004.

Li Qiqing 李耆卿. *Wenzhang jingyi* 文章精義. Beijing: Renmin chubanshe, 1983.

Li Shimin 李世民. "Di fan" 帝範. In *Di fan chen gui* 帝範臣規, ed. Yi Li 伊力. Changsha: Zhongzhou guji chubanshe, 1994, 1–39.

Li Xiaolong 黎小龍. "Yimen da jiating de fenbu yu zongzu wenhua de quyu tezheng" 義門大家庭的分布與宗族文化的區域特征. *Lishi yanjiu* 1998, no. 2: 54–63.

Li Xinchuan 李心傳. *Dao ming lu* 道命錄. Zhibuzu zhai congshu, 1872.

———. *Dao ming lu* 道命錄. Songshi ziliao cuibian. Taibei: Wenhai chubanshe, 1981.

Li Yuangang 李元綱. *Shengmen shiye tu* 聖門事業圖. Baichuan xuehai. Shanghai: Bogu zhai, 1921.

Li Zhuoran 李卓然. "Zhi guo zhi dao: Ming Chengzu ji qi *Shengxue xinfa*" 治國之道—明成祖及其聖學心法. *Hanxue yanjiu* 漢學研究 9, no. 1 (1991): 211–27.

Liang Gengyao 梁庚堯. *Songdai shehui jingji shi lunji* 宋代社會經濟史論集. Taibei: Yunzhen wenhua shiye, 1997.

Lin Qingzhang 林慶彰. "*Wujing daquan* zhi xiuzuan ji qi xiangguan tanjiu" 《五經大全》之修纂及其相關問題探究. *Zhongguo wenzhe yanjiu jikan* 中國文哲研究集刊 1 (1991): 361–83.

Lin Qingzhang 林慶彰 et al., eds. *Zhuzi xue yanjiu shumu* 朱子學研究書目. Taibei: Wenjin chubanshe, 1992.

Liu Chang 劉敞. *Gongshi ji* 公是集. Yingyin Wenyuange Siku quanshu. Taibei: Taiwan Shangwu yinshuguan, 1983.

Liu Dake 劉達可. *Bishui qunying daiwen huiyuan* 璧水羣英待問會元. Xuxiu Siku quanshu. Shanghai: Shanghai guji chubanshe, 1995.

Liu Guanglin. "Wrestling for Power: The State and Economy in Later Imperial China, 1000–1770." Ph.D. diss., Harvard University, 2005.

Liu, James T. C. *China Turning Inward: Intellectual-Political Changes in the Early Twelfth Century.* Cambridge: Council on East Asian Studies, Harvard University, 1988.

———. "How Did a Neo-Confucian School Become the State Orthodoxy?" *Philosophy East and West* 23 (1973): 483–505.

———. *Ou-yang Hsiu: An Eleventh Century Neo-Confucianist.* Stanford: Stanford University Press, 1967.

———. *Reform in Sung China: Wang An-shih (1021–1086) and His New Policies.* Cambridge: Harvard University Press, 1959.

———. "The Sung Views on the Control of Government Clerks." *Journal of the Economic and Social History of the Orient* 10, no. 2–3 (1967): 317–44.

Liu Jingzhen 劉靜貞. *Bei Song qianqi huangdi he tamen de quanli* 北宋前期皇帝和他們的權力. Taibei: Daoxiang chubanshe, 1996.

Liu, Kwang-Ching. "Socioethics as Orthodoxy: A Perspective." In *Orthodoxy in Late Imperial China,* ed. idem. Berkeley: University of California Press, 1990, 53–100.

Liu Liyan (Lau Nap-yin) 柳立言. "He wei 'Tang Song biange'?" 何謂「唐宋變革」? *Zhonghua wenshi luncong* 中華文史論叢 81 (2006): 125–71.

Liu Shuxun 刘树勋. *Minxue yuanliu* 闽学源流. Fuzhou: Fujian jiaoyu chubanshe, 1993.

Liu Xun 劉壎. *Yin ju tong yi* 隱居通議. Yingyin Wenyuange Siku quanshu. Taibei: Taiwan Shangwu yinshuguan, 1983.

Liu Yi 劉毅. "Songdai huangling zhidu yanjiu" 宋代皇陵制度研究. *Gugong bowu yuan yuankan* 故宮博物院院刊 1 (1999): 66–82.

Lo, Winston. *The Life and Thought of Yeh Shih.* Hong Kong: Chinese University of Hong Kong, 1974.

Lou Yao 樓鑰. *Gong kui ji* 攻媿集. Congshu jicheng chubian. Shanghai: Shangwu yinshuguan, 1935.

Lu Ge 盧格. *He ting bian lun* 荷亭辯論. Siku quanshu cunmu congshu. Ji'nan: Qi Lu shushe chubanshe, 1997.

Lu Jiuyuan 陸九淵. *Lu Jiuyuan ji* 陸九淵集. Beijing: Zhonghua shuju chubanshe, 1980.

Lu Miaw-fen (Lü Miaofen 呂妙芬). "Practice as Knowledge: Yang-ming Learning and *Chiang-hui* in Sixteenth-Century China." Ph.D. diss., University of California, Los Angeles, 1997.

————. *Yangming xue shiren shequn: lishi, sixiang yu shijian* 陽明學士人社群: 歷史, 思想與實踐. Taibei: Zhongyang yanjiu yuan, Jindai shi yanjiu suo, 2003.

Lü Pu 呂浦. *Zhu xi gao* 竹溪稿. Xu Jinhua congshu. Yongkang: Yongkang Hu shi Mengxuan lou, 1924.

Lu You 陸游. *Lao xue an biji* 老學庵筆記. Shanghai: Hanfen lou, 1912.

————. *Lu Fangweng quanji* 陸方翁全集. Beijing: Zhongguo shudian, 1986.

Lü Zujian 呂祖儉. *Donglai Lüshi ji* 東萊呂氏集. Xu Jinhua congshu. Yongkang: Yongkang Hu shi Mengxuan, 1924.

Lü Zuqian 呂祖謙. *Donglai Lü taishi wenji* 東萊呂太史文集. Xu Jinhua congshu. Yongkang: Yongkang Hu shi Mengxuan lou, 1924.

————. *Lidai zhidu xiangshuo* 歷代制度詳說. Jiangsu: Jiangsu guangling guji, 1990.

Luo Jiaxiang 羅家祥. *Bei Song dangzheng yanjiu* 北宋黨爭研究. Taibei: Wenjin chubanshe, 1993.

Lynn, Richard John. "Chu Hsi as Literary Theorist and Critic." In *Chu Hsi and Neo-Confucianism*, ed. Wing-tsit Chan. Honolulu: University of Hawai'i Press, 1986, 337–54.

Ma Duanlin 馬端臨. *Wenxian tongkao* 文獻通考. Shi tong. Taibei: Xinxing shuju, 1963.

Ma Jigao 馬积高. *Song Ming lixue yu wenxue* 宋明理学与文学. Changsha: Hunan shifan daxue chubanshe, 1989.

Mabuchi Masaya 馬淵昌也. "Gen Minsho seirigaku no ichi somen: Shushigaku no biman to Sun Saku no shisō" 元明初性理學の一側面: 朱子學の瀰漫と孫作の思想. *Chūgoku tetsugaku kenkyū* 中國哲學研究 4 (1992): 60–131.

Maemura Yoshiyuki 前村佳幸. "Goseichin no naibu kōzō: Sōdai Kōnan shichin shakai bunseki" 烏青鎮の内部構造—宋代江南市鎮社會分析. In *Sōdaibito no ninshiki: sōgosei to nichijō kūkan* 宋代人の認識—相互性と日常空間, ed. Sōdaishi kenkyūkai 宋代史研究會. Tokyo: Kyūko shoin, 2001, 57–90.

Makeham, John. *Transmitters and Creators: Chinese Commentators and Commentaries on the* Analects. Cambridge: Harvard University Asia Center, 2003.

Massey, Thomas P. "Chu Yuan-chang, the Hu-Lan Cases, and Early Ming Confucianism." Unpublished paper. 2000.

McDermott, Joseph, and Shiba Yoshinobu. "Economic Change During the Song (draft dated 2003)." In *Cambridge History of China*, vol. 5, pt. 2. Cambridge: Cambridge University Press, forthcoming.

McKnight, Brian E. "Fiscal Privileges and the Social Order in Sung China." In *Crisis and Prosperity in Sung China*, ed. John Winthrop Haeger. Tuscon: University of Arizona Press, 1975, 79–100.

———. *Village and Bureaucracy in Southern Sung China*. Chicago: University of Chicago Press, 1972.

Mencius. Trans. D. C. Lau. Harmondsworth, Eng.: Penguin Books, 1970.

Meng Peiyuan 蒙培元. *Lixue de yanbian: cong Zhu Xi dao Wang Fuzhi Dai Zhen* 理学的演变: 從朱熹到王夫之戴震. Taibei: Wen jin chubanshe, 1990.

Meskill, John. *Academies in Ming China*. Monographs of the Association for Asian Studies. Tucson: University of Arizona Press, 1982.

Metzger, Thomas A. *Escape from Predicament: Neo-Confucianism and China's Evolving Political Culture*. New York: Columbia University Press, 1977.

Min, Byounghee. "The Republic of the Mind: Zhu Xi's 'Learning (*Xue*)' as a Sociopolitical Agenda and the Construction of Literati Society." Ph.D. diss., Harvard University, 2007.

Mingchao kaiguo wenxian 明朝開國文獻. Taibei: Xuesheng shuju, 1967.

Miura Shūichi 三浦秀一. *Chūgoku shingaku no ryōsen: Genchō no chishikijin to ju dō butsu sankyō* 中国心学の稜線: 元朝の知識人と儒道仏三教. Tokyo: Kenbun shuppan, 2003.

Miyakawa Hisayuki. "An Outline of the Naitô Hypothesis and Its Effects on Japanese Studies of China." *Far Eastern Quarterly* 14, no. 4 (1955): 533–52.

Miyazaki Ichisada 宮崎市定. "Sōdai no shifu" 宋代の士風. In idem, *Miyazaki Ichisada zenshū* 宮崎市定全集. Tokyo: Iwanami shoten, 1992 [1953], 11: 339–75.

———. *Tōyōteki no kinsei* 東洋的の近世. Tokyo: Kyuiku taimususha, 1950.

Miyazawa Tomoyuki 宮澤知之. *Sōdai Chūgoku no kokka to keizai: zaisei, shijō, kahei* 宋代中國の國家と經濟——財政, 市場, 貨幣. Tokyo: Sōbunsha, 1998.

———. "Songdai dizhu yu nongmin de zhuwenti" 宋代地主與農民的諸問題. In *Riben xuezhe yanjiu Zhongguoshi lunzhu xuanyi* 日本學者研究中國史論著選譯. Beijing: Zhonghua, 1993, 2: 424–52.

Monod, Paul Kléber. *The Power of Kings: Monarchy and Religion in Europe, 1589–1715*. New Haven: Yale University Press, 1999.

Mori Masao 森正夫. "Sōdai igo no shitaifu to chiiki shakai" 宋代以後の士大夫と地域社會. In *Chūgoku shitaifu kaikyū to chiiki shakai to sono kankei ni tsuite no sōgō teki kenkyū* 中國士大夫階級と地域社會とその關系についての綜合的研究, ed. Tanigawa Michio 谷川道雄. Showa 57 nendo kagaku kenkyūhi bukin sōgō kenkyū. Kyoto: Kyōto daigaku, 1983, 95–103.

Mote, Frederick W. "Fang Hsiao-ju." In *Dictionary of Ming Biography*, ed. L. Carrington Goodrich and Chaoying Fang. New York: Columbia University Press, 1976, 426–33.

———. *Imperial China, 900–1800*. Cambridge: Harvard University Press, 1999.

Munro, Donald J. *A Chinese Ethics for the New Century: The Ch'ien Mu Lectures in History and Culture, and Other Essays on Science and Confucian Ethics.* Chi'en Mu Lectures. Hong Kong: Chinese University Press, 2005.

―――. *Images of Human Nature: A Sung Portrait.* Princeton: Princeton University Press, 1988.

Nakajima Gakushō 中島楽章. *Mindai kyōson no funsō to chitsujo: Kishū monjo o shiryō to shite* 明代郷村の紛争と秩序：徽州文書を史料として. Tokyo: Kyūko shoin, 2002.

―――. "Ruisei dōkyo kara sōzoku keisei e: Sōdai Kishū no chiiki kaihatsu to dōso ketsugō" 累世同居から宗族形成へ―宋代徽州の地域開發と同組結合. In *Sōdai shakai no kūkan to komyunikēshon* 宋代社会の空間とコミュニケーション, ed. Hirata Shigeki 平田茂樹, Endō Takatoshi 遠藤隆俊, and Oka Motoshi 岡元司. Tokyo: Kyūko shoin, 2006, 215–50.

Neskar, Ellen G. *The Politics of Prayer: Shrines to Local Former Worthies in Song China.* Cambridge: Harvard University, Asia Center, forthcoming.

―――. "Shrines to Local Former Worthies." In *Religions of China in Practice*, ed. Donald S. Lopez, Jr. Princeton: Princeton University Press, 1996, 293–305.

Oh Kuemsung 吳金成. *Mindai shakai keizaishi kenkyū: shinshisō no keisei to sono shakai keizaiteki yakuwari* 明代社會經濟史研究―紳士層の形成とその社會經濟的役割. Trans. Watari Masahiro 渡昌弘. Tokyo: Kyuko shoin, 1990.

Oka Motoshi 岡元司. "Nan Sō ki kakyo no shikan o meguru chiikisei: Settō shusshintachi no ichizuke o chūshin ni" 南宋期科舉の試官をめぐる地域性―浙東出身者の位置づけを中心に. In *Sōdai shakai no nettowāku* 宋代社会のネットワーク, ed. Sōdaishi kenkyūkai 宋代史研究会. Tokyo: Kyūko shoin, 1998, 233–74.

Okada Takehiko 岡田武彦. *Sō Min tetsugaku no honshitsu* 宋明哲學の本質. Tokyo: Mokujisha, 1984.

Ong, Chang Woei. "Men of Letters Within the Passes: Guanzhong Literati from the Tenth to Eighteenth Centuries." Ph.D. diss., Harvard University, 2004.

―――. "The Principles Are Many: Wang Tingxiang and Intellectual Transition in Mid-Ming China." *Harvard Journal of Asiatic Studies* 66, no. 2 (2006): 461–94.

Ouyang Xiu 歐陽修. *Ouyang Xiu quanji* 歐陽修全集. Taibei: Shijie shuju, 1961.

―――. *Ouyang Xiu quanji* 歐陽修全集. Beijing: Zhongguo shudian, 1986.

―――. *Shi ben yi* 詩本義. Yingyin Wenyuange Siku quanshu. Taibei: Taiwan Shangwu yinshuguan, 1983.

Ouyang Xiu 歐陽修 and Song Qi 宋祁. *Xin Tang shu* 新唐書. Beijing: Zhonghua shuju, 1975.

Oyama Masaaki 小山正明. *Min Shin shakai keizaishi kenkyu* 明清社會經濟史研究. Tokyo: Tokyo daigaku shuppankai, 1992.

Pan Liyong 潘立勇. *Zhuzi lixue meixue* 朱子理學美學. Beijing: Dongfang chubanshe, 1999.

Peterson, Willard J. "Another Look at *Li.*" *Bulletin of Sung and Yuan Studies* 18 (1986): 13–32.

———. "Confucian Learning in Late Ming Thought." In *The Cambridge History of China*, vol. 8, pt. 2, *The Ming Dynasty, 1368–1644*, ed. Denis Twitchett and Frederick W. Mote. Cambridge: Cambridge University Press, 1998, 708–88.

———. "Squares and Circles: Mapping the History of Chinese Thought." *Journal of the History of Ideas* 49, no. 1 (1988): 47–60.

Pinker, Steven. *The Blank Slate: The Modern Denial of Human Nature.* New York: Viking, 2002.

Plaks, Andrew H. Ta Hsüeh *and* Chung Yung (*The Highest Order of Cultivation and On the Practice of the Mean*). Penguin classics. London and New York: Penguin Books, 2003.

Qi Xia 漆俠. *Songxue de fanzhan he yanbian* 宋学的发展和演变. Shijiazhuang: Hebei renmin chubanshe, 2002.

———. "Song Yuan shiqi Puyang Zhengshi jiazu zhi yanjiu" 宋元時期浦陽鄭氏家族之研究. In idem, *Zhi kun ji* 知困集. Shijiazhuang: Hebei jiaoyu chubanshe, 1992, 196–210.

Qian Bocheng 钱伯城 et al., eds. *Quan Ming wen* 全明文. Shanghai: Shanghai guji chubanshe, 1992.

Qian Mu 錢穆. "Du Mingchu kaiguo zhuchen shi wen ji" 讀明初開國諸臣詩文集. *Xinya xuebao* 新亞學報 6, no. 1 (1964): 245–326.

Qiao Chuan 樵川, Qiao Sou 樵叟, and Hai Rui 海瑞, eds. *Qingyuan dangjin* 慶元黨禁. Shanghai: Shangwu yinshuguan, 1939.

Qiu Jun 丘濬. *Daxue yanyi bu* 大學衍義補. Yingyin Wenyuange Siku quanshu. Taibei: Taiwan Shangwu yinshuguan, 1983.

Rao Lu 饒魯. *Rao Shuangfeng jiangyi* 饒雙峯講義. Siku weishoushu jikan. Ed. Wang Chaoqu 王朝渠. Beijing: Beijing chubanshe, 1997.

Rong Zhaozu 容肇祖. *Zhongguo lidai sixiang shi*, 5, *Mingdai juan* 中國歷代思想史, 5, 明代卷. Taibei: Wenjin chubanshe, 1993.

Rossabi, Morris, ed. *China Among Equals: The Middle Kingdom and Its Neighbors, 10th–14th Centuries.* Berkeley: University of California Press, 1983.

Ruan Yuan 阮元. *Shisan jing zhushu: fu jiaokan ji* 十三經註疏: 附校勘記. Scripta Sinica ed. Nanchang: Nanchang fu xue 南昌府學, 1815.

Saeki Tomi 佐伯富. *Sōshi shokkan shi sakuin* 宋史職官志索引. Tōyōshi kenkyū sōkan 11. Kyoto: Tōyōshi kenkyūkai, 1963.

Sakai Tadao. "Confucianism and Popular Educational Works." In *Self and Society in Ming Thought*, ed. Wm. Theodore de Bary. New York: Columbia University Press, 1970, 331–66.

Sangren, P. Steven. "Traditional Chinese Corporations: Beyond Kinship." *Journal of Asian Studies* 43, no. 3 (1984): 391–416.

Saussy, Haun. *The Problem of the Chinese Aesthetic*. Stanford: Stanford University Press, 1993.

Schirokauer, Conrad. "Chu Hsi's Political Thought." *Journal of Chinese Philosophy* 5, no. 2 (1978): 127–48.

———. "Chu Hsi's Sense of History." In *Ordering the World: Approaches to State and Society in Sung Dynasty China*, ed. Robert Hymes and Conrad Schirokauer. Berkeley: University of California Press, 1993, 193–220.

———. "Neo-Confucians Under Attack: The Condemnation of Wei-hsueh." In *Crisis and Prosperity in Sung China*, ed. John Winthrop Haeger. Tuscon: University of Arizona Press, 1975, 163–98.

Schneewind, Sarah. *Community Schools and the State in Ming China*. Stanford: Stanford University Press, 2006.

———. "Visions and Revisions: Village Policies of the Ming Founder in Seven Phases." *T'oung Pao* 87, no. 3–5 (2001): 317–59.

Selover, Thomas Whitfield. *Hsieh Liang-tso and the* Analects *of Confucius: Humane Learning as a Religious Quest*. American Academy of Religion academy series. Oxford and New York: Oxford University Press, 2005.

Shen Liao 沈遼. *Yunchao bian* 雲巢編. In *Shen shi san xiansheng wenji* 沈氏三先生文集. Sibu congkan.

Shiba, Yoshinobu 斯波義信. *Commerce and Society in Sung China*. Abridged trans. Mark Elvin. Ann Arbor: University of Michigan, Center for Chinese Studies, 1970.

———. "Nan Sō ni okeru 'chūkan ryōiki' shakai no tōjō" 南宋における"中間領域"社會の登場. In *Sō Gen jidaishi no kihon mondai* 宋元時代史の基本問題, ed. Satake Yasuhiko 佐竹靖彦 et al. Tokyo: Kyuko shoin, 1996, 185–204.

———. *Sōdai Kōnan keizaishi no kenkyū* 宋代江南經濟史の研究. Tokyo: Kyūko shoin, 2001.

———. "Sōdai no toshika wo kangaeru" 宋代の都市化を考える. *Tōhōgaku* 東方学 102 (2001): 1–19.

———. "Urbanization and the Development of Markets in the Lower Yangtse Valley." In *Crisis and Prosperity in Sung China*, ed. John Winthrop Haeger. Tuscon: University of Arizona Press, 1975, 13–48.

Shimada Kenji 島田虔次. "Sōgaku no tenkai" 宋學の展開. In *Sekai rekishi* 世界歷史, vol. 9. Tokyo: Iwanami shoten, 1970, 423–47.

Sima Guang 司馬光. *Sima Wenzheng gong chuan jia ji* 司馬文正公傳家集. Wan-you wenku. Shanghai: Shangwu yinshuguan, 1937.

Skinner, G. William. "Introduction: Urban Development in Imperial China." In *The City in Late Imperial China*, ed. G. William Skinner. Stanford: Stanford University Press, 1977, 3–32.

Skonicki, Douglas Edward. "Cosmos, State and Society: Song Dynasty Arguments Concerning the Creation of Political Order." Ph.D. diss., Harvard University, 2007.

(Smith), Joanna F. Handlin. *Action in Late Ming Thought: The Reorientation of Lü K'un and Other Scholar-Officials*. Berkeley: University of California Press, 1983.

———. "Benevolent Societies: The Reshaping of Charity During the Late Ming and Early Ch'ing." *Journal of Asian Studies* 46, no. 2 (1987): 309–37.

Smith, Paul. *Taxing Heaven's Storehouse: Horses, Bureaucrats, and the Destruction of the Sichuan Tea Industry, 1074–1224*. Cambridge: Council on East Asian Studies, Harvard University, 1991.

So, Billy K. L. *Prosperity, Region, and Institutions in Maritime China: The South Fukien Pattern, 946–1368*. Cambridge: Harvard University Asia Center, 2000.

Song, Cze-tong, and Julia Ching. "Hsüeh Hsüan." In *Dictionary of Ming Biography, 1368–1644*, ed. L. Carrington Goodrich and Chao-ying Fang. New York: Columbia University Press, 1976, 616–19.

Song, Jaeyoon. "Shifting Paradigms in Theories of Government: Histories, Classics, and Public Philosophy in 11th–14th Century China." Ph.D. diss., Harvard University, 2007.

Song Lian 宋濂. *Song Lian quanji* 宋濂全集. Hangzhou: Zhejiang guji chubanshe, 1999.

Su Boheng 蘇伯衡. *Su Pingzhong wenji* 蘇平仲文集. Yingyin Wenyuange Siku quanshu. Taibei: Taiwan Shangwu yinshuguan, 1983.

Su Che 蘇轍. *Longchuan lue zhi* 龍川略志. Baichuan xuehai. Shanghai: Bogu zhai, 1921.

———. *Luan cheng ji* 欒城集. Shanghai: Shanghai guji, 1987.

Su Shi 蘇軾. *Su Dongpo ji* 蘇東坡集. Guoxue jiben congshu. Shanghai: Shangwu yinshuguan, 1933.

Su Xun 蘇洵. *Jiayou ji* 嘉祐集. Sibu beiyao.

Su Yuezong 蘇耀宗. "Cong 'zun wang rang yi' dao 'rang yi zun wang': lun Wang Fuzhi dui Hu Anguo de piping" 從 "尊王攘夷" 到 "攘夷尊王"—論王夫之對胡安國的批評. *Xianggang daxue Zhongwen xi jikan* 香港大學中文系集刊 4 (2000): 182–213.

Sue Takashi. "The Shock of the Year Hsuan-ho 2: The Abrupt Change in the Granting of Plaques and Titles During Hui-tsung's Reign." *Acta Asiatica* 84 (2003): 80–125.

Sun Hongsheng 孙洪升. *Tang Song chaye jingji* 唐宋茶业经济. Beijing: Shehui kexue wenxian chubanshe, 2001.

Sun Yingshi 孫應時. *Zhuhu ji* 燭湖集. N.p.: Jing yuan xuan 静遠軒, 1803.

Szonyi, Michael. *Practicing Kinship: Lineage and Descent in Late Imperial China.* Stanford: Stanford University Press, 2002.

Taiping Lü shi zongpu 太平呂氏宗譜. Yongkang, Daoguang 道光 era.

Taiwan xuesheng shuju 臺灣學生書局, ed. *Mingdai dengkelu huibian* 明代牌科錄彙編. Taibei: Taiwan xuesheng shuju, 1969.

Takahashi Yoshirō 高橋芳郎. "Sōdai no shijin mibun ni tsuite" 宋代の士人身分について. *Shirin* 史林 69, no. 3 (1986): 351–82.

Tanaka Masaki 田中正樹. "So shi Shokugaku kō: shuppan kara mita Sogaku no ryūkō ni tsuite" 蘇氏蜀學考—出版から見た蘇学の流行について. In *Sōdaibito no ninshiki: sōgosei to nichijō kūkan* 宋代人の認識—相互性と日常空間, ed. Sōdaishi kenkyūkai 宋代史研究會. Tokyo: Kyūko shoin, 2001, 227–58.

The T'ang Code. 2 vols. Trans. Wallace Johnson. Princeton: Princeton University Press, 1979, 1997.

Tanigawa Michio 谷川道雄. "Problems Concerning the Japanese Periodization of Chinese History." *Journal of Asian History* 21 (1987): 150–68.

———. "Zhongguo shehui gouzao de tezhi yu shidafu de wenti" 中國社會構造的特質與士大夫的問題. In *Riben xuezhe yanjiu Zhongguo lishi lunzhu xuanyi* 日本學者研究中國歷史論著選譯. Beijing: Zhonghua, 1993, 2: 177–98.

Tao, Jing-shen. *Two Sons of Heaven: Studies in Sung-Liao Relations.* Tucson: University of Arizona Press, 1988.

Taylor, Romeyn. "Official and Popular Religion and the Political Organization of Chinese Society in the Ming." In *Orthodoxy in Late Imperial China*, ed. Kwang-Ching Liu. Berkeley: University of California, 1990, 126–57.

Teraji Jun 寺地遵. "Nihon ni okeru Sōshi kenkyū no kichō" 日本における宋史研究の基調. *Chūgoku shigaku* 中國史學 1 (1991): 191–210.

———. "Sōdai seijishi kenkyū hōhō shiron" 宋代政治史研究方法試論. In *Sō Gen jidaishi no kihon mondai* 宋元時代史の基本問題, ed. Satake Yasuhiko 佐竹靖彦 et al. Tokyo: Kyūko Shoin, 1996.

Theiss, Janet M. *Disgraceful Matters: The Politics of Chastity in Eighteenth-Century China.* Berkeley: University of California Press, 2004.

Tian Xi 田錫. *Xian ping ji* 咸平集. Yingyin Wenyuange Siku quanshu. Taibei: Taiwan Shangwu yinshuguan, 1983.

Tillman, Hoyt Cleveland. *Ch'en Liang on Public Interest and the Law.* Honolulu: University of Hawai'i Press, 1994.

———. *Confucian Discourse and Chu Hsi's Ascendancy*. Honolulu: University of Hawai'i Press, 1992.

———. "Confucianism in the Chin and the Impact of Sung Confucian Tao-hsüeh." In *China Under Jurchen Rule: Essays in Chin Intellectual and Cultural History*, ed. idem and Stephen West. Albany: SUNY, 1995, 71–114.

———. "A New Direction in Confucian Scholarship: Approaches to Examining the Differences Between Neo-Confucianism and *Tao-hsueh*." *Philosophy East & West* 42, no. 3 (1992): 455–74.

———. *Utilitarian Confucianism: Ch'en Liang's Challenge to Chu Hsi*. Cambridge: Council on East Asian Studies, Harvard University, 1982.

Toda Hiroshi 戸田裕司. "Kō Shin no Kōtokugun shasō kaikaku: Nan Sō shasō no kentō" 黄震の廣德軍社倉改革—南宋社倉の檢討. *Shirin* 史林 73, no. 1 (1990): 105–36.

Tonami Mamoru 礪波護. *Tōdai seiji shakaishi kenkyū* 唐代政治社會史研究. Kyōto: Dōhōsha, 1986.

Tsuchida Kenjirō 土田健次郎. *Dōgaku no keisei* 道学の形成. Tokyo: Sōbunsha, 2002.

———. "Shakai to shisō: Sō Gen shisō kenkyū oboegaki" 社會と思想—宋元思想研究覺書. In *Sō Gen jidaishi no kihon mondai* 宋元時代史の基本問題. Ed. Satake Yasuhiko 佐竹靖彦 et al. Tokyo: Kyūko shoin, 1996, 427–52.

Tu, Wei-ming. *Neo-Confucian Thought in Action: Wang Yang-ming's Youth (1472–1509)*. Berkeley: University of California Press, 1976.

Tuotuo 脱脱, ed. *Jin shi* 金史. Beijing: Zhonghua shuju, 1975.

———. *Song shi* 宋史. Beijing: Zhonghua shuju, 1977.

Twitchett, Denis Crispin. *The Writing of Official History Under the T'ang*. Cambridge and New York: Cambridge University Press, 1992.

Übelhör, Monica. "The Community Compact (*Hsiang-yüeh*) of the Song and Its Educational Significance." In *Neo-Confucian Education: The Formative Stage*, ed. Wm. Theodore de Bary and John Chaffee. Berkeley: University of California Press, 1989, 371–88.

Uno Tetsuto 宇野哲人. *Shina tetsugakushi: kinsei jugaku* 支那哲學史: 近世儒學. Tokyo: Hōbunkan, 1954.

Uno Tetsuto 宇野哲人, Yasuoka Masahiro 安岡正篤, and Araki Kengo 荒木見悟. *Yōmeigaku binran: Ō Yōmei seitan gohyakunen kinen* 陽明學便覽: 王陽明生誕五百年記念. Yōmeigaku taikei, vol. 12. Tokyo: Meitoku shuppansha, 1974.

van Ess, Hans. "The Compilation of the Works of the Ch'eng Brothers and Its Significance for the Learning of the Right Way of the Southern Sung Period." *T'oung Pao* 90, no. 4 (2004): 264–98.

Virág, Curie K. "That Which Encompasses the Myriad Cares: Subjectivity, Knowledge, and the Ethics of Emotion in Tang and Song China." Ph.D. diss., Harvard University, 2004.

von Glahn, Richard. "Chu Hsi's Community Granary in Theory and Practice." In *Ordering the World: Approaches to State and Society in Sung Dynasty China*, ed. Robert P. Hymes and Conrad Schirokauer. Berkeley: University of California Press, 1993, 221–54.

———. *Fountain of Fortune: Money and Monetary Policy in China, 1000–1700*. Berkeley: University of California Press, 1996.

———. "Imagining Pre-modern China." In *The Song-Yuan-Ming Transition in Chinese History*, ed. Paul Jakov Smith and Richard von Glahn. Cambridge: Harvard University Asia Center, 2003, 35–70.

———. "Ming Taizu *ex Nihilo*?" *Ming Studies* 55 (2007): 113–41.

Waltner, Ann Beth. *Getting an Heir: Adoption and the Construction of Kinship in Late Imperial China*. Honolulu: University of Hawai'i Press, 1990.

Walton, Linda. *Academies and Society in Southern Song China*. Honolulu: University of Hawai'i Press, 1999.

———. "Charitable Estates as an Aspect of Statecraft in Southern Sung China." In *Ordering the World: Approaches to State and Society in Sung Dynasty China*, ed. Robert P. Hymes and Conrad Schirokauer. Berkeley: University of California Press, 1993, 255–79.

Wang Anshi 王安石. *Linchuan xiansheng wenji* 臨川先生文集. Beijing: Zhonghua shuju, 1959.

Wang Bo 王柏. *Yan ji tu* 研幾圖. Jinhua congshu. Hu shi Tuibu zhai 胡氏退補齋, 1862.

Wang Deyi 王德毅. "Nan Song yi yi kao" 南宋義役考. In *Song shi yanjiu lunji* 宋史研究論文集, ed. Wang Deyi 王德毅. Taibei: Taiwan Shangwu yinshuguan, 1993 [1968], 253–83.

Wang Maode 王懋德 and Wu Xiangxiang 吳相湘. *Jinhua fu zhi* 金華府志. Taibei: Taiwan xuesheng shuju, 1965 [1578].

Wang Ruilai 王瑞來. "Lun Songdai huangquan" 論宋代皇權. *Lishi yanjiu* 1989, no. 1: 144–60.

———. "Lun Songdai xiangquan" 論宋代相權. *Lishi yanjiu* 1985, no. 2: 106–20.

———. *Sōdai no kōtei kenri to shidaifu seiji* 宋代の皇帝權力と士大夫政治. Tokyo: Kyūko shoin, 2001.

Wang Shu 王恕. *Shiqu yi jian* 石渠意見. Xuxiu Siku quanshu 171. Shanghai: Shanghai guji chubanshe, 1995.

Wang Shuizhao 王水照. *Songdai wenxue tonglun* 宋代文学通论. Kaifeng: Henan daxue chubanshe, 1997.

Wang Wei 王褘. *Huachuan zhi ci* 華川卮辭. Jinhua congshu. Hu shi Tuibu zhai 胡氏退補齋, 1862.

———. *Wang Zhongwen gong ji* 王忠文公集. Congshu jicheng chubian. Shanghai: Shangwu yinshuguan, 1936.

Wang Yang-ming 王陽明. *Instructions for Practical Living, and Other Neo-Confucian Writing, by Wang Yang-ming*. Trans. Wing-tsit Chan. New York: Columbia University Press, 1963.

———. *Wang Yangming* Chuan xi lu *xiangzhu jiping* 王陽明傳習錄詳註集評. Introduced and annotated by Wing-tsit Chan (Chen Rongjie) 陳榮捷. Taibei: Taiwan xuesheng shuju 臺灣學生書局, 1983.

———. *Wang Yangming quanji* 王陽明全集. Ed. Wu Guang 吳光. Shanghai: Shanghai guji chubanshe, 1992.

Wei Cheng-t'ung. "Chu Hsi on the Standard and the Expedient." In *Chu Hsi and Neo-Confucianism*, ed. Wing-tsit Chan. Honolulu: University of Hawai'i Press, 1986, 255–72.

Wei Liaoweng 魏了翁. *Heshan ji* 鶴山集. Yingyin Wenyuange Siku quanshu. Taibei: Taiwan Shangwu yinshuguan, 1983.

Wei Zheng 魏徵 and Linghu Defen 令狐德棻. *Sui shu* 隋書. Beijing: Zhonghua shuju, 1973.

Welter, Albert. "A Buddhist Response to the Confucian Revival: Tsan-ning and the Debate over *Wen* in the Early Sung." In *Buddhism in the Sung*, ed. Peter Gregory and Daniel A. Getz, Jr. Honolulu: University of Hawai'i Press, 1999, 21–61.

Wilhelm, Helmut. "On Ming Orthodoxy." *Monumenta Serica* 29 (1970–71): 1–26.

Wilson, Edward O. *Consilience: The Unity of Knowledge*. New York: Knopf, 1998.

Wilson, Thomas. *Genealogy of the Way: The Construction and Uses of the Confucian Tradition in Late Imperial China*. Stanford: Stanford University Press, 1995.

Wood, Alan T. *Limits to Autocracy: From Sung Neo-Confucianism to a Doctrine of Political Rights*. Honolulu: University of Hawai'i Press, 1995.

Wright, Arthur F. "Propaganda and Persuasion in Imperial and Contemporary China." *Rice University Studies* 59, no. 4 (1973): 9–18.

Wright, David Curtis. *From War to Diplomatic Parity in Eleventh-Century China: Sung's Foreign Relations with Kitan Liao*. Boston: Brill, 2005.

Wu, Pei-yi. *The Confucian's Progress: Autobiographical Writing in Traditional China*. New York: Columbia Univeristy Press, 1990.

———. "Self-Examination and Confession of Sins in Traditional China." *Harvard Journal of Asiatic Studies* 39, no. 1 (1979): 5–38.

Wu Shidao 吳師道. *Jing xiang lu* 敬鄉錄. Xu Jinhua congshu. Yongkang: Hu shi Meng xuan lou, 1924.

Wu Songdi 吳松弟. *Beifang yimin yu Nan Song shehui bianqian* 北方移民與南宋社會變遷. Taibei: Wenjin chubanshe, 1993.

———. *Zhongguo renkou shi: Liao Song Jin Yuan shiqi* 中國人口史: 遼宋金元時期. In Zhongguo renkou shi 中國人口史, ed. Ge Jianxiong 葛劍雄. Shanghai: Fudan daxue chubanshe, 2002.

Wu Wanju 吳萬居. *Songdai shuyuan yu Songdai xueshu zhi guanxi* 宋代書院與宋代學術之關係. Taibei: Wenshizhe chubanshe, 1991.

Wu Yining 吳以寧. *Zhu Xi ji Song Yuan Ming lixue: fu gudai shuyuan yanjiu ziliao* 朱熹及宋元明理學: 附古代書院研究資料. Songshi yanjiu tongxun 16. N.p.: Zhongguo Songshi yanjiuhui, 1989.

Wu Yubi 吳與弼. *Kangzhai ji* 康齋集. Yingyin Wenyuange Siku quanshu. Taibei: Taiwan Shangwu yinshuguan, 1983.

Wu Zeng 吳曾. *Nenggai zhai manlu* 能改齋漫錄. Shanghai: Shanghai guji chubanshe, 1979.

Wyatt, Don J. *The Recluse of Loyang: Shao Yung and the Moral Evolution of Early Sung Thought*. Honolulu: University of Hawai'i Press, 1996.

Xiao Gongquan 蕭公權. *Zhongguo zhengzhi sixiang shi* 中國政治思想史, vol. 2. Taibei: Zhongguo wenhua xueyuan chubanbu, 1980.

Xiao Qiqing 蕭啓慶. "Yuandai de ruhu: rushi diwei yanjinshi shang de yizhang" 元代得儒戶—儒士地位演進史上的一章. *Journal of Oriental Studies* 16, no. 1–2 (1978): 151–78.

Xu Hongxing 徐洪興. *Sixiang di zhuanxing: lixue fasheng guocheng yanjiu* 思想的轉型: 理学发生过程研究. Shanghai: Shanghai renmin chubanshe, 1996.

Xu Qian 許謙. *Du Sishu congshuo* 讀四書叢説. Sibu congkan. Shanghai: Shangwu yinshuguan, 1934.

Xu Song 徐松, ed. *Song huiyao jigao* 宋會要輯稿. Beijing: Zhonghua shuju, 1957.

Xu Xuan 徐鉉. *Xu Qisheng ji* 徐騎省集. Guoxue jiben congshu. Changsha: Shangwu yinshuguan, 1939.

Xu Zi 徐梓. *Yuandai shuyuan yanjiu* 元代書院研究. Beijing: Shehui kexue wenxian chubanshe, 2000.

Xue Xuan 薛瑄. *Xue Jingxuan ji* 薛敬軒集. Zhengyi tang quanshu. Fuzhou: Zhengyi shuyuan 正誼書院, 1868.

Yamanoi Yū 山井湧. *Min Shin shisōshi no kenkyū* 明清思想史の研究. Tokyo: Tōkyō daigaku shuppankai, 1980.

Yang Shiwen 楊世文. "Ruiyi lilun yu Songdai zhengzhi" 瑞異理論與宋代政治. In *Songdai wenhua yanjiu* 宋代文化研究, vol. 6. Chengdu: Sichuan daxue, 1996: 71–85.

Yang Weisheng 楊渭生 et al. *Liang Song wenhua shi yanjiu* 兩宋文化史研究. Hangzhou: Hangzhou daxue chubanshe, 1998.

Yao Dali 姚大力. "Jinmo Yuanchu lixue zai beifang de chuanbo" 金末元初理學在北方的傳播. In *Yuanshi luncong* 元史論叢, vol. 2. Beijing: Zhonghua shuju, 1983, 217–24.

———. "Yuanchao keju zhidu de xingfei ji qi shehui beijing" 元朝科舉制度的興廢及其社會背景. *Yuanshi ji beiminzu yanjiu jikan* 元史及北民族研究季刊 6 (1982): 26–59.

Yao Mingda 姚名達. *Cheng Yichuan nianpu* 程伊川年譜. Zhongguo shixue congshu. Shanghai: Shangwu yinshuguan, 1937.

Yao Xinzhong. *An Introduction to Confucianism*. Cambridge: Cambridge University Press, 2000.

Yao Xuan 姚鉉. *Tang wen cui* 唐文粹. Sibu congkan. Shanghai: Shangwu yinshuguan, 1929.

Yao Yingting 姚瀛艇. "Shilun lixue de xingcheng" 試論理學的形成. In *Lun Song Ming lixue* 論宋明理學, ed. Zhongguo zhexue shi xuehui 中國哲學史學會 and Zhejiang sheng shehui kexue yanjiu suo 浙江省社會科學研究所. Hangzhou: Zhejiang renmin chubanshe, 1983, 1–13.

Yaxi Lu shi jiacheng 雅溪盧氏家乘. Dongyang: Yaxi Lu shi, 2004.

Ye Mengde 葉夢得. *Shilin yan yu* 石林燕語. Congshu jicheng xubian. Shanghai: Shanghai shudian, 1994.

Ye Shi 葉適. *Ye Shi ji* 葉適集. Beijing: Zhonghua shuju, 1961.

Ye Tan 葉坦. *Da bian fa: Song Shenzong yu shiyi shiji de gaige yundong* 大變法: 宋神宗與十一世紀的改革運動. Beijing: Shenghuo Dushu Xinzhi sanlian shuju, 1996.

Ye Xiaoxin 叶孝信. *Zhongguo fazhi shi* 中国法制史. Shanghai: Fudan daxue chubanshe, 2002.

Yü, Chün-fang. *The Renewal of Buddhism in China: Chu-hung and the Late Ming Synthesis*. New York: Columbia University Press, 1981.

Yu Wenbao 俞文豹. *Chui jian lu waiji* 吹劍錄外集. Yingyin Wenyuange Siku quanshu. Taibei: Taiwan Shangwu yinshuguan, 1983.

Yu Ying-shih 余英時. "Intellectual Breakthroughs in the T'ang-Sung Transition." In *The Power of Culture*, ed. Willard J. Peterson, Andrew Plaks, and Yu Ying-shih: Chinese University of Hong Kong, 1994, 158–71.

———. "Morality and Knowledge in Chu Hsi's Philosophical System." In *Chu Hsi and Neo-Confucianism*, ed. Wing-tsit Chan. Honolulu: University of Hawai'i Press, 1986, 228–54.

———. *Zhu Xi de lishi shijie: Songdai shidafu zhengzhi wenhua de yanjiu* 朱熹的歷史世界: 宋代士大夫政治文化的研究. Taibei: Yunchen wenhua shiye, 2003.

Yuan Fu 袁甫. *Meng zhai ji* 蒙齋集. Wuyingdian ju zhenban quanshu. N.p.: Guangya shuju 廣雅書局, 1875.

Yuan Zheng 袁征. *Songdai jiaoyu: Zhongguo gudai jiaoyu de lishixing zhuanzhe* 宋代教育—中國古代教育的歷史性轉折. Guangdong: Guangdong gaodeng jiaoyu chubanshe, 1991.

Zeng Gong 曾鞏. *Zeng Gong ji* 曾鞏集. Beijing: Zhonghua shuju, 1984.

Zhan Ruoshui 湛若水. *Xin lun* 新論. Bailing xueshan. Shanghai: Shangwu Hanfen lou, 1938 [1568].

Zhang Fangping 張方平. *Le quan ji* 樂全集. Yingyin Wenyuange Siku quanshu. Taibei: Taiwan Shangwu yinshuguan.

Zhang Jiushao 張九韶. *Lixue leibian* 理學類編. Yuzhang congshu. Nanchang: Delu, 1916.

Zhang Liwen 張立文. *Dao* 道. Zhongguo zhexue fanchou jingcui congshu. Taibei: Hanxing shuju, 1994.

———. *Li* 理. Zhongguo zhexue fanchou jingcui congshu. Taibei: Hanxing shuju, 1994.

———. *Qi* 氣. Zhongguo zhexue fanchou jingcui congshu. Taibei: Hanxing shuju, 1994.

———. *Xin* 心. Zhongguo zhexue fanchou jingxuan congshu. Taibei: Hanxing shuju, 1996.

Zhang Shi 張栻. *Nanxuan ji* 南軒集. Taibei: Guangxue yinshuguan, 1975.

Zhang Yide 张义德. *Ye Shi pingzhuan* 叶适评传. Nanjing: Nanjing daxue chubanshe, 1994.

Zhang Yixi 張藝曦. *Shequn, jiazu yu Wang xue de xiangli shijian: yi Ming zhong wan qi Jiangxi Jishui, Anfu liang xian wei li* 社群, 家族與王學的鄉里實踐: 以明中晚期江西吉水, 安福兩縣為例. Taibei: Guoli Taiwan daxue chuban weiyuanhui, 2006.

Zhang Yong 張詠. *Guai yai ji* 乖崖集. Yingyin Wenyuange Siku quanshu. Taibei: Taiwan Shangwu yinshuguan, 1983.

Zhang Zai 張載. *Zhang Zai ji* 張載集. Beijing: Zhonghua shuju, 1978.

Zhen Dexiu 真德秀. *Daxue yanyi* 大學衍義. Yingyin Wenyuange Siku quanshu. Taibei: Taiwan Shangwu yinshuguan, 1983.

———. *Wenzhang zhengzong* 文章正宗. Yingyin Wenyuange Siku quanshu. Taibei: Taiwan Shangwu yinshuguan, 1983.

Zheng Juzhong 鄭居中. *Zhenghe wu li xinyi* 政和五禮新儀. Yingyin Wenyuange Siku quanshu. Taibei: Taiwan Shangwu yinshuguan, 1983.

Zheng Xuan 鄭玄 and Kong Yingda 孔穎達. *Li ji zhengyi* 禮記正義: *Zhong yong* 中庸. In *Shisan jing zhushu: fu jiaokan ji* 十三經註疏: 附校勘記, ed. Ruan Yuan 阮元. Nanchang: Nanchang fu xue 南昌府學, 1815, 52.19b–29b.

Zheng Yu 鄭玉. *Shishan xiansheng wenji* 師山先生文集. Yingyin Wenyuange Siku quanshu. Taibei: Taiwan Shangwu yinshuguan, 1983.

Zhou Dunyi 周敦頤. *Zhou Lianxi xiansheng quanji* 周濂溪先生全集. Guoxue jiben congshu. Shanghai: Shangwu yinshuguan, 1937.

Zhou Mengjiang 周梦江. *Ye Shi yu Yongjia xuepai* 叶适与永嘉学派. Hangzhou: Zhejiang guji chubanshe, 2005.

Zhou Mi 周密. *Gui xin za zhi* 癸辛雜識. Beijing: Zhonghua shuju, 1988.

Zhou Yuwen 周愚文. *Songdai de zhou xian xue* 宋代的州縣學. Taibei: Guoli bianyi guan, 1996.

Zhu Chuanyu 朱傳譽. *Songdai xinwen shi* 宋代新聞史. Taibei: Zhongguo xueshe zhuzuo jiangzhu weiyuanhui, 1967.

Zhu Di 朱棣. *Shengxue xinfa* 聖學心法. Siku quanshu cunmu congshu. Ji'nan: Qilu shushe, 1995.

Zhu Hanmin 朱汉民. *Song Ming lixue tonglun: yizhong wenhuaxue de quanshi* 宋明理学通论: 一种文化学的诠释. Changsha: Hunan jiaoyu chubanshe, 2000.

Zhu Mu 祝穆. *Gujin shiwen leiju* 古今事文類聚. Yingyin Wenyuange Siku quanshu. Taibei: Taiwan Shangwu yinshuguan, 1985.

Zhu Xi 朱熹. *Changli xiansheng ji kaoyi* 昌黎先生集考異. Shanghai: Shanghai guji chubanshe and Anhui jiaoyu chubanshe, 2001.

———. *Chu ci ji zhu* 楚辭集注. Yingyin Wenyuange Siku quanshu. Taibei: Taiwan Shangwu yinshuguan, 1983.

———. *Introduction to the Study of the* Classic of Change (*I-hsüeh ch'i-meng*). Bilingual Texts in Chinese History, Philosophy, and Religion, no. 1. Provo, Utah: Global Scholarly Publications, 2002.

——— [Chu Hsi]. *Learning to Be a Sage: Selections from the* Conversations of Master Zhu, Arranged Topically. Trans., with commentary, Daniel K. Gardner. Berkeley: University of California Press, 1990.

———. *Shi ji zhuan* 詩集傳. Zhonghua zaizao shanben ed. Beijing: Beijing tushuguan chubanshe, 2004.

———. *Sishu zhangju jizhu* 四書章句集注. Shanghai: Shanghai guji chubanshe, 2001.

———. *Yi Luo yuan yuan lu* 伊洛淵源錄. Yingyin Wenyuange Siku quanshu. Taibei: Taiwan Shangwu yinshuguan, 1983.

———. *Yi xue qi meng* 易學啓蒙. Taibei: Yiwen yinshuguan, 1969.

———. *Zhou yi ben yi* 周易本義. Zhonghua zaizao shanben ed. Beijing: Beijing tushuguan chubanshe, 2003.

———. *Zhu Xi ji* 朱熹集. Chengdu: Sichuan jiaoyu chubanshe, 1996.

———. *Zhuzi yulei* 朱子語類. Ed. Li Jingde 黎靖德. Beijing: Zhonghua shuju, 1988.

———. *Zizhi tongjian gangmu* 資治通鑑綱目. Zhonghua zaizao shanben ed. Beijing: Beijing tushuguan chubanshe, 2003.

Zhu Xi 朱熹, Huang Gan 黄幹, and Yang Fu 楊復. *Yi li jing zhuan tongjie* 儀禮 經傳通解. Yingyin Wenyuange Siku quanshu. Taibei: Taiwan Shangwu yinshuguan, 1983.

Zhu Xi 朱熹 and Li Youwu 李幼武. *Song ming chen yan xing lu* 宋名臣言行錄. Taibei: Wenhai chubanshe, 1967.

Zhu Xi 朱熹 and Lü Zuqian 呂祖謙. *Jin si lu* 近思錄. Yingyin Wenyuange Siku quanshu. Taibei: Taiwan Shangwu yinshuguan, 1983.

——— [Chu Hsi] and ——— [Lü Tsu-ch'ien], eds. *Reflections on Things at Hand: The Neo-Confucian Anthology*. Trans., with notes, by Wing-tsit Chan. New York: Columbia University Press, 1967.

Zhu Zhen 朱震. *Hanshang yi zhuan* 漢上易傳. Sibu congkan. Shanghai: Shangwu yinshuguan, 1934.

Zürcher, Erik. "Christian Social Action in Late Ming Times: Wang Zheng and His "Humanitarian Society." In *Linked Faiths: Essays on Chinese Religions and Traditional Culture in Honor of Kristofer Schipper*, ed. Jan A. M. De Meyer and Peter M. Engelfriet. Leiden and Boston: Brill, 2000, 268–86.

———. "Confucian and Christian Religiosity in Late Ming China." *Catholic Historical Review* 83, no. 4 (1997): 614–53.

Character List

An Lushan (ca. 703–57) 安祿山
Antian yi shu 安田義塾

Ban Gu (32–92) 班固
bao jia 保甲
bo xue 博學

Cai Shen (1167–1230) 蔡沈
Cai Xiang (1012–76) 蔡襄
Cao Duan (1376–1434) 曹端
Chen Chun (1159–1223) 陳淳
Chen Fuliang (1137–1203) 陳傅良
Chen Liang (1143–94) 陳亮
Chen Longzheng (1585–1645)
　陳龍正
Chen Xianzhang (1428–1500)
　陳獻章
cheng (integrity, sincerity) 誠
Cheng Duanli (1271–1345)
　程端禮
Cheng Duanmeng (1143–91)
　程端蒙
Cheng Hao (1032–85) 程顥

Cheng Minzheng (ca. 1445–ca. 1500)
　程敏政
Cheng Rongxiu (fl. 1333)
　程榮秀
Cheng Yi (1033–1107) 程頤
Chengzu (r. 1402–24) 成祖
Chuanxin tang 傳心堂
Chunqiu zun wang fa wei 春秋尊
　王發微
community drinking ceremony
　鄉飲酒禮

Da gao 大誥
dao 道
daoli 道理
dao tong 道統
dao xin 道心
Dao xue 道學
Da Song guo 大宋國
Da tong / *Da tong* 大同
da yi 大義
dexing 德行
dexing zhi zhi 德性之知

353

di wang zhi xue　帝王之學
Donglin Academy　東林書院
Dongyang　東陽
Du Fu (712–70)　杜甫

Essential Meanings of the Analects
　論語精義

fa　法
fan　蕃
Fan Zhongyan (989–1052)
　范仲淹
Fan Zuyu (1041–98)　范祖禹
Fang Xiaoru (1357–1402)　方孝孺
fengjian　封建
Fu she　復社
Fu Yin　傅寅
Fuzhou, Fujian　福州

Gao Panlong (1562–1626)　高攀龍
Gaozong　高宗
ge wu　格物
gong　公
gongxin haoyi zhi shi　公心好義之士
Gu Xiancheng (1555–1612)
　顧憲成
guan　貫
Guo　郭
Guo Qinzhi　郭欽止
gu-wen　古文

Han　漢
Han ren　漢人
Han Yu (764–824)　韓愈
Hangzhou　杭州
He Xinyin (1517–79)　何心隱
Hongdao Academy　宏道書院
Hongwu　洪武
hu　戶
Hu Anguo (1074–1128)　胡安國

Hu Hong (1105–1155)　胡宏
Hu Juren (1434–84)　胡居仁
Hu Yuan (993–1059)　胡瑗
Hu Ze (963–1069)　胡則
Huang Gan (1152–1221)　黃榦
Huang Zongxi (1610–95)
　黃宗義
huang di　皇帝
huang ji　皇極
hua xia　華夏
hu ren　胡人
Huizong　徽宗
hunran titong zi zai qi zhong　混然
　體統自在其中
huoran guantong　豁然貫通

jia　家
Jiajing　嘉靖
jiang hui　講會
jiang xue　講學
Jianning　建寧
Jianwen　建文
jiaohua　教化
jiao min bang wen　教民榜文
Jin Lüxiang (1232–1308)
　金履祥
jing (classic, constant)　經
jing (inner mental attentiveness,
　reverence)　敬
jing shen　敬身
Jinhua　金華
jinshi　進士
Jiu yi hui guan　九邑
　會館
Jizhou　吉州
jue　絕
junzi　君子

Kaifeng　開封
Ke'an　可庵

ke yi 克一
Kongzi 孔子

Lanxi xianzhi 蘭溪縣志
lao ren 老人
li (coherence) 理
li (profit, advantage, interests) 利
li (ritual) 禮
Li Gou (1009–59) 李覯
Li Tong (1093–1163) 李侗
Li Xinchuan (1166–1243)
　　李心傳
Li Yuangang (fl. 1172) 李元鋼
Li Zhi (1527–1602) 李贄
liang min 良民
liang shui fa 兩稅法
liang xin 良心
liang zhang 量長
liang zhi 良知
li hui / li-hui 理會
li jia 里甲
Lin Zhao'en (1517–98) 林兆恩
Liu Chang (1019–68) 劉敞
Liu dian 六典
liu nei guan 流內官
liu wai guan 流外官
Li xue 理學
li yi fen shu 理一分殊
Lize Academy 麗澤書院
li zhang 里長
Lu Rong 1413–89 盧溶
Lu You (1125–1210) 陸游
Lü Dajun (1031–82) 呂大鈞
Lü Dalin (1046–92) 呂大臨
Lu Jiuyuan (1139–94) 陸九淵
Lü Kun (1536–1618) 呂坤
Lü Pu (fl. 1346) 呂浦
Lü Zuqian (1137–81) 呂祖謙
lü ling ge li 律令格例
Luo Rufang (1515–88) 羅汝芳

Ming dao Academy 明道書院
ming jing 明經
Mirror of Song Literature 宋文鑒
Mou Zongsan 牟宗三
mu zu 睦族

nan ren 南人

Ouyang Shoudao (fl. 1264) 歐陽
　　守道
Ouyang Xiu (1007–72) 歐陽修

Pan Haogu (1101–70) 潘好古
Pan Jinggui (1127–1201+)
　　潘景珪
Pan Jingkui 潘景夔
Pan Jinglian 潘景連
Pan Jingliang 潘景良
Pan Jingxian (1134–90) 潘景憲
Pan Jingyu 潘景愈
Peng Fei (fl. 1330) 彭飛

qi 氣
qian and *kun* 乾坤
Qian xu 潛虛
Qin 秦
Qin Gui (1090–1155) 秦檜
qing 情
qiong li 窮理
Qisong (1007–72) 契嵩
Qiu Jun (1420–95) 邱浚
quan 權
Quan Zuwang (1705–55)
　　全祖望

Rao Lu (late 13th c.) 饒魯
ren (humaneness) 仁
renwen 人文
ren xin 人心
Ru 儒

sandai hou zhi sandai 三代後之三代

Sandai zhi shuai 三代之衰

Shao Yong (1011–77) 邵雍

she cang 社倉

Shen Liao (1032–85) 沈遼

sheng 生

shengren zhi dao 聖人之道

sheng wang 聖王

Sheng xue 聖學

shengyuan 生員

she xue 社學

shi (literatus) 士

shi (stone) 石

Shi Kangnian (fl. 1200) 施康年

Shi Shaozhang (fl. 1263) 時少章

Shi ben yi 詩本義

shidafu 士大夫

Shidong shuyuan 石洞書院

shiren 士人

shi zhe 十哲

shi zi 士子

shi-zu 士族

shu (atruism, reciprocity) 恕

shu (history) 書

shuai 衰

shuo 説

shuyuan 書院

si ke 四科

Sima Guang (1019–86) 司馬光

Sima Qian (ca. 145–ca. 85 B.C.) 司馬遷

si-wen 斯文

Song Lian (1301–81) 宋濂

Song Qi (998–1061) 宋祈

Song ren 宋人

Su Che (1039–1112) 蘇轍

Su Shi (1037–1101) 蘇軾

Su Xun (1009–66) 蘇洵

Sun Fu (992–1057) 孫復

Sun Yingshi (1154–1206) 孫應時

Suzhou 蘇州

taiji 太極

Taizhou 台州

Taizhou (school) 泰州

Taizu 太祖

Tang 唐

Tang Zhongyou (1136–88) 唐仲友

Tian di wan wu 天地萬物

tian li 天理

tian ming 天命

tian-wen 天文

tianxia 天下

tong 通

tong daode yi fengsu 同道德一風俗

tong shan hui 同善會

Tong shu 通書

tongzhi 同志

tongzhi hui 同志會

Wang Anshi (1021–86) 王安石

Wang Bo (1197–1274) 王柏

Wang Gen (1483–1541) 王艮

Wang Mang (45 B.C. –A.D. 23) 王莽

Wang Shu (1416–1508) 王恕

Wang Yangming (1472–1529) 王陽明

Wei Liaoweng (1178–1237) 魏了翁

Wei Su (1303–72) 危素

wei guan zhe 爲官者

wei ji zhi xue 爲己之學

wei ren zhi xue 爲人之學

wei shi zhe 爲士者

wei wen 爲文

wei zheng 爲政

wen 文
Wen Jiweng (fl. 1273) 文及翁
wen-jiao 文教
Wen miao 文廟
wen-xue 文學
wen-zhang 文章
Wu Cheng (1249–1333) 吳澄
Wu Pu (1363–1426)
Wu Wenbing 吳文炳
Wu Yubi (1391–1469) 吳與弼
Wu jing zheng yi 五經正義
Wuzhou 婺州

xian 縣
xiang 鄉
xiang yue 鄉約
xian juezhe 先覺者
Xian wang 先王
xiao 效
Xiao xue 小學
Xie Liangzuo (1050–1103) 謝良佐
xin 心
xing 性
Xing li xue 性理學
Xin xue 心學
Xu Heng (1209–81) 許衡
Xu Ji 徐畸
Xu Qian (1270–1337) 許謙
xue 學
Xue Xuan (1389–1464) 薛瑄
xungu 訓詁

Yan Fu (1853–1921) 嚴復
Yan Jun (1504–96) 顏鈞
yang 陽
Yang Dongming (1548–1624) 楊東明
Yang Jian (1141–1226) 楊簡
Yang Shi (1053–1135) 楊時

Yang Weizhen (1296–1370) 楊維楨
yang qi 陽氣
Yangzhou 揚州
Yanzhou 嚴州
Ye Shi (1150–1223) 葉適
yi (conception, intention, idea) 意
yi (righteousness, moral principle, significance, meaning) 義
yi (unity) 一
yi cang 義倉
yi guan 一貫
yili 義理
yin 陰
Yin Tun (1071–1142) 尹焞
yin qi 陰氣
yi yi 義役
Yi zhuan 易傳
yi zhuang 義莊
Yongkang 永康
Yong le 永樂
You Zuo (1053–1123) 游酢
yu (desire) 慾
yubei cang 預備倉
Yuan Cai (fl. 12th c.) 袁采
"Yuan dao" 原道
Yuan Huang (1533–1606) 袁黃

Zeng Gong (1019–83) 曾鞏
Zhan Ruoshui (1466–1560) 湛若水
Zhang Fangping (1007–91) 張方平
Zhang Jiucheng (1092–1159) 張九成
Zhang Juzheng (1525–82) 張居正
Zhang Mou (1437–1522) 章懋

Zhang Ruyu (early 13th c.)　章如愚

Zhang Shi (1130–80)　張栻

Zhang Zai (1020–77)　張載

Zhao Fu (fl. 1240)　趙復

Zhao Kuangyin (Song Emperor
　Taizu, r. 960–76)　趙匡胤

Zhen Dexiu (1178–1235)　眞德秀

Zheng family commune　鄭氏義門

Zhenghe wu li xin yi　政和五禮新儀

zheng tong　正統

zheng-shi　政事

zhi li　支離

zhong　忠

Zhong guo　中國

zhong tu　中土

zhong yuan　中原

zhou　州

Zhou Dunyi (1017–73)　周敦頤

Zhou zhi shuai　周之衰

Zhu Di (1360–1424)　朱棣

Zhu Xi (1130–1200)　朱熹

Zhu Yuanzhang (1328–98; Ming
　Taizu, r. 1368–99)　朱元璋

Zhu Zhen (1072–1138)　朱震

Zhuhong (1535–1615)　袾宏

ziran zhi li　自然之理

Zi shuo　字說

zong　宗

Zonggao Dahui (1089–1163)
　宗杲大慧

zu　族

Zu Zezhi (11th c.)　祖擇之

Index

Harvard East Asian Monographs
(*out-of-print)

Harvard East Asian Monographs

Harvard East Asian Monographs

Harvard East Asian Monographs

Milton Keynes UK
Ingram Content Group UK Ltd.
UKHW032154071124
450892UK00001B/77